Lecture Notes in Business Information Processing

41

Series Editors

Witold Abramowicz   Robert Tolksdorf (Eds.)

Business Information Systems

13th International Conference, BIS 2010
Berlin, Germany, May 3-5, 2010
Proceedings

Volume Editors

Witold Abramowicz
Poznań University of Economics
Department of Information Systems
Al. Niepodległości 10, 61-875 Poznań, Poland
E-mail: W.Abramowicz@kie.ue.poznan.pl

Robert Tolksdorf
Freie Universität Berlin
Department of Mathematics and Computer Science
Institute for Computer Science
Networked Information Systems
Königin-Luise-Str. 24-26, 14195 Berlin, Germany
E-mail: tolk@ag-nbi.de

Library of Congress Control Number: 2010925419

ACM Computing Classification (1998): J.1, H.4, H.3

ISSN 1865-1348
ISBN-10 3-642-12813-0 Springer Berlin Heidelberg New York
ISBN-13 978-3-642-12813-4 Springer Berlin Heidelberg New York

springer.com

Printed in Germany

Typesetting: Camera-ready by author, data conversion by Scientific Publishing Services, Chennai, India
Printed on acid-free paper 06/3180 5 4 3 2 1 0

Preface

BIS 2010 held on 3–5 May 2010 in Berlin, Germany was the 13th in a series of international conferences on Business Information Systems. The BIS conference series has been recognised by professionals from its very beginning as a forum for the exchange and dissemination of topical research in the development, implementation, application and improvement of computer systems for business processes.

The theme of the conference was "Future Internet Business Services." A number of new initiatives are already underway to address the challenges related to explosive development of Internet applications, hence the conference topics: Search and Knowledge Sharing, Data and Information Security, Web Experience Modelling. Although many people announced that SOA was dead there is undoubtedly a strong need for service-orientation. This was addressed by a topic: Services and Repositories. More and more effort is put on explaining and understanding complex processes as could be seen in topics: Business Processes and Rules, Data Mining for Processes, Visualisation in BPM. Finally, the classical business aspects were covered in session: ERP and SCM.

Altogether, a set of 25 papers illustrating these trends were selected for the presentation during the main event, grouped in 8 sessions. The Program Committee consisted of almost 100 members who carefully evaluated all the submitted papers. Each submission was reviewed on the average by 3.1 programme committee members. Only the best quality papers were selected, resulting in an acceptance rate of less than 30%.

During the conference we hosted two keynote speakers: Steffen Staab (University of Koblenz-Landau) and Thomas F. Gordon (Fraunhofer FOKUS).

BIS 2010 was kindly supported by Semantic Technology Institute International.

May 2010

Witold Abramowicz
Robert Tolksdorf

Conference Organization

BIS 2010 was Organized by

Freie Universität Berlin, Networked Information Systems
Poznań University of Economics, Department of Information Systems

Program Chairs

Witold Abramowicz
Robert Tolksdorf

Programme Committee

Ajith Abraham
Harith Alani
Dimitris Apostolou
Diego Calvanese
Gerardo Canfora
Longbing Cao
Jorge Cardoso
Wojciech Cellary
Dickson K.W. Chiu
Witold Chmielarz
Oscar Corcho
Flavio Corradini
Sergio de Cesare
Nirmit Desai
Tommaso Di Noia
Asuman Dogac
Marlon Dumas
Schahram Dustdar
Dieter Fensel
Bogdan Franczyk
Ulrich Frank
Johann-Christoph Freytag
Jerzy Gołuchowski
Jon Atle Gulla
Hele-Mai Haav
Mohand-Said Hacid
Axel Hahn
Martin Hepp
Knut Hinkelmann
Jack Hsu
Marta Indulska
Pontus Johnson
Paweł J. Kalczyński
Uzay Kaymak
Gary Klein
Ralf Klischewski
Jacek Koronacki
Ryszard Kowalczyk
Marek Kowalkiewicz
Helmut Krcmar
Maurizio Lenzerini
Peter Lockemann
Peter Loos
Alexander Löser
Zakaria Maamar
Leszek Maciaszek
Yannis Manolopoulos
Yutaka Matsuo
Florian Matthes
Heinrich C. Mayr
Wagner Meira
Günter Müller
Adam Nowicki
Markus Nüttgens
Andreas Oberweis
Mitsunori Ogihara
José Palazzo M. de Oliveira
Marcin Paprzycki

Eric Paquet
Vassilios Peristeras
Arnold Picot
Jakub Piskorski
Jaroslav Pokorny
Elke Pulvermueller
Hajo Reijers
Ulrich Reimer
Gustavo Rossi
Massimo Ruffolo
Shazia Sadiq
Juergen Sauer
Alexander Schill
Douglas Schmidt
Munindar P. Singh
Elmar Sinz
Il-Yeol Song
Kilian Stoffel
Vojtech Svatek
Sergio Tessaris
Barbara Thoenssen
Olegas Vasilecas
Herna Viktor
Hans Weigand
Hannes Werthner
Mathias Weske
Roel Wieringa
Stanisław Wrycza
Vilas Wuwongse
Hui Xiong
Yun Yang
Yiyu Yao
Qi Yu
Sławomir Zadrożny
John Zeleznikow
Jozef Zurada

Local Organization

Szymon Łazaruk	Poznań University of Economics
Monika Starzecka	Poznań University of Economics
Piotr Stolarski	Poznań University of Economics
Małgorzata Mochól (Co-chair)	Freie Universität Berlin
Adam Walczak	Poznań University of Economics
Krzysztof Węcel (Co-chair)	Poznań University of Economics

External Reviewers

Aidas Smaizys
Algirdas Laukaitis
Chen Li
Chiara Ghidini
Daneva Maya
Diana Kalibatiene
Ermelinda Oro
Ezio Bartocci
Floriano Scioscia
Francesco Riccetti
Francesco De Angelis
Ioan Toma
Jacek Chmielewski
Jürgen Geuter
Laden Aldin
Marco Zapletal
Maria Rita Di Berardini
Markus Buschle
Maya Daneva
Nick Gehrke
Nikos Loutas
Philipp Liegl
Pia Gustafsson
Rahmanzadeh Heravi
Rainer Schuster
Silja Eckartz
Teodor Sommestad
Thomas Motal
Ulrik Franke
Xiaomeng Su
Zimeo Eugenio

Table of Contents

Session 1. Search and Knowledge Sharing

Session 2. Data and Information Security

Session 3. Web Experience Modelling

Session 4. Business Processes and Rules

Session 5. Services and Repositories

Session 6. Data Mining for Processes

Session 7. Visualisation in BPM

Session 8. ERP and SCM

Faceted Wikipedia Search

Rasmus Hahn[1], Christian Bizer[2], Christopher Sahnwaldt[1], Christian Herta[1], Scott Robinson[1], Michaela Bürgle[1], Holger Düwiger[1], and Ulrich Scheel[1]

[1] neofonie GmbH
Robert-Koch-Platz 4, 10115 Berlin, Germany
firstname.lastname@neofonie.de
http://www.neofonie.de
[2] Freie Universität Berlin
Garystraße 21, 14195 Berlin, Germany
chris@bizer.de
http://www.wiwiss.fu-berlin.de/en/institute/pwo/bizer/

Abstract. Wikipedia articles contain, besides free text, various types of structured information in the form of wiki markup. The type of wiki content that is most valuable for search are Wikipedia infoboxes, which display an article's most relevant facts as a table of attribute-value pairs on the top right-hand side of the Wikipedia page. Infobox data is not used by Wikipedia's own search engine. Standard Web search engines like Google or Yahoo also do not take advantage of the data. In this paper, we present Faceted Wikipedia Search, an alternative search interface for Wikipedia, which facilitates infobox data in order to enable users to ask complex questions against Wikipedia knowledge. By allowing users to query Wikipedia like a structured database, Faceted Wikipedia Search helps them to truly exploit Wikipedia's collective intelligence.

Keywords: Faceted search, faceted classification, Wikipedia, DBpedia, knowledge representation.

1 Introduction

This paper presents *Faceted Wikipedia Search*, an alternative search interface for the English edition of Wikipedia. *Faceted Wikipedia Search* allows users to ask complex questions, like "Which rivers flow into the Rhine and are longer than 50 kilometers?" or "Which skyscrapers in China have more than 50 floors and were constructed before the year 2000?" against Wikipedia knowledge. Such questions cannot be answered using keyword-based search as provided by Google, Yahoo, or Wikipedia's own search engine.

In order to answers such questions, a search engine must facilitate structured knowledge which needs to be extracted from the underlying articles. On the user interface side, a search engine requires an interaction paradigm that enables inexperienced users to express complex questions against a heterogeneous information space in an exploratory fashion.

W. Abramowicz and R. Tolksdorf (Eds.): BIS 2010, LNBIP 47, pp. 1–11, 2010.

For formulating queries, *Faceted Wikipedia Search* relies on the faceted search paradigm. Faceted search enables users to navigate a heterogeneous information space by combining text search with a progressive narrowing of choices along multiple dimensions [6,7,5]. The user subdivides an entity set into multiple subsets. Each subset is defined by an additional restriction on a property. These properties are called the facets. For example, facets of an entity "person" could be "nationality" and "year-of-birth". By selecting multiple facets, the user progressively expresses the different aspects that make up his overall question. Realizing a faceted search interface for Wikipedia poses three challenges:

1. Structured knowledge needs to be extracted from Wikipedia with precision and recall that are high enough to meaningfully answer complex queries.
2. As Wikipedia describes a wide range of different types of entities, a search engine must be able to deal with a large number of different facets. As the number of facets per entity type may also be high, the search engine must apply smart heuristics to display only the facets that are likely to be relevant to the user.
3. Wikipedia describes millions of entities. In order to keep response times low, a search engine must be able to efficiently deal with large amounts of entity data.

Faceted Wikipedia Search addresses these challenges by relying on two software components: The *DBpedia Information Extraction Framework* is used to extract structured knowledge from Wikipedia [4]. *neofonie search*, a commercial search engine, is used as an efficient faceted search implementation.

This paper is structured as follows: Section 2 describes the *Faceted Wikipedia Search* user interface and explains how facets are used for navigating and filtering Wikipedia knowledge. Section 3 gives an overview of the *DBpedia Information Extraction Framework* and the resulting DBpedia knowledge base. Section 4 describes how the efficient handling of facets is realized inside *neofonie search*. Section 5 compares *Faceted Wikipedia Search* with related work.

2 User Interface

This section describes how queries are formulated as a series of refinements within the *Faceted Wikipedia Search* user interface. *Faceted Wikipedia Search* is publicly accessible at `http://dbpedia.neofonie.de`. Several example queries are found at `http://wiki.dbpedia.org/FacetedSearch`. Figure 1 shows a screen shot of the interface. The main elements of the interface are:

1. *Text Search:* Free-text search terms can be entered into this search field.
2. *Faceted Navigation:* The most frequent values of the relevant facets are displayed in the faceted navigation. The user can define filters by selecting or entering values.
3. *Your Filters:* A breadcrumb navigation displays the selected facet values and search terms. Facets and search terms can be disabled independently of each other by clicking on the corresponding delete button.

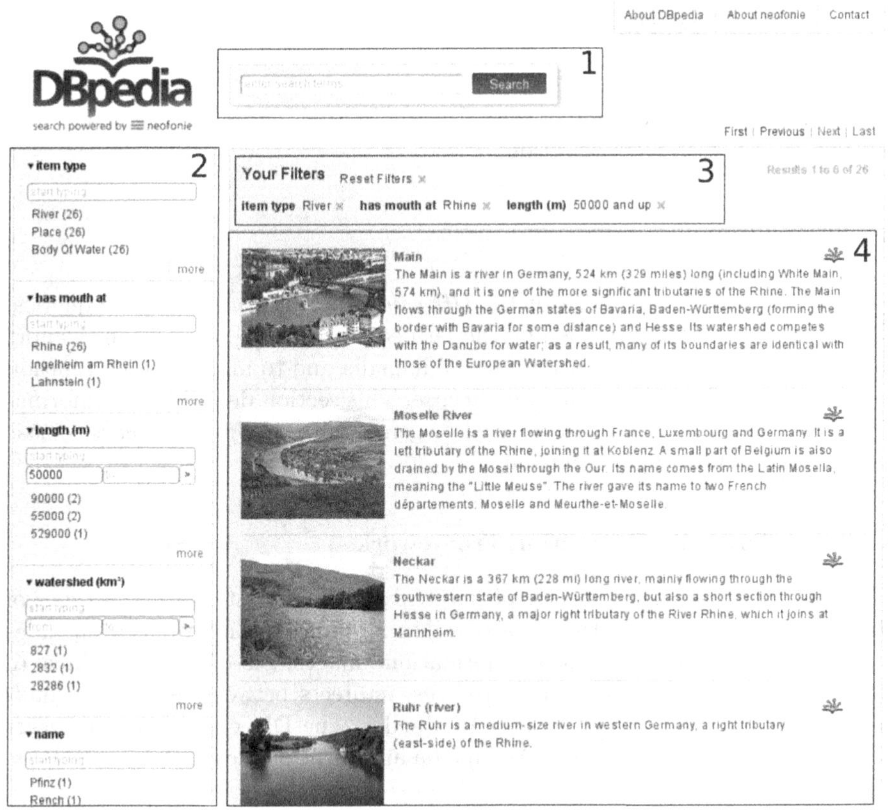

Fig. 1. Screen shot of the *Faceted Wikipedia Search* user interface. The facets are shown in the leftmost area of the screen. The numbers in brackets are the number of results corresponding with each facet value. *Your Filters:* (Area 3) displays the breadcrumb of the selected facet values: `item type` *River* with properties `has mouth at` *Rhine* and `length more than` *50000.*

4. *Search Results:* The search results contain the titles of the matching Wikipedia articles, a teaser of each articles' text, and an image from each article (if existent).

To formulate the question "Which rivers flow into the Rhine and are longer than 50 kilometers?", a user would go through the following steps:

1. On the start page of the *Wikipedia Faceted Browser*, the user would type the value "River" into the facet `item type`. As a result, 12,432 "River" entities are shown.
2. With the selection of "More Facets", the `has mouth at` facet will be displayed. The user types "Rhine" into "has mouth at" entry field, which restricts the results to the 32 rivers which flow into the Rhine.

3. To define the numeric-range constraint, he types 50000 in the "from" field of the facet `length (m)`. As result 26 entities which match the complete query are returned.

In addition to the exploration of the entity space using facets, users can also mix full-text search with facet selection.

3 DBpedia

Faceted Wikipedia Search relies on the *DBpedia knowledge base* to answer queries. The knowledge base is provided by the DBpedia project [4], a community effort to extract structured information from Wikipedia and to make this information available on the Web under an open license. This section describes the information extraction framework that is used to generate the *DBpedia knowledge base* as well as the knowledge base itself.

3.1 The DBpedia Extraction Framework

Wikipedia articles consist mostly of free text, but also contain various types of structured information in the form of wiki markup. Such information includes infobox templates, categorization information, images, geo-coordinates, links to external Web pages, disambiguation pages, redirects between pages, and links across different language editions of Wikipedia. The DBpedia project extracts this structured information from Wikipedia and turns it into an RDF knowledge base [9].

The type of Wikipedia content that is most valuable for the DBpedia extraction are infoboxes. Infoboxes display an article's most relevant facts as a table of attribute-value pairs on the top right-hand side of the Wikipedia page. The Wikipedia infobox template system has evolved over time without central coordination. Therefore, different communities of Wikipedia editors use different templates to describe the same types of things (e.g. `infobox_city_japan`, `infobox_swiss_town` and `infobox_town_de`). Different templates use different names for the same property (e.g. `birthplace` and `place-of-birth`). As many Wikipedia editors do not strictly follow the recommendations given on the page that describes a template, property values are expressed using a wide range of different formats and units of measurement.

In order to deal with the problems of synonymous attribute names and multiple templates being used for the same type of things, the DBpedia project maps Wikipedia templates onto an ontology using a custom mapping language. This ontology was created by manually arranging the 550 most commonly used infobox templates within the English edition of Wikipedia into a subsumption hierarchy consisting of 205 classes and by mapping mapping 3200 infobox attributes to 1843 properties of these classes. The property mappings define fine-grained rules on how to parse infobox values and define target datatypes, which help the parsers to process property values. For instance, if a mapping defines the target datatype to be a list of links, the parser will ignore additional text which may be present in the property value. The ontology currently uses 55 different datatypes. Deviant units of measurement are normalized to one of these datatypes.

3.2 The DBpedia Knowledge Base

The DBpedia knowledge base currently consists of around 479 million RDF triples, which have been extracted from the English, German, French, Spanish, Italian, Portuguese, Polish, Swedish, Dutch, Japanese, Chinese, Russian, Finnish, Norwegian, Catalan, Ukrainian, Turkish, Czech, Hungarian, Romanian, Volapük, Esperanto, Danish, Slovak, Indonesian, Arabic, Korean, Hebrew, Lithuanian, Vietnamese, Slovenian, Serbian, Bulgarian, Estonian, and Welsh versions of Wikipedia. The knowledge base describes more than 2.9 million entities. For 1.1 million out of these entities, the knowledge base contains clean infobox data which has been extracted using the mapping-based approach described above. The knowledge base features labels and short abstracts in 30 different languages; 609,000 links to images; 3,150,000 links to external web pages; 415,000 Wikipedia categories, and 286,000 YAGO categories [12]. Table 1 gives an overview of common DBpedia classes, and shows the number of instances and some example properties for each class.

Besides being provided for download in the form of RDF dumps, the DBpedia knowledge base is also accessible on the Web via an public SPARQL endpoint and is served as Linked Data [2]. In order to enable DBpedia users to discover further information, the DBpedia knowledge base is interlinked with various other data sources on the Web according to the Linked Data principles [2]. The knowledge base currently contains 4.9 million outgoing data links that point at complementary data about DBpedia entities, as well as meta-information about media items depicting an entity. Altogether, the Web of interlinked data around DBpedia provides approximately 13.1 billion pieces of information (RDF triples) and covers domains such as geographic information, people, companies, films, music, genes, drugs, books, and scientific publications [1].

In the future, the data links between DBpedia and the external databases will allow applications like *Faceted Wikipedia Search* to answer queries based not only on Wikipedia knowledge but based on a world wide web of databases.

4 Faceted Search Implementation

This section gives an overview of the requirements that had to be met by the *Faceted Wikipedia Search* implementation as well as the approach that is used to select the potentially relevant subset of facets that is displayed to the user and the approach that is used to represent facet values in memory.

4.1 Requirements

In *Faceted Wikipedia Search*, each document is ordered to an item type, which the facets are then assigned to. For example, a document about a person may

Table 1. Common DBpedia classes with the number of their instances and example properties

Ontology Class	Instances	Example Properties
Person	282,000	name, birthdate, birthplace, employer, spouse
Artist	54,262	activeyears, awards, occupation, genre
Actor	26,009	academyaward, goldenglobeaward, activeyears
MusicalArtist	19,535	genre, instrument, label, voiceType
Athlete	74,832	currentTeam, currentPosition, currentNumber
Politician	12,874	predecessor, successor, party
Place	339,000	lat, long
Building	23,304	architect, location, openingdate, style
Airport	7,971	location, owner, IATA, lat, long
Bridge	1,420	crosses, mainspan, openingdate, length
Skyscraper	2,028	developer, engineer, height, architect, cost
PopulatedPlace	241,847	foundingdate, language, area, population
River	12,432	sourceMountain, length, mouth, maxDepth
Organisation	119,000	location, foundationdate, keyperson
Band	14,952	currentMembers, foundation, homeTown, label
Company	20,173	industry, products, netincome, revenue
Educ.Institution	29,154	dean, director, graduates, staff, students
Work	189,620	author, genre, language
Book	15,677	isbn, publisher, pages, author, mediatype
Film	44,680	director, producer, starring, budget, released
MusicalWork	101,985	runtime, artist, label, producer
Album	74,055	artist, label, genre, runtime, producer, cover
Single	24,597	album, format, releaseDate, band, runtime
Software	5,652	developer, language, platform, license
TelevisionShow	10,169	network, producer, episodenumber, theme

have a property *nationality*, but this property makes little sense when ordered to a document about a celestial body. But, a facet *age* would make sense for both documents. Therefore, a collection of documents consisting of a large variety of themes, like Wikipedia, will need a large total number of facets, but only a small number of facets per document will be needed. The statistical characteristics of the documents are shown in Table 2. In other scenarios, for example, an online shop, a much smaller number of total facets would be required, but documents would have more facets in common, e.g. price.

For the user, only two aspects of a faceted-search system are readily apparent:

- *Facet Display*: For any set of documents (e.g. search result set) the facets and facet values are displayed. For example, a user is returned a set of documents, some of which correspond to the item type person. The user would be presented the *first-name* facet of the document set. The user would then see that there are 53 persons named *John*, and 63 people named *James*, etc.

Table 2. Statistical characteristics of the documents of *Faceted Wikipedia Search*

Property	Value
number of documents	1134853
number of types	205
number of different facets	1843
average number of unique facets per document	14.8
number of values	24368625
number of unique values	5569464
average number of values per document	21.5
average number of values per facet	13222

– *Faceted Search*: The user can narrow the set of chosen documents based on the value of one or more facets by selecting a facet value. Technically, this is the intersection of one set of documents with another set which has the specific, selected values to the corresponding facets. Generally, for an implementation of a faceted-search system, this means that when the user selects a facet value, the search results reflect this selection.

4.2 Actual Implementation

In our implementation of faceted search these two aspects were implemented independently from one another to a large extent. This is mainly due to the fact that both aspects were implemented in an existing information retrieval engine[1], which already had various methods for document selection. Most notably, the possibility of performing boolean queries [10] is a previously existing feature of the search engine. Some adaptations were necessary to index facet values within documents (no normalization, special tokenization). In the case of faceted search, however, the user only selects the values that are presented to him, without requiring him to enter keywords. Therefore, there is no need for normalization and tokenization.

Facet Display

The selection of the facet values which are to be displayed is dependent on the number of corresponding documents in the currently displayed document set. This set is determined by a previous search. *Wikipedia Faceted Search* offers the user two possibilities of search: first, through the selection of facet values and second, through a traditional full-text search.

The facet values are presented to the user as a list. The order of the values presented is dependent on the number of documents concerning a particular facet value. That means, for the selected document set the number of documents with the same facet value for any facet is counted. The values are then ordered by the absolute number of documents corresponding to a particular facet.

[1] We used our proprietary full text retrieval system for the implementation.

This ordering of values by number of occurrences of facet values is not necessarily the only or most comprehensible for the user; there are many facets which have a natural order (mainly numeric facets like e.g. *year*), but in the DBpedia Search we do not use this.

Due to limitations of the user interface and diversity of documents, not all facets and their values can be presented in a user friendly way. Therefore, the facet values which are displayed are limited to a set that can clearly be represented. The set of facets which is retrieved from the system is preselected at the time of the query. These we define as the target facets. This selection is primarily done to keep the number of round trips, and the amount of data transferred, small. This issue is readily apparent in the DBpedia system, as the documents are heterogeneous, i.e. many facets are only defined for a small subset of documents and only a few facets are shared between all documents.

To determine the target facets which are queried, we distinguish between three cases:

1. At the start of the user-session (without any search or selection) only the item type facet is displayed.
2. If there is no *item type* selected, the most generic facets, *item-type*, *location* and *year-of-appearance* etc. are target facets, since these are facets of the majority of documents.
3. If the user has selected an *item type*, the most frequent facets of the *item type* are target facets.

The resulting target facets (of 2, 3) are ranked according to their most frequent facet value. Only the target facets with the highest value frequencies are displayed.

Faceted Search

Conceptually, the facet information in the data is a set of tuples of document, facet and value, where a tuple (f, d, v) represents that a document d has a value v in the facet f. After the selection of a subset of documents D_q as a result of a query q, and a choice of the facets F_q, the set of resulting facet values must be calculated. For each facet and value the number of documents for this combination is returned as a response to the query. That is, given a subset of documents D_q and a subset of facets F_q we must calculate $|\{(f, d, v)|d \in D_q\}|$ for each v and $f \in F_q$ efficiently. We do not know the set of documents D_q in advance, which leads to the difficulty in calculating the number of these tuples. We also do not know the set of facets F_q in advance, but as there are not many facets in total, this does not pose much of a problem. However, as we have a sizable amount of documents, this forces us to use a data representation which allows us to represent the facet values efficiently. To accomplish this, we use a (sparse) tree.

In the tree, the facet values are stored in a hierarchical data structure with three levels, the first level being the facets, the second level being the documents and the third level the values. This particular ordering is not strictly mandatory, but since the query output is ordered by facet first, it is more memory-efficient to reflect this in the data-structure, since each facet can then be calculated independently. This also allows for more efficient memory usage in the case that not all facets are queried, as we only need facets to be in the memory when they are being used.

As it turns out, this design is especially useful for the DBpedia use case where there is a large number of facets in relation to the number of documents. By having the facets in the first level of the tree structure, the amount of data to be examined is efficiently reduced.

5 Related Work

The following section is dedicated to discussing a sample of the related work on faceted search and Wikipedia information extraction.

Faceted Search. An early faceted search prototype was the "flamenco" [5] system developed at the University of California. "flamenco" is implemented on top of a SQL-database and uses the `group by`-command and specific optimizations [3]. This setup was developed without a full-text search engine.

In Yitzhaz et. al. [14], a hierarchically faceted search implementation in the *Lucene* search library is described. The facet value-information for the documents is stored in the *Payload* of a dedicated posting list (*FacetInfo*). The values are counted with a customized `HitCollector` for the target facets. The main difference to our approach is that their method aggregates by document first while our approach aggregates by facet. In our opinion, our implementation is better suited for the Wikipedia document collection (see 4.2).

Today, many commercial websites use faceted search. Examples include eBay and Amazon. A faceted search system that works on similar content as Faceted Wikipedia Search is Freebase Parallax[2]. Parallax focuses on extending faceted search to a chained-sets navigation paradigm, while Faceted Wikipedia Search aims at providing a simple, self-explanatory search interface for Wikipedia.

Extraction of structured Wikipedia content. A second Wikipedia knowledge extraction effort is the Freebase Wikipedia Extraction (WEX) [11]. Freebase[3] is a commercial company that builds a huge online database which users can edit in a similar way as editing Wikipedia articles. Freebase employs Wikipedia knowledge as initial content for their database that will afterwards be edited by Freebase users. By synchronizing the DBpedia knowledge base with Wikipedia, DBpedia in contrast relies on the existing Wikipedia community to update content. Since November 2008, Freebase is published as Linked Data, and DBpedia as well as Freebase include data links pointing to corresponding entities in the respective other data source. These links allow applications to fuse DBpedia and Freebase knowledge.

---

[2] `http://www.freebase.com/labs/parallax/`

[3] `http://www.freebase.com`

A third project that extracts structured knowledge from Wikipedia is the YAGO project [12]. YAGO extracts 14 relationship types, such as `subClassOf`, `type`, `diedInYear`, `bornInYear`, `locatedIn` etc. from Wikipedia category system and from Wikipedia redirects. YAGO does not perform an infobox extraction like DBpedia. The YAGO and DBpedia projects cooperate and we serve the resulting YAGO classification together with the DBpedia knowledge base.

In [13] the KOG system is presented, which refines existing Wikipedia infoboxes based on machine learning techniques using both SVMs and a more powerful joint-inference approach expressed in Markov Logic Networks. In conjunction with DBpedia, KOG gives Wikipedia authors valuable insights about inconsistencies and possible improvements of infobox data.

NLP-based knowledge extraction. There is a vast number of approaches employing natural language processing techniques to obtain semantics from Wikipedia. Yahoo! Research Barcelona, for example, published a semantically annotated snapshot of Wikipedia[4], which is used by Yahoo for entity ranking [15]. A commercial venture, in this context, is the Powerset search engine[5] which uses NLP for both understanding queries in natural language as well retrieving relevant information from Wikipedia. Further potential for the DBpedia extraction as well as for the NLP-field in general lies in the idea of using huge bodies of background knowledge — like DBpedia — to improve the results of NLP-algorithms [8].

6 Conclusion

We have presented *Faceted Wikipedia Search*, an alternative search interface for Wikipedia, which facilitates infobox data in order to enable users to ask complex queries against Wikipedia. The answers to these queries are not generated using key word matching like the search engines Google or Yahoo, but are generated based on structured knowledge that has been extracted and combined from many different Wikipedia articles.

In future projects, we plan to extend the user interface of *Faceted Wikipedia Search* with more sophisticated facet value selection components like maps, timeline widgets and the automatic binning of numerical and date values. We also plan to complement and extend the application's knowledge base by fusing Wikipedia infobox data with additional data from external Linked Data sources.

References

1. Bizer, C.: The emerging web of linked data. IEEE Intelligent Systems 24, 87–92 (2009)
2. Bizer, C., Heath, T., Berners-Lee, T.: Linked data - the story so far. Int. J. Semantic Web Inf. Syst. 5(3), 1–22 (2009)

---

[4] `http://www.yr-bcn.es/dokuwiki/doku.php?id=semantically_annotated_snapshot_of_wikipedia`

[5] `http://www.powerset.com`

3. Chen, K.: Computing query previews in the flamenco system. Technical report, University of Berkeley (2004)
4. Bizer, C., et al.: Dbpedia - a crystallization point for the web of data. Journal of Web Semantics 7(3), 154–165 (2009)
5. English, J., Hearst, M., Sinha, R., Swearingen, K., Yee, K.-P.: Flexible search and navigation using faceted metadata. Technical report, University of Berkeley (2002)
6. Hearst, M., Elliott, A., English, J., Sinha, R., Swearingen, K., Yee, K.-P.: Finding the flow in web site search. Commun. ACM 45(9), 42–49 (2002)
7. Hearst, M.A.: Uis for faceted navigation: Recent advances and remaining open problems. In: HCIR 2008 Second Workshop on Human-Computer Interaction and Information Retrieval. Microsoft (October 2008)
8. Kazama, J., Torisawa, K.: Exploiting wikipedia as external knowledge for named entity recognition. In: Joint Conference on Empirical Methods in Natural Language Processing and Computational Natural Language Learning (2007)
9. Klyne, G., Carroll, J.: Resource description framework (rdf): Concepts and abstract syntax - w3c recommendation (2004), `http://www.w3.org/TR/2004/REC-rdf-concepts-20040210/`
10. Manning, C.D., Raghavan, P., Schütze, H.: Introduction to Information Retrieval. Cambridge University Press, New York (2008)
11. Metaweb Technologies. Freebase wikipedia extraction (wex) (2009), `http://download.freebase.com/wex/`
12. Suchanek, F.M., Kasneci, G., Weikum, G.: Yago: A large ontology from wikipedia and wordnet. Journal of Web Semantics 6(3), 203–217 (2008)
13. Wu, F., Weld, D.: Automatically Refining the Wikipedia Infobox Ontology. In: Proceedings of the 17th World Wide Web Conference (2008)
14. Yitzhak, O.B., Golbandi, N., Har'el, N., Lempel, R., Neumann, A., Koifman, S.O., Sheinwald, D., Shekita, E., Sznajder, B., Yogev, S.: Beyond basic faceted search. In: WSDM 2008: Proceedings of the international conference on Web search and web data mining, pp. 33–44. ACM, New York (2008)
15. Zaragoza, H., Rode, H., Mika, P., Atserias, J., Ciaramita, M., Attardi, G.: Ranking very many typed entities on wikipedia. In: CIKM 2007: Proceedings of the sixteenth ACM conference on Conference on information and knowledge management, pp. 1015–1018. ACM, New York (2007)

A Model of Cross-Functional Coopetition in Software Development Project Teams

Shahla Ghobadi, Farhad Daneshgar, and Graham Low

Information Systems, Technology & Management, Australian School of Business,
University of New South Wales, 2052
Sydney NSW Australia
Shahlaghobadi@gmail.com, F.daneshgar@unsw.edu.au,
G.low@unsw.edu.au

Abstract. Building high-performing software development teams increases the likelihood that firms can meet the expectations of software development projects. Due to the cross-functional nature of the majority of software development projects, the required knowledge for project completion is distributed among stakeholders from different functional units. This implies the importance of efficient interaction and knowledge sharing among different parties involved in the project. To investigate the mechanisms behind effective knowledge sharing among members of this kind of software development projects, the current study combines the game theoretical model of knowledge sharing and the social interdependence theory as a foundation for developing a conceptual model for this study. The integration of these theories as a conceptual basis will help in identifying the constructs that represent effective knowledge sharing. A preliminary model for the constructs' measures is developed through a number of steps. This study proposes a two-step research design process. The results of the first phase are briefly discussed and a number of major issues in the second phase are also explained.

Keywords: Software development teams, Coopetition, Cross-functionality, Knowledge sharing.

1 Introduction

Software development is increasingly becoming an important driver of successful technology-based products and needs to be examined as both a social/behavioral as well as a technological process. However, the research on software development has primarily focused on mechanisms such as software development methodologies and overlooks the importance of social and behavioral processes [1]. Since performance is the result of the interactions and dynamics among team members, teams as the primary vehicle of continuous innovation and learning across projects should be deeply studied, alongside technological factors [2]. In this regard, a theme of literature points to the importance of building high-performing software development teams in increasing the likelihood that firms can meet the ever-expanding expectations of software development projects [2].

W. Abramowicz and R. Tolksdorf (Eds.): BIS 2010, LNBIP 47, pp. 12–22, 2010.

The dynamic nature of software development projects requires multiple perspectives and diverse skills of specialists. Therefore, cross–functional (CF) teamwork is necessary for dealing with the dynamic nature of the software development projects. Distribution of required knowledge among various stakeholders for the completion of software development projects indicates the necessity of effective knowledge sharing among different functions [1]. Therefore these projects are strongly dependant on the effective collaboration and knowledge sharing of cross-functional team members [3, 4]. However, the cross-functionality aspect of software development projects has not yet found sufficient attention and empirical testing. Such a lack of attention into this matter has led to overlooking a considerable amount of conflict among cross-functional team members as highlighted in a number of studies [5]. This paper addresses these issues by providing insights for how cross-functional software development projects could be managed to facilitate effective knowledge sharing among cross-functional team members. In order to explain knowledge sharing in these types of teams, the present study provides a theoretical basis for specifying the constructs that comprise effective knowledge sharing among cross-functional team members.

The proposed conceptual model integrates social interdependence theory [6] and the coopetitive model of knowledge sharing [7]. The rationale behind such integration is to enable investigation of knowledge sharing process among cross-functional software development team members that is driven by forces of cooperation and competition. The proposed model is expected to provide richer understanding of how software development projects should be managed in terms of providing appropriate blend of different interdependencies as well as cooperative and competitive behaviors.

2 Literature Review

Majority of the extant literature sets forth on explaining the first challenge and its impact on knowledge sharing among software development team members or software development project's performance [3, 8]. A number of studies point to the interdepartmental politics and competing interdependencies among different team member representatives [5]. This is in alignment with the cross-functional project (CFP)'s literature that argues competing social identities and loyalties, related to politics and competition between departments, make CFP's members to identify more strongly with their function, both socially and psychologically, than with their group and even the organization [9]. This alongside different functional objectives, priorities, and agendas that could often be in conflict, make team members from different functional areas unable to exploit their diverse expertise. However, there is little investigation on examining the simultaneous effects of different interdependencies on determining different patterns of knowledge sharing behaviors (e.g., goal, reward, and task).

The nature of the cooperative environment in cross-functional teams suggests that project members are supposed to cooperate, whereas the cross functionality implies a kind of competition among team members[10, 11]. Such competition is particularly related to their social identity and association with different departments [10, 11]. The above phenomenon has many similarities with the term, cross-functional coopetition that is defined as the simultaneous cooperation and competition among functional units within a firm [10]. According to Luo et al (2006), cross-functional coopetition conveys the idea that while functional units might cooperate with each other in gaining knowledge and learning from each other, they might compete in many aspects (tangible, intangible, strategic power, organisational chart).

There are different viewpoints toward both concepts of cooperation and competition. A number of studies suggest the existence of a trade-off between cooperation and competition, and other environmental and/or structural factors [12]. Some scholars have noticed the synergy of cooperation and competition in producing various benefits, including learning, and innovation [13]. The existing literature has arisen the importance of a model for cooperative and competitive behaviors that can explain the ideal blend of cooperative and competitive behaviors [14] but it has not yet found sufficient attention by the scholars. Despite a dawning recognition of the importance of coopetitive behaviors, to date there has been a lack of empirical studies that focus on the elements that comprise coopetitive behaviors particularly at the intra-organisational level. In fact, recently the simultaneous existence of cooperative and competitive behaviors is investigated rather than their separate impacts [9]. Research in this area is hamstrung by inconsistent conceptualization of the nature of this phenomenon and inconsistent treatment of related constructs.

Social interdependence theory [15] provides an appropriate explanation for cooperative and competitive behaviors in collaborative contexts. This theory indicates that the structure of interdependencies among individuals determines the degree of cooperative and/or competitive interactions that in turn determine the potential outcomes. With regard to the collaborative context of software development projects, this theory is in congruence with software development processes [3]. According to the latter theory, the structure of the interdependencies between team members (positive or negative) determines the degree to which cooperative or competitive interactions occur among them [3]. Where positive interdependence results in a process of efficient promotive interaction, the negative interdependence results in a process of contrient or oppositional interaction.

A few scholars have applied the concept of interdependencies to explain positive or negative interdependencies (e.g., different goals, rewards) among SD team members driving cooperative and competitive behaviors [3]. For example, Pee et al (2008) discussed that when subgroups' goals are interdependent, they tend to promote mutual goal attainment by coordinating and cooperating with each other. But if the conflict becomes a dominating concern, the subgroups may behave uncooperatively towards each other to prevent others from achieving their goals. That is because one's success is at the expense of the other.

There are three major group of interdependencies: outcome (goal and reward), means (task, resource, role), and boundary (sense of identity, friendship, environmental closeness) [16]. However, the existing literature is limited to investigating the impacts of a few sets of interdependencies (e.g., goal, reward). This overlooks providing a thorough examination of the simultaneous impacts of different interdependencies.

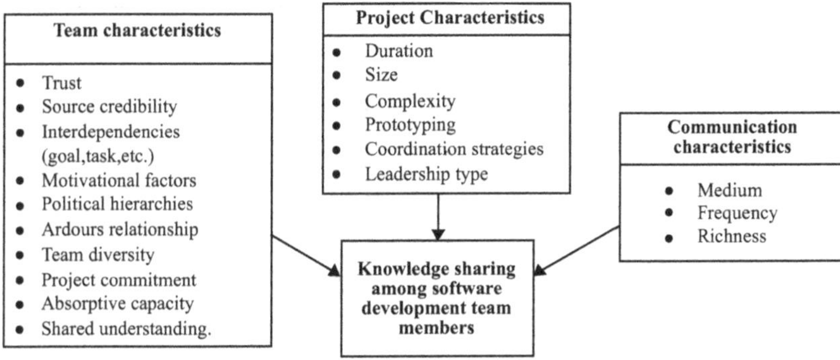

Fig. 1. Factors affecting knowledge sharing among software development team members

To identify factors that affect knowledge sharing among software development team members, a systematic review was conducted. Certain keywords were used to search a number of well-known databases (e.g., Web of Science, ScienceDirect , SpringerLink) and identify empirical and conceptual studies that have investigated factors that influence knowledge sharing among software development team members. The key references in the findings were also checked. The findings of these studies were thoroughly examined and as a result three groups of factors were identified as depicted in Figure 1.

3 Theoretical Modeling

The conceptual framework guiding this study is presented in Figure 2. The logics of the hypotheses are framed in the context of social interdependence theory [15] and the coopetitive model of knowledge sharing [7]. It applies coopetitive model of knowledge sharing [7] to explain different patterns of knowledge sharing driven by two forces of cooperation and competition between cross-functional software development team members. In addition, social interdependence theory [15] is borrowed for explaining the antecedences of cooperative and competitive behaviors among individuals. This section describes the proposed hypothesises as well as the preliminary model of constructs measures.

3.1 Hypothesises

Guided by the social interdependence theory, the current research proposes that interdependencies account for the extent of cooperation and competition among cross-functional software development team members. More specifically, higher positive levels of interdependencies account for higher levels of cooperation, whereas higher levels of negative interdependencies account for higher levels of competition.

According to the reviewed literature, there are three sets of interdependencies including: outcome, means, and boundary interdependence. This study defines the outcome interdependence among cross-functional team members as: the degree to which

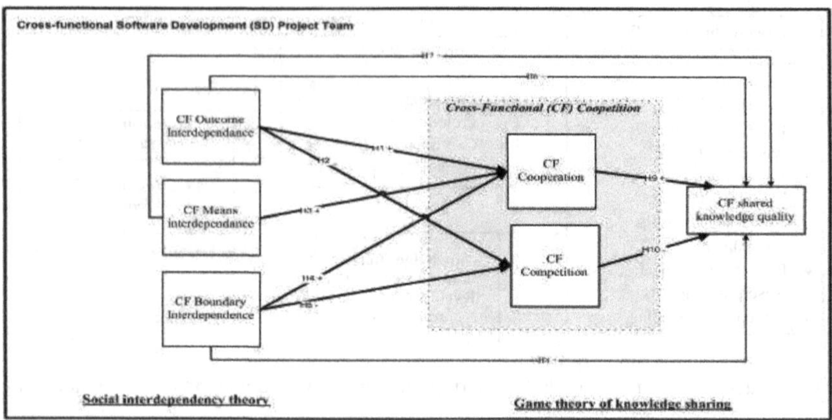

Fig. 2. Conceptual model

cross-functional team members perceived that their outcomes are interdependent with each other. This interdependence could be explained by the degree to which their goals and rewards will be achieved only when the goals/rewards of the other cross-functional members are also met [16]. Similarly, means interdependence among cross-functional team members could be defined as: the degree to which cross-functional team members perceived that they depend on the means of other cross-functional team members to achieve mutual team outcomes. This dependency could be explained by the degree to which cross-functional team members depend on the tasks, roles, and resources of other cross-functional team members to achieve their mutual outcomes [3, 16]. Finally, boundary interdependence among cross-functional team members is defined as: the degree to which cross-functional team members perceived that they have continuous relations among themselves. This includes having friendship, having sense of identity, and having environmental closeness [16]. According to the definition of these concepts, the degree of outcome and boundary interdependencies could be positive, negative, or no interdependence.

This study applies cross-functional cooperation and cross-functional competition concepts to represent levels of cooperation and competition among cross-functional software development team members. There are numerous terms and phrases that have been used analogously with cross-functional cooperation, such as cross-functional collaboration, and cross-functional coordination [9]. Therefore depending on the respective studies, cross-functional cooperation could mean different things. This study defines it as: the extent of similar or complimentary coordinated actions taken by cross-functional team members in interdependent relationships to achieve mutual outcomes or singular outcomes [9, 10]. To explain this concept, the three dimensions introduced by Pinto et al (1993) are used: communication, interpersonal relations, and task orientations. Similarly, this study defines cross-functional competition as : the degree to which cross-functional team members have the tendency of rivalry with each other for limited resources and values [10].

In this regard, this study proposes that higher positive levels of outcome and boundary interdependencies account for higher levels of cooperation, whereas their higher levels of negativity account for higher levels of competition. However, means interdependence could be only positive or no interdependence. Therefore, this study proposes that higher positive levels of means interdependencies account for higher levels of cooperation. The above propositions shape H1,2,3,4,5 in Figure 2.

It has been shown that interdependencies facilitate the development of insightful thoughts and discoveries through promotive interaction [16]. Through increasing shared understanding, higher reasoning strategies and efficient promotive interaction among individuals lead to more effective knowledge sharing that is essential for improvements and encouraging other team members. The knowledge sharing literature has mentioned the concept of knowledge quality as an indicator of effective knowledge sharing.

This study adopts this concept to explain the effectiveness of knowledge sharing among cross-functional software development team members and defines it as: the quality of the shared knowledge among cross-functional team members. This concept could be explained by the degree of rigor, soundness, usefulness and innovativeness of the knowledge being shared among individuals [17]. Therefore, this study proposes that higher positive levels of interdependencies will increase the effectiveness of knowledge sharing among cross-functional team members. This argument is shown thorough H6, 7, 8.

Game theoretical model of knowledge sharing [7] suggests that the knowledge sharing phenomenon is deeply influenced by the value of the knowledge being shared. This model suggests that individuals share knowledge according to the payoffs they get or loose in the phenomena of knowledge sharing. Therefore, in cooperative situations, they are more likely to share their knowledge, whereas competitive contexts make them more reserved in sharing valuable knowledge. In addition, cooperative behaviors will result in increasing shared understanding among individuals that is a major prerequisite for sharing the knowledge that has innovative characteristics for others [4]. In this regard, cooperation will result in sharing high-quality knowledge among team members. Whereas tension that as the result of competition, might impede the effective knowledge sharing in terms of sharing high-quality knowledge. The above arguments are shown by H9, 10.

3.2 Development of the Preliminary Model of Constructs Measurers

After reviewing the extant literature, in order to select the appropriate measures and questions for the constructs, five steps are taken: creating pool of measures, consolidating measures and questions, measures and questions refinement (face validity), developing reflective and formative measures and questions, and final measures and questions refinement.

Firstly, according to the definition of each construct, the related measures in the previous studies were put together. If no explicit definition of a measure was provided in the literature, the original manuscript was carefully investigated and based on the provided sample questions, a short description was provided. To avoid considering a concept twice in the final instrument, measures that were repeated in different instruments were identified and removed from the pool. Measures that reflected the same concept were consolidated by reviewing their definition. Having the list of measures, the related questions to capture the value of each measure were developed. The results were discussed in several meetings with professionals from both academia and industry to screen the items, evaluate face validity, and note ambiguous or redundant items.

A number of software developers were also asked to review the items and note any item that they perceived as unclear or unimportant. As a result, the questions were revised. In addition, a number of reflective measures were developed for each construct to ensure the future statistical results.

4 Research Methodology

In consistency with the research objectives, the research process of the current study is guided by a pluralist approach [18], which employs case study research to validate and enrich the design of the survey research. Qualitative approach is employed to re-examine, confirm, and enrich the quantitative part of the research. This is also consistent with the sequential triangulation approach that validates results by combining a range of data sources and methods [19]. An overview of these two phases is shown in Figure 3.

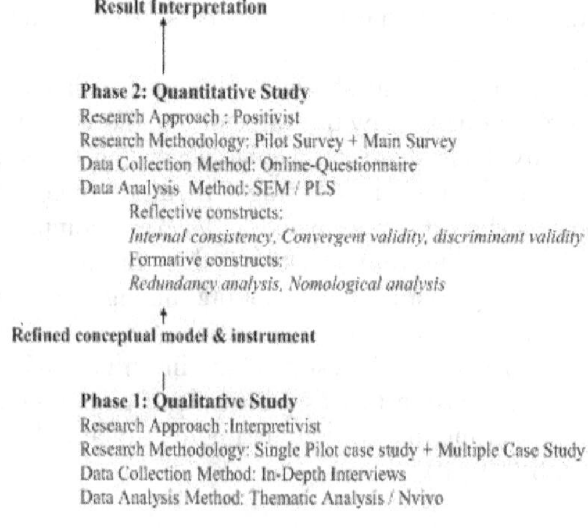

Fig. 3. Methodology sections

4.1 Multiple Case-Studies

The first phase that is multiple case studies included a single pilot case study followed by a more explanatory, cross-case analysis of a number of software development project managers who had the experience of managing cross-functional software development projects within the last three years.

Semi-structured interviews constituted the method of data collection for this phase [20]. Conducting interviews had four purposes including: (i) testing the presence of coopetitive behaviors within cross-functional software development projects, (ii) to enrich the conceptual model and its variables (for any reduction/extension to the variables), (iii) to re-examine measures of the proposed variables (for any reduction/extension/or change to the measures), and (iv) to test the appropriateness of the hypothesises. As this phase aimed at providing support for the initial model and implementing possible modifications, a limited number of interviews were conducted.

Five interviews were conducted with five software development managers (P1, P2, P3, P4, and P5) with the experience of at least managing one cross-functional software development project within the last three years. Following similar key informant research to identify a person who would be highly knowledgeable about team events and practices, project managers were targeted. Table 1 demonstrates a brief description of the cases relevant to each project manager (Case1, Case 2, Case 3, Case 4, and Case 5). The interviews had three sections. In the first section, the interviewees answered a number of questions that aimed at describing the project they were involved in.

Table 1. Cases descriptions

Project factors	Case 1	Case 2	Case 3	Case 4	Case 5
Sector	Private	Private	Private	Government	Government
Project type	In-house	Outsourced	Outsourced	Outsourced	Outsourced
Project duration	1.5yrs	6months	4months	6 months	6 months
Project size **Num. team members** **Num. functional units involved**	 20 4	 8 4	 7 5	 16 8	 12 7
Project manager experience	15yrs	20 yrs	13 yrs	12 yrs	10 years

In the second section, interviewees explained the major factors that had significant impacts on the dependant constructs of the model as well as their perception about the constructs measures. In this section, all the interviewees' perceptions about the constructs' characteristics were mapped with the proposed measures. The result showed the adequacy and relevancy of almost all the measures. However, it was found that the major indicators of knowledge quality were usefulness, innovativeness, and reliability. In fact, instead of preciseness and soundness, reliability was found to be closer to the interviewees' perceptions: "I guess it should be accurate in articulating the user's requirements.

In terms of factors that affect the dependent variables, the model was confirmed by the interviewees. All interviewees pointed to different interdependencies (outcome, tasks, environmental closeness, friendship, etc.) as the determinants of cooperative interactions. Negative outcome interdependence, negative boundary interdependence, limited resources, and departmental issues (shining in front of the top executives, etc.) were also found as the major sources of competitive attitudes. The interviewees stressed the impact of different dimensions of cooperation (communication, interpersonal relations, and task orientations), interdependencies (e.g., environmental closeness, friendship), team characteristics (e.g., commitment, team members capabilities), and project characteristics (e.g., cross-functionality) on the quality of knowledge being shared. In the third section, the interviewees confirmed the appropriateness of majority of the model hypotheses and relations. However, there were some inconsistencies for H2, H7, and H10. First, negative outcome interdependence was found to result in competitive behaviors (H2).

However, according to P4 and P5, negative outcome interdependence resulted in time delays rather than arising competitive behaviors. It could be because of the governmental nature of these projects in which team members avoid showing competitive attitudes.

Second, P2, P4, and P5 expressed that during the project, each department had been given specific responsibilities. Therefore, team members had to transfer the required knowledge regardless of the degree of the means interdependence (contrast with H7). This study plans to test this hypothesis in a broader context and by the use of quantitative data.

Third, in alignment with the existing literature on constructive competition [10], all the interviewees except P3 believed that competition was to some degree helpful and positive (contrast with H10). This points to the existing literature on coopetition that suggests the synergy of cooperation and competition [10]. For example, P1 expressed that: 'Competition is not by itself a bad thing. If competition goes far beyond the line then it becomes the negative competition which is destructive for the project otherwise it is always good to have competitive spirit among team members'. The latter work has used the multiplication of the cooperation and competition as an indicator of the synergy between these two forces. This study plans to set forth on analyzing different patterns of simultaneous cooperation and competition and their impacts on the knowledge quality in the quantitative phase of the research. Similarly, categorizing cooperation, competition, and interdependencies to qualitative groups (e.g., low, high) will be one of the possible choices in the next phase.

4.2 Survey Study

In the second phase, the online questionnaire will allow to get the quantitative data and test the model. It will be sent to the members of a number of IT associations. Questions will use several scales (7 point Likert scale and semantic differential scales) to avoid the common method bias . In the first round, which is pilot study, the research consolidates and prepares the questions for the main survey.

Structural Equation Modeling (SEM) will be employed to investigate the causal relationships between the variables. This study will use partial least squares (PLS) that uses a principal component-based estimation approach, to test the hypotheses. The choice of PLS has several reasons and mainly comes back to the inclusion of formative measures in the model that PLS is able to account for [21]. It is planned to assess the adequacy of formative measures by following a flow offered by [22] that takes into account the redundancy analysis. For the reflective constructs, the procedure by [23] will be followed, including: determining reliability, and using multitrait-multimethod techniques (MMT) to assess validity. For these steps, this study will take account for internal consistency, convergent validity, and discriminant validity. The questionnaire will be finalized based on the results and will be prepared for the main survey.

5 Research Limitations and Conclusion

It is recognized that there are restrictions in gathering data from all members of the cross-functional software development teams. Therefore, the current study proposes that data to be collected from key informants rather than all of the team members. This might overlook different opinions and viewpoints that exist within the project. In addition, in the quantitative part, a number of IT associations have been targeted that might not be perfect representatives of the target population for the sake of generalisability. Third, it is believed that the interdependencies change during software development projects. However, the current study targets completed software development projects and asks the levels of interdependencies in general. Having longitudinal studies might discover interesting results that are not the subject of the current research. The research is in progress for conducting the survey research.

References

1. Patnayakuni, R., Rai, A., Tiwana, A.: Systems development process improvement: A knowledge integration perspective. IEEE Transactions on Engineering Management 54, 286–300 (2007)
2. He, J.: Knowledge impacts of user participation: a cognitive perspective. In: SIGMIS conference on Computer personnel research: Careers, culture, and ethics in a networked environment. ACM, New York (2004)
3. Pee, L.G., Kankanhalli, A., Kim, H.W.: Examining Knowledge Sharing in IS Development Projects: A Social Interdependence Perspective. In: 3rd International Research Workshop on Information Technology Project Management (IRWITPM), France, Paris, pp. 61–72 (2008)
4. Nelson, K.M., Cooprider, J.G.: The contribution of shared knowledge to IS group performance. MIS Quarterly, 409–432 (1996)
5. Curtis, B., Krasner, H., Iscoe, N.: A field study of the software design process for large systems. Communications of the ACM 31 (1988)
6. Deutsch, M.: Cooperation and competition. In: The handbook of conflict resolution: Theory and practice, Jossey Bass (2000)
7. Loebecke, C., Van Fenema, P.C., Powell, P.: Co-Opetition and Knowledge Transfer. The DATA BASE for Advances in Information Systems 30 (1999)
8. He, J., Butler, B.S., King, W.R.: Team Cognition: Development and Evolution in Software Project Teams. Journal of Management Information Systems 24, 261–292 (2007)
9. Pinto, M.B., Pinto, J.K., Prescott, J.E.: Antecedents and consequences of project team cross-functional cooperation. Management Science, 1281–1297 (1993)
10. Luo, X., Slotegraaf, R.J., Pan, X.: Cross-Functional 'Coopetition': The Simultaneous Role of Cooperation and Competition Within Firms. Journal of Marketing 70, 67–80 (2006)
11. Tsai, W.: Social Structure of "Coopetition" Within a Multiunit Organization: Coordination, Competition, and Intraorganizational Knowledge Sharing. Organization Science 13, 179–190 (2002)
12. Song, X.M., Montoya-Weiss, M.M., Schmidt, J.B.: Antecedents and consequences of cross-functional cooperation: a comparison of R&D, manufacturing, and marketing perspectives. An international publication of the product development & management association 14, 35–47 (1997)
13. Lado, A.A., Boyd, N.G., Hanlon, S.C.: Competition, Cooperation, and the Search for Economic Rents: A Syncretic Model. The Academy of Management Review 22, 110–141 (1997)
14. Beersma, B., Hollenbeck, J.R., Humphery, S.E., Moon, H., Conlon, D.E., Ilgen, D.R.: Cooperation, Competition, And Team Performance: Toward A Contingency Approach. Academy of Management Journal 46, 572–590 (2003)
15. Deutsch, M.: A theory of cooperation and competition. Human Relations 2, 129–152 (1949)

16. Johnson, D.W., Johnson, R.T.: New developments in social interdependence theory. Genetic, social, and general psychology monographs 131, 285–358 (2006)
17. Haas, M.R., Hansen, M.T.: Different knowledge, different benefits: toward a productivity perspective on knowledge sharing in organizations. Strategic Management Journal 28, 1133–1153 (2007)
18. Mingers, J.: Combining IS research methods: towards a pluralist methodology. Information Systems Research 12, 240–259 (2001)
19. Tashakkori, Teddlie, A.C.: Handbook of mixed methods in social & behavioral research. Sage Pubns., Thousand Oaks (2002)
20. Remenyi, Williams, D.B.: The nature of research: qualitative or quantitative, narrative or paradigmatic? Information Systems Journal 6, 131–146 (1996)
21. Chin, W.W.: Issues and opinion on structural equation modeling. Management Information Systems Quarterly 22, 7–16 (1998)
22. Chin, W.W.: How to write up and prepare PLS analysis. In: Hand Book of Partial Least Squares: Concepts, Methods and Applications (2009)
23. Churchill Jr., G.A.: A paradigm for developing better measures of marketing constructs. Journal of Marketing Research, 64–73 (1979)

Using Probabilistic Topic Models in Enterprise Social Software

Konstantinos Christidis and Gregoris Mentzas

National Technical University of Athens,
Iroon Polytechniou 9 Zografou Athens, 157 80 Greece
{kchrist,gmentzas}@mail.ntua.gr

Abstract. Enterprise social software (ESS) systems are open and flexible corporate environments which utilize Web 2.0 technologies to stimulate participation through informal interactions and aggregate these interactions into collective structures. A challenge in these systems is to discover, organize and manage the knowledge model of topics found within the enterprise. In this paper we aim to enhance the search and recommendation functionalities of ESS by extending their folksonomies and taxonomies with the addition of underlying topics through the use of probabilistic topic models. We employ Latent Dirichlet Allocation in order to elicit latent topics and use the latter to assess similarities in resource and tag recommendation as well as for the expansion of query results. As an application of our approach we extend the search and recommendation facilities of the Organik enterprise social system.

Keywords: Probabilistic Topic Models, Latent Dirichlet Allocation, Enterprise Social Software, Recommender Systems.

1 Introduction

The Web 2.0 term has been extensively used to describe the use of the World Wide Web as a platform for social interactions [1]. The change of culture and usage patterns in the public part of the Web has also had a significant effect on related developments within the borders of enterprises, giving rise to the topics of Enterprise 2.0[2] and of Enterprise Social Software. According to Gartner, Enterprise Social Software (ESS) provide "an open and flexible environment to stimulate participation through informal interactions and aggregate these interactions into a structure that reflects the collective attitudes, dispositions and knowledge of the participants"[3].These software technologies provide innovative approaches for discovering, collecting, organizing, managing and distributing data and information and typically include blogs, wikis, feeds and syndication systems, social bookmarking applications and discussion forums.

An inherent challenge in ESS is to discover, organize and manage the structure of topics found within the "knowledge base" of the enterprise. Traditionally, e.g. in corporate information portals, this problem has been tackled with the use of corporate taxonomies [4], i.e. classification schemes organised in hierarchical tree structures which model entities and 'is–a' relationships and are typically engineered in a top-down approach where the subject area is divided into increasingly narrower and more

W. Abramowicz and R. Tolksdorf (Eds.): BIS 2010, LNBIP 47, pp. 23–34, 2010.

detailed systematically enumerated categories, However, enterprise social software are based on the use of folksonomies ([5],[6]), i.e. collaborative, user-generated metadata that offer an informal way of online information categorisation, search and sharing. Folksonomies are created bottom-up, in a way where the subject area is divided into individual concepts which can be composed to construct complex subjects via appropriate sets of rules [7].

A central problem in ESS is that both the structure of taxonomies, which may become obsolete due to the rapidly changing conditions in the business environment, and folksonomies, which are by definition arbitrary and evolving, fail to identify latent topics existing in the system. This can lead to an inferior quality of search and recommendation results.

Our motivation in the present paper is to improve the search and recommendation functionalities of ESS by extending the folksonomy and taxonomy structure with the addition of underlying topics through the use of probabilistic topic models. Probabilistic topic models are based upon the idea that documents are mixtures of topics, where a topic is a probability distribution over words. Statistical methods can be used in order to discover this model which provides a probabilistic procedure by which documents can be generated ([8], [9]). Specifically we use Latent Dirichlet Allocation (LDA) [10] in order to elicit latent topics and use them to identify similarities for use in resource and tag recommendation as well as for the expansion of query results. As application test-bed we extend the search and recommendation facilities of an enterprise social system we have developed called OrganiK.

The remainder of this paper is organized as follows. The next section provides a brief overview of the probabilistic topic models and specifically of Latent Dirichlet Allocation. Section three describes how this analysis can be utilized in order to support search and recommendation facilities. In section four, the implementation of the latent topic model and integration with recommendation and search is discussed. Subsequently, results are presented and discussed.

2 Probabilistic Topic Models

In this section we discuss general principles of Probabilistic Topic Models and move on to describe Latent Dirichlet Allocation and its application.

2.1 Basic Assumptions

In text processing, words are filtered: stop-words are removed and stemming is taken into account. However no special consideration is made about the position and the order of words. This bag-of-words assumption is common in natural language processing models, including Latent Semantic Analysis (LSA).

It is also assumed that a generative model can sufficiently describe the document corpus and this model can be discovered. It is hypothesized that there is a way to generate the documents by using latent topic variables and simple probabilistic sampling techniques, i.e. documents can be generated by sampling topics from a distribution of topics over documents and sampling words from a distribution of words over each topic. In order to describe the model these distributions need to be identified.

However, the process we describe in the following section operates on documents and observed words only. Therefore, statistical inference is used in order to approximate the underlying model, which is most probable to have generated this data.

2.2 Latent Dirichlet Allocation

Latent Semantic Analysis (LSA) was the first technique to analyze documents and the words that they contain in order to generate a set of concepts that relate to both of them. Probabilistic Latent Semantic Analysis, as proposed by Hoffmann in [8], is an evolution of the previous model that incorporated a probabilistic foundation. Latent Dirichlet Allocation [10] was then proposed, assuming that both word-topic and topic-document distributions have a Dirichlet prior.

LDA is based on sound probabilistic principles and overcomes problems previously encountered in pLSA. Topic mixture weights are not individually calculated for each document, but are treated as a k-parameter hidden random variable (where k is the number of topics). Therefore the method is naturally generalized to new documents. Additionally the parameters needed are not growing with the size of the training corpus.

In this work we use a variant of the model that places a Dirichlet prior on both distribution of topics over documents and of words over topics as applied in [11].

2.3 Training and Using LDA

LDA is a statistical model which requires training in order to converge to a generative model. Afterwards, this model can be used in applications.

The graphical model in Figure 1, as found in [9], illustrates in plate notation the generative model: z and d variables identify topics and documents, while θ(d) is the distribution over topics for a document d and φ(z) is the distribution over words for a topic z. These distributions can be used to generate documents in the form of a collection of words (w). D is the number of documents, T is the number of topics in the corpus and N_d the topics found in each document. Hyperparameters α and β identify the Dirichlet priors of the above multinomial distributions respectively. These hyperparemeters can be changed in order to control the smoothing of the distributions.

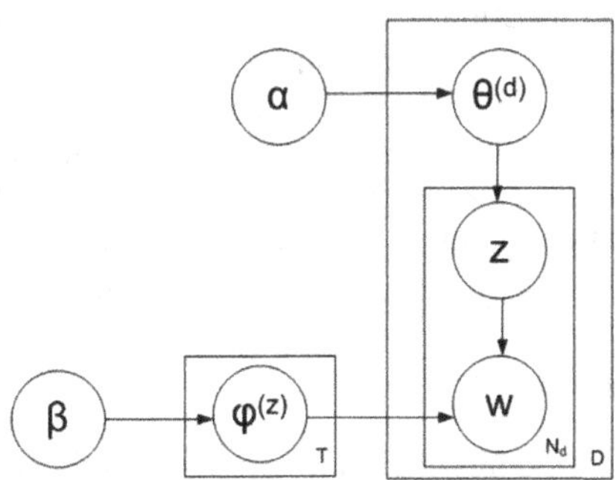

Fig. 1. LDA Plate Notation

Instead of directly estimating the two required distributions, θ and φ, it is advisable to estimate directly the posterior distribution over z (assignment of word tokens to topics.) [9]. A Gibbs sampler, which is a special case of a Monte Carlo Markov Chain, is used for this approximation of p(z), which subsequently is used to estimate φ and θ. Iterative evaluation of (1), after a burn-in period, leads to a sampling convergence to an estimate of z. Then using (2) the topic-word and document-topic distributions can be calculated. C^{WT} and C^{DT} are matrices of counts: $C^{WT}_{w_i j}$ contains the number of times word w is assigned to topic j, not including the current instance i and $C^{DT}_{d_i j}$ contains the number of times topic j is assigned to some word token in document d, not including the current instance i.

$$P(z_i = j \mid z_{-i}, w_i, d_i, \cdot) \propto \frac{C^{WT}_{w_i j} + \beta}{\sum_{w=1}^{W} C^{WT}_{wj} + W\beta} \frac{C^{DT}_{d_i j} + \alpha}{\sum_{t=1}^{T} C^{DT}_{d_i j} + T\alpha} \tag{1}$$

$$\phi'^{(j)}_i = \frac{C^{WT}_{ij} + \beta}{\sum_{k=1}^{W} C^{WT}_{kj} + W\beta}, \quad \theta'^{(d)}_j \frac{C^{DT}_{d\,j} + \alpha}{\sum_{k=1}^{T} C^{DT}_{d_i k} + T\alpha} \tag{2}$$

It is important to note that the topics generated by this method are not epistemologically claimed to be more than latent multinomial variables, nevertheless are capturing probability distribution of words. Additionally these distributions are exchangeable, i.e. after the document re-training no assumptions can be made to relate topics from the previous with topics from the current model.

After the topics have been trained, it is possible to infer the distribution that could have generated a new, previously unseen, item.

3 Applying Topic Analysis in Recommender Systems and Search

For enterprise information portals, the ability to use both pull and push technologies ensures that ‘‘the right information is available or distributed to the right people at the right time’’ [12].Two technologies that support the abovementioned strategies are recommender systems and search. Recommender Systems address the need for pushing information from the system to the employee, while the search component facilitates the (re)discovery of resources in the corporate knowledge base.

In this section we explore specific implementations of these technologies, based on probabilistic topic models and specifically Latent Dirichlet Allocation.

3.1 Recommender Systems

Recommender Systems are addressing, in the most general expression, the problem of estimating the utility or the ratings of items that have not yet been seen by the user [13]. To address this problem different types of recommender systems have been researched, content-based or collaborative, utilizing models or heuristics.

Business interest in this area started from early adopting electronic businesses, such as Amazon.com [14] bookstore collaborative filtering recommendations, and is growing since [15]. Recommender Systems can be transferred from the universe of the e-commerce and social web to enterprise social software, where the problem is redefined as estimating the relevance and usefulness of a previously unseen information resource or keyword.

Latent Semantic Analysis and Latent Dirichlet Allocation have been successfully applied in the field of recommender systems ([16], [17]).

3.1.1 Using LDA in Resource Recommendation

Since probabilistic topic analysis employs processing of textual resources to identify latent topics, the latter can be used for resource recommendation, as for example in [18].

Latent Dirichlet Allocation, when trained, produces two probabilistic distributions: topics over words and documents over topics which are approximated as illustrated in section 2.3. The documents over topics distributions induced by the probabilistic methods are used as similarity measures for relevant resource suggestion. In the case of the import of a new resource to the model, it is possible to use the model to infer which of the latent topics are related to the previously unseen resource and describe their distribution.

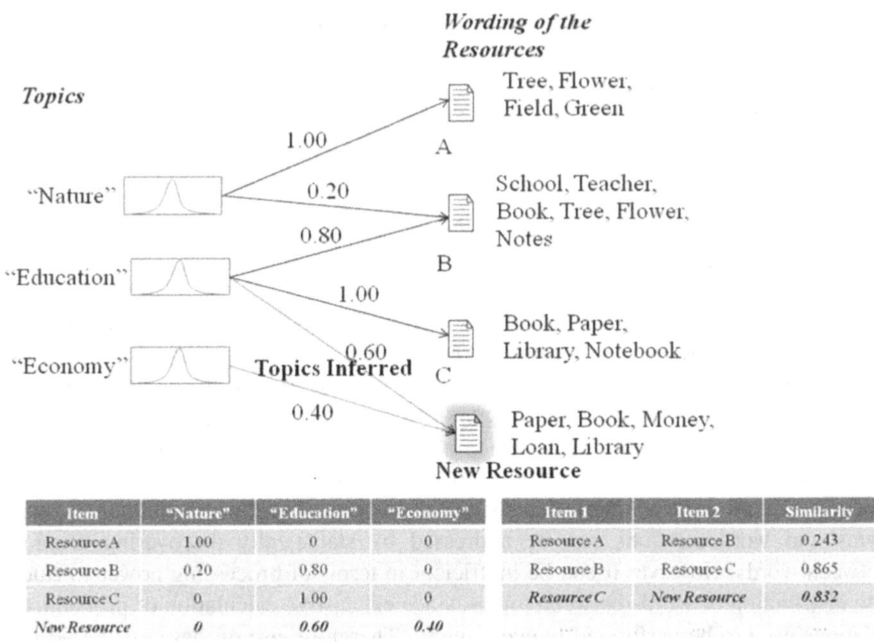

Item	"Nature"	"Education"	"Economy"
Resource A	1.00	0	0
Resource B	0.20	0.80	0
Resource C	0	1.00	0
New Resource	*0*	*0.60*	*0.40*

Item 1	Item 2	Similarity
Resource A	Resource B	0.243
Resource B	Resource C	0.865
Resource C	*New Resource*	*0.832*
...	...	...

Fig. 2. LDA item recommendation - adding a new resource

This extraction of topic distribution and use as similarity measure is illustrated in a simplified example in Figure 2. A new resource is added to the system and the topic distribution is inferred based on the words observed. The topic distribution for the new resource is considered as an identifier of its semantic content and the distance to the distributions of the other resources is considered a measure of similarity.

Latent topic detection approach for content recommendation is unsupervised and provides a number of benefits, compared to other supervised and model based methods. It is not depending on an external knowledge structure such as a taxonomy or ontology and does not require effort by the user in order to categorize the resources. Additionally, it can scale to accommodate evolving corporate knowledge bases and is less dependent on the wording of the text than other text-analysis techniques, since words with multiple meanings can be found in different topics.

3.1.2 Using LDA in Tag Recommendation

Tagging is the assignment of a keyword to a resource. Words that can be assigned as metadata to a resource can be either freely chosen by the user or selected from ordered lists or trees of categories. Social applications in their majority allow for free tagging (forming folksonomies), however it shouldn't be overseen that most corporate environments use some kind of taxonomy or catalogue.

Process and analysis of folksonomies is a field that has been intensely researched as in [19], [20]. Additionally a number of techniques have been examined in order to combine unsupervised probabilistic latent semantic analysis with folksonomies and specifically, Latent Dirichlet Allocation has been evaluated in folksonomies [21] for tag recommendation, outperforming state of the art association rules mining. In [21] the distribution of words for each topic is used as the source for tag recommendations. The details of our implementation are presented in section 4.2

3.2 Using LDA in Search

Search is one of the major functions performed inside a corporate portal. Search enables the users to access the ever-expanding and evolving knowledge base of the company.

Searching inside a corporate portal is a challenging application. The words used in the queries sometimes are not accurately found in the results expected by the user. Additionally, use of synonyms and idiosyncratic terms can greatly impair the efficiency of text-based search functionality. Suggestions to address these problems have been proposed including semantic search and query expansion, for example in [22], [23].

Probabilistic topic models can be used as an unsupervised technique to topic extraction and subsequent query expansion, where issues like word ambiguity, synonyms and word relations can be addressed by statistically discovering relations between words. However it can be inefficient in terms of processing power to calculate distribution of words between topics, since exhaustive calculation of probabilistic relations need to be performed in every query. Therefore, use of thesaurus based systems has been proposed [24].

In this case, even though the probabilistic topics are used to conclude the underlying similarities, subsequently a simpler word index is used in order to improve the speed of the query expansion.

4 Topic Analysis in Enterprise Social Software

In this section we describe our approach for integration of knowledge structures with latent topics and the specifics of the recommender systems and search implementations. Afterwards, we proceed to describe an indicative usage scenario of the applications in an enterprise.

4.1 Knowledge Structures and Latent Topics

Enterprise Social Software is supported by knowledge structures, which can vary on their level of documentation and top down imposition. Different kinds of ontologies have been proposed and each of them can be placed on a semantic continuum, ranging from lightweight to rigorously formalized ones, as illustrated for example in [25]. Additionally, there is a varying degree of arbitrary intervention, i.e. how much users are allowed to dynamically contribute to the refinement and extension of the structure.

In this spectrum we assume that the system can use a combination of both taxonomies and folksonomies. We then extend the system, using latent topics as presented in the Figure 3.

This system described is a combination of structured taxonomies, folksonomies and unsupervised latent topics. It supports the periodic processing of resources and discovery of latent topics. The discovered topics are then used as a basis for functionalities intentioned to assist the user, i.e. the search and recommendation functionality. Indirectly these functionalities affect the resources and the knowledge model of the system.

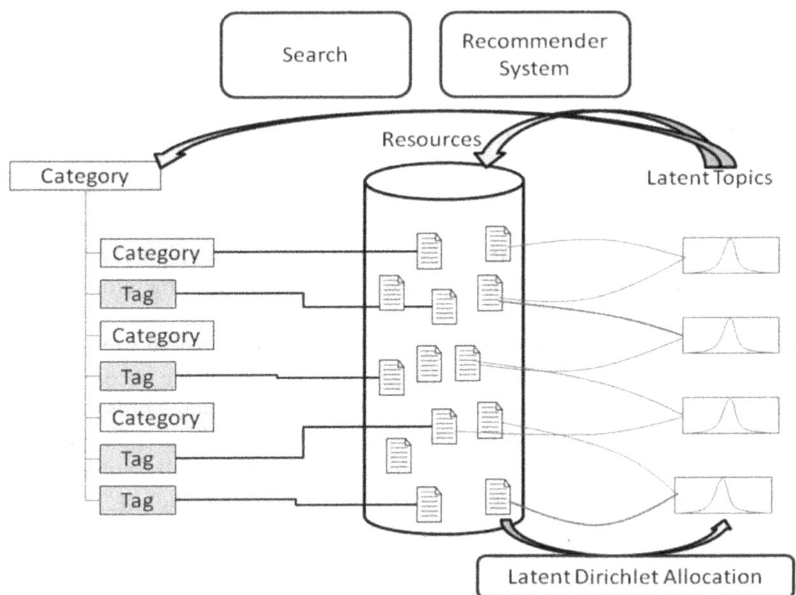

Fig. 3. Knowledge Structures and Latent Topics

Search and Resource Recommender is guiding the user to take into account latent topics. The search results and the recommendations can lead to creation and linking of related resources based on the analysis performed.

Tag Recommendation can influence the creation of knowledge structures in the portal; the recommendation of tags for the model can help the corporate categorization system evolve to describe emerging topics. As new documents are inserted into the system, new latent topics are detected in them as the probabilistic topic model is reassessed to match the document corpus. Dominant words in these topics are constantly suggested as keywords for the new related resources, therefore proposing refinements and extensions in the underlying knowledge structure to better describe the discovered topics.

4.2 Implementation

In this section we elaborate on the features of our implementation of recommender systems and search expansion for the OrganiK enterprise social system.

Resource Recommendation

The resource recommendation is implemented as content-based, related items functionality. When an item is read by the user, the system either retrieves the topic distribution or, in the case of a new item, infers the underlying topic distribution. Then, items that have a similar distribution of documents are suggested. To compare the similarity between the topic distributions of the documents, a cosine metric is used. Alternatively Kullback Leibler divergence metric could be applied [26].

Resource recommendation as a user interaction is currently limited to a recommender, in the form of a list of related resources next to the resource currently being read. However, it can be additionally applied to a subscription/notification system or to corporate newsletters.

Tag Recommendation

The Tag recommender system we propose can combine both formal and informal tagging approaches.

The first approach of tag suggestion derives from the similarity measures calculated as described in 3.1.1. The system infers the related resources from the topic distribution, and then proposes the tags already assigned to highly relevant items (item-to-item similarity).This approach reuses highly used tags, therefore reinforcing the model of terms used before in the system.

The second approach is based on the fact that topics that emerge from the analysis are represented by distributions of words. In the context of tag recommendations, these distributions can become the keyword pools. The dominant words of a topic can be used in order to categorize resources that are in some degree generated by this topic. For example, as in Figure 2, a latent topic that we can call *"nature"*, is modelled by the system in the form of a list: *{"green", "tree", "flower", "field", ...}*, where the words are placed in order of probabilistic importance. If a resource is closely related to this topic, then these dominant words are suggested as possible annotation keywords.

These two approaches are combined to propose the list of tags using a weighted combination approach. This hybrid recommender can both support an existing taxonomy and suggest new keywords based on dominant words in an evolving knowledge base.

Search

Our system implements a thesaurus-based solution. In this approach, words that are found together in a latent topic, are considered similar and are stored together with their similarity measure, after a threshold and pruning process is followed. Later, when the user executes a query including a number of terms, his query is expanded by some of the highly related terms.

To compute each document's score we use (3) as described in [24].

$$S_d(Q) = \mu S_d(E) + (1-\mu)S_d(Q) \tag{3}$$

In (3) Q is the query terms and E is the expansion based on the topic model thesaurus. S_d is the document scoring results as received by the underlying social software and μ ($0<\mu<1$) is the mixing parameter.

4.3 Walkthrough of the System

In this section we present how the above mentioned applications are integrated in an enterprise 2.0 system. As a platform we use the OrganiK Knowledge Management system [27], an enterprise social system intended for use in small and medium knowledge-intensive companies. The mallet [28] open-source implementation of Latent Dirichlet Allocation has been used.

All resources are recurrently analyzed and topics are created in the corporate portal. The topic distributions are saved in the system database, as well as the model than can be used in order to infer topics from a previously unseen document. The words are indexed and associated in a thesaurus.

An employee finds a new resource in the World Wide Web that is of interest to the enterprise. He inserts it together with his personal comments in the enterprise collaborative platform in the text area of a blog (Region 1 of Figure 4). The text content of the resource is analyzed in the background and relations to the existing topics are inferred.

The user can then locate related resources, which are suggested based on the latent topics. Suggestions appear at the Region 2 of Figure 4 and evolve as the user types in new information. The user can enhance the content of his resource by adding information from other relevant items or linking to them.

As the user types in text in the page, tags are suggested (Region 3 of Figure 4). The recommender is assisting the employee to categorize this resource. Tags are derived from both the corporate taxonomy and the latent topic wording.

A few minutes later, another user looks for *hazard*. This word is not contained in the page that the previous user wrote, however using latent topics for query expansion, related articles emerge – including the previous one. The query is expanded to cover related documents by using closely related words based on the latent topics.

The OrganiK Knowledge Management System, including the probabilistic topic analysis presented in this work, is currently under evaluation within five companies; they include two information technology service companies, a content provider, a translation/localisation services company and a maritime consulting company (we expect to have concrete results from an in-depth evaluation of our approach until the conference takes place).

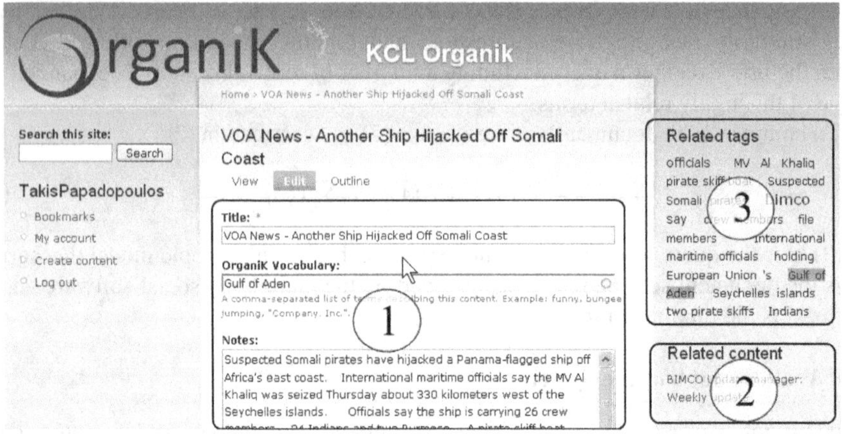

Fig. 4. Tag and Resource Recommendation

5 Related Work

Recommendation and search systems have been used to support the participation of employees in enterprise social software. In [29] the application of lightweight semantics is proposed to enhance the results of enterprise search, while [30] uses text and social network analysis to support search for experts. [31] demonstrates how utilising user annotations can improve the quality of an intranet search and [32] proposes an enterprise knowledge recommender system based on semantic matching and rules that can be adapted to different users. To the best of our knowledge, our work is the first effort for applying probabilistic topic models to support search and recommendation in enterprise social software.

6 Conclusions and Further Work

In this work we have demonstrated how probabilistic topic models as an integral part of an enterprise social system can enhance the recommendation processes and improve the efficiency of the search functionality. The specific method we propose addresses problems in query expansion and can enrich the results with related items. It also provides a sound basis for item-to-item collaborative and content-based recommendations. Our approach does not require significant effort from the employees as the documents evolve to cover diversifying subjects and is easily scalable to a large number of documents.

The qualities of such a probabilistic foundation can become evident in an enterprise social platform, established on a combination of ontologies of varying formality. This probabilistic topic analysis can improve flexibility and stability, as the corporate knowledge structure and the arbitrarily dynamic refinements and extensions are complemented with the latent topics.

Further work needs to be done in the applications of Latent Dirichlet Allocation. Challenges such as the currently required predefined number of topics and the relations between topics are addressed in the field of Information Retrieval. Furthermore the processing of user generated content such as text, terms and comments and user behaviour remains to be further explored and enhanced. Finally, the link between collaboratively created folksonomies and taxonomies is a field of intense research.

In this paper we have described the framework and the application of Latent Dirichlet Allocation as an extension of the underlying knowledge models and as a basis for recommendation and search functionality in enterprise social software. We have described and implemented specific query expansion, resource recommendation and a hybrid tag-recommendation technique. We have also presented an early implementation of the system, and then denoted the issues that should be addressed as probabilistic topic models are adopted in enterprise social software.

Acknowledgments. Research reported in this paper has been partially financed by the European Commission in the OrganiK project (FP7: Research for the Benefit of SMEs, 222225).

References

1. Reilly, T.: What is Web 2.0: Design patterns and business models for the next generation of software
2. McAfee, A.P.: Enterprise 2.0: The dawn of emergent collaboration. MIT Sloan Management Review 47, 21 (2006)
3. Eid, T.: The Enterprise Social Software Market Continues to Expand Gartner (2008)
4. Gilchrist, A.: Corporate taxonomies: report on a survey of current practice. Online Information Review 25, 94–103 (2001)
5. Folksonomy Coinage and Definition, `http://www.vanderwal.net/folksonomy.html`
6. Shirky, C., Butterfield, S., et al.: Folksonomy, or How I Learned to Stop Worrying and Love the Mess. (2005)
7. Dotsika, F.: Uniting formal and informal descriptive power: Reconciling ontologies with folksonomies. International Journal of Information Management 29, 407–415 (2009)
8. Hofmann, T.: Probabilistic latent semantic indexing. In: Proceedings of the 22nd ACM SIGIR conference on Research and development in information retrieval, pp. 50–57 (1999)
9. Steyvers, M., Griffiths, T.: Probabilistic topic models. In: Handbook of Latent Semantic Analysis, pp. 424–440 (2007)
10. Blei, D.M., Ng, A.Y., Jordan, M.I.: Latent dirichlet allocation. The Journal of Machine Learning Research 3, 993–1022 (2003)
11. Steyvers, M., et al.: Probabilistic author-topic models for information discovery. In: Proceedings of the tenth ACM SIGKDD international conference on Knowledge discovery and data mining, pp. 306–315 (2004) doi:10.1145/1014052.1014087

12. Shilakes, C.C., Tylman, J.: Enterprise information portals. Merrill Lynch (November 16, 1998)
13. Adomavicius, G., Tuzhilin, A.: Toward the next generation of recommender systems: A survey of the state-of-the-art and possible extensions. IEEE transactions on knowledge and data engineering 17, 734–749 (2005)
14. Linden, G., Smith, B., York, J.: Amazon.com recommendations: item-to-item collaborative filtering. Internet Computing, IEEE 7, 76–80 (2003)
15. Schafer, J.B., Konstan, J., Riedi, J.: Recommender systems in e-commerce. In: Proceedings of the 1st ACM conference on Electronic commerce, pp. 158–166 (1999)
16. Jin, X., Zhou, Y., Mobasher, B.: Web usage mining based on probabilistic latent semantic analysis. In: Proceedings of the tenth ACM SIGKDD international conference on Knowledge discovery and data mining, pp. 197–205 (2004) doi:10.1145/1014052.1014076
17. Chen, W.Y., et al.: Collaborative filtering for orkut communities: discovery of user latent behavior. In: Proceedings of the 18th international conference on World wide web, pp. 681–690 (2009)
18. Haruechaiyasak, C., Damrongrat, C.: Article Recommendation Based on a Topic Model for Wikipedia Selection for Schools. Digital Libraries: Universal and Ubiquitous Access to Information, 339–342 (2008)
19. Schmitz, C., et al.: Mining Association Rules in Folksonomies. Data Science and Classification, 261-270 (2006), http://dx.doi.org/10.1007/3-540-34416-0_28
20. Hotho, A., et al.: Information retrieval in folksonomies: Search and ranking
21. Krestel, R., Fankhauser, P., Nejdl, W.: Latent dirichlet allocation for tag recommendation. In: Proceedings of the third ACM conference on Recommender systems, pp. 61–68 (2009)
22. Voorhees, E.M.: Query expansion using lexical-semantic relations. In: Proceedings of the 17th annual international ACM SIGIR conference on Research and development in information retrieval, pp. 61–69 (1994), http://portal.acm.org/citation.cfm?id=188508
23. Xu, J., Croft, W.B.: Query expansion using local and global document analysis. In: Proceedings of the 19th annual international ACM SIGIR conference on Research and development in information retrieval, pp. 4–11 (1996)
24. Park, L.A., Ramamohanarao, K.: The sensitivity of latent dirichlet allocation for information retrieval. In: Buntine, W., Grobelnik, M., Mladenić, D., Shawe-Taylor, J. (eds.) ECML PKDD 2009. LNCS, vol. 5782, pp. 176–188. Springer, Heidelberg (2009)
25. Uschold, M., Gruninger, M.: Ontologies and semantics for seamless connectivity. SIGMOD Rec. 33, 58–64 (2004)
26. Lin, J.: Divergence measures based on the Shannon entropy. IEEE Transactions on Information theory 37, 145–151 (1991)
27. Bibikas, D., et al.: A Sociotechnical Approach to Knowledge Management in the Era of Enterprise 2.0: The case of OrganiK. Scalable Computing: Practice and Experience 9, 315–327 (2008)
28. McCallum, A.K.: MALLET: A Machine Learning for Language Toolkit (2002), http://mallet.cs.umass.edu
29. Passant, A., et al.: Semantic Search for Enterprise 2.0
30. Ehrlich, K., Lin, C., Griffiths-Fisher, V.: Searching for experts in the enterprise: combining text and social network analysis. In: Proceedings of the 2007 international ACM conference on Supporting group work, pp. 117–126 (2007)
31. Dmitriev, P.A., et al.: Using annotations in enterprise search. In: Proceedings of the 15th international conference on World Wide Web, pp. 811–817 (2006)
32. Zhen, L., Huang, G.Q., Jiang, Z.: An inner-enterprise knowledge recommender system. Expert Systems with Applications 37, 1703–1712 (2010)

Using SPARQL and SPIN for Data Quality Management on the Semantic Web

Christian Fürber and Martin Hepp

Universität der Bundeswehr München, E-Business & Web Science Research Group
Werner-Heisenberg-Weg 39, 85577 Neubiberg, Germany
c.fuerber@unibw.de, mhepp@computer.org

Abstract. The quality of data is a key factor that determines the performance of information systems, in particular with regard (1) to the amount of exceptions in the execution of business processes and (2) to the quality of decisions based on the output of the respective information system. Recently, the Semantic Web and Linked Data activities have started to provide substantial data resources that may be used for real business operations. Hence, it will soon be critical to manage the quality of such data. Unfortunately, we can observe a wide range of data quality problems in Semantic Web data. In this paper, we (1) evaluate how the state of the art in data quality research fits the characteristics of the Web of Data, (2) describe how the SPARQL query language and the SPARQL Inferencing Notation (SPIN) can be utilized to identify data quality problems in Semantic Web data automatically and this within the Semantic Web technology stack, and (3) evaluate our approach.

Keywords: Semantic Web, Linked Data, Data Quality Management, SPARQL, SPIN, RDF, Ontologies, Ontology-Based Data Quality Management.

1 Introduction

Due to the tight coupling of real-world processes and data, poor data quality may lead to errors in business processes or to wrong decisions, both causing additional costs. Also, data quality can impact product and service quality and the satisfaction of customers and employees [3]. According to *Redman*, the average total costs of poor data quality are as high as 8-12 % of a company's revenues [20]. In 2002, the Data Warehousing Institute estimated that poor data quality costs U.S. companies more than 600 billion US Dollar annually [19]. Those estimates are strong indicators for the significant impact of data quality on business success.

Semantic Web technologies aim to attach data structure, typed links, and axiomatically represented implicit facts to such data that is available on the Web. The goal is to empower computers to better extract, combine, interpret, and reuse the data [4]. A major share of such data originates from existing relational databases and is being lifted by mapping database schema elements to Web ontologies. Ontologies are commonly understood as conceptual models of a domain of interest that (1) aim at representing a model agreed among multiple individuals and organizations, and valid for

W. Abramowicz and R. Tolksdorf (Eds.): BIS 2010, LNBIP 47, pp. 35–46, 2010.

multiple contexts, and that (2) contain formal axioms to reduce the ambiguity of the conceptual elements [5].

Businesses and public institutions have already started to publish significant amounts of non-toy data on the Web using Web ontologies. For example, BestBuy Inc., one of the largest US retail chains for consumer electronics products, has started to publish its full catalog [6] using the GoodRelations ontology [7]. O'Reilly Media has also begun to expose their products using GoodRelations in the RDFa syntax [24]. In addition to the growing number of data published directly by the owners of the data source, the enterprise OpenLink Software has released a middleware technology called "Sponger cartridges" that creates, on the fly, RDF representations of Amazon, eBay, and other commerce sites using the GoodRelations ontology by accessing vendor-specific APIs [12]. This makes an unprecedented amount of actual business data available on the Web of Linked Data.

However, the process of lifting existing data sources to the RDF data model and Web ontologies like GoodRelations usually replicates existing data quality problems from the original representation. While sophisticated conversion scripts and middleware components can filter out some of the problems, the negative impact of data quality issues will grow on the Web of Data, because the data will be used in more applications and in more different contexts. The amount and impact of any problems will increase accordingly.

In this paper, we describe how data quality problems in Semantic Web data originating from relational databases can be identified and classified, and this within the Semantic Web technology stack. Our approach is motivated by three main assumptions: (1) quality checks based on ontologies are highly reusable, in particular in multiple-source scenarios that utilize ontologies as means for data integration, (2) the application of Semantic Web technologies facilitates the collective emergence of data quality knowledge on the Web, and (3) it is likely that many relational data sources will be exposed to the Semantic Web without previously applying strong quality checks. Our proposal can also be applied to relational databases inside closed settings, e.g. within a single enterprise.

While existing data quality management tools usually hide the rules inside application code or regular expressions, our approach makes the rules much more accessible and easier to maintain, extend, and share, because the rules are kept in the form of a library of SPARQL queries that are human-readable and platform-neutral.

2 Overview of Data Quality Problems

A common, but rather generic definition of high data quality is when it is "fit for use", i.e. that the data meets the required purpose [1]. This popular definition of data quality is based on the subjective perception of data quality by data consumers, encompassing several dimensions, such as accessibility, completeness, and relevance; see [1] for a complete list of established data quality dimensions. Despite the importance of data consumers' perception of data quality, this perspective is not solely sufficient for the development of algorithmic approaches for identifying data quality problems. A more technical understanding of quality is to require data to be "free of defects" [2]. While still rather generic, this allows categorizing data quality problems according to their cause or effect. In the following, we summarize the work of [8-11] and provide a typology of data quality problems (see Table 1).

We trace back the types of quality problems found in literature to four basic types, namely inconsistency, lack of comprehensibility, heterogeneity, and redundancy. In the following sections, we describe these basic types of data quality problems. For a detailed discussion of the original data quality problems, we refer to [8-11].

Our current main interest is to improve the quality of literal values in ontology-based knowledge representations, which have so far not attracted a lot of interest from the formal ontology communities. In this paper, we focus on data quality problems in single-source scenarios, i.e. such within one database. So far, we have developed generally usable identification rules for syntactical errors, missing values, unique value violations, out of range values, and functional dependency violations, all of which are explained in more detail in section 3.

Ontologies also promise significant benefits when data from multiple sources is being combined during retrieval or integration, e.g. as described in [21], but that is part of our ongoing research. Also, we did not yet investigate problems within the conceptual model of ontologies themselves.

Table 1. Common data quality problems in single-source scenarios [8-11]

Data Quality Problem	Basic Type
Word transposition/Syntax violation	Inconsistency
Outdated values	Inconsistency
False values	Inconsistency
Misfielded values	Inconsistency
Meaningless values	Comprehensibility
Missing values	Inconsistency
Out of range values	Inconsistency
Invalid substrings	Inconsistency
Mistyping / Misspelling errors	Inconsistency
Imprecise values	Comprehensibility
Unique value violation	Inconsistency
Violation of a functional dependency	Inconsistency
Referential integrity violation	Inconsistency
Incorrect reference	Inconsistency
Contradictory relationships	Inconsistency
Existence of synonyms	Heterogeneity, Redundancy
Existence of homonyms	Comprehensibility
Approximate duplicate tuples	Redundancy
Inconsistent duplicate tuples	Redundancy, Inconsistency
Business domain constraint violation	Inconsistency
Outdated conceptual elements	Inconsistency

2.1 Representational Inconsistency

Inconsistency subsumes all data quality problems that originate from an actual state σ' of an element E to differ from the required state σ for E. Thereby, the element E can be (1) syntax, (2) the lexical representation of a value, (3) a data type, (4) a schema element, or (5) a relationship. For example, the value for an attribute "date" may require a syntax (E) of state DD/MM/YYYY (σ), but the syntax (E) of a value could actually have the state YYYY/DD/MM (σ'). So if $\sigma'(E) \neq \sigma(E)$, we call σ' inconsistent to σ. In other words, the actual state of the element is inconsistent to the required state of the element. Functional dependency violations are not fully covered by this formula. According to [13], functional dependencies exist if a value v_1 of an attribute α_1 requires specific values v_n of one or more other attributes α_n in the representation. Hence, in contrast to other inconsistency problems, functional dependencies encompass states of more than one element. This also applies for referential integrity violations, incorrect references, inconsistencies among duplicate tuples, and for certain types of business domain constraint violations.

2.2 Comprehensibility

We define comprehensibility as the condition of data to be correctly interpreted by other applications or users. We further break down comprehensibility into ambiguity and vacuity. Ambiguity is if an instance or a schema element can represent two or more meanings that are treated differently by any consumer of the data. A typical case is the usage of homonyms without providing any context. We consider instances or schema elements that have no meaning at all in the presented context as vacuous. It is usually difficult to define hard criteria for comprehensibility, because this property often depends on the amount of context attached to the data and on the amount of background knowledge available to the interpreting agent. Data that is comprehensible within a closed enterprise setting may become incomprehensible when consumed on a Web scale due to the lack of contextual information.

2.3 Heterogeneity

Heterogeneity as a type of data quality problems subsumes all cases in which the representation of identical information varies. Heterogeneity mostly heavily occurs in multiple-source scenarios and can be broken down into *structural* heterogeneity and *semantic* heterogeneity. In cases of structural heterogeneity, the same real-world domain is represented by different schema elements. Semantic heterogeneity also constitutes a difference in the intension of the compared schemata with overlapping elements [9].

2.4 Redundancy

Redundancy problems exist when the same real-world entity or relationship is represented more than once and are not constrained to multiple-source scenarios. Inconsistency problems frequently co-occur with redundancy problems if some of the attribute values of the redundant tuples differ in meaning.

3 Identifying Data Quality Problems with SPARQL and SPIN

In this section, we describe our approach to identify data quality problems in Semantic Web data through the use of the SPARQL Inferencing Notation (SPIN) [17]. First, we describe the architecture of our approach. Next, we show how respective rules for the automatic identification of data quality problems in Semantic Web data can be designed and used. Finally, we evaluate our approach and outline open issues and limitations.

3.1 Architecture for Ontology-Based Data Quality Management (OBDQM)

A key goal of our approach is to handle data quality problems entirely within the Semantic Web technology stack and to employ existing technologies from the Semantic Web community. This allows using the Semantic Web itself for the collective emergence of data quality rules, i.e., users can create, improve, and share knowledge about spotting and curing data quality problems on the Semantic Web.

For the extraction of relational data we use D2RQ[1]. With D2RQ, we can extract data from a relational database into an RDF representation. This step will be optional for data that is already published as RDF. After extracting the data, we can import the data file into TopBraid Composer Free Edition[2] or another environment that supports SPIN[3]. SPARQL[4] is a query language for querying RDF data. SPIN is a framework that utilizes SPARQL to facilitate the definition of constraints and inference rules in ontologies. When applying the constraints on the ontology, SPIN can flag all problematic data elements and list them in a report. The defined rules can be attached to a class of entities in the form of SPARQL queries. With the use of SPARQL query templates in SPIN, it is possible to define generic queries with high reusability [17].

When lifting relational data to RDF automatically, we usually get very simple ontology structures based on the elements of the database. This requires refinements to enable more sophisticated reasoning. For example, the domain and range definitions of properties are usually not available from the extraction. In single-source scenarios, such can be added directly to the extracted ontology using an ontology editor. In multiple-source scenarios, however, it might be more suitable to create a global ontology with mappings to the local database schemata to enable reasoning with a source-independent vocabulary [18]. The mappings from the local database schemata to the global ontology can be created with D2RQ as well. Figure 1 illustrates the basic approach.

To facilitate the identification of data quality problems, we have to create formalized definitions of the expected data quality problem types. For this purpose, we employ SPARQL query templates. The templates have to be customized and can be attached to the class of entities that contains the data to be checked. They are attached using SPIN constraints. After the creation of the query templates and its customization, SPIN can be used to identify, flag, and report each data quality problem. Thus, further

[1] `http://www4.wiwiss.fu-berlin.de/bizer/d2rq/`
[2] `http://www.topquadrant.com/products/TB_Composer.html#free`
[3] `http://spinrdf.org/spin.html`
[4] `http://www.w3.org/TR/2008/REC-rdf-sparql-query-20080115/`

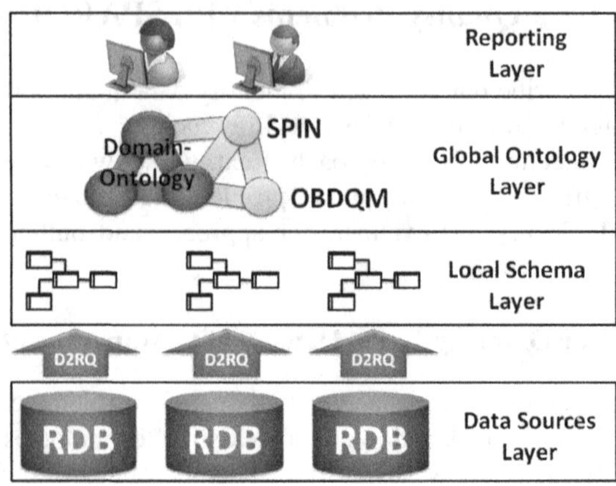

Fig. 1. Architecture of ontology-based data quality management

analysis of the presented data quality problems can be performed by domain experts; alternatively, heuristics for solving the problems can be triggered automatically.

3.2 Identification of Data Quality Problems with SPIN

With the proposed architecture, we can focus on the main problem, i.e., the automated identification of data quality problems. For that, we define generic SPARQL query templates based on the typology of data quality problems from section 2.

As explained in section 2, inconsistency in the representation exists if the real state of an element does not meet the expected state of an element. Thus, in order to identify data quality problems with SPARQL queries, we need to express nearly all states of an element that do not meet the expected state. In other words, every SPARQL query template used to identify data quality problems has to define either all legal or all illegal states of an element. In the case of OWL object properties, the amount of axioms determines the effort for spotting respective problems. A greater formal account of the ontology, e.g. by including disjointness axioms, simplifies the rules design for data quality management. For OWL datatype properties, the use of intervals, regular expressions, and negations can reduce a lot of manual effort.

We define ASK and CONSTRUCT queries in the property `spin:body` of the generalized query template with variables, as depicted in Figure 2. The element types of the variables have to be defined in the property `spin:constraint` in order to support customization of the query. Typical element types in this case are classes, properties, or literals. Since the answer of ASK queries can only be true or false, they are especially suitable to simply flag data quality problems. When the query result returns true, the problems will be flagged by SPIN tools automatically. If the query contains more than one triple in the WHERE clause, i.e. class, property, and literal combinations, it is recommended to use a CONSTRUCT query statement with the properties `spin:ConstraintViolation`, `spin:violationRoot`, and `spin:violationPath` to correctly flag the data quality problem where it occurs.

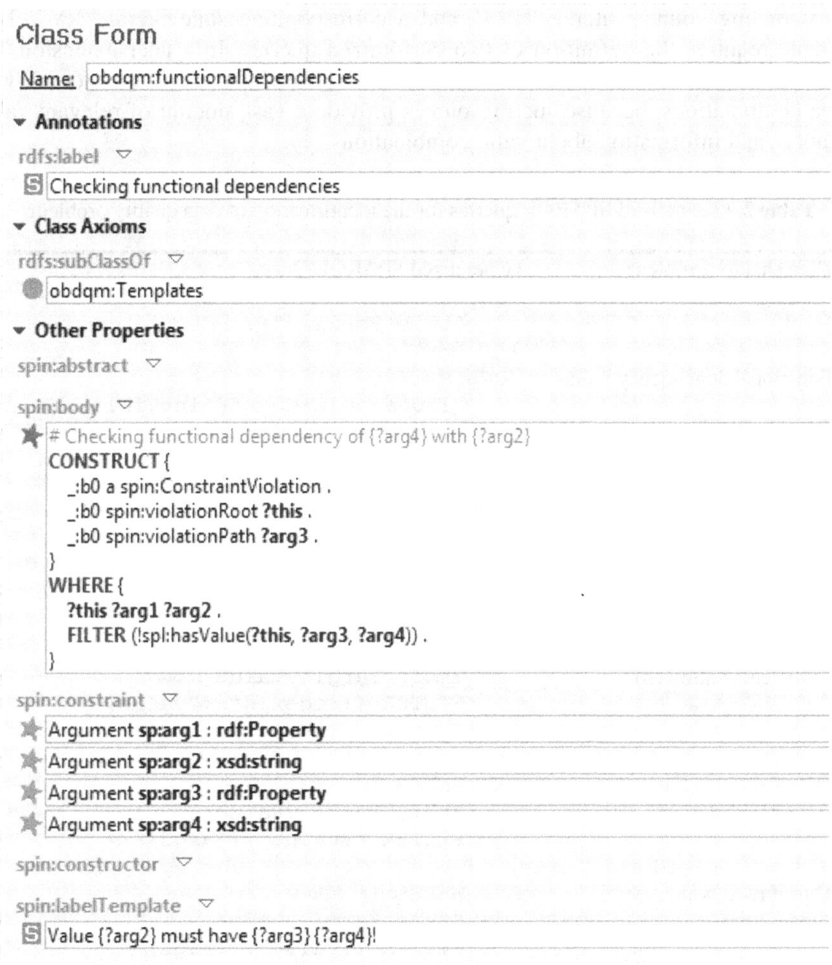

Class Form

Name: obdqm:functionalDependencies

▾ Annotations

rdfs:label

Checking functional dependencies

▾ Class Axioms

rdfs:subClassOf

obdqm:Templates

▾ Other Properties

spin:abstract

spin:body

```
# Checking functional dependency of {?arg4} with {?arg2}
CONSTRUCT {
   _:b0 a spin:ConstraintViolation .
   _:b0 spin:violationRoot ?this .
   _:b0 spin:violationPath ?arg3 .
}
WHERE {
   ?this ?arg1 ?arg2 .
   FILTER (!spl:hasValue(?this, ?arg3, ?arg4)) .
}
```

spin:constraint

Argument **sp:arg1 : rdf:Property**

Argument **sp:arg2 : xsd:string**

Argument **sp:arg3 : rdf:Property**

Argument **sp:arg4 : xsd:string**

spin:constructor

spin:labelTemplate

Value {?arg2} must have {?arg3} {?arg4}!

Fig. 2. Properties of a SPARQL query template in TopBraid Composer

Finally, we only have to define an error message in the property spin:labelTemplate that will be shown with the flagged data quality problem.

For the identification of syntax violations in literals, we use regular expressions in the SPARQL query in order to define the allowed characters in the literal and simply negate it. SPIN tools will flag all literals with syntactical states that do not satisfy the regular expression.

For the identification of functional dependency violations, we focused on defining bilateral dependencies in the generic query template, i.e., a value v_1 of attribute α_1 requires a certain value v_2 for attribute α_2. This can be extended to multilateral relationships by using this query template multiple times. In our example we would additionally define that value v_1 of attribute α_1 also requires a certain value v_3 for attribute α_3. For instance, we can define that the city "Las Vegas" can only have a corresponding country literal "USA" and a corresponding state literal "NV". This example requires the definition of two customized queries. In a later extension, we will tap existing Linked Open Data resources like DBPedia as references for allowed value combinations, because such resources provide a vast amount of relevant value instances and information about valid combinations.

Table 2. Generalized SPARQL queries for the identification of data quality problems

Data Quality Problem	Generalized SPARQL Query

Missing values	ASK WHERE {
	    ?this ?arg1 "" .
	}

Functional dependency violation	CONSTRUCT {
	    _:b0 a spin:ConstraintViolation .
	    _:b0 spin:violationRoot ?this .
	    _:b0 spin:violationPath ?arg3 .
	}
	WHERE {
	    ?this ?arg1 ?arg2 .
	    FILTER (!spl:hasValue(?this,
	?arg3, ?arg4)) .
	}

Syntax violation
(only letters allowed)
	ASK WHERE {
	    ?this ?arg1 ?value .
	    FILTER (!regex(str(?value),
	"^([A-Za-z,.])*$")) .
	}

Out of range value
(lower limit)
	ASK WHERE {
	    ?this ?arg1 ?value .
	    FILTER (?value < ?arg2) .
	}

Out of range value
(upper limit)
	ASK WHERE {
	    ?this ?arg1 ?value .
	    FILTER (?value > ?arg2) .
	}

Unique value violation	CONSTRUCT {
	    _:b0 a spin:ConstraintViolation .
	    _:b0 spin:violationRoot ?a .
	    _:b0 spin:violationPath ?arg1 .
	}
	WHERE {
	    ?a ?arg1 ?uniqueValue .
	    ?b ?arg1 ?uniqueValue .
	    FILTER (?a != ?b) .
	}

We also created generic queries for the identification of missing values, unique value violations, and out of range values. Missing values can be detected with a simple query searching for empty literal values. This works for numeric and string data types.

The identification of unique values requires a search of equal literals in the same data type property of a different tuple. Since we are again using more than one triple pattern in the WHERE clause, it is necessary to define the location of the potential violation in a CONSTRUCT statement so that the URI of the problem can be reported. Finally, out of range values can only occur with numeric data types. Hence, they can easily be detected with the relational operators "less than" or "greater than", as long as datatypes are properly attached to the RDF literals. For more flexibility, we created two queries to identify out of range values, one for values surpassing the upper limit and one for values below the lower limit. Hence, it is possible to define the legal range either as a single point boundary or in the form of an interval. The limits have to be set during the customization of the queries. All of our queries are summarized in table 2.

4 Related Work

Data quality problems have been addressed by database research for over a decade. In the Semantic Web research community, the problem of data quality is a rather new topic. With growing adoption of the Semantic Web, the diversity of data sources that will be lifted to RDF and the loss of contextual information when reusing data on a Web scale will increase the importance of data quality research for the Web of Linked data. Most existing work from the Semantic Web does not address data quality at the instance level. In particular, errors that are not directly accessible at the logical level received little attention. In the following, we summarize the most relevant previous works.

Ji et al. describe a plug-in called RaDon (Repair and Diagnosis on Ontology Networks) for ontology modeling software, which tries to extend capabilities of existing reasoners to detect inconsistencies [16]. RaDon focuses on logical contradictions when mapping ontologies to each other. The tool assumes that the single ontologies are already consistent and coherent, and focuses on repairing mappings between ontologies. *Hartig* proposed a provenance model for Web data [22]. It is based on the finding that information on the provenance of data can be used to predict the perceived quality of data by its consumers. This provenance model considers data access and data creation. In [23], he complements that work by a framework to extent Semantic Web data with trust values. The trust values are based on subjective perceptions about the query object. Although the latter two approaches provide more transparency about the underlying data sources and its potential trustworthiness, they do not directly identify data quality problems. Hence, they do not provide enough information to spot and repair data quality problems on the instance level.

The approach described by *Wang et al.* in [14] uses a task ontology for describing data cleansing tasks to be performed over existing information systems. Users are required to define a "cleaning" goal, which is translated into queries on the knowledge base to identify adequate cleaning methods. Based on the query results, an appropriate cleansing algorithm can be applied. *Grüning* describes a domain-specific example of data quality management for energy companies that partly uses ontologies [15]. In a training phase, domain experts have to flag data that exhibit data quality problems. Based on the annotations of the training phase, algorithms can be trained to identify and annotate data quality problems automatically. Unfortunately, this excellent approach currently focuses on data quality management for the energy industry only. Moreover, it only considers outlier analysis, redundancies, functional dependency violations, and suspicious timestamps. Although the use of learning algorithms saves a lot of effort, wrongly trained algorithms may limit the impact of that work.

To the best of our knowledge, there is currently no holistic approach that (1) provides a domain-independent data quality management methodology for Semantic Web data, and that (2) handles those problems entirely within the Semantic Web technology stack.

5 Evaluation

In order to evaluate our approach, we created a small sample MySQL database consisting of four tables with data about products and their inventory locations. For the evaluation scenario, we assumed that we want to publish the data on the Semantic Web. The sample data contained errors for different inconsistency problems, e.g. the city "Las Vegas" was wrongly located in the country of "France". We dumped the database completely into an RDF/XML file using a script from D2RQ. The script created individual ontology classes for each of the database tables, data type properties for each of the table columns, and RDF literals from the attribute values. After the extraction of the data, we refined the raw ontology in TopBraid Composer. First, we changed the `rdf:type` to `owl:Class` for the "table-classes", defined the four classes as subclasses of `owl:Thing`, and assigned domains and ranges to the datatype properties.

After refining the extracted ontology, we customized the generic queries for our ontology. The exclamation marks in Fig. 3 show the identified data quality problems of a certain tuple. In this example, we defined a functional dependency between the city "Las Vegas" and the country "USA". Moreover, we defined that the properties `vocab:location_COUNTRY` and `vocab:location_STREET` should only contain letters and that the property `vocab:location_STREETNO` must always have a literal value. Finally, we defined that the property `vocab:location_ID` must only contain unique values. Any new data of this class underlies the same quality checks.

The evaluation based on the sample data shows that the developed generic rules are suitable to identify data quality problems in literals. Since we are at an early stage of research, we have not yet developed algorithms for all data quality problems from table 1. In the future, we will design additional rules for the identification of comprehensibility problems, redundancy problems, and heterogeneity problems. The identification of certain data quality problems, e.g. false values or outdated values, may likely require additional annotations in the ontology. At present, we have no formal evidence about the scalability of our approach. However, existing commercial databases for RDF data, e.g. Virtuoso from OpenLink Software, contain powerful optimizations for regular expressions and scale well up to at least 8 billion triples. We are planning a more formal evaluation on real-world data sets to prove practical applicability.

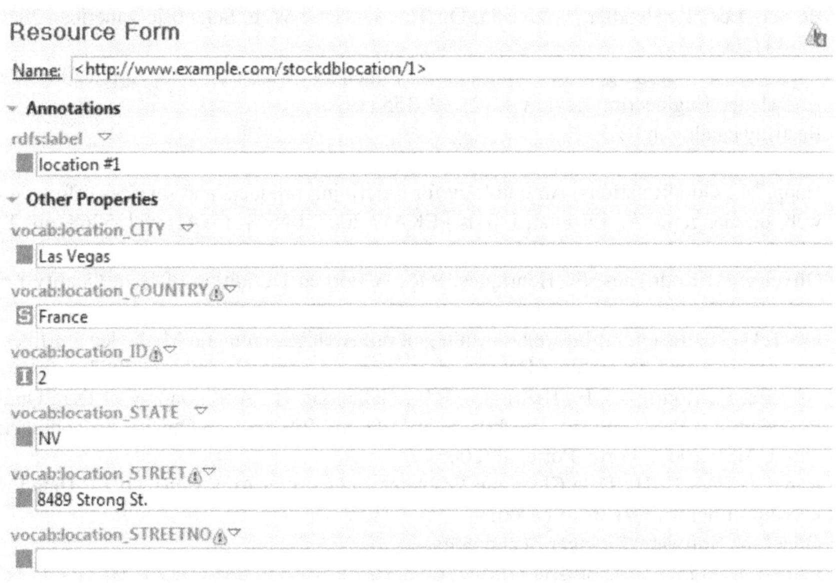

Fig. 3. Identification of data quality problems

6 Conclusion and Outlook on Future Work

The proposed approach provides a set of generally usable query templates that allow the identification of data quality problem types, as known from data quality research, in relational database content lifted to RDF, and to native RDF knowledge bases alike, independently of a specific domain or source system. Therefore, it is theoretically suitable for any Semantic Web data before or after its publication on the Web.

So far, we have developed query templates for the identification of syntax errors, missing values, unique value violations, out of range values, and functional dependency violations. Future work will address the development of additional identification rules for other data quality problems. Moreover, we plan to develop correction heuristics for the automated repair of some of the identified data quality problems. It is also planned to evaluate our approach using large-scale real-world data sets to prove the practical applicability. Additionally, we will soon expand the scope of our approach to multi-source scenarios that will be suitable for data quality management of master data distributed in heterogeneous data sources.

References

1. Wang, R.Y., Strong, D.M.: Beyond accuracy: what data quality means to data consumers. Journal of Management Information Systems 12(4), 5–33 (1996)
2. Redman, T.C.: Data quality: the field guide. Digital Press, Boston (2001)
3. Redman, T.C.: Data quality for the information age. Artech House, Boston (1996)

4. Berners-Lee, T., Hendler, J., Lassila, O.: The Semantic Web. Scientific American 284(5), 34–43 (2001)
5. Uschold, M., Gruninger, M.: Ontologies: Principles, Methods, and Applications. The Knowledge Engineering Review 11(2), 93–155 (1996)
6. BestBuy catalog in RDF, `http://products.semweb.bestbuy.com/sitemap.xml`
7. Hepp, M.: GoodRelations: An ontology for describing products and services offers on the web. In: Gangemi, A., Euzenat, J. (eds.) EKAW 2008. LNCS (LNAI), vol. 5268, pp. 329–346. Springer, Heidelberg (2008)
8. Oliveira, P., Rodrigues, F., Henriques, P.R.: A Formal Definition of Data Quality Problems. In: International Conference on Information Quality (2005)
9. Leser, U., Naumann, F.: Informationsintegration: Architekturen und Methoden zur Integration verteilter und heterogener Datenquellen. dpunkt-Verlag, Heidelberg (2007)
10. Oliveira, P., Rodrigues, F., Henriques, P.R., Galhardas, H.: A Taxonomy of Data Quality Problems. In: Proc. 2nd Int. Workshop on Data and Information Quality (in conjunction with CAiSE 2005), Porto, Portugal (2005)
11. Rahm, E., Do, H.-H.: Data Cleaning: Problems and Current Approaches. IEEE Data Engineering Bulletin 23(4), 3–13 (2000)
12. OpenLink Software: Sponger Technology, `http://virtuoso.openlinksw.com/dataspace/dav/wiki/Main/VirtSponger`
13. Olson, J.: Data quality: the accuracy dimension. Morgan Kaufmann Publishers, San Francisco (2003)
14. Wang, X., Hamilton, H.J., Bither, Y.: An ontology-based approach to data cleaning. Dept. of Computer Science, University of Regina, Regina (2005)
15. Grüning, F.: Datenqualitätsmanagement in der Energiewirtschaft. Oldenburger Verlag für Wirtschaft, Informatik und Recht, Oldenburg (2009)
16. Ji, Q., Haase, P., Qi, G., Hitzler, P., Stadtmüller, S.: RaDON – Repair and Diagnosis in Ontology Networks. In: 6th European Semantic Web Conference on The Semantic Web: Research and Applications (2009)
17. Knublauch, H.: SPIN – SPARQL Inferencing Notation (2009), `http://spinrdf.org/` (retrieved December 4, 2009)
18. Alexiev, V., Breu, M., de Bruin, J., Fensel, D., Lara, R., Lausen, H.: Information integration with ontologies: experiences from an industrial showcase. Jon Wiley & Sons, Ltd., Chichester (2005)
19. Eckerson, W.: Data Quality and the Bottom Line: Achieving Business Success through a Commitment to High Quality Data. Report of The Data Warehousing Institute (2002)
20. Redman, T.C.: The impact of poor data quality on the typical enterprise. Communications of the ACM 41, 79–82 (1998)
21. Kedad, Z., Métais, E.: Ontology-Based Data Cleaning. In: Proceedings of the 6th International Conference on Applications of Natural Language to Information Systems-Revised Papers (2002)
22. Hartig, O.: Provenance Information in the Web of Data. In: Linked Data on the Web (LDOW 2009) Workshop at the World Wide Web Conference, WWW (2009)
23. Hartig, O.: Querying trust in RDF data with tSPARQL. In: Aroyo, L., Traverso, P., Ciravegna, F., Cimiano, P., Heath, T., Hyvönen, E., Mizoguchi, R., Oren, E., Sabou, M., Simperl, E. (eds.) ESWC 2009. LNCS, vol. 5554, pp. 5–20. Springer, Heidelberg (2009)
24. O'Reilly catalog in RDF, `http://oreilly.com/catalog/9780596007683`

Quality in Blogs: How to Find the Best User Generated Content

Rafael Hellmann, Joachim Griesbaum, and Thomas Mandl

University of Hildesheim, Germany
rafael.p.hellmann@gmail.com,
joachim.griesbaum@uni-hildesheim.de,
thomas.mandl@uni-hildesheim.de

Abstract. As the popularity of weblogging continues to grow, the automatic quality assessment of user generated content shifts more and more into the focus of scientific and commercial discussions. This paper examines Web Mining and machine learning methods for these purposes. Based on automatically detectable features, various blog-specific quality models are trained using machine learning methods. Data from several thousand blogs in three languages has been collected. Along with the assessment of their efficiency, the most useful attributes are identified. Thus, this work points at the characteristics of high-quality blogs and develops basic ideas for their automatic analysis.

Keywords: Quality Retrieval, Web Mining, Blogs, Quality Models, Metrics.

1 Introduction

Weblogging continues to become increasingly popular. Technorati has tracked 112 Million blogs in 2008 with 120 thousand being created every day [1]. In 2006 their number has doubled every six months [2]. Blogs are considered a particularity of grassroots journalism [3], enabling everybody to publish, re-publish, read and discuss information directly without the need to have it reviewed or proofread. Blogs are a typical instance of User Generated Content and bring about high subjectivity and extremely varying qualities of published information. However at the very core of the blogosphere, there is a relatively small number of highly frequented and frequently referenced blogs, which are sometimes referred to as A-Listers [4]. They usually top popular national or international blog rankings as Technorati, and are known by names as *Huffington Post, TechCrunch* or *Engadget*. But what exactly is this concept of quality, making us humans able to tell apart high quality from lower quality blogs? Can features of high quality blogs be exploited in a way that we are able to use them to train systems to assess the quality of blogs automatically?

This abstract, blog-specific definition of quality is analyzed throughout this paper. While there are plenty of qualitative studies on the structure, quality and contents of blogs, the number of large, quantitative analyses has been very limited so far. On the basis of AQUAINT [5], we have studied the correlation of blog features and the perceived quality of blogs. Several (to some extent experimental) blog features were modeled in Java and assessed for their usefulness as quality-determining characteristics in

W. Abramowicz and R. Tolksdorf (Eds.): BIS 2010, LNBIP 47, pp. 47–58, 2010.

quality models, which were developed throughout machine learning features. Thus, this work does on the one hand evaluate the accuracy of machine learning models in quality classification tasks. On the other hand it helps us understand which blog characteristics contribute to a blog's objective quality and how they could be exploited for quality blog retrieval tasks in the future.

The remainder of the paper is organized as follows. The next section discusses related work and shows the shortcomings of previous approaches. Section 3 describes how the quality features were modeled and finally exploited from blog collections. Section 4 gives an overview on the performance of the developed quality models. A resume and an outlook close the paper.

2 Related Work

Quality can be interpreted as the degree of desirability of a page by a user of a search service. Many definitions for the quality of information products have been discussed in the literature. The user interface and the content are inseparable on the web and as a consequence, their evaluation cannot always be separated easily. As a consequence, content and interface are usually considered to form two aspects of quality and they are jointly assessed for web pages. A helpful quality definition in this context is provided by Huang et al. [6]. It is shown in table 1.

Table 1. Categories of information quality (IQ) [6]

IQ Category	IQ Dimensions
Intrinsic IQ	Accuracy, objectivity, believability, reputation
Contextual IQ	Relevancy, value-added, timeliness, completeness, amount of information
Representational IQ	Interpretability, ease of understanding, concise representation, consistent representation
Accessibility IQ	Access, security

Many researchers in the area of automatic quality assessment agree that an objective notion of quality cannot be found. Nevertheless, quality can be treated as independent of relevance. Relevance describes the situational value of a document in a search setting. Quality describes aspects of documents independent of any current information need.

It is not yet fully understood which aspects humans value the most when they assess the overall quality of web pages. However, experiments show that layout and design aspects are very important for quality decisions [7]. Consequently, automatic quality analysis systems should rely heavily on the detection and analysis of design aspects in order to distinguish high quality from low quality pages.

The assignment of quality to Web pages does not seem to be universally constant. Design and content features which humans consider important for their quality decisions are culturally dependent. Lists of quality criteria from several countries proved to partially contain different criteria and to assign different importance to the same criteria. A survey in Peru and Germany revealed great differences [8].

2.1 Link Analysis

Link analysis is the approach most often discussed for automatic quality assessment in information retrieval. Some search engines claim that they implement link analysis in their ranking algorithm.

The most popular algorithm is PageRank. The basic assumption of PageRank and similar approaches is that the number of in- or back-links of a web page can be used as a measure for the popularity and consequently for the quality of a page [9]. PageRank assigns an authority value to each Web page, which is primarily a function of its back links. Additionally, it assumes that links from pages with high authority should be weighed higher and should result in a higher authority for the receiving page. To account for the different values each page has to distribute, the algorithm is carried out iteratively until the result converges [9].

2.2 Page Content and Design

Assessing the quality of individual web pages is the aim of many approaches. One of the earliest automatic quality assessment systems originated in web engineering and did HTML syntax checking. Syntax checkers for HTML and other web standards analyze the quality of Web pages from the perspective of software engineering [10]. Some systems consider the human-computer interaction of web sites. Recently, some systems emphasize aspects of accessibility[1].

Many lists of criteria for the quality of web pages have been developed from the perspective of library and information science. These lists intend to support the user during quality decision processes. Their criteria are often vague and it is often not even clear whether a rule indicates high or low quality.

A study on the age and timely relevance of web pages uses a decay measure as a quality metric [11]. Similar to PageRank, the decay of a page is defined as the number of dead links on pages to which it links. This decay measure needs to be calculated iteratively. A content oriented definition of quality inspired by information retrieval metrics is proposed by Tang et al. [11]. In a user experiment, 350 high quality pages from the medical domain were identified by humans. Relevance feedback was used to direct a crawler toward other high quality pages. The crawler used relevance feedback measures on the high quality set to find typical terms for high quality pages.

2.3 Machine Learning Approaches

The approach implemented by Zhu & Gauch explicitly integrates quality assessment into an information retrieval system. Six criteria for quality are extracted from web pages: “currency, availability, information–to-noise ratio, authority, popularity, and cohesiveness“ [12]. These criteria are used to influence the ranking of documents in retrieval. It was shown that the average precision of the rankings including quality

---

[1] E.g. http://www.webxact.com/

measures outperformed those which relied solely on traditional information retrieval measures in some cases. However, this evaluation does not take the quality of the results into account but only the relevance of the pages in the result list.

Zhu & Gauch explicitly integrate quality assessment into an information retrieval system. Six criteria for quality are extracted from web pages: "currency, availability, information–to-noise ratio, authority, popularity, and cohesiveness" [12].

Amento et al. also stress the importance of a distinction between relevance and quality. An experiment involving some 1,000 web pages suggests, that the human perception of the quality of Web pages can be predicted by four formal features. These four features include link analysis measures and the total number of in-links. However, simple features like the number of pages on a site and the number of graphics on a page also correlated highly with the human judgments [13].

The system WebTango extracts more than 150 atomic and simple features from a web page and tries to reveal statistical correlations to a set of sites rated as excellent [14]. The extracted features are based on the design, the structure and the HTML code of a page. The data was extracted form an internet design award for popular pages. Pages adjudged the award were considered to be high quality pages. The data sets contained 5400 pages from 639 sites. A third fell into the categories good, average and poor. Classifiers could learn this assignment with an accuracy of 94% in the test set [14].

2.4 Automatic Assessment of User Generated Content

Information on the web does vary in both format and quality. This applies even more for User Generated Content, amongst the most popular representatives of which are counted weblogs and wikis. They all share a high focus on user participation and collaborative creation of contents, which are considered characteristics of the Web 2.0. The special features of the information, which has been worked out by users throughout social processes, may demand special techniques of analysis which account for the aspects which may not be distinctive in traditional web publication formats. In this section, we present some approaches which have inspired us during our work.

Nanno et al. [15] introduce a rule-based blog filtering and monitoring system. It uses a range of hypertext-based features as well as date markups to discriminate blogs from non-blog web content. The implementation of various heuristic rules leads to a classification accuracy of 94% for a collection of 300 Japanese weblogs.

Elgersma & de Rijke [16] demonstrate how machine learning approaches can be used to discriminate blogs from other web sites. They identify 46 attributes, which serve the algorithms as basis for the classification experiments. They go from the number of posts to the verification of characteristic expression as "archives" or "comments". While manual classifications using these attributes usually have baseline accuracies of 80%, Elgersma & de Rijke [16] come up with high automatic classification accuracies ranging from 90% for Naive Bayes to 94.75% for SMO.

Li et al. [17] show that machine learning methods may profit from the additional information incorporated in blog comments. Throughout their clustering experiments the comments of blogs turned out be better indicators than the corresponding titles of the blog posts themselves. Li et al. [17] conclude that the effectiveness of machine learning methods can be improved if comments and their timestamps are used for indexing purposes.

As Macdonald & Ounis [18] argue, the increasing pervasiveness of syndication formats offers additional prospects for the automatic recognition of documents. Using a collection of 100,649 blogs they compare the retrieval effectiveness for XML-feed indices and traditional HTML-indices. While retrieval methods using mere XML-feeds tremendously profit from the reduced index-size in regard to efficiency, they tend not to reach up to the retrieval quality of methods using HTML-indices.

Agichtein et al. [19] introduce an approach to the automatic quality classification of User Generated Content, which is based on textual features as well as on the popularity of the users in the social network and usage statistics. They use a collection from the social network Yahoo! Answers to train binary classification models. The models are based on a range of features, which are characteristic for Social Media. To verify the discriminative power of the metrics, Agichtein et al. [19] classified the collections using machine learning methods. They could discriminate high quality content from the used collection with accuracies from 73% to 79% using decision-tree algorithms. The average user ratings, punctuation rate, the length of postings and the average access-frequency of the content were especially useful features.

3 Blog Analysis

Weblogs feature distinct characteristics, which are typical for User Generated Content and other rich internet applications. While it is possible to analyze features, which are commonly used for the quality classification of traditional websites, findings by Agichtein et al. [19] show, that the complementary usage of UGC-specific attributes may allow high classification accuracies. Blog-specific quality model will be based on different features than generic quality concepts [5], while the overall approach to the automatic quality analysis is very similar.

Our models are based on supervised learning algorithms. We are using two separate populations to train and assess the resulting algorithm accuracy. The controlled collection can be considered the reference collection of high quality blogs and is used by the classifier to learn the quality model through the features of the instances of the blog-collection. The second collection is a set of random blogs collected by querying a search engine. The high quality blogs are automatically compared to the random blogs. Simultaneously the ability of the model to discriminate the blogs through the recognition scheme derived from the reference collection's set of features is assessed. A highly specialized blog crawler compiles the collections on which the quality models are based.

This crawler is JAVA (J2SE) 6.0 based and used to crawl the blogs from both sources and to analyze them at runtime. Its functionalities are derived from classes from a modified version of the open-source crawler JoBo 1.4 [20]. Our adaption features additional characteristics to facilitate the analysis of blogs and their characteristics in a more specialized way than the AQUAINT system, but uses some classes derived from it [5]. The blog crawler converts HTML-documents into a Document Object Model (DOM), which allows for the structural analysis of the HTML-document [5]. It is configured to only consider HTML-documents on the highest possible level of an URL ("Home"). This way we decide to access the web page, which usually lists several blog, posts and is most representative for the blogs contents in its recent past. Blogs use standardized style sheets and layouts, so there is little need to crawl the pages on lower hierarchy levels, as significant structural differences are unlikely to occur. In addition, the crawler is able to access the available XML-representations as RSS-feeds, which offer more structure and enable us to access the blogs metadata fairly easily. This kind of web crawling does not correspond to a complete web-site analysis, however it reaches far beyond the simple analysis of the top hierarchy level HTML-page.

An overall number of about 150 attributes is extracted for each blog while the crawler works his way through a given collection. Previous work on the usefulness of features for quality web retrieval were of influence [5], as well as findings from social media research [17,18,19,21].

On the one hand, functionality had been implemented which analyzed traditional web metrics as file measures, link based-measures, markup frequency, color markups, table measures and list measures as well as language-based measures. For the model creation, the efficiency did matter much as several thousand HTML-pages had to be downloaded and analyzed at run time. As a consequence, complex link analysis measures were not included because they require full knowledge about the link structure and a specific link index. However, we used wrappers to access measures from several search engines as Technorati or Google to get hints on the impact of the blogs popularity. These features can be grouped into the following categories:

- **File measures:** number of DOM elements, length of URL, length of HTML title, file size.
- **Link based measures:** Number of out-links, link-label-lengths, number of Google-In-links, Technorati rank.
- **Markup frequency:** H1, H2, H3, layer, table, frameset, frequency of a set of text style tags.
- **Measures based on HTML lists:** number of lists, average, median and deviation of the number of <li> tags per list.
- **Measures based on HTML** tables**:** number of embedded tables, number of tables divided by file size, average, median and deviation of the number of <tr> and <td> tags per table.
- **Colors:** number of colors, number of unique colors, RGB values of most frequent color, text color, background color.
- **Language-based features:** number of words, number of unique words, number of stopwords, number of sentence markers, relation between words and stopwords.
- **Calculated measures and relations between atomic measures:** number of out-links to file size, number of graphics to DOM elements, number of graphics to text length, number of words to DOM elements.

On the other hand we integrated blog specific metrics based on tag and category information, update intervals, comments as well as several markups from syndication formats. Furthermore we took He et al.'s [22] approaches as an inspiration to try and analyze internal thematic coherences considering /tag- and /category-pages the blogs' concept-representations of each covered topic. The resulting blog-specific features can be grouped into the following categories:

- **Coherence measures:** Mean similarity of tag pages, mean similarity of category pages.
- **Syndication based measures:** mean feed update interval, number of creators, number of comments in feed, mean amount of comments per perma-link in feed.

Currently, there is only limited knowledge about which of these metrics are useful indicators for objective blog quality. The huge number of measures we assess is partly due to the lack of empirical scientific evidence. Some of them surely do have an experimental character. What is more, the amount of gathered blog attributes makes it hard to determine exact relations between the considered features. We focus primarily on the accuracy of the quality prediction, while the transparency and intuitive understandability of the models only play a minor role.

4 Quality Model Development

We are using WEKA (Waikato Environment for Knowledge Analysis) to generate the quality models [23]. This data mining tool offers various learning algorithms as well as methods to analyze and classify unstructured data. Moreover, it is available as Open Source software. Elgersma & de Rijke 2006 have used it in comparable experimental settings. Apart from classification algorithms WEKA's functionalities to identify highly discrimative blog features are of special interest to us [16].

To generate the quality models we have used various collections, which had been crawled and logged by our specialized blog crawler. In WEKA, both a high quality collection and a low quality collection are delineated from one another through their features.

In the work presented, different training and test collections are used to generate quality models for blogs in German, English and Russian. The blogs have been crawled and logged between 14 February 2009 and 6 May 2009. Prior to each crawl we have manually changed the stopword list configuration, so the language based features could be analyzed correctly and considered in our models. The collections must not be regarded country-specific, as we cannot figure out from where a blog is maintained. This is not only due to country-independent language areas but also to different language preferences of bloggers [24]. Thus, our results do not allow for conclusions about culture-specific characteristics of blogging.

We are using so-called A-listers ranked by blog-tracking services as collections of high-quality blogs [4]. A-Lists are often operationalized as collections of outstanding blogs and can be considered the benchmarks for popular blogs [25], although the assessment criteria of most blog tracking services are somewhat vague [5]. While such lists are not always explicitly based on the quality of the ranked blogs and usually come from machine ratings, they are a good indicator for the features of outstanding and popular blogs [26]. What is more, the ratings are mostly based on link analysis, which reflects very effectively the subjective quality perception of web site users as is argued by [13]. Link-based rankings are hence well suited for the generation of high quality collections.

We used the blogtracking service Wikio[2] to create a training collection of 300 high quality blogs in German (con_de). Wikio is based on link-based ranking algorithms and is thus well fit as the basis of high quality blog collection [13]. After data cleansing the collection contained 275 blogs. To create a large English-speaking training collection we merged the Wikio-ranking for blogs from the UK and the US to come by with a cleansed collection of 436 instances (con_en). Our third, Russian-speaking collection is based on a ranking by the popular Russian blog tracking service Yandex[3] and consists of 314 blogs (con_ru).

To generate collections containing instances of lower quality blogs, we are using a JAVA-based tool to extract random blogs from Google Blog Search in German (rnd_de, 2,929 instances), English (rnd_en, 2,554 instances) and Russian (rnd_ru, 2,473 instances). While the controlled collections are very clear and of limited size, the collection of randomly extracted blogs may be less clean and homogenous. Due to the functionality of the random blog search engine, this collection might contain single instances of high quality blogs, which could reduce the accuracy of the learned models. However, our analysis has shown that these inaccuracies are of little statistical impact and they hardly affect the quality of the learned models. Further details on the collection can be found in [27].

5 Performance of the Trained Quality Models

The WEKA machine-learning package offers us several algorithms to train and evaluate classifiers. They all require a target feature set serving as reference, which the instances of the collections are related to through their set of features. In all of our experiments we have defined the class label of the collections' instances as target features. Some algorithms required nominal label definitions and enabled us to measure the models' relative precisions by percentage. All experiments were carried out with ten-fold cross validation. Table 2 shows the predictive accuracies for the German-speaking training collection consisting of high quality blogs (con_de) and lower quality blogs (rnd_de). An accuracy of 90% indicates that 90 of 100 blogs were correctly attributed to their initial class label on the basis of the classification model derived from the collection.

The results for nominal classification are in general very satisfying and support related findings in this field of research. They show that it is possible to learn to distinguish between the high and low quality blogs as we have defined them. All of the algorithms besides one lead to models with accuracies higher than 90%. *IBk* is an algorithm very susceptible to unclean data and leads to a significantly lower classification performance. However, as we have proved in later experiments using merely a reduced set of features selected through WEKA's algorithm *CfsSubsetEval,* the accuracy of models derived through this learning method could be again raised to 97.82%. This shows that our data set tends to be somewhat unclean and that algorithms other than *Ibk* allow for a more robust classification of our collections.

Other algorithms allowed for numerical prediction but required numeric target values, so we interpreted the high quality class labels as 1.0 and the lower quality class

[2] http://www.wikio.com

[3] http://www.yandex.ru

Table 2. Quality Model Accuracies for *con_de*

Learning methods for classification	% of correctly classified blogs from con_de[4]	% of wrongly classified blogs from con_de
NaiveBayes	94.91%	4.36%
DecisionTable	98.18%	1.82%
RBFNetwork	94.18%	5.82%
J48	98.55%	1.45%
IBk[5]	66.55%	33.45%
NBTree[6]	98.91%	1.09%

Table 3. Results for numerical learning methods for *con_de* and *rnd_de*

Learning methods for numerical prediction	Correlation
Decision Table	0.957
REPTree	0.863
LWL (Locally Weighted Learning)	0.979
Decision Stump	0.975
SVMreg[7]	0.817

labels as 0.0 respectively [5]. Table 3 shows results for the numerical value prediction. The predicted values exhibit a high correlation to the original data. It can be stated that the numerical methods also lead to good results on this data set.

While models, which are based on a huge number of features, allow for extensive analysis, they still have some disadvantages. They are computationally intensive and subject to data irregularities. What is more, it is questionable if they lead to good generalization of the results. As a consequence, it is of high interest to determine the accuracy for models based on a reduced set of features. WEKA offers algorithms to determine the features which are most important to the discrimination of a given data set. Through this, the most important attributes can be identified, which allows for the reduction of the information available to the training algorithms on these factors. In this work we have used *CfsSubsetEval* to choose the most important features [26]. We have trained new models with merely the identified attributes for the given German-speaking collection. Their accuracy is presented in Table 4. It is interesting that the accuracy of all models increased for the reduced feature set.

Furthermore, we dealt with the question if the generated quality models could be compared in between different linguistic areas and if the results were similar for the collections in Russian and English. Various studies have elaborated and tried to explain culture-specific peculiarities of blogs [8,24]. Through language-specific collections this work aims at discovering possible linguistic dependencies of the generated quality models. Our experiments had unexpected results.

4 n=275.

5 Instance-Based Classifier, 1 nearest neighbor.

6 Naive Bayes Tree.

7 Support Vector Machine Regression, linear kernel.

Table 4. Accuracies of reduced attribute quality models for *con_de*

Learning methods for classification	% of correctly classified blogs from con_de[8]	% of wrongly classified blogs from con_de
NaiveBayes	97.82%	2.18%
DecisionTable	98.91%	1.09%
RBFNetwork	96.36%	3.64%
J48	98.55%	1.45%
IBk[9]	97.82%	2.18%
NBTree[10]	99.27%	0.73%

The overall accuracies of the models resulting from *con_ru* ranged up to about 80% and were thus only slightly lower than the accuracies for the corresponding German-language collection. However, the quality models for the English collection *con_en* were of much lower accuracies with very high confusion rates for *rnd_en*. While the attribute reduction using *CfSSubseEval* raised the accuracies for *con_ru*, which proves to some extent the impurities of our Russian-language database, *con_en* has hardly profited from the reduced number of attributes. Thus we do not unquestionably ascribe the strongly diverging results to mere impurities of the data. The heterogeneity of the English-language collection due to a wider use of English in the blogosphere may lead to a reduced accuracy in classification tasks. However, we cannot exclude that the attributes chosen for German blogs are less fit for the description of the English collection. It is obvious that more extensive studies are needed to prove and explain the variation of performance for quality models based on different language collections.

In an additional test setting we evaluated the accuracy of quality models based on human estimation. We asked 15 participants to subjectively rate the quality of 407 blogs randomly chosen from the German blog directory *bloggerei.de*[11]. Each participant rated 10 blogs according to a 6-point ordinal scale. Thus we supposed to gain indicators for the reliability of our investigations. Our calculations resulted in a *Kendall's W of* 0.2609, which signifies a low interrater reliability for the ratings on the ordinal scale. While there was some agreement on the quality of the assessed instances, still considerable interpersonal differences in quality perception are obvious. Thus we expected a very low accuracy for models trained on the basis of the human ratings. We trained models with the subjective user ratings being the numeric target value for the classification task. As estimated the correlations of the predicted values to the original data were very low with correlations not exceeding K= 0.25. The classification performance was quite similar to the accuracy of the models which Mandl trained using a manually rated collection [5]. As the concordance is very low, the mean classification performance may not only be affected by the chosen training collection, but also by the fact that the raters perceived and valued characteristics of the blogs in very different ways. Further details on the learning process and results can be found in [27].

---

[8] n=275.

[9] Instance-Based Classifier, 1 nearest neighbor.

[10] Naive Bayes Tree.

[11] http://www.bloggerei.de

6 Conclusion and Future Work

The greatly varying quality and the great economic importance of social media show that there is need for automatic quality rating in social media. The most promising approaches for automatic quality assessment are based on machine learning. We defined a set of features, which is well suited for determining the quality of blogs. Our classification experiments and our user experiments show that such a system can be implemented and work successfully for a substantially large data set. Further experiments to validate the parameters are necessary. Applications in economic settings need to be developed now to prove the advantages of automatic quality determination for User Generated Content.

References

1. Ebersbach, A., Glaser, M., Heigl, R.: Social Web, p. 56. UTB, Stuttgart (2008)
2. Technorati: State of the Blogosphere (2008), `http://technorati.com/blogging/state-of-the-blogosphere/` (Updated: 27.02.2009. Verified: 27.02.2009)
3. Gillmor, D.: We the Media. Grassroots Journalism by the People, for the People, ch. 2 (2004), `http://oreilly.com/catalog/wemedia/book/ch02.pdf` (Verified: 1.3.2009)
4. Herring, S., Kouper, I., Paolillo, J., Scheidt, L.-A., Tyworth, M., Welsch, P., Wright, E., Yu, N.: Conversations in the Blogosphere: An Analysis "From the Bottom Up". In: Proceedings of the Thirty Eigth Hawaii International Conference on System Sciences (HICSS-38) (2005)
5. Mandl, T.: Implementation and Evaluation of a Quality Based Search Engine. In: ACM Conference on Hypertext and Hypermedia (HT 2006) Odense, Denmark. pp. 73–84 (2006)
6. Huang, K.-T., Lee, Y., Wang, R.: Quality Information and Knowledge. Prentice Hall, Upper Saddle River (1999)
7. Fogg, B., Marable, L., Stanford, J., Tauber, E.: How Do People Evaluate a Web Site's Credibility? Results from a Large Study. In: Consumer Web Watch 2002 (2002)
8. Mandl, T., de la Cruz, T.: International Differences in Web Page Evaluation Guidelines. Intl. Journal of Intercultural Information Management (IJIIM) 1(2), 127–142 (2009)
9. Brinkmeier, M.: PageRank revisited. ACM Trans. Internet Technol. 6(3), 282–301 (2006)
10. Brajnik, G.: Towards Valid Quality Models for Websites. In: Seventh Conference Human Factors & the Web (HFWEB) (2001), `http://www.dimi.uniud.it/~giorgio/papers/hfweb01.html`
11. Tang, T., Hawking, D., Craswell, N., Griffiths, K.: Focused crawling for both topical relevance and quality of medical information. In: ACM Conf. on Information and Knowledge Management (CIKM), pp. 147–154 (2005)
12. Zhu, X., Gauch, S.: Incorporating quality metrics in centralized/distributed information retrieval on the World Wide Web. In: SIGIR Conf. on Research and Development in Information Retrieval, pp. 288–295 (2000)
13. Amento, B., Terveen, L., Hill, W.: Does "authority" mean quality? predicting expert quality ratings of Web documents. In: SIGIR Conf. on Research and Development in Information Retrieval, pp. 296–303 (2000)
14. Ivory, M.Y., Megraw, R.: Evolution of web site design patterns. ACM Trans. Inf. Syst. 23(4), 463–497 (2005)

15. Nanno, T., Suzuki, Y., Fujiki, T., Okamura, M.: Automatic Collection and Monitoring of Japanese Weblogs. In: Proceedings of the 13th international World Wide Web conference. Alternate track papers & posters (WWW 2004), pp. 320–321 (2004)
16. Elgersma, E., de Rijke, M.: Personal vs Non-Personal Blogs: Initial Classification Experiments. In: SIGIR Conf. on Research and Development in Information Retrieval, pp. 723–724 (2008)
17. Li, B., Xu, S., Zhang, J.: Enhancing clustering blog documents by utilizing author/reader comments. In: Proceedings of the 45th Annual Southeast Regional Conf., pp. 94–99 (2007)
18. Macdonald, C., Ounis, I.: Key blog distillation: ranking aggregates. In: Proc. 17th ACM Conf. on information and Knowledge Management (CIKM 2008), pp. 1043–1052 (2008)
19. Agichtein, E., Castillo, C., Donato, D., Gionis, A., Mishne, G.: Finding high-quality content in social media. In: Conf Web Search and Web Data Mining (WSDM), pp. 183–194 (2008)
20. Matuschek, D.: JoBo (2006), `http://www.matuschek.net/jobo/` (Updated: 16.12.2006; Verified: 17.04.2009)
21. Mandl, T.: Comparing Chinese and German Blogs. In: ACM Conference on Hypertext and Hypermedia (HT 2009), pp. 299–308 (2009)
22. Witten, I., Frank, E.: Data Mining. In: Technical Machine Learning Tools and Techniques with Java Implementations. Morgan Kaufmann, San Francisco (2000)
23. He, J., Weerkamp, W., Larson, M., de Rijke, M.: Blogger, Stick to your Story: Modeling Topical Noise in Blogs with Coherence Measures. In: Proceedings of the second workshop on Analytics for noisy unstructured text data, pp. 39–46 (2008)
24. Shchipitsina, L.: Sprachliche und textuelle Aspekte in russischen Weblogs. In: Schlobinski, P., Siever, T. (eds.) Sprachliche und textuelle Merkmale in Weblogs (2005), `http://www.mediensprache.net/de/networx/docs/networx-46.asp`
25. Carrol, D.: Technorati Authority and Rank (Updated: 05.05.2007. Verified: 01.03.2009) (2007), `http://technorati.com/weblog/2007/05/354.html`
26. Hall, M.A.: Correlation-based Feature Subset Selection for Machine Learning. PhD Thesis, The University of Waikato (1999), `http://www.cs.waikato.ac.nz/~mhall/thesis.pdf`
27. Hellmann, R.: Qualitätsmodelle und Web Mining in Blogs. Master Thesis, University of Hildesheim. International Information Management (2009)

Avoiding Inconsistency in User Preferences for Data Quality Aware Queries

Naiem Khodabandehloo Yeganeh and Shazia Sadiq

School of Information Technology and Electrical Engineering
The University of Queensland, St Lucia. QLD 4074, Australia
{naiem,shazia}@itee.uq.edu.au

Abstract. In situations where for a single query, multiple sources of information are available or needed, quality of data sources should be considered. We introduce a framework called data-quality aware query systems (DQAQS) that factors in the quality of data in the query answering process. Query is answered by taking quality of elements of data into account against the user's data-quality preferences such as completeness, currency, etc. User preferences may convey inconsistency which compromises the query response. In this paper we propose a method to graphically capture user preferences and visually feedback user on consistency of the query, through an efficient algorithm for detecting inconsistency in real-time, thus improving user satisfaction in DQAQS.

Keywords: Data Quality, Information Quality Framework, Consistency, User Preferences.

1 Introduction

User satisfaction from a query response is a complex problem encompassing various dimensions including both the efficiency as well as the quality of the response. This satisfaction can not be achieved without considering user preferences as part of the query. Data quality aware query systems (DQAQS) [10] are querying systems where quality of data sets are measured, user preferences on data quality are understood and considered in the query, and data sources are ranked to satisfy or to do best effort to satisfy the user's quality requirements.

Consider for example a virtual store that is compiling a comparative price list for a given product (such as Google products, previously known as froogle) through a meta search (a search that queries results of other search engines and selects best possible results amongst them). It obviously does not read all the millions of results for a search and does not return millions of records to the user. It normally selects top k results (where k is a constant value) from each search engine and finally returns top n results after the merge.

In the above scenario, when a user queries for a product, the virtual store searches through a variety of data sources for that item and ranks and returns the results. For example the user may query for "Canon PowerShot". In turn the virtual store may query camera vendor sites and return the results. The

W. Abramowicz and R. Tolksdorf (Eds.): BIS 2010, LNBIP 47, pp. 59–70, 2010.

value that the user associates with the query result is clearly subjective and related to the user's intended requirements, which go beyond the entered query term, namely "Canon PowerShot" (currently returns 91,345 results from Google products). For example the user may be interested in comparing product prices, or the user may be interested in information on latest models.

More precisely, suppose that the various data sources can be accessed through a view consisting of columns ("Item Title", "Item Description", "Numbers Available", "Price", "Tax", "User Comments"). A user searching for "Canon PowerShot" may actually be interested to:

- Learn about different items (products) - the user may not care about the "Numbers Available" and "Tax" columns. "Price" is somewhat important to the user although obsoleteness and inaccuracy in price values can be tolerated. However, consistency of "Item Title" and completeness within the populations of "User Comments" in the query results, is of the highest importance.
- Compare prices - the user is sure about the item to purchase but is searching for the best price. Obviously "Price" and "Tax" fields have the greatest importance in this case. They should be current and accurate. "Numbers Available" is also important although slight inaccuracies in this column are acceptable as any number more than 1 will be sufficient.

Above examples indicate that selection of a good source for data is subjected to what does the term "good" mean to the user. Data quality aware query answering is a multi-faceted problem. Aggregations across multiple large data sets are infeasible due to the scale of data. Further, ranking approaches based on generic user feedbacks gives a constant rank to the quality of a data source and does not factor in user/application specific quality ranking. A DQAQS is a system that provides answers for the following questions: 1) How to obtain information about the generic data quality of data sources? 2) How to model and capture user specific data quality requirements? 3)How to conduct the quality aware query? and 4) How to rank results based on the quality aware query?

Figure 1 illustrates a quality aware query system's architecture within a generic information system. Each data source (could be an organization or department within an organization) consists of a base (relational) database and

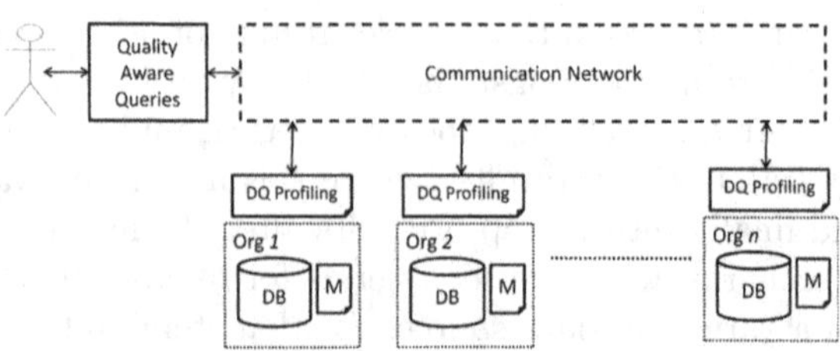

Fig. 1. Quality aware query processing architecture

certain metadata. The meta data includes Data Quality profiles, which are measurements indicating the quality of data. We assume that each source is responsible for providing data quality profiles at attribute level for each table of the database.

Modelling user preferences is a challenging problem due to the inherent subjective nature. Intuitively preferences are regarded as sets of partial orders [11]. For example "I like coffee more than tea" or "I like juice more than coffee" are partial order clauses that can describe user preferences. To be more precise, a partial order clause can convey strength of a preference. For example "I like coffee much more than tea" and "I like juice slightly more than coffee". People expresses the strength of each preference with subjective adjectives such as "very strongly", "strongly", "slightly", etc.

Several models have been developed to model the user preferences in decision making theory and database community. Models which have been based on partial orders are shown to be effective in many cases [11]. Different extensions to the standard SQL are also proposed to define a preference language [12] [3] [16].

Inconsistencies in user preferences often happen. Current studies on user preferences in database systems assume that existence of inconsistency is natural (and hard to avoid) for user preferences and a preference model should work even when user preferences are inconsistent, hence; they deliberately opt to ignore it.

Nevertheles, studies do not confirm this assumption. Human science and decision making studies show that people struggle with an internal consistency check and they will almost always avoid inconsistent preferences if they are a given proper tool. [8] believes inconsistency in user preferences is mostly human-mistakes caused by confusion.

In DQAQS, due to hierarchical nature of preferences, the uncertainty that happens as a result of inconsistency in user preferences is noticeable since uncertainties propagate to lower levels of preference hierarchy, thus eventually compromising query response. This paper aims to address this problem.

The remaining of this paper is structured as follows: In Sec. 2 related works are studied. In Sec. 3 we formulate and model quality aware queries, then in Sec. 4 we propose methods to detect different types of inconsistencies in DQAQs. Finally, Sec. 5 concludes the paper after presenting a querying GUI for DQAQS framework and studying the efficiency of the proposed algorithms.

2 Related Works

In this section we present related works on data quality and preference modeling as such aspects are closely related to this paper.

Consequents of poor quality of data have been experienced in almost all domains. From the research perspective, data quality has been addressed in different contexts, including statistics, management science, and computer science. To understand the concept, various research works have defined a number of quality dimensions [18].

Data quality dimensions characterize data properties e.g. accuracy, currency, completeness etc. Many dimensions are defined for assessment of quality of data that give us the means to measure the quality of data. Data Quality attributes can be very subjective (e.g. ease of use, expandability, objectivity, etc.).

To address the problems that stem from the various data quality dimensions, the approaches can be broadly classified into investigative, preventative and corrective. Investigative approaches essentialy provide the ability to assess the level of data quality and is generally provided through data profiling tools (See e.g. IBM Quality Stage). Many sophisticated commercial profiling tools exist [6], and hence we do not provide further details in this regard. Suffice to say that in this paper we focus on a selected set of data quality dimensions which can be profiled using typical profiling tools.

A variety of solutions have also been proposed for preventative and corrective aspects of data quality management. These solutions can be categorized into following broad groups : **Semantic integrity constraints** [5] . **Record linkage** solutions. Record linkage has been addressed through approximate matching , de-duplicating and entity resolution techniques [1]. **Data lineage or provenance** solutions are classified as annotation and non-annotation based approaches where back tracing is suggested to address auditory or reliability problems . **Data uncertainty** and probabilistic databases are another important consideration in data quality [15].

The research literature on preferences is extensive . It encompasses preference logics , preference reasoning , decision theory , and multi criteria decision making [17] (the list is by no means exhaustive).

The issue of user preferences in database queries dates back to 1987 [14]. Preference queries in deductive databases are studied in [7]. A new operator called Skyline is proposed in [3] that extends generic SQL statements with some powerful preference definitions. In [11] and [4] a logical framework for formulating preferences and its embedding into relational query languages are proposed.

Existing literature on user preferences in database systems, ignores the problem of inconsistency in user preferences. Since user preferences are considered as wish list [11], and there is no guarantee to satisfy a wish; any preference system should still work in presence of inconsistency in user preferences.

Nevertheless, studies show that consistency in preference defined as partial orders by user has a direct relation with rationality of the query. In the presence of inconsistency levels of uncertainty exists when evaluating the query [13]. In fact, existence of inconsistency in user preferences tends to reduce valuable information about user preferences captured by the query.

In [9], 80 decision makers were asked the same 100 pairwise comparison questions on two separate occasions with 3-5 days of separation, and the consistency rates for each person ranged from 60-90%. As concluded in [9], the respondents were certainly not answering the questions randomly, else the consistency rate would have been around 50% (since there is a 50% chance that the random answers to any of the 100 questions from both rounds would match). In another study [13] , subjects where asked the same 42 questions twice, with the second time coming immediately after the first time. Consistency rates were well under 100%. The economic choice theory researchers concluded in [8] that the most likely source of these inconsistencies was "stochastic choice," or what one might call "error" or "mistakes" on the part of the decision makers.

In addition, as noted in [8] , people struggle with the internal consistency of decisions and the empirical accuracy of decisions based on multiple fallible indicators. It is argued in [8] that the integration of consistency and accuracy be viewed in the context of rationality. Identifying these inconsistencies or "mistakes" as denoted in [8], and correcting them is one of the objectives of the work in this paper.

3 Quality-Aware Queries

Our approach is based on the generic information systems as in Fig. 1. Each data source (could be an organization or department within an organization) consists of a base (relational) database and certain meta data. The meta data consists of two main components: i) Schema and ii) Data Quality profiles, which are results obtained through data profiling processes, or what we can term quality-aware metadata (more details in Sec. 3.1). Each source is responsible for providing data quality profiles at attribute level for each table of the database. Profiling can be a periodic task or it can be incrementally updated each time data is modified.

3.1 Quality-Aware Metadata

We consider the following data quality metrics (also referred to as dimensions): completeness, consistency, accuracy, and currency. Consider an example data set as below relating to the virtual store example presented previously.

Completeness of an attribute is calculated by counting the nulls over the number of all records. Consistency of the attribute is calculated by counting the number of items conforming to consistency constraints over the number of all records. For example, a consistency constraint on "Item Title" can be defined to ensure that all values have an exact match with a given master data list of item titles. Accuracy of the attribute is calculated by counting the number of values which are not in the correct format over the number of all records. Currency of a value is calculated by checking the timestamp that DBMS records each time a value is changed (e.g. dividing the last modified timestamp by a constant normalizing factor).

Definition 1. *Let relation $R(A)$ be a relation of attributes $a \in A$. $M = \{m_1..m_k\}$ is the set of k data quality metrics and $a.m := \sigma_m(a)$ where σ_m returns the calculated data quality metric value for metric m over attribute a and $0 \leq \sigma_m(a) \leq 1$.*

3.2 Quality-Aware SQL

Consider an information system as given in Fig. 1, wherein an instance of information can be selected from each source, and the quality aware metadata

(data profile) is available for each source. User queries relation $R(A)$ that can be accessed from any source $S_1..S_n$ where n is the number of sources. The data quality metrics allow the user to query for any attribute $a_i \in A_i$ from any source S_i plus the value of any data quality metric $a_i.m$.

For purpose of simple illustration we allow using quality-aware metadata, to query any metric as *[Column Name.Metric Name]* as part of the SQL query formulation. For example the query `SELECT Title, Price FROM ShopItem WHERE Title.Completeness>0.8` queries sources only if the completeness of the column Title from table ShopItem is more than 80%. Or query `SELECT Title, Title.Accuracy, Price FROM ShopItem ORDER BY Price.Accuracy` sorts the results based on the accuracy of column price in data source. It also returns the accuracy of the column title from the source as a result.

Generic SQL is not capable of modeling complicated user preferences of higher complexity. Though clause `ORDER BY Price.Accuracy` models a one dimensional preference that indicates sources with higher price accuracy are preferred, a two dimensional preference can not be intuitively achieved. Further, users may prioritize the various dimensions differently. Therefore, in Sec. 3.3 we propose an extension to the generic SQL (called Hierarchy Clause) to model complicated user preferences relating to data quality.

3.3 Modelling User Preferences

Preference modelling is in general a difficult problem due to the inherent subjective nature. Typically, preferences are stated in relative terms, e.g. "I like A better than B", which can be mapped to strict partial orders [11]. In quality-aware queries, a mixture of preferences could be defined, e.g. the accuracy of the price and completeness of the user comments should be maximized.

The notion of **Hierarchy** in preferences is defined in the literature as prioritized composition of preferences. For example; completeness of user comments may have priority over completeness of prices. We use the term Hierarchy to define prioritised composition of preferences which can form several levels of priority i.e. a hierarchy. The hierarchy over the preference relations is quantifiable such as: a is strongly more important than b, or a is moderately more important than b.

Definition 2. *Let relation $R(A)$ be a relation of attributes $a \in A$. Let $M = m_1..m_k$ be the set of k data quality metrics. Let $S = S_1...S_n$ be a set of possible sources for relation $R(A)$. A preference formula (pf) $C(S_1, S_2)$ is a first order formula defining a preference relation denoted as $\succ$, namely $S_1 \succ S_2$ iff $C(S_1, S2)$.*

Consider the Relation $ShopItem(Title, Price, UserComments)$ from source S denoted as $R_S(t,p,u)$, quality metric completeness is denoted as m_1 and completeness of the price is denoted as $p.m_1$. A preference relation can thus be defined as C:

$$(t,p,u) \in R_s \succ (t',p',u') \in R_{S'} \equiv p.m_1 > p'.m_1$$

Where $p.m_1$ is from the source S and $p'.m_1$ is from the source S'. Letter t, p, u represent relation attributes.

A hierarchy (prioritized order) of preferences is defined as below:[4].

Definition 3. *Consider two preference relations* $\succ_1$ *and* $\succ_2$ *defined over the same schema. The prioritized composition* $\succ_{1,2} := \succ_1 \rhd \succ_2$ *of* $\succ_1$ *and* $\succ_2$ *is defined as:*

$$S_1 \succ_{1,2} S_2 \equiv S_1 \succ_1 S_2 \vee (\neg S_2 \succ_1 S_1 \wedge S_1 \succ_2 S_2).$$

The formal notions above are translated below into pseudo-SQL in order to illustrate the quality aware query. A specialized `HIERARCHY` clause is defined to identify the hierarchy of preferences. It is assumed that sources with maximial value of a data quality metric are preferred (i.e. source S_k where $\sigma_m(a)$ is greater than or equal to $\sigma_m(a)$ of all $S_i \in \mathrm{S}|i : 1..n$), thus, there is no need to explicitly define this preference in the query. Only hierarchy (prioritized order) of those preferences are written in the query.

The example hierarchy clause `HIERARCHY(ShopItem.p) p.Currency OVER (p.Completeness)` is defined as below, let p be the "Price" attribute, m_1 and m_2 be currency and completeness metrics and $p.m_1$ and $p'.m_1$ be the currency of the column "Price", from quality-aware meta data related to source S and S':

$$\begin{array}{c}(t, p, u) \succ_0 \rhd \succ_1 (t', p', u'),\\ (t, p, u) \in S \succ_0 (t', p', u') \in S' \equiv p.m_1 > p'.m_1,\\ (t, p, u) \in S \succ_1 (t', p', u') \in S' \equiv p.m_2 > p'.m_2\end{array}$$

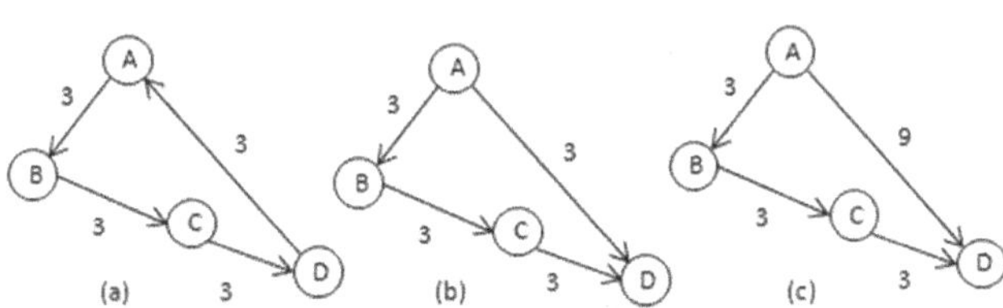

Fig. 2. (a)Circular inconsistency (b) Path inconsistency (c)Consistent graph

A Hierarchy clause can be modelled as a directed weighted graph, in which nodes represent items, directed links represent preferences, and preference intensities represent link weights. Preference graph is defined as follows:

$$N := \{a_i \| 1 \leq i \leq n\}$$

$$G := \{(a, a', d) \| a, a' \in N \wedge a \neq a' \wedge d \in \{1..9\}\}$$

Where n is the number of nodes or items in the preference, N is the set of all items, and G is the graph representing preferences.

3.4 Inconsistent Partial Order Graphs

As discussed earlier partial orders in DQAQs include a numeric intensity as representives for quantitative words like very strongly, strongly, slightly, etc. In [17] represented in numbers from 1 to 9.

Accordingly we define cumulative transitivity over preferences as below:

Definition 4. *If A OVER B n, and B OVER C m holds then A OVER C m+n holds, where* $a \in \{m, n, m+n\} \in \{1..9\} \wedge \forall a, a > 9 \rightarrow a = 9$.

Accumulative transitivity can be assumed for most real-world preferences, for example if someone loves coffee, likes coke, and hates tea; he strongly prefers coffee to coke, strongly prefers coke to tea, thus; very strongly prefers coffee to tea. It does not make sense if he specifies that he prefers coffee to tea slightly. In this paper, we assume accumulative transitivity holds in all cases.

Two types of inconsistencies can be found in a preference graph:

- **Circular inconsistency:** A graph has circular inconsistency when a circular loop exists in the graph. In this situation, there would be at least two nodes n, n' that both clauses "n is preferred to n'" and "n' is preferred to n" can be inferred from the graph. Figure 2(a) depicts a set of preferences that make an inconsistent state because taking any two nodes e.g. A and B, both following clauses can be inferred from the graph: A is preferred to B and B is preferred to A.
- **Path inconsistency:** A graph has path inconsistency when there is a pair of nodes n and n' that can be connected with at least two different paths with different accumulative weights. In this situation, it is inferred that n is preferred to n' but with different intensities which does not make sense. Graph in Fig. 2(b) is in an inconsistent state since considering two nodes A and C, both of the following clauses can be inferred from the graph: A is slightly preferred to C and A is highly preferred to C.

Algorithm 1. Inconsistency detection in quality aware query systems

Data: $G := \{(a, a', d) \| a, a' \in N \wedge a \neq a' \wedge d \in \{0..9\}\}$

$$d(x', y') \in \left\{ \begin{array}{ll} 0 & x' = y' \\ n & (x', y', n) \in G \\ -n & (y', x', n) \in G \\ \phi & else \end{array} \right\}$$

Result: True or False

```
Define M[n,n] matrix of (0..9)
for k:=1 to n do
    i:= k-1
    while M_{i,k} ≠ φ ∧ M_{i,k} ≠ 0 do
        i:=i - 1
    end
    for j:=1 to n do
        if M_{i,j} ≠ φ then
            M_{i,j} := M_{i,j} - M_{i,k}
        end
        else
            M_{k,j} := d(a_k, a_j)
        end
    end
    for j:=1 to n do
        if M_{k,j} ≠ d(a_k, a_j) then
            return False
        end
    end
end
return True
```

4 Inconsistency Detection

Definition 5. *A directed weighted graph G is inconsistent if either; either a loop exists in the graph or at least a pair of nodes* $n, n' \in N$ *exist which are connected by at least a pair of paths* P_k, P'_k *where* $w_k \neq w'_k$ *assuming P is the set of all paths from* $P_1, P_2, \ldots, P_k; P'_k, \ldots$ *with weight* $w_1, w_2; \ldots, w_k, w'_k, \ldots$

We call the process of checking the consistency of graph with searching for existance of a loop or a pair of inconsistent paths as inconsistency check. Brut-force searching for inconsistent paths in graph is exhaustive. There is $n * (n-1)/2$ combination of node pairs where all possible paths between any pair should be tested.

Alternatively consistency check can be described as follows: Given the graph G, check if: 1) No loop exists in G. 2)For any arbitrary pair of nodes n_k, n'_k, shortest connecting path and longest connecting path are of the same weight.

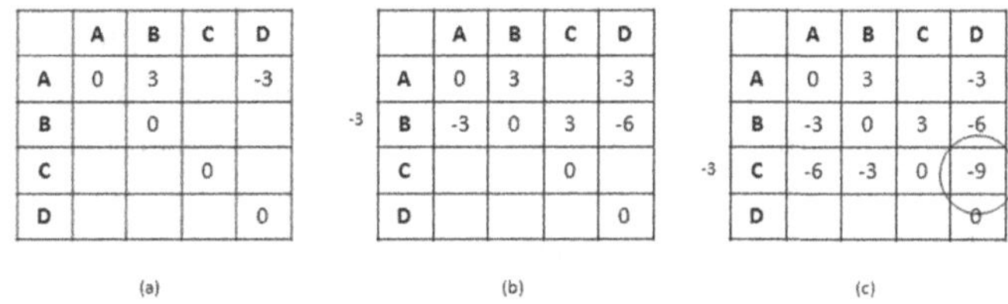

(a)

	A	B	C	D
A	0	3		-3
B		0		
C			0	
D				0

(b) -3

	A	B	C	D
A	0	3		-3
B	-3	0	3	-6
C			0	
D				0

(c) -3

	A	B	C	D
A	0	3		-3
B	-3	0	3	-6
C	-6	-3	0	-9
D				0

Fig. 3. Graph G with a circular inconsistency and its relevant distance matrix

Despite the fact that the first part of consistency check is the classic loop detection problem in graph with complexity of $O(n)$, second part of the consistency check is hard. Previous studies prove that both problems of searching for shortest path and longest path are NP-hard problems [2].

Since weights are only numeric representations of the subjective priority of preferences, accumulated weights have an upper limit and will never pass that limit, thus; our problem will reduce to an approximated version of shortest and longest path (or the accumulative weight in this paper) identification which is bound to a strict upper bound. Additionally, we do not really need to find both shortest and longest paths or exhaustively search for all possible paths between any two nodes. As soon as we get to a point that inconsistency is inevitable we can judge that the graph is inconsistent.

Considering above specificities , we propose an algorithm that detects inconsitencies in the preference graph in $O(n^2)$ time (This can be seen by looking at the number of nested loops in the algorithm). Algorithm 1 gets the preference graph as input and determines if the graph consists of inconsistent preferences. It checks for both circular and path inconsistencies.

We illustrate now the execution of this algorithm through the example graph given in Fig. 2(a). Consider $N := \{a_i || 1 \leq i \leq n\}$ to be all the nodes of the preference graph G where n is the number of nodes. We define matrix $M_{n \times n}$ as accumulative distance matrix of graph G where $M_{i,j}$ is the accumulative distance between nodes i and j. Accumulative distance between two nodes in the graph represents accumulated preference weight of one item over another in the actual preference query.

Consider graph G of Fig.2(a) with four nodes A, B, C, D, Fig. 3 illustrates it's accumulative distance matrix. Accumulative distance matrix M will be formed with main diagonal consisting of zero since the distance between each node and itself is zero. Starting from node A, Fig 3(a) displays distance between nodes A, B, and D in matrix M at this stage distance from A to C is not known since there is no direct link between A and C.

The second row of matrix M in Fig 3(b) displays distance between node B and other nodes. It is generated by adding the first row with -3 which is the distance from node B to A. Distance from node B to nodes A and C from the graph should be same as the nodes calculated in matrix M.

The third row of matrix M in Fig 3(c) displays distance between node C and other nodes. It is calculated by adding second row with -3 which is the distance from node C to B. Third matrix row identifies that distance from C to D should be -9, but the real distance from C to D in graph G is 3. This difference indicates that there is an inconsistency in the graph. In the same way inconsistent paths between all nodes including ones that are not directly conneced can be detected.

5 Evaluation and Conclusion

In order to provide an environmental testbed for research results, we have developed a system called Data Quality Aware Query Studio (DQAQS). DQAQS runs on a simulated cooperative information systems where multiple data sources are available for user queries (See Fig. 1).

The Data Quality Aware Query System is able to rank different available data sources based on the Data Quality Aware Query specified by user [16]. A comparision study in [16] shows that for different queries, data source ranked as first by DQAQS has the highest data quality which satisfies user preferences the most. Figure 4 (b) depicts a snapshot of DQAQS querying form.

We have further designed an interactive graphical user interface for DQAQS to effectively capture user data quality preferences. Figure 4 (a) shows a screenshot of this user interface for a simple query from "Shopping Items". A natural hierarchy of the query attributes and their quality metrics is represented as a tree of connected circles. Size of a circle compared to other circles identifies its priority.

User can see all the attributes being queried as circles connected to the query with lines. To avoid confusion for user the underneath subtree (i.e. data quality metrics) appears on clicking on an attribute, and disappears as the user moves away from it, thus at each instance of time, the user has to deal with limited number of circles.

In Fig. 4 (a) user requires a few clicks to define the following DQAQ hierarchy statement: *Hierarchy (ShoppingItems) userComments OVER (tax) 5, userComments OVER (price) 2, Hierarchy (userComments) completeness OVER (consistency, accuracy) 4.*

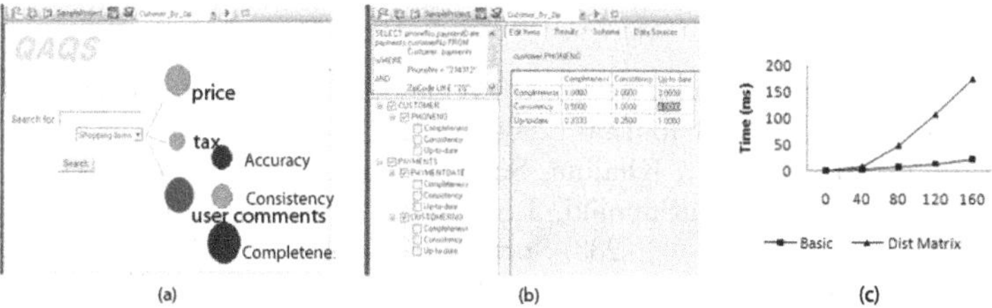

Fig. 4. (a) Interactive user interface to query user DQ preferences, (a) is modified for readability (b) DQAQS environment (c) Comparision of the efficiency of the proposed algorithms

With every click, consistency of the system is tested using the proposed algorithm 1, and as soon as the query becomes inconsistent, mutual items causing it start blinking. In section 3 we mentioned that in most (near 100%) cases, inconsistency is a result of user mistake. Users psychologically struggle with their internal consistency check, and the intuitive feeling of the proposed DQAQS user interface helps them to avoid mistakes. As of Fig. 4 (c) , the proposed algorithm also provides a significant improvement in speed over the basic algorithm. The graph shows the average speed of consistency detection for randomly injected inconsistencies to consistent preferences where x axis defines the number of items within the preference.

In conclusion we observe that in most of today's information systems, various sources of information are available and quality of data varies amongst them. One data source may return high quality results for a specific query while it may return low quality result for another query. Users have different data quality preferences for different queries. We introduced the Data Quality Aware Query System (DQAQS) as a framework which takes user preferences on data quality into account when processing query result. User preferences are prone to inconsistency while studies show that inconsistent user preferences compromise the query and should be avoided when possible. DQAQS contains a set of tools to interface user and conduct queries over the system. DQAQS captures the quality of data in the format of metadata blocks called Data Quality Profiles. In order to capture user preferences on data quality, we model user preferences as an extension to generic SQL called Data Quality Aware SQL. The entered user preference is then used to select the best data sources to continue processing the query. Our other studies show that DQAQS is able to select high quality data sources based on user requirements to improve user satisfaction.

In this paper we have proposed a method and an efficient algorithm to detect inconsistenies.

We further propose a graphical user interface to improve user experience and reduce the chances of inconsistent user preference specification. The proposed GUI, uses our inconsistency detection algorithm to detect inconsistencies as soon as they appear and co-operate with user to resolve inconsistent preferences when needed.

References

[1] Benjelloun, O., Garcia-Molina, H., Su, Q., Widom, J.: Swoosh: A generic approach to entity resolution. VLDB Journal (2008)

[2] Bjorklund, A., Husfeldt, T., Khanna, S.: Approximating longest directed paths and cycles. In: Díaz, J., Karhumäki, J., Lepistö, A., Sannella, D. (eds.) ICALP 2004. LNCS, vol. 3142, pp. 222–233. Springer, Heidelberg (2004)

[3] Borzsonyi, S., Kossmann, D., Stocker, K.: The skyline operator. In: Proc. of ICDE, pp. 421–430 (2001)

[4] Chomicki, J.: Querying with Intrinsic Preferences. LNCS, vol. 2287, pp. 34–51. Springer, Heidelberg (2002)

[5] Cong, G., Fan, W., Geerts, F., Jia, X., Ma, S.: Improving data quality: consistency and accuracy. In: Proceedings of the 33rd international conference on Very large data bases, pp. 315–326 (2007)

[6] Friedman, T., Bitterer, A.: Magic Quadrant for Data Quality Tools. Gartner Group (2006)

[7] Govindarajan, K., Jayaraman, B., Mantha, S.: Preference Queries in Deductive Databases. New Generation Computing 19(1), 57–86 (2000)

[8] Hey, J.D.: Do Rational People Make Mistakes? In: Game Theory, Experience, Rationality: Foundations of Social Sciences, Economics and Ethics: in Honor of John C. Harsanyi, p. 55 (1998)

[9] Hey, J.D., Orme, C.: Investigating generalizations of expected utility theory using experimental data. Econometrica: Journal of the Econometric Society, 1291–1326 (1994)

[10] Khodabandehloo, N.Y., Sadiq, S.: A study of Data Quality issues in mobile telecom operators (2008)

[11] Kießling, W.: Foundations of preferences in database systems. In: Proceedings of the 28th international conference on Very Large Data Bases, pp. 311–322. VLDB Endowment (2002)

[12] Kießling, W., Köstler, G.: Preference SQL: design, implementation, experiences. In: Proceedings of the 28th international conference on Very Large Data Bases, vol. 28, pp. 990–1001 (2002)

[13] Kulok, M., Lewis, K., Asme, M.: A Method to Ensure Preference Consistency in Multi-Attribute Selection Decisions. Journal of Mechanical Design 129, 1002 (2007)

[14] Lacroix, M., Lavency, P.: Preferences: Putting More Knowledge into Queries. In: Proceedings of the 13th International Conference on Very Large Data Bases, pp. 217–225. Morgan Kaufmann Publishers Inc., San Francisco (1987)

[15] Lakshmanan, L.V.S., Leone, N., Ross, R., Subrahmanian, V.S.: ProbView: a flexible probabilistic database system. ACM Transactions on Database Systems (TODS) 22(3), 419–469 (1997)

[16] Yeganeh, N.K., Sadiq, S., Deng, K., Zhou, X.: Data quality aware queries in collaborative information systems. In: Li, Q., Feng, L., Pei, J., Wang, S.X., Zhou, X., Zhu, Q.-M. (eds.) APWeb/WAIM 2009. LNCS, vol. 5446, pp. 39–50. Springer, Heidelberg (2009)

[17] Saaty, T.L.: Multicriteria Decision Making: The Analytic Hierarchy Process: Planning, Priority Setting, Resource Allocation. RWS Publications (1996)

[18] Scannapieco, M., Missier, P., Batini, C.: Data quality at a glance. Datenbank-Spektrum 14, 6–14 (2005)

Textractor: A Framework for Extracting Relevant Domain Concepts from Irregular Corporate Textual Datasets

Ashwin Ittoo, Laura Maruster, Hans Wortmann, and Gosse Bouma

Faculty of Economics and Business, University of Groningen
9747 AE Groningen, The Netherlands
{r.a.ittoo,l.maruster,j.c.wortmann,g.bouma}@rug.nl

Abstract. Various information extraction (IE) systems for corporate usage exist. However, none of them target the product development and/or customer service domain, despite significant application potentials and benefits. This domain also poses new scientific challenges, such as the lack of external knowledge resources, and irregularities like ungrammatical constructs in textual data, which compromise successful information extraction. To address these issues, we describe the development of Textractor; an application for accurately extracting relevant concepts from irregular textual narratives in datasets of product development and/or customer service organizations. The extracted information can subsequently be fed to a host of business intelligence activities. We present novel algorithms, combining both statistical and linguistic approaches, for the accurate discovery of relevant domain concepts from highly irregular/ungrammatical texts. Evaluations on real-life corporate data revealed that Textractor extracts domain concepts, realized as single or multi-word terms in ungrammatical texts, with high precision.

Keywords: Natural Language processing, term extraction, information extraction, corporate industrial data, product development, customer service.

1 Introduction

Many product development and customer service organizations are struggling with the rising number of customer complaints due to soft-failures. These failures arise from mismatches between products' specifications and customers' expectations. Previous studies [13] suggested that the information in product development and customer service data sources could provide insights on causes of soft-failures. However, this information is often expressed in natural language free-text. Its analysis requires natural language processing (NLP) techniques, such as Information Extraction (IE). For example, IE techniques could serve as a precursor to business intelligence (BI) by extracting relevant concepts pertaining to soft-failures from textual data, and thus, enable the development of better quality products.

Various IE systems exist for corporate usage [12]. However, none of them targeted the product development and/or customer service (PD-CS) domain despite the

W. Abramowicz and R. Tolksdorf (Eds.): BIS 2010, LNBIP 47, pp. 71–82, 2010.

numerous application opportunities and benefits to be accrued. Our interest in this domain is also attributed to the scientific challenges that it poses to extant IE systems. A major challenge is the quasi-inexistence of knowledge resources, such as ontologies, upon which traditional IE systems relied to identify relevant concepts from text. Creating such resources in PD-CS organizations is impeded by the perpetually evolving product lines and business models. Existing resources are neither machine-readable (e.g. diagrams on paper), nor reliable since different organizational departments maintain conflicting domain conceptualizations due to their diverging business perspectives. Exploiting general knowledge repositories like Wikipedia is also not warranted due to the specific PD-CS terminologies. This is in stark contrast to traditional IE application areas, with readily available and authoritative resources such as Yahoo! Finance [12] or Unified Medical Language System (UMLS)[18] to support IE activities. Another challenge pertains to irregularities of PD-CS data that compromise traditional IE systems. One such irregularity is terminological variations due to subtle language patterns. For example, identifying domain concepts from semantically ambiguous phrases, as in "cooling fan" from "device cooling fan", is difficult especially in the absence of knowledge resources. Another type of inconsistency in the data which hinders IE is ungrammatical constructs. For example, the absence of sentence boundaries in "customer helpdesk collimator shutter" hinders the identification of the two distinct terms "customer helpdesk" and "collimator shutter". These difficulties are compounded by the presence of both valid and invalid multi-word terms, such as "processor connection cable" and "status check ok". Creating extraction rules to deal with these inconsistencies is not always viable. They do not guarantee the capture of all inconsistencies, and their hand-crafting is tedious. Another characteristic of PD-CS datasets that poses additional challenges to accurate term extraction is their multilingual contents generated by customers and engineers worldwide.

To address these issues, and enable PD-CS organizations to fully exploit IE capabilities in their business intelligence efforts, we develop and present a framework for extracting relevant concepts from corporate datasets with textual contents that exhibit the aforementioned irregularities. We realize our methodology in the Textractor term extraction application that we implemented as part of the DataFusion initiative[1]. DataFusion aims at facilitating the creation of better quality products by aligning customers' expectations to products' specifications.

Our major contributions in this paper are novel algorithms that, by applying linguistic and statistical approaches in an ensemble, accurately extract relevant domain concepts realized as terms of arbitrary length in irregular narrations. The extracted information can be fed to various BI models to support activities such as analyzing soft-failure causes. Textractor consists of independent modules, performing various tasks for successful IE, such as multi-language standardization, and data preprocessing. The modules are easily adaptable for other application domains, although we focused on PD-CS. Our framework, depicting various IE activities and Textractor's architecture, could serve as blueprints for organizations in their IE endeavors. We evaluated Textractor on real-life industrial datasets provided by industrial partners

[1] The DataFusion or "Merging of Incoherent Field Feedback Data into Prioritized Design Information" initiative is a collaboration between academia and industry, sponsored by the Dutch Ministry of Economic Affairs under the IOP-IPCR program.

in the DataFusion project. The high precision obtained during evaluation suggests that Textractor is indeed suitable for extracting relevant information from irregular corporate textual data, and that it can support various forms of BI.

This paper is organized as follows. Section 2 presents and compares related work. Our framework and the underlying methodology are discussed in Section 3. We present results of experimental evaluations in Section 4, before concluding and highlighting future work in Section 5.

2 Related Work

Term Extraction (TE) is a form of information extraction (IE) to automatically extract linguistic realizations of relevant concepts, i.e. terms, from domain text. Literature mentions three forms of TE approaches. Linguistic approaches [1] identify terms based on their linguistic properties (e.g. parts-of-speech). Statistical approaches employ techniques like mutual information [19], log-likelihood [19,22], and term frequency-inverse document frequency [9] for computing the saliency of terms. Hybrid approaches [7] combine linguistic and statistical techniques to accurately recognize terms from texts. Most current TE and general IE rely on knowledge resources like Wikipedia [21] or UMLS [10] to identify generic (e.g. Persons) or bio-medical concepts (e.g. genes) from specialized texts.

IE applications targeted at corporate usage have also been developed. The h-TechSight system [11] uses domain ontologies to extract information such as employment trends. Nexus [14] relies on the Politically Motivated Violent Events ontology to extract facts from online news articles. Xu et al. [22] use GermaNet for financial information extraction. MUSING [12] extracts information from corporate datasets and resources like Yahoo! Finance based on domain ontologies.

Compared to the classical application areas listed above, term extraction from product development and/or customer service (PD-CS) datasets presents new challenges. As already mentioned, existing knowledge resources, like ontologies, are quasi-inexistent. PD-CS datasets also exhibit more irregularities than those (e.g. bio-medical, finance data) traditionally targeted by existing IE systems. For example, inconsistent and ungrammatical language constructs are likelier in texts entered by (frustrated) customers or helpdesk officers with their personal jargon than in texts of bio-medical or financial experts. To address the challenges of term extraction from the product development and/or customer service domain, and to enable organizations fully exploit IE capabilities for business intelligence, we develop the Textractor application.

3 Textractor Framework

We now describe our methodology and its implementation in the Textractor application for extracting relevant domain concepts from corporate datasets with irregular textual contents. The various phases of our methodology are realized by independent but interoperable modules in Textractor's architecture, depicted in Figure 1 (Dotted objects are not part of Textractor, they depict the input and output). Textractor's

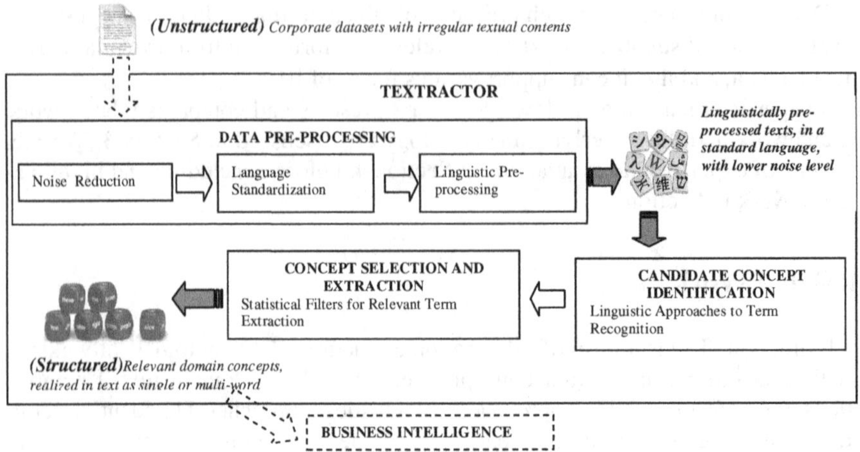

Fig. 1. Textractor Architecture

design follows the Service-Oriented-Architecture (SOA) paradigm, with each of its modules providing specific services. They are discussed in the following sub-sections. As our major contributions, the Candidate Concept Identification, and Concept Selection and Extraction phases (modules) are treated more extensively. The modules were implemented as standalone and web-based applications in Java, Perl and (Java) Servlets running under the Tomcat server.

3.1 Data Pre-processing

Our approach starts with data pre-processing, which lowers the noise level, standardizes the languages for multi-lingual texts, and performs basic linguistic operations on the textual data.

Noise Reduction

We implemented wrapper-like techniques [3] based on regular expression rules to discard noisy entities from our texts. Entities that our rules target include identifiers like “<EOL>”, which are automatically inserted by data-entry software, words with less than two letters, and irrelevant symbols entered by humans in their narrations (e.g. “,”{,},#...). The rules' authoring was done with domain experts so that only noisy entities are targeted, without dropping any relevant facts from the data.

Language Detection and Standardization

The narrations in our data were expressed in the major European and Asian languages. To facilitate information extraction, we implemented a language detection algorithm, based on [4], which automatically determines the language in which texts are written. Our algorithm predicts the language of textual records by computing their distances from category profiles that define various languages. The language with the smallest distance is predicted. While we maintain the core of the technique presented in [4], our algorithm only targets the languages (viz. English, Dutch, German, French, Spanish, Italian, and Portuguese) present in our dataset, and achieves higher accuracy than [4] on these selected few languages. It also annotates texts containing elements of more than one language with the label "inter-lingual". We omit further details of this algorithm in this paper.

Linguistic Pre-processing
Although NLP tools for other languages exist, in this work, we restrict ourselves to English texts for ease of evaluation by the authors and industrial partners. Also, we believe that formal grammars in English and their associated NLP tools are more mature than those in other languages.

We apply standard NLP techniques to segment our textual records into individual sentences, to tokenize the sentences, and to determine the parts-of-speech (PoS)-tags of these tokens. PoS-tags are later used to identify candidate terms (Section 3.2). We also determine the lemmas (roots) of inflected words-forms. PoS-tagging and lemmatization were achieved with the Stanford maximum entropy tagger and morphological analyzer [17].

The output of this phase is linguistically processed textual records, in a standard language, and with lower noise levels. The data is now amenable for term identification and extraction.

3.2 Candidate Concept Identification

This phase of our methodology recognizes terms in text based on contiguous sequences of parts-of-speech (PoS)-tags, called term signatures.

Various term signatures are mentioned in literature. However, existing term signatures are susceptible to PoS-tagging errors, which are common in our corporate datasets due to their irregular texts with subtle language patterns and malformed sentences. We noted that in semantically ambiguous phrases, some nouns were wrongly tagged by standard tools [5,17] as progressive-verbs (VBG). This led to inaccurate term identification by existing signatures as they always look for sequences of adjectives and nouns. For instance, "device cooling fan" was PoS-tagged as "device/N cooling/VBG fan/N", and misled existing term signatures to inaccurately suggest "device" and "fan" as terms, instead of "cooling fan". As a brute-force countermeasure, we devised a PoS-signature that considers as terms, any phrase with a progressive verb (VBG) or adjective (A) that precedes nouns (N). A simplified version is shown in the regular expression of equation (1). Note that ?,+, and * are regular expression cardinality operators, and =~ is the "matching" operator. Experimental evaluations (Section 4.2) reveal that our signature accurately identifies candidate terms even in the presence of PoS-tag errors.

$$\text{term} =\sim \ (\text{VBG}?)\,(\text{A}^*)(\text{N}+). \tag{1}$$

Another limitation of term signatures is their inability to recognize valid terms, particularly if term (or sentence) boundaries are not explicit. For example, the ungrammatical construct "customer helpdesk collimator shutter" contains two terms, "customer helpdesk" and "collimator shutter" in two sentences, which are not explicitly demarcated by boundaries. PoS-tagging yields the (correct) sequence "N N N N", which causes term signatures to wrongly suggest "customer helpdesk collimator shutter" as a term, instead of "customer helpdesk" and "collimator shutter". Dealing with such intricacies and other invalid terms requires statistical analyses.

3.3 Concept Selection and Extraction

This stage applies two statistical filters in an ensemble to address the short-comings of the previous linguistic filter, to discriminate between valid and invalid terms, and to measure the terms' relevancy.

The first statistical filter in our ensemble is based on the term frequency-inverse document frequency (tf-idf) [15] metric. It determines the relevancy of a candidate term *t* in a document (i.e. textual record of our dataset) *d* as

$$\mathrm{tf-idf}(t_d) = f_t \times \log\left(\frac{N}{Df_t}\right) \tag{2}$$

where f_t is the frequency of *t* in *d*, Df_t is the number of records containing *t*, and *N* is the total number of records.

Higher scores are assigned to terms occurring frequently in a few documents. Terms are considered relevant (i.e. they designate salient domain concepts) if their scores exceed experimentally set thresholds. We used tf-idf to determine relevant single-word terms.

Identifying relevant multi-word terms requires measuring the collocation strength between their individual lexical elements (word tokens). To this aim, we applied the cubed mutual information technique (MI3), which was shown to achieve highest precision and recall compared to other collocation measures [6,19]. MI3 computes the collocation strength between words *x* and *y* in a term "*x y*" as

$$\mathrm{MI3}(t) = \log \frac{\left(\frac{F(x,y)}{N}\right)^3}{\frac{\sum F(x)}{N} \times \frac{\sum F(y)}{N}} \tag{3}$$

where *F(x,y)* is the co-occurrence frequency of words *x* and *y*, *F(x)* is the frequency of *x* and *N* is the number of candidate multi-word terms identified by the Candidate Concept Identification phase.

Collocation techniques are designed only for 2-word terms (bi-grams). They are unable to compute the collocation strength for longer terms (general n-grams, n>2), like "disk image power supply unit", which are prominent in corporate domains. To address this issue, we present an innovative algorithm based on dynamic programming to calculate the collocation strength of a term *t*, consisting of an arbitrary number of words (n-gram, n >=2). A simplified version of our algorithm is listed below.

```
Procedure collocation_mi3 (Term t)
1. n = length of t;
2. if n == 2 then
3.   score=MI3(t); //note: according to equation (3)
4.   add (t,score) to hash_n; //note: n=term's length
5. else
6.   sTermSet= get subterms of t with length m=2…(n-1);
7.   for each sTerm of length m, element of sTermSet
8.       if hash_m contains(sTerm)then
9.          score+=retrieve score of sTerm from hash_m;
10.      else
11.         score += collocation_mi3(sTerm);
12.  score = score/(size of sTermSet);
13.  add (t,score) to hash_n;
```

Our iterative procedure starts by computing the collocation scores between the elements of bi-grams using MI3. Bi-grams and their scores are indexed in a look-up (hash) table (lines 3-4). In each subsequent iterations, we consider terms with one additional word. For example, tri-grams (3-word terms) are processed after bi-grams. To deal with general n-word terms (n>2), we reformulate the statement that "terms are composed of words" [16] to posit that n-word terms (n>2) are composed of sub-terms, each of which can consist of at least 2 and at most (n-1) words. Our algorithm operates upon the premise that if a multi-word term *t* is relevant, its sub-terms must also be relevant. Thus, given any n-word term (n>2), our algorithm first decomposes them into sub-terms (line 6). For example, sub-terms of "control rack power supply" are "control rack", "control power", "control supply", "rack power", "rack supply", "power supply", "control rack power", and "rack power supply". Next, lookup tables of previous iterations are inspected to determine whether the sub-terms' collocations are already computed (line 8). If so, the scores are retrieved and accumulated (line 9). Otherwise, we compute the scores of the sub-terms in a recursive manner (line 11). Finally, the collocation score of an n-word term (n>2) is calculated by normalizing the accumulated collocations of its sub-terms (line 12). The term and its score are stored in a look-up table, which will be inspected in future iterations when processing longer terms (e.g. with n+1 words). We consider (multi-word) terms as domain relevant if their collocation scores are higher than an experimentally set threshold. Experiments (Section 4.3) reveal that our algorithm not only accurately identifies valid multi-words terms of arbitrary length, but also discards invalid ones. It is also able to identify individual terms from ungrammatical constructs, which for example, lack explicit term boundaries.

The output of this stage is a set of salient domain concepts, manifested in text as single-word or multi-word terms with relevancy and collocation scores above experimentally set thresholds.

4 Evaluation

Experiments were conducted on real-life corporate data provided by our industrial partners to gauge the performance of Textractor. The datasets contained 143,255 text records of customer complaints captured at helpdesks, and repair actions of service engineers. The contents exhibited typical peculiarities of corporate data, namely high noise level, multi-lingual narratives, subtle language patterns with nested terms, ungrammatical constructs, and valid and invalid multi-word terms. We only report the evaluation of the language detector, candidate concept identification and concept selection and extraction phases, emphasizing on the latter two major contributions..

4.1 Language Detector

Around 65% of our corpus consisted of English texts. Italian documents constituted around 20%, while the remaining 15% of the corpus was almost equally distributed among documents in the French, Dutch, German, Spanish and Portuguese languages. We found out that, on average, our detector correctly predicted the language of a given text with an accuracy of 95%. Sample outputs are in Figure 2, with the first narration correctly identified as Dutch, the second one as "inter-lingual" due to the presence of both English and Italian words, and the last one as English.

```
Materiaal vanaf oktober in de locker...{dutch(0.75)}

Funziona ne la scopia e ne grafia: modification call...{inter-lingual(0.93)}

New ethernet switch cover sensor sent to site...{english (0.75)}
```

Fig. 2. Sample output of language detector

4.2 Candidate Concept Identification

The PoS-tag pattern that we propose as signature for term recognition (Section 3.2) was less susceptible to PoS-tagging errors in identifying terms from ill-formed sentences. For example, despite the PoS-tagging errors in "device/N cooling/VBG fan/N", it correctly induced "cooling fan" as a candidate domain concept. Other similar examples are listed in Table 1. PoS-tag errors are marked with *.

Table 1. Correctly induced candidate terms in the presence of PoS-tag errors

Original Phrase (with PoS-tags)	Candidate Term Identified
unit/N viewing/VBG* console/N	viewing console
testing/VBG archiving/VBG* device/N	archiving device
italy/N flickering/VBG* monitor/N	flickering monitor

However, our term signature fails to recognize terms from ungrammatical sentences without boundaries, such as the terms "customer helpdesk" and "collimator shutter" from "customer helpdesk collimator shutter". Such intricacies are dealt with in the next statistical filtering stage.

4.3 Concept Selection and Extraction

Table 2 illustrates some results of our 2-stage statistical filtering (Section 3.3). Pertinent single-word terms were identified based on their relevancy scores using tf-idf. Relevancy scores for multi-word terms (i.e. n-word terms, n>=2) were computed using our dynamic programming algorithm based on MI3. The maximum tf-idf score (single-word term) we obtained was 84.32, while for MI3 (multi-word term) the maximum score was 143.43.

Table 2. Sample multi-word terms extracted by statistical filter

Term	Term Length	Score: tf-idf and MI3
headset	1	33.71
collimator shutter	2	26.75
customer helpdesk	2	30.45
cpu circuit breaker	3	44.56
control rack power supply	4	33.21
video tube window cover	4	33.67
audio console keyboard circuit board	5	30.50
disk image power supply unit	5	25.91
Status check ok	invalid	0
quality ppl_gb ppl_gb	invalid	0
customer helpdesk collimator shutter	invalid	0

The single and multi-word terms, in Table 2, extracted by our technique, indicate that our approach successfully identifies relevant domain terms of arbitrary lengths, and does not suffer from limitations of traditional statistical techniques that are intended only for 2-word terms. Our technique also separates individual terms embedded in ungrammatical texts that lack sentence/term boundaries. For example, it assigns significantly higher scores to the terms "customer helpdesk" and "collimator shutter" than to "customer helpdesk collimator shutter", the latter being an ungrammatical sentence in which the terms appear. Thus, based on relevancy scores, "customer helpdesk" and "collimator shutter" are suggested as domain terms, while "customer helpdesk collimator shutter" is discarded. Other invalid terms, like "quality ppl_gb ppl_gb" are also discarded due to their low relevancy scores as computed by our technique.

Evaluation was manually performed by domain experts from our industrial partners as no external resources for gold-standards were available. The precision [12], *P*, of Textractor in extracting relevant single and multi-word terms was measured according to equation (4) as the percentage of extracted terms that are considered domain relevant.

$$P = \frac{true\_positive}{true\_positive + false\_positive} \tag{4}$$

where *true_postive* is the number of relevant domain terms identified by Textractor and confirmed by the domain experts, and *false_positive* is the number of terms suggested by Textractor but deemed irrelevant by the experts. The highest precision obtained was 91.5%. with the threshold of the tf-idf filter set to 25 (i.e. only considering single-word terms with tf-idf score > 25) and that for the MI3 filter set to 15 (i.e. only considering muti-word terms with scores > 15). In the absence of any gold-standard, we selected a small sub-corpus, with 500 known entities in the domain, realized as both single and multi-word terms, and computed the recall score, *R*, of our technique as

$$R = \frac{true\_positive}{true\_positive + false\_negative} \tag{5}$$

where false_negative is the number of known relevant domain concepts that our approach could not detect. By lowering thresholds for both the tf-idf and MI3 filters to 5, we achieved a nearly perfect recall of 99%. However, as expected, these low thresholds entailed significant precision losses. We thus computed the F-score to determine the optimal trade-off between precision and recall as

$$F - score = \frac{2 \times P \times R}{P + R} \tag{6}$$

The maximum F-score obtained was 87.7 %, with the thresholds for the tf-idf and MI3 filters set to 23 and 10 respectively, which resulted in a precision of 85.3% and recall of 90.4. Our scores, obtained in extracting terms from noisy, irregular corporate texts, are comparable to other related work, such as [12], which reports average precision, recall and F-measure of respectively 85.6, 93.6 and 84% in company/country profile information extraction, [22], which reports a precision of 61% for financial term extraction, and [14] with precision ranging from 28-100% for news event extraction.

5 Conclusion and Future Work

We have described the design and implementation of Textractor, an application to extract relevant domain concepts, realized as single or multi word terms, from text. Textractor enables business organizations to fully exploit capabilities of information extraction (IE) in order to overcome the difficulties in uncovering critical knowledge hidden within textual data to subsequently support business intelligence activities.

Unlike previous information extraction (IE) systems, Textractor does not rely on external resources (e.g. ontologies). It employs novel algorithms to accurately extract relevant domain concepts, realized as terms of arbitrary lengths, from corporate datasets. Our algorithms efficiently overcome the challenges posed by textual contents of corporate datasets such as terminological variations, subtle language patterns, ungrammatical constructs and the presence of valid and invalid multi-words terms. The high precision obtained during experimental evaluation by domain experts illustrates Textractor's suitability as a pre-cursor to business intelligence activities in corporate settings, especially in the domain of product development and/or customer service.

Future work will extract relations between the concepts identified by Textractor. We will then learn ontologies, which are crucial for semantically integrating heterogeneous, but complementing, data sources into a comprehensive basis. Ontologies facilitate the effective access and usage of information, so that organizations induce more meaningful insights from their business intelligence activities. In the domain of product development and customer service, ontology-based integration could lead to the discovery of soft-failures causes and a better understanding of customer complaints. This knowledge will allow organizations develop better quality products and ensure financial returns. Although we focused on a specific corporate domain in this paper, our algorithms are generic to be applicable in other corporate or even “open” domains, especially to deal with extracting multi-word terms from ungrammatical texts, such as from online forums and blogs.

Acknowledgement

This work is being carried out as part of the project "Merging of Incoherent Field Feedback Data into Prioritized Design Information (DataFusion)", sponsored by the Dutch Ministry of Economic Affairs under the IOP IPCR program.

References

1. Ananiadou, S.: A methodology for automatic term recognition. In: 15th Conference on Computational Linguistics, pp. 1034–1038. Association for Computational Linguistics, Morristown (1994)
2. Bourigault, D.: Surface grammatical analysis for the extraction of terminological noun phrases. In: 14th Conference on Computational Linguistics, pp. 977–981. Association for Computational Linguistics, Morristown (1992)
3. Buitelaar, P., Cimiano, P., Frank, A., Hartung, M., Racioppa, S.: Ontology-based Information Extraction and Integration from Heterogeneous Data Sources. International Journal of Human Computer Studies 66, 759–788 (2008)
4. Cavnar, W.B., Trenkle, J.M.: N-Gram-Based Text Categorization. In: Third Annual Symposium on Document Analysis and Information Retrieval, pp. 161–175. UNLV Publications/Reprographics, Las Vegas (1994)
5. Cunningham, H., Maynard, D., Bontcheva, K., Tablan, V.: GATE: A Framework and Graphical Development Environment for Robust NLP Tools and Applications. In: 40th Anniversary Meeting of the Association for Computational Linguistics (2002)
6. Daille, B., Gaussier, E., Lange, J.M.: Towards automatic extraction of monolingual and bilingual terminology. In: 15th conference on Computational Linguistics, pp. 515–521. Association for Computational Linguistics, Morristown (1994)
7. Frantzi, K.T., Ananiadou, S.: Extracting nested collocations. In: 16th Conference on Computational Linguistics, pp. 41–46. Association for Computational Linguistics, Morristown (1996)
8. Justeson, J., Katz, S.M.: Technical terminology: some linguistic properties and an algorithm for identification in text. Natural Language Engineering 1, 9–27 (1995)
9. Koyama, T., Kageura, K.: Term extraction using verb co-occurrence. In: 3rd International Workshop on Computational Terminology (2004)
10. Maynard, D., Ananiadou, S.: Identifying terms by their family and friends. In: 18th conference on Computational Linguistics, pp. 530–536. Association for Computational Linguistics, Morristown (2000)

11. Maynard, D., Yankova, M., Kourakis, A., Kokossis, A.: Ontology-based information extraction for market monitoring and technology watch. In: ESWC Workshop End User Aspects of the Semantic Web, Heraklion, Crete (2005)
12. Maynard, D., Saggion, H., Yankova, M., Bontcheva, K., Peters, W.: Natural Language Technology for Information Integration in Business Intelligence. In: Abramowicz, W. (ed.) BIS 2007. LNCS, vol. 4439, pp. 366–380. Springer, Heidelberg (2007)
13. Petkova, V.: An analysis of field feedback in consumer electronics industry. PhD thesis, Eindhoven University of Technology
14. Piskorski, J., Tanev, H., Oezden-Wennerberg, P.: Extracting Violent Events from On-line News for Ontology Population. In: Abramowicz, W. (ed.) BIS 2007. LNCS, vol. 4439, pp. 287–300. Springer, Heidelberg (2007)
15. Salton, G.: Developments in automatic text retrieval. Science, 974–979 (1991)
16. Schone, P., Jurafsky, D.: Is knowledge-free induction of multiword unit dictionary headwords a solved problem? In: Lee, L., Harman, D. (eds.) Conference on Empirical Methods in Natural Language Processing, pp. 100–108 (2001)
17. Stanford Tagger: `http://nlp.stanford.edu/software/index.shtml`
18. Unified Medical Language System (UMLS), `http://www.nlm.nih.gov/research/umls/`
19. Vivaldi, J., Rodriguez, H.: Improving term extraction by combining different techniques. Terminology 7, 31–48 (2001)
20. Wright, S.E., Budin, G.: Term Selection: The Initial Phase of Terminology Management. In: Handbook of Terminology Management, vol. 1, pp. 13–23 (1997)
21. Wu, F., Weld, D.S.: Autonomously semantifying Wikipedia. In: sixteenth ACM conference on Conference on information and knowledge management, pp. 41–50. ACM, New York (2007)
22. Xu, F., Kurz, D., Piskorski, J., Schmeier, S.: Term Extraction and Mining of Term Relations from Unrestricted Texts in the Financial Domain. In: Abramowicz, W. (ed.) Businesss Information Systems. Proceedings of BIS 2002, Poznan, Poland (2002)

Comparing Intended and Real Usage in Web Portal: Temporal Logic and Data Mining

Jérémy Besson[1], Ieva Mitašiūnaitė[2], Audronė Lupeikienė[1], and Jean-François Boulicaut[3]

[1] Institute of Mathematics and Informatics, Vilnius, Lithuania
[2] Faculty of Mathematics and Informatics, Vilnius University, Lithuania
[3] INSA Lyon, LIRIS CNRS UMR 5205, France

Abstract. Nowadays the software systems, including web portals, are developed from a priori assumptions about how the system will be used. However, frequently these assumptions hold only partly and are defined also partially. Therefore one must be capable to compare the a priori assumptions with the actual user behavior in order to decide how the system could be improved. To tackle this problem, we consider a promising approach to employ the same formalism to express the intended usage, the web portal model and the frequent real usage patterns, extracted from the experimental data by data mining algorithms. This allows to automate the verification whether the frequent real usage patterns satisfy the intended usage in the web portal model. We propose to use temporal logic and Kripke structure as such a common formalism.

Keywords: Intended Usage, Real Usage, Web Portal Model, Linear Temporal Logic, Pattern Mining.

1 Introduction

Nowadays the software systems, including web portals, are developed from a priori assumptions about how the system will be used. However, frequently these assumptions hold only partly and are defined only partially. Therefore one must be capable to compare the a priori assumptions with the actual user behavior in order to decide how the system should be improved. We intend to develop a tool that helps to compare the intended usage of a web portal specified by the web portal designers, and its real (frequent) usage. This would allow to point out some design decisions that led to the development of a web portal whose real usage does not correspond to the intended usage.

We focus on corporate portals that present information about an organization, its activities, people, etc. Such a portal is a set of client-oriented web sites that personalize the portals tools and information to the specific needs and characteristics of the person who is visiting this web site, searching information that is presented directly in the web sites or in the associated databases. As a rule, it provides a standard set of tools. Corporate portals promote the gathering, sharing, and dissemination of information throughout the intranet, extranet and

W. Abramowicz and R. Tolksdorf (Eds.): BIS 2010, LNBIP 47, pp. 83–93, 2010.

Internet. However, the traditional approaches to portal design often ignore the information needs, searching practices and personalities of users. As a result, the corporate portals suffer from quality problems that prevent or inhibit their use (for example, impossibility to find information, poor navigation or inappropriate display of information). To overcome this problem, one not only need to consider the structure of the portal in terms of web pages and their links between one another, but also additional knowledge and information, e.g., what is the goal of the user while navigating through a given path of the portal and what category the user belongs to.

To allow automatic reasoning and verification on the indented usage and the real usage, the system must be represented in a formal way. A formal representation of a system called Model must check certain Properties of the System in order to reproduce its behavior under various conditions. Considerable work has been done to develop methods of constructing such models. In most of these approaches (e.g., [1], [2], [3]) properties are already known, i.e., they come from literature and/or intuition and insights of the application domain experts. Much less approaches in the domain of system modeling consider the issue of finding out the Properties of the System, necessary to build a Model. Generally, knowledge about the System is acquired by performing the Experiments on it, and thereby it is the Experiments that inform on Properties. We suggest that there is a place here for Data Mining - an art of finding knowledge (e.g., patterns and Properties) from data (e.g., experimental data and experiments).

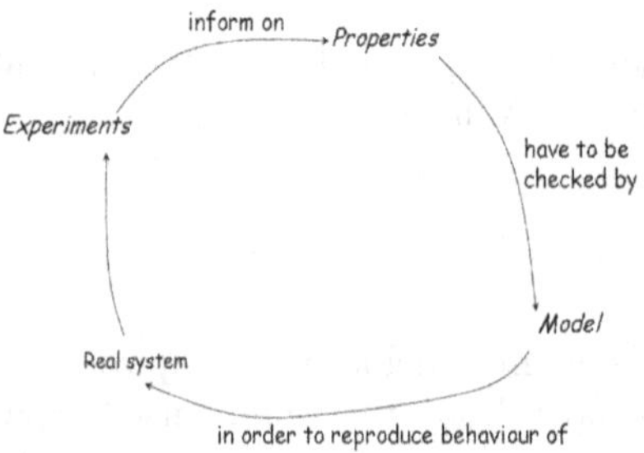

Fig. 1. Model - Properties - Experiments

We consider that the integration of the two issues, i.e., "Properties have to be checked by the Model in order to reproduce the behavior of the real System" and "Experiments inform on Properties" into one cycle of "Experiments or Experimental data inform on Properties that have to be checked by the Model in order to reproduce the behavior of the real System" (see Figure 1) is a promising research goal. This goal can be achieved by employing the same formalism to express the properties, extracted from experimental data by data mining algorithms, and to reason on/verify/learn models using these properties.

In our context, three different elements must be considered: the model, real usage (Experiments) and intended usage (Properties). The model represents the possible usages (behavior) of the system and can be seen as a set of local transitions between states of the user browsing. A real usage is a sequence of transitions in the model. An intended usage is a global constraint on the possible sequences of transitions in the real system. In this context, we seek to be able to express a web portal in terms of both local transitions and global behavior (intended usage), and then to check if they are compatible, i.e., if the local transitions lead to the intended global behavior. Intended usage are here considered as requirements and must be satisfied by the real usage. If it is not the case, then some design decisions was spurious and must be modified, in order to converge toward a web portal model that exhibits the needed global behavior.

We propose the use of linear temporal logic (LTL) and Kripke structure as such a common formalism. It is widely used in many application domains and well adapted to express dynamic properties of non-deterministic finite transition systems. Examples of interesting properties of real systems, such as attainability of a state or property, inevitability of a property, the invariants, chaining of properties can be easily expressed in temporal logic.

The rest of the paper is organized as following. Section 2 presents the Linear Temporal Logic and Kripke structure formalisms that are employed in this article. Section 3 presents the method of modeling a web portal, its intended and real usages. Afterwards, in Section 4 we describe how intended and real usage are compared. Finally, Section 5 concludes the work.

2 LTL over a Kripke Structure as a Common Formalism

Temporal logic extends propositional logic (used for describing the states) with operators for reasoning over time and non-determinism. Systems of temporal logic are classified along a number of axes: propositional versus first order, branching versus linear, points versus intervals, global versus compositional, and past versus future tense [4]. Temporal logic was shown to be a powerful formalism for expressing the dynamic properties of a system [5,6], thus we consider LTL (Linear Temporal Logic) as a convenient formalism to express intended usage.

Several temporal operators are introduced in LTL: X ϕ means ϕ is true at next transition, G ϕ means ϕ is always true, F ϕ means ϕ finally true, and ϕ U ψ means ϕ is always true until ψ becomes true. A LTL formula is true if every path of the Kripke structure, starting from a starting node, satisfies the LTL formula.

With LTL one can express the interesting properties, such as reachability, safety, mutual exclusion and responsiveness, thus it can typically be used to express intended usage. In the following we give several examples. A state is called reachable if there is a computation path from an initial state leading to a state that satisfies a propositional expression P, what can be written in LTL as $F\ P$. A system is called safe if one cannot reach a state for which an undesirable property holds ($!P$), what can be written as $G\ !P$. Mutual exclusion means that a system is not allowed to hold two (or more) critical properties (P_1 and P_2), what can be written in LTL as $G\ !(P_1\ \wedge\ P_2)$. A system is called responsive if, when a property $P1$ holds, then there will be a given answer $P2$, what can be written in LTL as $G(P_1 \rightarrow F(P_2))$. To express that P_1 must remain true until the answer P_2 is given, one can use the formula $G(P_1 \rightarrow P_1 \bigcup P_2)$. The formula $G(P_1 \rightarrow (P_1 \wedge !P_2) \bigcup (!P_1 \wedge P_2))$ means that P_1 and P_2 must be exclusive once P_1 holds.

Semantics of LTL formulas can be implemented on a Kripke Structure. A Kripke structure is a finite-state automaton. A set of discrete variables are defined (Boolean, enumeration, bounded integer [a...b]), such that an instantiation of all the variables defines a state in the automaton. Then the transitions between the variable instantiations (states) are defined. The semantics of the Kripke structure is given by the set of its trajectories (also named paths or executions), i.e., the set of sequences of states of the Kripke structure. For example, two discrete variables named "B" and "E" can be defined in a Kripke structure where "B" is a Boolean variable and "E" is an enumeration variable that can take one of the two values: either "e1" or "e2". Three states (S1, S2 and S3) may be defined with the following instantiations: S1= (B=true,E=e1), S2 = (B=false,E=e1) and S3 = (B=false,E=e2). Transitions in the Kripke structure can be defined, e.g., from S1 to S2, from S2 to S3 and from S3 to S3. This Kripke structure defines the model of the system for which one can check its dynamic properties.

Interestingly, with such a formalism, we can at the same time (a) model a (web portal) system with a set of discrete variables and a finite-state automaton and (b) define LTL constraints over this model. For example, one can model a web portal as a Kripke structure, where the set of states is the set of all tuples of values denoting the set of characteristics of a web portal navigation. Then, intended usage and real usage can be expressed with LTL formulas.

Here are examples of a priori interesting system properties that can be defined in LTL over a Kripke structure:

- A user is of the category X;
- In the initial state, every user of the category X has some information, but the users goal (i. e., what information he/she needs) is unknown;
- Each user of the category X has a goal to find definitions of some terms;
- Any reachable (from initial) state, in which the property p_1 is true, has a path from it on which the property p_2 is eventually true, and until the property p_3 is true;
- Any portal state should always be characterized as follows: no links to already deleted documents.

3 Modeling a Web Portal to Verify Intended and Real Usages

We seek to propose a tool that can answer the question: Are the frequent usages of a web portal coherent w.r.t. the web portal model and the intended usage? For doing that, we propose to model the intended usage, the real usage and the web portal model with the same formalism. If succeeded, one could specify and compare the intended and real usage in a unified way. Thereby, our approach is qualitatively different from the ad-hoc methods that glue different applications solving distinct parts of the problem. We also underline that a web portal analysis is only one of the possible applications of the proposed method, and thus we seek genericity.

In the process mining research domain, important work was realized on discovery, conformance and extension of the models w.r.t. experimental data. The main addressed problems are the following: "How to discover a model from the real usage data?", "Is the model conform w.r.t. the real usage data?" and "How to extend the model w.r.t. to the real usage data?". In these questions, two entities are considered: the model and the real usage data. We seek to add another entity in our analysis: the intended usage. In our context, the model represents all the possible usages of the system. The system-usage data is the concrete real usage of the system (i.e., how the system behaves). The intended usage states how the system should be used (i.e., what the expected behavior is).

We model a web portal as a set of discrete variables whose instantiations form the states of the browsing process, and the possible transitions between these states. Indeed, employing such a formalism, the model can be transformed into a Kripke structure on which LTL formulas that represent intended and real usage can be evaluated. The intended usage represents the correct usages of the system, among the possible usages (where all possible usages make a web portal model). By definition, the web portal cannot restrict the usage of the web portal to only those of the intended usages.

Summing up, to compare intended and real usage, we propose the following methodology:

- To specify a web portal model (see Section 3.1).
- To specify intended usage (see Section 3.2).
- To extract frequent usage employing frequent sequence pattern mining algorithms (see Section 3.3).
- To transform the web portal model, intended usage and frequent usage patterns into a Kripke structure and LTL formulas, and finally to apply a symbolic model checker to verify the intended and real usage w.r.t. to a web portal model (see Section 4).

3.1 Web Portal Model

To express the possible usages of a web portal, we propose to model web portals by the means of a Kripke structure, i.e., a finite-state transition system. Kripke structure contains discrete variables whose instantiations form the states of the browsing process. Among these variables we distinguish a principal one that represents the current web page browsed by the user. However we need to consider not only the web portal structure in terms of web pages and their links between each other, but also additional information, such as the goal of the navigation through a given path and his/her category. Other examples are period of the day, day of the week, quality of services, and meta-data on the browsed pages. All this additional information can be taken into account through additional discrete variables in the Kripke structure.

Following are several examples of web portal possible usages that we seek to represent:

- Ex1: From the page "P1", a user can go to pages "P2", "P3" and "P4".
- Ex2: When a user arrives to the web page "P1", he/she should have the goal named "G".
- Ex3: When a user sends an email and has the goal named "G", then it is probable that the goal "G" is reached.
- Ex4: When a user of the category "C" goes to the page "P1", he/she has the goal "G2".
- Ex5: The web pages "P1" and "P2" are pages of the same category "C1"

Interestingly, all these usages can be defined in a Kripke structure. More generally, any information that can be expressed by the means of discrete variables can be included in such a model.

Example 1. Figure 2 presents a web portal model with four web pages (P1, P2, P3 and P4) and two user's goals (G1 and G2) that can become new or reached for some web pages (G1 is new in P1 and reached in P4 and G2 is new in P2 and reached in P3). This web portal model can be formalized by a Kripke structure with three state variables: $page \in \{P1, P2, P3, P4, P5\}$, $G1 \in \{True, False\}$ and $G2 \in \{True, False\}$ where "True" means that the user has this goal and "False" means that the goal is reached or that the user does not have this goal. The Kripke structure is defined as following:

- start($page$) = P1, P2, P3, P4 or P5.
- start($G1$) = False.
- start($G2$) = False.
- next($page$) = (P2 or P3) if $page = P1$, P4 if ($page = P2$ or $page = P3$), $P2$ if $page = P4$ or $P5$ if $page = P2$.
- next($G1$) = True if $page = P1$, False if $page = P4$ else $G1$.
- next($G2$) = True if $page = P2$, False if $page = P3$ else $G2$.

The "start" function gives the possible initial values of a state variable and the "next" function provides the possible values of a state variable for the next Kripke state.

3.2 Intended Usage

To express the intended usage, we use LTL formulas over the Kripke structure, i.e., the web portal model. In general, because of design decisions and incompatible choices to fulfill the requirements and specifications, a model contains navigational paths that do not satisfy the intended usage. Thus by intended usage we mean the constraints that must be satisfied by the frequent usage of the portal.

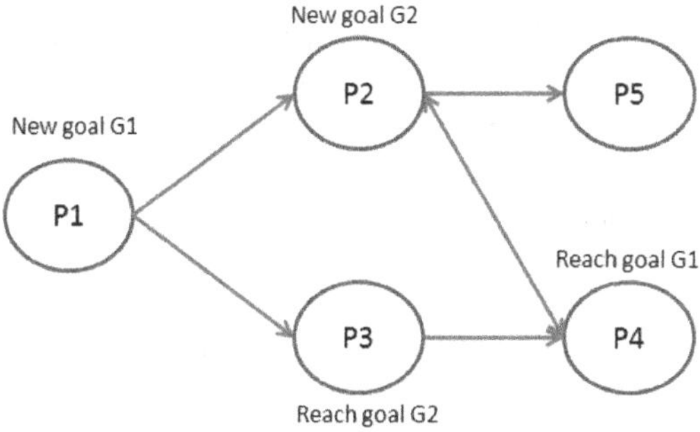

Fig. 2. Example of a web portal model

Activity diagrams and use cases are documents commonly written while specifying a software system. They can be used as the basis of the intended usage. Activity diagrams are used to model the behaviors of a system and the way in which these behaviors are related in an overall flow of the system. Activity diagrams are similar to flowcharts, but they allow the specification of concurrent parallel processing paths. Activity diagrams are used to model the behavior of a system and the way in which these behaviors are related in an overall flow of the system, while state machine diagrams illustrate how an element can move between states classifying its behavior, according to transition triggers, constraining guards, and so on.

In addition, behavioral constraints can be defined to specify the acceptable behavior without considering the specific web portal. For example, each new goal must be reachable, user can have only a maximum given number of goals to reach, user should not go too many times to the same web page and any browsing should contain a reached goal.

Example 2. Referring to Example 1, following are examples of use cases:

- Use case "UC1": User has the new goal G1, then has the new goal G2 then reaches the goal G2 and finally reaches the goal G1.
- Use case "UC2": User has the new goal G1, then reaches the goal G1 and then goes to the web page P5.

One can define an intended usage in LTL that states that any browsing should follow one of the two use cases "UC1" or "UC2": $F(G1 = True \wedge F(G2 = True \wedge F(G2 = False \wedge F(G1 = False)))) \vee F(G1 = True \wedge F(G1 = False \wedge F(page = P5)))$.

3.3 Frequent Usage Patterns Discovery through Frequent Sequential Pattern Mining

To extract frequent usage patterns from event files (log files), one can use sequential pattern mining algorithms. Indeed, event files can be transformed into sets of sequences of nominal values. Each session can be seen as an ordered sequence of pages (nominal values) that was browsed by the user during its session. Sequences of nominal values can be mined to extract patterns of different pattern languages. Portal usages patterns can be revealed by extracting, e.g., episode rules [7], frequent sub-strings (e.g., [10] and [9]) and frequent sub-sequences ([8]). For example, a pattern "20% of users that reached the page P1 also go to the page P2" can be used as a frequent real usage and compared with the intended usage.

We propose to express the extracted frequent usage patterns using LTL. In the following we provide examples of different sequential patterns and their corresponding LTL formulas. We consider that the event file being mined contains three sequences {abaabcb, baacba, cbaa}. In the LTL formulas we use the notation S[1...n] that represents a pattern of n symbols where S[i] is its i-th symbol.

Frequent sub-string

- Pattern to extract: all the strings (consecutive elements) that appear in at least X% of the input sequences.
- Examples: "a", "b", "c", "aa", "baa" and "cb" appear in 100% of the input sequences. "cba" appears in 2/3 of the input sequences.
- LTL formula of a frequent sub-string S[1...n]: F(page=S[1] ∧ X(page=S[2] ∧ X(page=S[3] ∧ X(. . . ∧ X(page=S[n]))))).

Frequent sub-sequence

- Pattern to extract: all the sequences (not necessary successive elements) that appear in at least X% of the input sequences and such that the consecutive elements of the extracted sequence appear in the input sequences within a window of maximal size Y
- Example: "ca" appears in 2/3 of the input sequences with a maximal windows size of 2.
- LTL formula of a frequent sub-sequence S[1...n]: F(page=S[1] ∧ X F(page= S[2] ∧ X F(page=S[3] ∧ X F(. . . ∧ X F(page=S[n]))))).

Episode rule

- Pattern to extract: all the couples of sequences (S1,S2) such that if the sequence S1 is present then S2 is present afterwards with a confidence of at least X% and it appears in at least Y% of input sequences
- Example: When "baa" is present then later there is "cb" with a confidence of at least 2/3 and it appears in at least 2/3 of input sequences
- LTL formula of an episode rule pattern (S1[1...n],S2[1...n]): G (page=S1[1] ∧ X (page = S1[2] ∧ . . . ∧ page = S1[n] ∧ X F(page = S2[1] ∧ X (page = S2[2] ∧ . . . ∧ X(page = S2[m])))) ∨ ! (page=S1[1] ∧ X (page=S1[2] ∧ . . . ∧ page=S1[n]))).

Example 3. Referring to Example 1, following are examples of user browsing that can be obtained from the log file of the web portal:

- P1, P3, P4, P2, P5
- P1, P2, P4, P2
- P1, P2, P5
- P1, P2, P5

$\{P1, P4, P2\}$ and $\{P1, P2, P5\}$ are examples of frequent usage patterns in user browsing with a frequency threshold of 50% that can be transformed into LTL formulas: $F(page = P1 \wedge XF(page = P4 \wedge X(page = P2)))$ and $F(page = P1 \wedge X(page = P2 \wedge X(page = P5)))$.

4 Comparing Real Usage and Intended Usage

To verify the extracted frequent usage patterns w.r.t. the intended usage from a web portal model, we check if it exists a path in the Kripke structure that satisfies all the intended usages and the LTL formulas obtained from the frequent usage patterns. Thereby one can verify if the frequent usage patterns are coherent w.r.t. the intended usage.

Let C1, C2, ..., Cn be the LTL formulas specifying the intended usage, and Cp be the LTL formula obtained from a frequent usage pattern. To verify the intended usage w.r.t. the frequent usage we generate the following LTL formula "! (C1 ∧ C2 ∧ ... ∧ Cn ∧ Cp)". It is important to notice that a LTL formula is true if it is true in all initial states and for all the paths of the Kripke structure. But our objective is to check only if it exists one path that satisfies the LTL formula. Note that a LTL formula A holds on some computation path if and only if it is not true that formula !A holds on all computation paths. Vice versa, A holds on all computation paths if and only if it is not true that formula !A holds on some computation path. Thus we will check if "! (C1∧ C2 ∧ ... ∧ Cn ∧ Cp)" is false, i.e., if it is not true that the formula is true for all paths, what is equivalent to check if it exists a path such that the formula (C1 ∧ C2 ∧ ... ∧ Cn ∧ Cp) is true.

This LTL formula, generated from the intended usage and frequent usage, expresses the following "Does it exist a path in the Kripke structure model of a web portal that satisfies the intended usage and that follows the frequent usage pattern?". To be more concrete, we do not want to check if it exists a real usage (extracted from the event file) that satisfies the generated LTL formula, because the paths that satisfy the LTL formula may not be present in the event files. On the contrary, we want to check whether a frequent usage pattern leads to coherent or incoherent paths w.r.t. the intended usage. A frequent usage pattern is incoherent w.r.t. the intended usage, if no path can follow the frequent usage pattern while satisfying the intended usage. The frequent usage pattern is incoherent w.r.t. the intended usage, if the generated LTL formula is true. To check whether the generated LTL formula is true over the Kripke structure model of a web portal we use the NuSMV symbolic model checker.

Example 4. Referring to the web portal model of Example 1, the intended usage of Example 2 $(F(G1 = True \wedge F(G2 = True \wedge F(G2 = False \wedge F(G1 = False)))) \vee F(G1 = True \wedge F(G1 = False \wedge F(page = P5))))$ and of the frequent usage patterns of Example 3 $(F(page = P1 \wedge XF(page = P4 \wedge X(page = P2)))$ and $F(page = P1 \wedge X(page = P2 \wedge X(page = P5))))$, one can check if the real usage and the intended usage are compatible. Using our method, we can verify that the frequent usage pattern$F(page = P1 \wedge XF(page = P4 \wedge X(page = P2)))$ satisfies the intended usage. Indeed, the path (P1, P2, P4, P2, P5) follows the frequent usage pattern and satisfies the intended usage. The pattern $F(page = P1 \wedge X(page = P2 \wedge X(page = P5)))$ does not satisfy the intended usage. Indeed, it cannot reach any goal and then does not follow neither "UC1" nor "UC2".

5 The Whole Process

Figure 3 presents a global picture of our tool for comparing real usage and intended usage for a web portal. The web portal model is specified by the web portal designer/administrator. Then the intended usage is defined. Afterwards, the event file of the web portal is retrieved and pre-processed (session detection, transformation of pages into categories, removing robots, format transformation, etc). Frequent patterns are extracted from the event file and transformed into LTL formulas. Then, we use the Nusmv symbolic model checker to verify if a real usage fits with the intended usage of a web portal model. To accomplish this, we transform the web portal model, the intended usages and the extracted frequent usage patterns into a NuSMV files (input format of Nusmv).

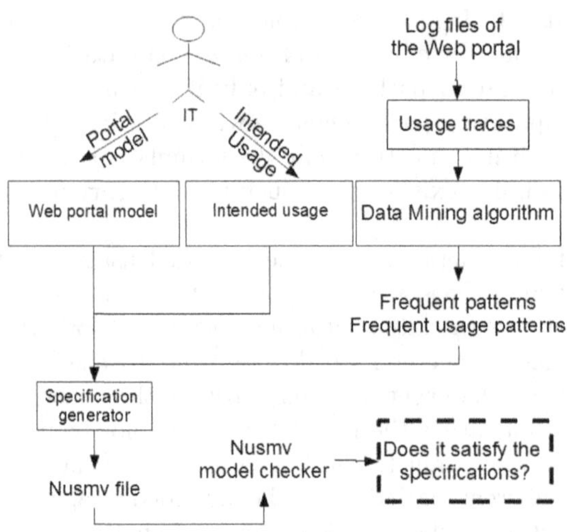

Fig. 3. Comparing intended usage and real usage

6 Conclusion

We present a method to compare intended usage and real usage in web portal employing the same unifying formalism: LTL and Kripke structure. We also employ Data Mining techniques to extract frequent usage patterns from event files (system usage data). This method is valid not only for web portal re-engineering but also for the analysis of other software systems.

Acknowledgment. This work is funded by the Lithuanian State Science and Studies Foundation under the grand V-33/2009 (Reg. Nr. V-09050) and by the French-Lithuanian bilateral program EGIDE PHC "Gilibert" under the grant 19976RM.

References

1. Bockmayr, A., Courtois, A.: Using hybrid concurrent constraint programming to model dynamic biological systems. In: Stuckey, P.J. (ed.) ICLP 2002. LNCS, vol. 2401, pp. 85–99. Springer, Heidelberg (2002)
2. Regev, A., Silverman, W., Shapiro, E.: Representation and simulation of biochemical processes using the pi-calculus process algebra. In: Proceedings of the 6th Pacific Symposium on Biocomputing, pp. 459–470 (2001)
3. Bernot, G., Comet, J.-P., Richard, A., Guespin, J.: Application of formal methods to biological regulatory networks: extending Thomas' asynchronous logical approach with temporal logic. Journal of theoretical biology 229(3), 339–347 (2004)
4. Emerson, E.A.: Temporal and Modal Logic. In: Formal Models and Semantics, pp. 995–1072. North-Holland Pub. Co./MIT Press, Cambridge (1990)
5. Pnueli, A.: System specification and refinement in temporal logic. In: Proceedings of Foundations of Software Technology and Theoretical Computer Science, pp. 1–38. Springer, Heidelberg (1992)
6. Dixon, C., Fisher, M., Konev, B., Lisitsa, A.: Efficient first-order temporal logic for infinite-state systems, Computing Research Repository, Cornell University (2007)
7. Méger, N., Rigotti, C.: Constraint-based mining of episode rules and optimal window sizes. In: Boulicaut, J.-F., Esposito, F., Giannotti, F., Pedreschi, D. (eds.) PKDD 2004. LNCS (LNAI), vol. 3202, pp. 313–324. Springer, Heidelberg (2004)
8. Agrawal, R., Srikant, R.: Mining Sequential Patterns. In: ICDE 1995: Proceedings of the Eleventh International Conference on Data Engineering, pp. 3–14. IEEE Computer Society, Los Alamitos (1995)
9. Dan Lee, S., De Raedt, L.: An efficient algorithm for mining string databases under constraints. In: Goethals, B., Siebes, A. (eds.) KDID 2004. LNCS, vol. 3377, pp. 108–129. Springer, Heidelberg (2005)
10. De Raedt, L., Jaeger, M., Dan Lee, S., Mannila, H.: A Theory of Inductive Query Answering. In: Proceedings IEEE ICDM 2002, pp. 123–130 (2002)
11. Mannila, H., Toivonen, H.: Levelwise search and borders of theories in knowledge discovery. In: Data Mining and Knowledge Discovery, vol. (1-3), pp. 241–258. Kluwer Academic Publishers, Dordrecht (1997)
12. Albert-Lorincz, H., Boulicaut, J.-F.: Mining frequent sequential patterns under regular expressions: a highly adaptative strategy for pushing constraints. In: Proceedings 3rd SIAM SDM 2003, pp. 316–320 (2003)

Capturing Eye Tracking Data for Customer Profiling

Robert Andrei Buchmann[1] and Radu Meza[2]

[1] Babes Bolyai University,
Faculty of Economic Sciences and Business Administration,
Business Information Systems Dpt., str. Teodor Mihali 58-60,
400591 Cluj Napoca, Romania
robert.buchmann@econ.ubbcluj.ro
[2] Babes Bolyai University,
Faculty of Political, Administrative and Communication Sciences,
Journalism Dpt., str. G-ral Traian Moşoiu 71,
400132 Cluj Napoca, Romania
mezaradu@yahoo.com

Abstract. In the context of user-centric design and customer profiling based on the persona paradigm, the paper proposes a Web application model focused on integrating eye tracking data and user-defined metadata with a profile repository. During user-computer interaction through an AJAX-driven graphic interface or interactive document, the user attention map is captured with eye tracking tools and converted in formats that are fit for mining and inferring on relationships between the key concepts that attracted the user's attention. For facile integration of metadata with HTML dynamically generated pages, solutions such as microformats and RDF in attributes are employed.

Keywords: Eye tracking, AJAX, profiling, RDF in attributes.

1 Introduction

The premise of our research is the eye tracking tools' potential of becoming mainstream domestic technology of general use, going beyond their current commercial target - people with disabilities and research projects. In a relative near future, the evolution of biometrics security and customization features will provide enough value for individuals, within the limits of rigorous privacy policies that will protect the right of the end-users to decide for or against engaging eye tracking during their computer-related activities.

In our research, web customization and profiling is approached as the convergence of two fields: *marketing*, with an established tradition in customer profiling, and *user-centered design*, promoted since the early 90s by usability pioneers [1] and culminating in the paradigm of *personas*, established by Alan Cooper [2], an idea that has shifted the self-centered approach of *user interface design* to a more extensive and integrated approach: *interaction design*. In the Web environment, concepts such as *user*, *visitor*, *client*, *customer* or *consumer* tend to overlap (ideally) thus the convergence between user-centered artifacts such as personas and marketing

W. Abramowicz and R. Tolksdorf (Eds.): BIS 2010, LNBIP 47, pp. 94–105, 2010.

profiling techniques. Both approaches are based on capturing data from the user/customer, both knowingly (through forms) and unknowingly (by behavior observation and recording).

Our paper proposes an application model for capturing inputs for profiling metrics through mainstream Web 2.0 technologies in an eye tracking environment. Our goals are to capture the eye tracking activity on the server side and to render it as an informational structure suited for mining and inferring, in order to enrich user/customer personas with a new level of behavioral knowledge. In order to express such knowledge, we engage tools such as JSON (the lightweight alternative to XML) for interoperability purposes and semantic representational models such as RDF, RDFa and improvised microformats.

The next sections of the paper briefly describe the problem context and some related works, the technology involved in our studies and, finally, the proposed model with some research prospects based on its potential.

2 Problem Context and Statement

A variety of profiling methodologies have been engaged both in software engineering and marketing. In *marketing*, the following milestones have been identified [3]:

- The definition of "markets" [4], as synthetic groups of targeted customers, and the target customer characterization [5] through insightful personal attributes;
- The customer "indivisualization" [6] - unlike descriptive profiles that provide an external projection of the customer, it's focused on how the customer sees himself, how he acknowledges his needs and what inspires his decision making;
- The customer image statements [7], based on sets of assertions that do not include direct expression of a desire or the suggestion of a solution (information derived from traditional customer research); instead, the image statements are linked together through relationships vaguely similar to those involved in ontological explicit conceptualization.

In *software development*, the evolution of user-centrism has been developing through several proposals:

- John Carroll's scenarios [8], focused on sequence of actions/tasks rather than actors, tend to be difficult to reuse;
- Hackos and Redish proposed classes of users, focusing on user attributes in the detriment of experiences, motivation and actions [9];
- User roles, addressed by software development processes as part of the requirements analysis phase;
- User archetypes (proposed by [10]) are an improvement of the concept of "user classes", by emphasizing goals on several levels of aggregation (not only task-level goals), including typical activities and domain knowledge;
- Alan Cooper established in 1999 the concept of **personas**, with roots in role-playing techniques; personas are "hypothetical archetypes of actual users… defined with significant rigor and precision" [2] and they are based on user goals and user knowledge, in addition to behavioral, task-level or demographic attributes; our

research is based on the idea that personas can be greatly improved with eye tracking patterns and semantically-enriched attention maps.

Eye tracking represents a recently emerged field and its supporting technology. It debuted in a medical context (optical and neurological), and was later adopted in a wide range of fields, mainly in visual communication research, including interaction design, assistive technologies, usability and marketing. Most eye tracking tools provide means of recording various aspects of the eye activity during interaction with a source of visual stimuli. Usually the eye activity is represented as a succession of fixations and saccades, represented in graph called *the scan path*. Other data such as *blinking*, *pupillary diameter* and *ocular vibration*, may be relevant in certain contexts [11]. The saccades are triggered by stimuli, or anchors, of several types [12]: visual, mnemonic, predicted or anti-anchors (that trigger anti-saccades).

Pupillary diameter variation was considered at some point in time a quantifiable emotional response [13], but a valid correlation is yet to be discovered. That doesn't make pupillary diameter irrelevant: several studies [14] confirmed that its variation is triggered by attention and emotional response (among other stimuli), but it doesn't correlate with the value of the variation.

One of the challenges in integrating eye tracking activity with user interaction is the so called *Midas touch*, named after the mythic figure that turned into gold everything he touched. Similarly, if eye tracking is integrated with user interface events, eye activity tends to trigger undesired events all over the interface surface. Some filtering criteria are needed in order to detect focus points that realistically reflect user attention. The literature recommends several methods for accomplishing this:

- Timing out hovering time over elements [15], our chosen solution;
- Selecting interface elements in a probabilistic manner [16];
- Issuing complementary commands by using the keyboard [17].

Although gaze reactive interfaces are usually marketed as assistive technology, our approach is motivated by the assumption that eye tracking tools will eventually be integrated with domestic technology (regulated by appropriate privacy policies), in order to provide higher customization and biometric features. In business-related research, eye tracking is mostly employed for measuring the effectiveness of visual stimuli (advertising) [18], while it clearly holds great potential in customer behavior monitoring and modeling.

In this paper, we approach the problem of capturing behavioral data relevant to on-line customer profiling in a user-centric e-business environment, using eye tracking graphs mapped on a strongly structured user interface. The mapped behavior is then transferred towards the server for profile development through an emulation of the Persona methodology. The scope of the paper covers the client mechanism of capturing the data in the context of the proposed architectural solution.

Browser event models that integrate gaze events with the browser interface are a fundamental concern in the field [19]. Our research does not focus on this aspect, but rather applies mouse-eye emulation drivers and mouse-contingent interaction in order to emulate gaze events through mouse events. More closely related research is the framework *Text 2.0*, presented in [20], a project oriented on augmented reading - the detection of comprehension difficulties and generation of helper elements with translations or Wikipedia hyperlinks. Also, EyePrint [21] is a system that enhances document access and comprehension through metadata generated during reading. These are mostly reading enhancement solutions, while our research focuses on capturing and modeling preferences in a Web 2.0 e-business environment, with potential for behavior mining and semantic interoperability.

3 Instrumentation

Eye tracking tools are widely available both in commercial products and in open-source or shareware tools. Prices are still prohibitive for domestic use and inclusion in everyday computers but as the field evolves and gains popularity, it's fairly predictable that eye tracking will become the basis for a new generation of biometric user interfaces [22]. Several low-cost, freeware and shareware tools involved in our studies are: Starburst/openEyes [23][24], openGazer [25], TrackEye [26], ITU Gaze Tracker [27], OGAMA (analysis tool) [28]. Advanced commercial solutions such as the products from Tobii Technology [29] eliminate any interference with the user experience by integrating the eye tracking receiver with a TFT monitor, and are complemented by a software development kit and software support for storing, converting and analyzing data. However, our research is still logistically limited to low-cost and freeware tools, as it focuses on prototype, model and metric development rather than conducting experiments with large sets of subjects.

As for the languages used in the proposed application model, there is a need to guarantee a certain level of interoperability, both syntactic (through JSON) and semantic (through RDFa / microformats).

4 The Proposed Model

The proposed framework is based on the premise that an eye-based browser event model is already working on the client-side. In the absence of such an event model, experiments can be made using mouse emulation drivers, which enable users to move the mouse cursor with their eyes (thus, mouse events emulate to a certain degree eye events). Mapping these events in order to avoid the Midas touch is a challenge in itself. However, for our proposed application, timing out MouseOver events is a fairly simple and fit solution in order to detect relevant fixations in the browser. A keyboard event complements the timed fixation event by triggering the display of a text box used for capturing element-level tagging-style metadata from the user, if he chooses so (instead of the ThinkAloud-style verbalization protocols, which are unrealistic in general use scenarios).

Another premise is that the Web user interface is built according to several widely accepted principles:

1. *The Web text readability and navigability principles* promoted by authors such as Jakob Nielsen [30] and Jenny Reddish [31].
2. *The Web 2.0 principle of structuring content* in a hierarchy of DIV and SPAN elements, easily manipulated with CSS styles and Dynamic HTML.

1. The essential principle in providing readability and minimizing the effort of information acquisition is to break text content in paragraphs with self-contained semantics. Each paragraph should reflect a single concept or idea about a single subject. The key concept of each paragraph should be semantically attached to the paragraph in a manner easily integrated with HTML. The most popular models for doing this (without delving in mature Semantic Web such as OWL or RDFS) are microformats and RDFa (RDF in attributes). These models allow for annotation of metadata in XHTML attributes, such as the CLASS, PROPERTY, REV, REL, HREF etc. The key elements are taxonomized in several categories such as *functional* (navigational) and *knowledgeable* (semantically rich).

Another content-related principle states that a hypertext interface must provide a taxonomical interaction structure. In a GUI context this is usually accomplished by breaking the access to various features in menus, submenus, tabbed option containers, options etc. In a document context, this translates to a hierarchical structure, from general to specific, i. e. a group of hyperlinks acting as a table of contents, with each hyperlink acting both as an abstract and as a gateway to more specialized content/semantics.

In this respect, two notions become relevant: *nanocontent* and *microcontent.* Nanocontent consists in the first characters of an emphasized text block (heading, paragraph, hyperlink etc.), on which light readers base their decision of reading further or skipping certain text blocks / list items. Nanocontent is particularly essential while searching (looking up) along a set of visual anchors. Also, text skimming relies heavily on nanocontent. Microcontent consists in small paragraphs with high semantic load (headings, hyperlinks) that must act as an abstract for more detailed content and, therefore, must be semantically independent of their context. Since nanocontent always appears at the beginning of microcontent, they can be delimited as juxtaposed elements. By translating best practices from on-line journalism, we can say that microcontent should be no more than the equivalent of two connected RDF assertions (which is usually sufficient for expressing the most simple sentences in natural language).

2. Most Web 2.0 interfaces are built as a hierarchy of DIV and SPAN elements, easily manipulated with CSS styles and Dynamic HTML. As AJAX applications have been accepted as mainstream, most Web interfaces followed the same principle of interface structuring, even for interfaces that do not use HTML elements (e.g. Flash components). Our model employs AJAX interfaces due to several key features, essential on the client-side:

AJAX (particularly the Document Object Model) represents the interface as a quasi-taxonomy of elements defined with HTML tagging, which easily supports semantic annotations with microformats and RDFa. The structural taxonomy can be mapped to a semantic network of concepts, attached to key elements using HTML attributes.

Most AJAX frameworks (Prototype being our choice) provide means of inserting dynamically generated elements on the fly. This feature is heavily used by our model for generating text boxes near a fixated element, when the user signals (by pressing a key) his desire to annotate his own semantic label to the element, thus contributing to the development of a folksonomy.

The asynchronous data interchange between the client and server is involved in two use cases:

1. While the user skims over the document / interface, a JavaScript object is built with data extracted from the elements that attracted his attention; at certain moments the object is serialized and passed to the server as JSON (see Fig.1 and its subsequent code sample);
2. When the user combines the fixation event with a key press, a Prototype object (Ajax.Updater) calls the text box code from the server and displays it in the proximity of the fixated element, for explicit tagging; the user-defined labels are appended to the JavaScript object representing a client-side attention map.

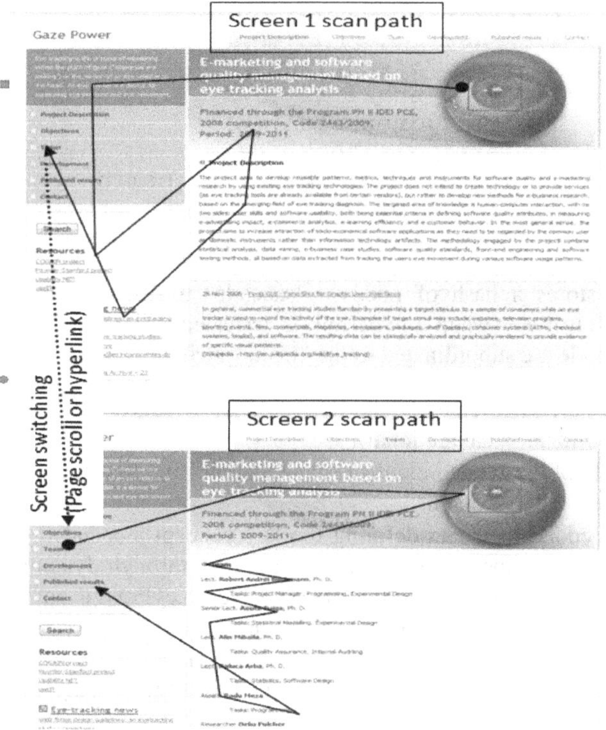

Fig. 1. An attention graph with a screen switching operation

The following JSON code partially expresses an attention graph, including a fixation on a text element presenting the Black Quill literary awards and a screen switching event triggered by an annotated hyperlink. Constructs such as scr1fix1 (screen 1, fixation 1) act as a qualifying namespace in order to discriminate between screens (and attention map resets):

```
attention={
          "user":"John Doe",
          "saccade":{
             "from":{
               "id":"scr1fix1",
               "type":"knowledgeable",
               "content":
               {"nano":"Black Quill",
                "micro":"Black Quill Awards announced!"},
               "pupildiam":7,
               "metadata":
                     {"concept":"Black Quill Award",
                     "tags":["nominees","wishlist"]},
             "to":"scr1fix2" },
          ................
          "screenswitch":{
               "from":"scr1link4",
               "to":"scr2fix1",
               "rel":"nextscr",
               "arrival":"home page",
               "departure":"detailed nominees",
               "rev":"prevscr"
               },..............}
```

The object stores a hash of nodes - "saccade" attributes and, occasionally, a "screenswitch" attribute (when a hyperlink is activated). The data points stored in an attention map node are subordinated to the "from" attribute (the starting fixation):

- The "id" of the fixated element and its type ("knowledgeable" - semantically relevant, or "functional" - navigational);
- The "content" of the fixated element (nanocontent - the first two words, microcontent - the text heading content);
- The pre-embedded metadata defining the key concept associated to each element ("concept") and the metadata attached by the user through dynamically generated text boxes triggered by the simultaneous EyeOver+KeyPress event ("tags");
- Attention metrics (pupillary diameter, fixation span);
- The rhetoric of arrival and departure for screen-switching events (hyperlinks, PageUp or PageDown), in the sense described by [32] (metadata acting as cross-referential semantics).

One specific challenge is to establish proper granularity for the JSON objects representing the client-level attention map, and the moment / event that triggers the asynchronous transfer. There are several ways of implementing the dynamic generation of the attention map:

Each so-called EyeOver event (relevant “fixation cluster” over a certain element) triggers an asynchronous server call, sending a data package for a single event. The data is appended to the attention map on the server side. For common Internet connections, this method has the potential to render the user interface clunky, theoretically unusable, due to the frequent HTTP requests. A better solution is to append new members/data points to a local JavaScript object, with each relevant event. This object dynamically expands with new attributes, thus becoming a client representation of the attention map. At the end of the session, the object is serialized as JSON and sent to the server. This is more feasible from a performance standpoint, but the object must be persistently available in the browser through the entire session. This can be easily accomplished for documents/interfaces built in a monolithic AJAX manner, with simulated hyperlinks that trigger Dynamic HTML transformations rather than HTTP requests. However, where HTTP requests break the user experience, portions of the attention map would be built locally as JavaScript objects and sent to the server for merging, at key moments (triggered by page-switching hyperlinks).

Fig.2 presents a general architecture of the application model:

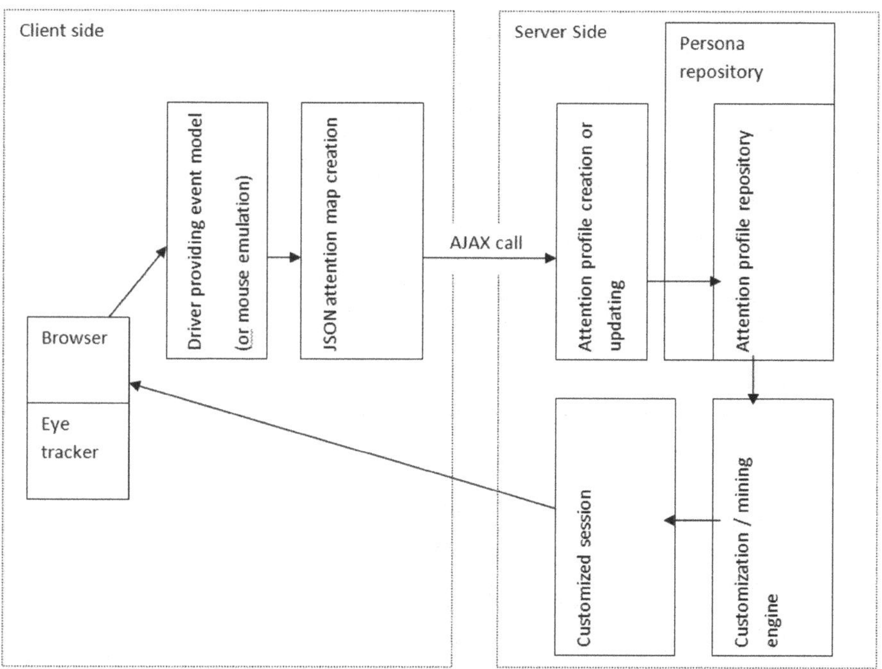

Fig. 2. The general architecture of the proposed model

On the server side, the attention map is stored in two versions:

- In the application database, as serialized JSON representation, for mining purposes and for dynamically generating HTML pages with embedded RDFa, through DOM manipulation;
- In the semantic repository, for semantic reuse, merging and querying, as proper RDF managed by a triplestore server/API (RDFLib for Python is our toolkit of choice).

The following code expresses parts of an attention map in HTML with embedded metadata from the JSON serialized object (for brevity, actual data was replaced with dots, URIs and namespaces were avoided):

```
<div class="attention" about="John Doe">
  <a href="#scr1fix2" rel="saccade">
    <div id="scr1fix1" class="fixated knowledgeable" ↵
about="keyconcept21">
      <div property="microcontent">
        <span property="nanocontent">
        ...............
        </span>
      ...............
      </div>
      <span property="metadata">
      ...............
      </span>
      <span property="pupildiam">
      ................
      </span>
    </div>
  </a>
................................
  <a href="#scr2fix1" rel="nextscr" rev="prevscr">
    <div id="scr1fix6" class="fixated functional" ↵
about="keyconcept26">
      <div property="microcontent">
        <span property="nanocontent">
        ................
        </span>
      ...............
      </div>
      <span property="metadata">
      ...............
      </span>
      <div property="rhet-arrival">
      ..............
      </div>
      <div property="rhet-depart">
      ..............
      </div>
      <span property="pupildiam">
      .......
      </span>
     </div>
  </a>
  .........
</div>
```

5 Profile Processing Prospects

A wide range of processing can be done once the attention map repository is built, depending on the degree of customization desired with respect to the business objectives. First of all, there is a need for crossing from the instance level consisting in the attention maps of specific users, to the more abstract persona level. This is accomplished by various clustering methods applied on the attention map repository, such as clustering users based on their attention span, over three predefined clusters: decision-makers guided by nanocontent, by microcontent or by heavy reading.

The main attributes would be the fixation span and pupillary diameter. In order to accomplish this, a factor to be considered is how the user adjusts and automates parts of his behavior after repeated interactions with the same interface. It is possible for someone who initially acts as a heavy reader, to become a nanocontent decision-maker after several sessions with the same interface or in certain conditions (time pressure). Because of this, the attention map from the repository is updated and its nodes are weighted with the frequency of their involvement in repeated sessions.

Different strategies of visual communication should be used for the three types of users (based on graphics, taxonomical hypertext interfaces or heavy text interfaces). Further studies will be employed to establish how different types of users interact with these communication strategies, based on efficiency and task analysis metrics. Several prospects for further development are, as follows:

- Clustering users based on sequence patterns. Sequential pattern and association rule mining are common in shopping cart analysis and other Web usage mining scenarios where navigational patterns are relevant. Attention maps captured by our model become a valuable resource for eye movement pattern analysis using algorithms such as *GSP* (for sequence patterns) [33] and *A priori* (for association rules) [34]. An attention map can be processed as a supersequence of eye movement patterns and their corresponding interface elements / key concepts;
- Applying self-organizing maps in the adjustment of attention maps after repeated interactions with the same user;
- Clustering users based on the key concepts that attracted their attention, using Jaccard/Tanimoto distance metrics;
- Detecting the most effective nanocontent and microcontent by measuring their frequency in the attention maps. Detecting counter-anchors that trigger frequent antisaccades;
- Inferring on the persona repository in order to draw conclusions regarding the relationship between a user class and key concepts, and commonalities among user classes.

6 Conclusions

Consumer action is determined by three types of factors - environmental, competitive and marketing-defined. Of these, the environmental factors determine needs, while the other factors most often determine desires. The consumer action is the result of a decision-making process which involves need recognition, preference recommendation, persuasion (including sensory stimulation) and prior action (reusable behavior).

Eye tracking helps to measure, to a certain degree, the process of information acquisition, before it triggers the consumer action. However, most eye tracking studies in marketing are oriented on the effectiveness of visual stimuli attributes (color, size, graphics, location) for specific test subjects. Our studies emphasize the integration of eye tracking on higher levels of abstraction, with preference recommendation and enriched customer profiling in order to provide reusable models and innovative segmentation criteria. Thus, the focus of eye tracking shifts from specific subjects to virtual personas whose preferred visual stimuli can be aggregated and mined. Further research will be invested in developing the persona management system, in order to raise the persona repository to a fully ontological level.

Acknowledgment. This paper represents results of the research project *E-marketing and Software Quality Management Based on Eye Tracking Analysis*, code 2443/2009 funded by the National Research Program IDEI, managed by Lect. Robert Andrei Buchmann Ph.D.

References

1. Nielsen, J.: Usability Engineering. Academic Press, Boston (1993)
2. Cooper, A.: The Inmates Are Running the Asylum. Macmillan, New York (1999)
3. Pruitt, K., Adlin, T.: The Persona Lifecycle. Morgan Kaufmann, San Francisco (2006)
4. Sissors, J.: What Is a Market? J. of Marketing 30, 17–21 (1966)
5. Moore, G.A.: Crossing the Chasm: Marketing and Selling High-Tech Products to Mainstream Customers. HarperCollins, New York (1991)
6. Upshaw, L.: Building Brand Identity: A Strategy for Success in a Hostile Marketplace. John Wiley and Sons, New York (1995)
7. Mello, S.: Customer-centric Product Definition: The Key to Great Product Development. AMACOM, New York (2002)
8. Carroll, J. (ed.): Scenario-based Design: Envisioning Work and Technology in System Development. John Wiley and Sons, Chichester (1995)
9. Hackos, J.T., Redish, J.C.: User and Task Analysis Techniques: User and Task Analysis for Interface Design. John Wiley and Sons, New York (1998)
10. Mikkelson, N., Lee, W.O.: Incorporating User Archetypes into Scenario-Based Design. In: 9th Annual Usability Professionals' Association Conference, Asheville (2000)
11. Duchowski, A.T.: Eye Tracking Methodology - Theory and Practice, 2nd edn. Springer, London (2007)
12. Rommelse, N.N., Van der Stigchel, S., Sergeant, J.A.: A Review on Eye Movement Studies in Childhood and Adolescent Psychiatry. Brain and Cognition 63(8), 391–414 (2008)
13. Hess, E.H., Polt, J.M.: Pupil Size as Related to Interest Value of Visual Stimuli. Science 132(3423), 349–350 (1960)
14. Beatty, J., Lucero-Wagoner, B.: The Pupillary System. In: Cacioppo, J.T., Tassinary, L.G., Berntson, G.G. (eds.) Handbook of Psychophysiology, pp. 142–162. Cambridge University Press, Cambridge (2000)

15. Jacob, R.J.K.: The Use of Eye-movements in Human-Computer Interaction Techniques: What You Look at is What You Get. ACM Transactions on Information Systems 9(2), 152–169 (1991)
16. Salvucci, D.D., Anderson, J.R.: Intelligent Gaze-added Interfaces. In: Proceedings of the Conference on Human Factors in Computing Systems, pp. 273–280. ACM Press, New York (2000)
17. Zhai, S., Morimoto, C., Ihde, S.: Manual and Gaze Input Cascaded (Magic) Pointing. In: Proceedings of the SIGCHI conference on human factors in computing systems, pp. 246–253. ACM Press, New York (1999)
18. Wedel, M., Pieters, R.: Eye tracking for Visual Marketing. Foundations and Trends in Marketing 1, 231–320 (2006)
19. Reeder, R.W., Pirolli, P., Card, S.K.: Web Eye Mapper and WebLogger: Tools for Analyzing Eye Tracking Data Collected in Web-use Studies. In: Proceedings of the Conference on Human Factors in Computing Systems, pp. 19–20. ACM Press, New York (2001)
20. Text 2.0, `http://text20.net/`
21. Ohno, T.: Eyeprint: Support of Document Browser with Eye Gaze Trace. In: Proc. ACM 6th International Conference on Multimodal Interfaces, pp. 16–23. ACM Press, New York (2004)
22. Ohno, T., Hammoud, R.I.: Gaze-based Interaction. In: Hammoud, R.I. (ed.) Passive Eye Monitoring, pp. 180–194. Springer, Heidelberg (2008)
23. Starburst 1.0.1, `http://joelclemens.colinr.ca/eyetrack/software.html`
24. openEyes - Eye Tracking for the Masses, `http://thirtysixthspan.com/openEyes/`
25. Opengazer, `http://www.inference.phy.cam.ac.uk/opengazer/`
26. TrackEye, `http://www.codeproject.com/KB/cpp/TrackEye.aspx`
27. ITU GazeGroup, `http://www.gazegroup.org/downloads/23-gazetracker`
28. Open Gaze and Mouse Analyzer, `http://didaktik.physik.fu-berlin.de/projekte/ogama/`
29. Tobii Technology, `http://www.tobii.com`
30. Nielsen, J., Loranger, H.: Prioritizing Web Usability. New Riders, Berkeley (2006)
31. Redish, J.: Letting Go of the Words. Morgan Kaufman, San Francisco (2007)
32. Landow, G.: Hypertext 3.0: Critical Theory and New Media in an Era of Globalization. The Johns Hopkins University Press, Baltimore (2006)
33. Srikant, R., Agrawal, R.: Mining Sequential Patterns: Generalizations and Performance Improvements. In: Proc. of the 5th Intl. Conf. Extending Database Technology, EDBT 1996, Avignon, France, pp. 3–17 (1996)
34. Agrawal, R., Srikant, R.: Fast Algorithms for Mining Association Rules. In: Proc. of the 20th Intl. Conf. on Very Large Data Bases, VLDB 1994, Santiago, Chile, pp. 487–499 (1994)

Consistency Checking of Compliance Rules

Ahmed Awad, Matthias Weidlich, and Mathias Weske

Business Process Technology Group
Hasso-Plattner-Institute, University of Potsdam, Germany
{ahmed.awad,matthias.weidlich,
mathias.weske}@hpi.uni-potsdam.de

Abstract. Compliance checking of business process models against regulation is inevitable. Due to various sources of compliance requirements, a conflict of interest of such requirements is very likely. Thus, it is crucial to analyze the relation between compliance rules to discover any possible conflicts before even checking such rules against process models. Although this step is important in the compliance management life cycle, there is almost no work that studied this direction. In this paper, we start by checking for consistency between execution ordering compliance rules expressed in linear temporal logic (LTL), addressing control and data flow aspects. To achieve this, we rely on the generation of Büchi automaton from LTL formulas. However, we show that domain-specific knowledge is of crucial importance to draw correct conclusions.

Keywords: Compliance Checking, Consistency Checking, Temporal Logic.

1 Introduction

Compliance checking of business process models has received growing attention in recent years. Financial scandals in large public companies led to legislative initiatives like SOX [1]. The purpose of these initiatives is the enforcement of certain controls on business. Controls can be in the form of, e.g., *executing* activities in certain order or separation of duty regarding financial transactions (a person who issues an order must not be the one to grant it). In addition to regulations, compliance requirements might be enforced by domain specific initiatives, e.g., BASEL II [28] in the banking sector.

Since then, compliance of a process model at design time has been addressed by different approaches. In such approaches either the process model creation is guided by compliance rules (e.g., [17, 16, 18]) or existing process models are *verified* against compliance rules (e.g., [3,12,23,31]). Still, most of the effort is spent on checking/enforcing compliance between a process model and a rule. Almost no work discussed how to automatically check consistency among various compliance rules. On the one hand, such inconsistencies might stem from ambiguous descriptions of compliance rules as they are typically described in natural language and, therefore, subject to interpretation. On the other hand, compliance requirements might originate from a variety of sources, e.g., in the form of regulations (SOX Act in the public sector), internal policies of the organization, or guidelines and best practices (e.g, BASEL II and guidelines for anti-money laundering [7] in the financial sector). Consequently, the chance for conflicting rules is

W. Abramowicz and R. Tolksdorf (Eds.): BIS 2010, LNBIP 47, pp. 106–118, 2010.

very likely. For instance, consider two rules, one stating that "in general, money needs to be transfered before shipment of the product", whereas the second states that "shipment of the product might happen before payment, if credit card details are already known for the customer". Clearly, there is a conflict that might be attributed to *misinterpretation* of the compliance requirements. That is, certain assumptions (e.g., that credit card details are not known in case of the first rule) are not made explicit.

One might argue that these conflicts between compliance rules are revealed once a process model is checked for compliance. However, it does not seem reasonable to spend effort on such a check that is bound to fail. Moreover, the negative compliance result might cause even more time consuming investigations of the particular process, even though conflicts in the compliance rules caused the compliance violation. Therefore, it is essential to provide support for automated conflict detection for compliance rules.

Our contribution in this paper is an automated approach to check consistency among rules that specify execution ordering constraints, potentially enriched with data-related aspects. These rules are expressed as temporal logic formulas [30, 32]. Although the notion of consistency checking among rules expressed in temporal logic has already been addressed in literature, it has been applied solely in the context of hardware specifications [8]. While our work is inspired by these approaches of checking consistency, we show that they cannot be applied for compliance rules of business process models in a straight-forward manner. Instead, additional domain knowledge needs to be leveraged.

The remainder of this paper is organized as follows. Section 2 provides preliminaries for our work, i.e., basic notions of execution ordering compliance rules and their formal grounding used for model checking. Afterwards, Section 3 shows that consistency checking of compliance rules is not straight-forward and illustrates the need for considering domain knowledge. Based thereon, we introduce the notion of a business context that captures domain knowledge in Section 4. Section 5 shows how the business context is applied to detect conflicting and inconsistent rules. Further on, we review related work in Section 6 and conclude the paper in Section 7.

2 Preliminaries

In this section we introduce the background of our work. First, Section 2.1 briefly summarizes linear temporal logic with past operators (PLTL). Second, Section 2.2 summarizes our previous work in the area of compliance checking. Afterwards, Section 2.3 gives details on the formal background of compliance checking using model checking.

2.1 Linear Temporal Logic with Past Operators (PLTL)

Linear Temporal Logic (LTL) allows expressing formulas about the future of systems. In addition to logical connectors ($\neg, \wedge, \vee, \rightarrow, \Leftrightarrow$) and atomic propositions, it introduces temporal operators, such as *eventually* (F), *always* (G), *next* (X), and *until* (U). PLTL [32] extends LTL by operators that enable statements over the past. That is, it introduces the *previous* (P), *once* (O), *always been* (H), and *since* (S) operators. Although the past operators do not increase expressiveness of the formalism, they enable convenient specification of predicates over the past [20].

2.2 Compliance Rules for Business Process Models

Compliance rules might require the execution of certain activities or enforce ordering constraints for a set of activities. Thus, these rules focus purely on the control flow perspective of process models. These rules might be further classified according to the scope they consider, which might be *global*, *before*, *after*, or *between* [10]. Within a scope rules can require the *existence* or *absence* of activities. In [3,6], we showed how compliance rules focusing on the control flow can be modeled in PLTL. We also showed how these rules can be verified using model checking techniques.

The aforementioned kinds of rules neglect data aspects of process models. It is well-known that this is not sufficient for real-world scenarios, as execution of an activity often changes data objects from one state to another [19]. Therefore, data aspects have to be taken into account in order to achieve holistic compliance checking, which we discussed in previous work [5].

The whole spectrum of compliance rules along with the respective PLTL expressions is illustrated in Table 1. With A as the set of activities of a process model, the PLTL expressions are based on the predicates $ready(a)$ and $executed(a)$. They capture the facts that an activity $a \in A$ is about to execute or has already executed, respectively. It is worth to mention that the predicate $executed(a)$ holds solely in *one* state. That is,

Table 1. Mapping of Compliance Rule Patterns into PLTL

	Rule Pattern	PLTL Formula
Control Flow	Global Scope Existence	$\mathsf{F}(executed(a))$
	Global Scope Absence	$\mathsf{G}(\neg executed(a))$
	Before Scope Absence	$\mathsf{G}(ready(b) \rightarrow \mathsf{H}(\neg executed(a)))$
	After Scope Absence	$\mathsf{G}(executed(a) \rightarrow \mathsf{G}(\neg executed(b)))$
	After Scope Existence	$\mathsf{G}(executed(a) \rightarrow \mathsf{F}(executed(b)))$
	Between Scope Absence	$\mathsf{G}(executed(a) \rightarrow (\neg executed(b))\ \mathsf{U}\ executed(c))$
	Before Scope Existence)	$\mathsf{G}(ready(b) \rightarrow \mathsf{O}(executed(a)))$
	Before Scope Absence	$\mathsf{G}(ready(c) \rightarrow (\neg executed(b))\ \mathsf{S}\ executed(a))$
Data	Data Flow	$\mathsf{G}(ready(a) \rightarrow \bigwedge_{d \in D}(\bigvee_{s \in S} state(d,s)))$
Mixed	Conditional After Scope Existence	$\mathsf{G}(executed(a) \wedge \bigwedge_{d \in D}(\bigvee_{s \in S} state(d,s)) \rightarrow \mathsf{F}(executed(b)))$
	Conditional After Scope Absence	$\mathsf{G}(executed(a) \wedge \bigwedge_{d \in D}(\bigvee_{s \in S} state(d,s)) \rightarrow (\neg executed(b))\ \mathsf{U}\ executed(c))$
	Conditional Before Scope Existence	$\mathsf{G}(ready(b) \rightarrow \mathsf{O}(executed(a) \wedge \bigwedge_{d \in D}(\bigvee_{s \in S} state(d,s))))$
	Conditional Before Scope Absence	$\mathsf{G}(ready(c) \rightarrow (\neg executed(b))\ \mathsf{S}\ (executed(a)) \wedge \bigwedge_{d \in D}(\bigvee_{s \in S} state(d,s)))$

the state that is reached by the execution of a. In other words, $executed(a)$ does *not* hold in all states after execution of activity a. In the line of the data access semantics defined in [2], we assume a set of data objects D and a set of data states S. Further on, the predicate $state(d, s)$ requires that a certain data object $d \in D$ is in state $s \in S$.

Global Scope rules require that a certain activity is either executed in all process instances (existence rule), or in $none$ of them (absence rule). An example for a global scope existence rule would be an insurance handling process, in which it is required that the case is $always$ archived.

Before / After Scope Absence rules require the absence of a certain activity either *before* or *after* the execution of another activity, i.e., mutual exclusion.

Leads to rules specify a causal dependency between two activities, such that one activity eventually follows the execution of another activity (existence rule). This case might also be interpreted as an *after scope existence* rule. Further on, a third activity might be requested not to occur in between (absence rule). As in case of the existence rule, the latter could be seen as a *between scope absence* rule.

Precedes rules specify a causal dependency between two activities, such that one activity has been executed whenever another activity is about to execute. Again, this kind of rules might be specified as an absence rule. That is, an activity has been executed whenever another activity is about to execute, while a third activity has not been executed in between.

Data Flow rules specify requirements for the execution of a certain activity in terms of combinations states of data objects. These requirements have to be met, whenever the activity is about to execute.

Conditional Leads to rules specify an execution ordering relation between activities that is further refined by data conditions. That is, a *leads to* rule as introduced above has to hold solely in case certain data conditions are met. Such a data condition might be considered in the case of existence rules as well as in case of absence rules.

Conditional Precedes rules also refine the aforementioned $precedes$ rules. That is, the causal dependency is required to hold solely if the data condition is met. Again, a data condition might be applied for existence rules and absence rules.

2.3 LTL Model Checking Based on Büchi Automata

Model checking techniques can be applied to check compliance rules that are specified in LTL. In particular, both, the actual compliance rule as well as the behavioral model of the system, a process model, might be represented as Büchi automata. A Büchi automaton for an LTL formula represents a computation to satisfy the formula, if there is one. Approaches like [14, 13][1] are capable of generating a Büchi automaton for a given LTL formula. Based on the set of words that is accepted by the automata of the formula *and* the system, we are able to conclude whether the system satisfies the compliance rule.

[1] An implementation of the algorithm presented in [13] is available from `http://www.lsv.ens-cachan.fr/~gastin/ltl2ba/index.php`

3 Checking Consistency for Compliance Rules

This section introduces our approach of checking consistency be means of exemplary compliance rules. The overall setting is depicted in Fig. 1. In general, there might be more than one set of compliance rule, e.g., rules related to anti money laundering and rules related to BASEL II. Some of these rules are related, i.e., they address a common set of business processes. In order to enable consistency checking of these rules, we have to include extra knowledge from the domain. Finally, the conjunction of all LTL formulas is created and its corresponding Büchi automaton is checked for having accepting states.

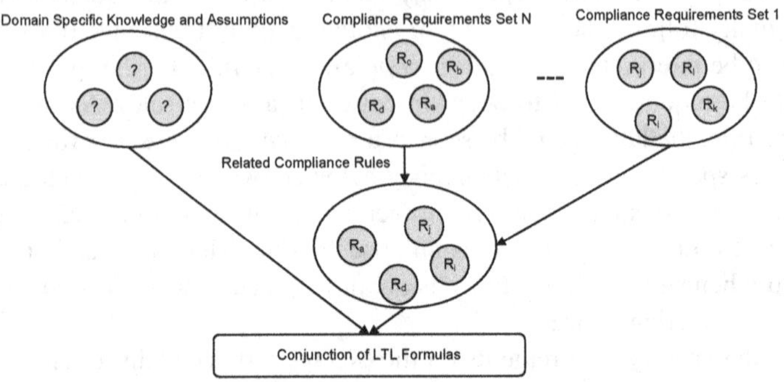

Fig. 1. The Approach of Consistency Checking

In order to motivate the need for taking domain knowledge into account, we introduce a set of example compliance rules. Following on the model checking approach as introduced in the previous section, we illustrate the resulting Büchi automaton for the conjunction of compliance rules. Of course, one would assume the compliance rules to be consistent, if the Büchi automaton has accepting runs, whereas inconsistent rules are indicated by an automaton that has no accepting runs. However, our examples show that detection of inconsistencies is not as straight-forward as expected.

Example 1 (Cyclic Dependency). Imagine two rules that consider the ordering of two activities, one specifying the payment of goods and the other describing the sending of goods. Let the first rule R1 state that payment must precede sending goods, whereas the second rule R2 states the opposite, i.e., sending goods precedes payment. It is obvious that the objectives behind the two rules are totally different. In the first one we need to guarantee that the money has been transferred before the goods are sent out. With respect to the second rule, the objective might be to gain new customers by relaxed payment conditions. If we represent the payment activity with a and the sending goods activity with b, the corresponding LTL formulas would be $G(executed(b) \rightarrow O(executed(a)))$ and $G(executed(a) \rightarrow O(executed(b)))$. Here, O is the past time LTL operator *once*.

The Büchi automaton generated for the conjunction of both formulas is illustrated in Fig. 2. Although R1 and R2 are clearly inconsistent, the respective Büchi automaton has accepting runs. In particular, the following runs are possible.

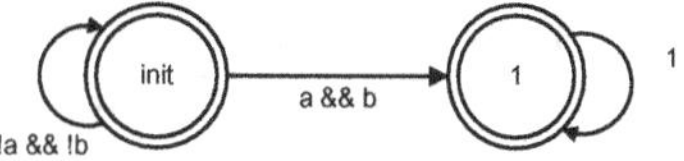

Fig. 2. Automaton for R1 and R2

1. Neither a nor b are executed at all, which is represented by the transition from state $init$ to itself.
2. Both activities, a and b are executed in a single step, which is represented by the transition from $init$ to $state1$.

The phenomena that led to the first accepting run is called vacuous satisfiability [8]. The set of compliance rules would be satisfied by all process models that contain neither a nor b. Obviously, that is not a valid solution in our context, as these compliance rules are specified for process models that contain these activities.

The second accepting run is invalid in our context either. Common process description languages, e.g., the Business Process Modeling Notation (BPMN) or Event-Driven Process Chains (EPC) assume interleaving semantics. That is, two activities cannot complete their execution at the very same time. That, in turn, is reflected in any behavioral model of a process model, which is derived by transformation to some intermediary representation, for instance, Petri nets (cf., [9]). These models do not contain a single state in which two activities finish their execution. For this reason, the second accepting run of the automaton in Fig. 2 is also invalid in our context.

Example 2 (Contradictions). Imagine two rules that have the same condition, but different implications. For instance, one rule R3 specifies that the reception of payment leads to the activity of sending goods by DHL. A second rule R4, in turn, states that after the reception of payment, the goods have to be sent by UPS. Further on, let a be the activity of receiving the payment, while the send activities are represented by b in case of DHL, and c in case of UPS, respectively. Then, the resulting LTL formula would be $G(executed(a) \rightarrow F(executed(b))) \wedge G(executed(a) \rightarrow F(executed(c)))$. The Büchi automaton, which was omitted due to its size, has accepting runs, owing to the vacuous satisfiability phenomena discussed above and state transitions with more than one activity being executed at a time. However, there are other accepting runs that might not be traced back to these phenomena. These runs correspond to scenarios, in which activity a is executed; thereafter activities b and c are executed in any order.

A process model fragment that shows such a behavior and, therefore, satisfies the compliance rules is illustrated in Fig. 3. However, this model would not be considered a valid solution for our compliance requirements from a business point of view. Goods might be send only once using either activity *Send Goods by DHL* or *Send Goods by*

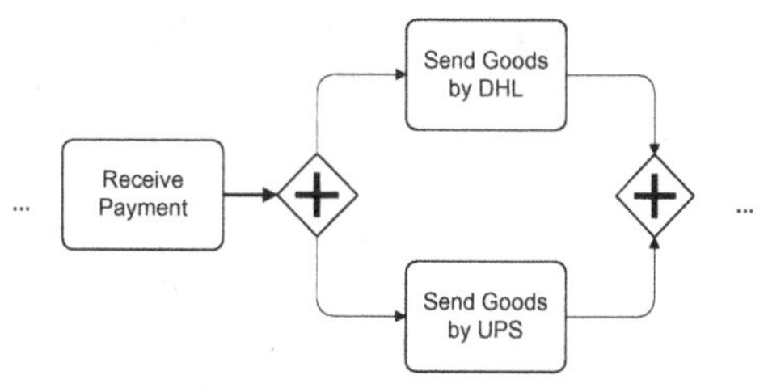

Fig. 3. A process fragment satisfying rules R3 and R4

UPS. Therefore, consistency checking for these kinds of compliance rules requires further information about the business domain.

Example 3. (Data Issues) The aforementioned aspects are also of relevance for data-related rules. As mentioned before, we assume a formalization of data flow for process models, such that a data object can be only one data state at a time. Thus, data states are exclusive.

Consider a compliance rule R5 that requires a purchase request to be in state $archived$ when the case is closed. Based on the predicates introduced in Section 2, this compliance requirement is expressed as $G(ready(a) \rightarrow state(d, archived))$ with a being the activity to close the case and d the data object representing the purchase request. Further on, a second rule R6 requires a purchase request to be either in state *accepted*, or $rejected$, i.e., $G(ready(a) \rightarrow state(d, accepted) \vee state(d, rejected))$, when the case is about to be closed.

Not surprisingly, the Büchi automaton for the conjunction of these rules has a lot of accepting runs (again, the figure was omitted due to its size) even though both rules are inconsistent. That results from the phenomena that were already discussed above for activities. That is, accepting runs violate the requirement of exclusive data states, require data objects to be in no state (vacuous satisfiability), or are invalid from a business perspective (e.g, the state of the purchase request might be set to both, *accepted* and $rejected$). Again, inconsistencies between two compliance rules cannot be identified by solely testing the generated Büchi automaton for the absence of accepting runs.

4 The Business Context

It is of crucial importance to include correct assumptions about the system/domain under investigation in order to correctly decide about the consistency of the specification [8]. We also illustrated this need by our examples in Section 3. Thus, reasonable consistency checking has to consider business context information.

The business context describes the domain specific knowledge. It reflects the way a business provides its added value. Moreover, it could be seen as the unified view of the domain among the participants. The context is a global process independent description of the business activities. Processes are composed from individual business activities from the context. Each business activity provides a value by its own. For instance, an activity *Payback claim by bank transfer* provides the value of transferring the amount of money claimed by a customer as its *effect*. However, execution of such an activity is based on assumptions about the input, there are *preconditions*. Moreover, having another activity *Payback claim by a cheque*, it would be part of the domain knowledge that it is not possible for the two payment activities to be *both* executed in the same process.

To make the concept of a context more familiar, one might think of the notion of service registries [27] in service oriented architecture as a sub-concept for the business context. There, each service is described independently in terms of its inputs and outputs on a syntactical level. In a business context, business activities are the counterpart of services in a registry. We require at least the following information to be part of the business context in terms of relations between business activities. 1) Preconditions: for each activity we need to know the preconditions, other activities required to execute previously. 2) Effect: the value added by executing a certain activity. 3) Contradiction: the set of activities that cannot be allowed to execute within the same process instance.

5 Detecting Compliance Conflicts

Given a set of compliance rules, it becomes necessary to check consistency among them. In particular, the business context (domain knowledge) has to be considered in the PLTL expressions in order to detect inconsistencies based on the respective Büchi automaton. Again, we assume a set of compliance rules to be inconsistent, if the Büchi automaton for the conjunction of the rules has no accepting runs. We illustrate the approach based on the examples presented in Section 3.

Example 1. (Cyclic Dependency) The first example contains two rules R1 and R2 that state a cyclic dependency between payment for goods, activity a and sending the goods, activity b, respectively. However, the Büchi automaton generated for the conjunction showed accepting runs, which required both activities not to be executed at all or to be executed in the same step. In order to cope with the first phenomenon, that is, vacuous satisfiability, we specify an additional rule, $F(executed(a))$, that enforces the execution of payment for goods activity. That, in turn, results in the automaton that is illustrated in Fig.4(a), which still accepts the concurrent execution of both activities. As discussed in Section 3 such concurrent execution conflicts with the assumption of interleaving semantics for process models. Therefore, another predicate that prohibits concurrent execution, $G(\neg(executed(a) \wedge executed(b)))$, is added. As mentioned in Section 2 the predicate $executed(a)$ holds only for one state, i.e., the state that is reached by executing the activity a. The updated automaton is shown in Fig. 4(b). This automaton has no accepting run. At this point, we conclude that the rules R1 and R2 are *inconsistent* given our knowledge about the process modeling domain. Thus, the additional formula that prohibits concurrent execution of activities is of a general nature and has to be added for consistency checking of any activity execution compliance rules.

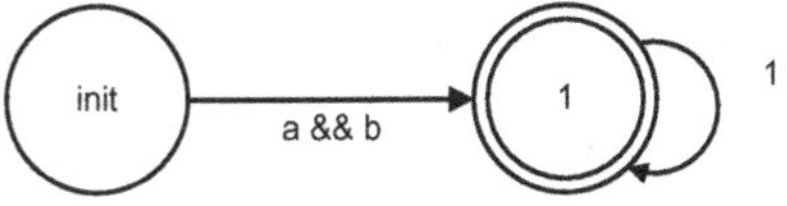

(a) Automaton for the conjunction of R1, R2, $F(executed(a))$, and $F(executed(b))$

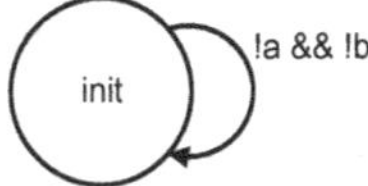

(b) Automaton for the conjunction of R1, R2, $F(executed(a))$, $F(executed(b))$, and $G(\neg(executed(a) \wedge executed(b)))$

Fig. 4. Büchi automata for R1 and R2 with additional conditions

Example 2 (Contradictions). The second example introduces two rules R3 and R4 with the same condition (reception of payment), activity a, but different implications (sending goods by DHL, activity b, or sending goods by UPS, activity c, respectively). However, enforcing the knowledge about non-concurrent execution of activities a, b, and c, as was discussed in Example 1, still generates a Büchi automaton that accepts all runs in which activity a is executed; thereafter, activities b and c are executed in any order. However, according to the business context, we figure out that activities *Send Goods by DHL* and *Send Goods by UPS* contradict each other. This fact has to be reflected in consistency checking. That is, both activities are considered to be mutually exclusive. Therefore, we add the following two LTL formulas to the conjunction, $G(executed(b) \rightarrow G(\neg executed(c)))$ and $G(executed(c) \rightarrow G(\neg executed(b)))$. The resulting Büchi automaton has no accepting run. Again, the automaton was omitted due to its size. We conclude that there cannot be a process model that would satisfy R3 and R4 under the information given by the business context. Thus, we detected an inconsistency between both compliance rules.

Similar to the two examples above, data access semantics for data elements have to be reflected in the LTL formulas for consistency checking. That is, for our case, the fact that each data object can assume a single value (state) at a time has to be considered. Moreover, the knowledge about contradicting data values has to be incorporated.

So far, we showed through examples how consistency checking between different compliance rules can be reduced to a check of accepting runs (accepting states) in a Büchi automaton generated from an LTL formula. Using the business context, additional knowledge was injected in the LTL formula in order to reflect domain-specific compliance requirements. Based thereon, we generalize the approach to any given set of compliance rules for which consistency checking is required. The requirement of separate execution states is captured as follows.

Definition 1 (Separate Execution States). *For any set of activities A, each activity completes its execution in a separate execution state, i.e.,* $\bigwedge_{a,b \in A, a \neq b} G(\neg(executed(a) \wedge executed(b)))$.

Non-vacuous satisfiability for compliance rules has to be ensured. Therefore, we introduce the following LTL formula.

Definition 2 (Non Vacuous Satisfiability). *Process models that would satisfy compliance rules regarding a set of activities A have to satisfy them non-vacuously. That is,* $\bigwedge_{a \in A} F(executed(a))$, *if and only if a appears in the condition of a compliance rule.*

Further on, contradicting activities as well as mutual exclusive data states as defined by the business context have to be treated accordingly.

Definition 3 (Contradicting Activities). *If two activities a and b are known to be contradicting, exclusive, from the business context, the LTL formula to avoid contradicting activities is defined as* $G(executed(a) \rightarrow G(\neg executed(b)))$.

Definition 4 (Mutual Exclusive Data States). *Let D be the universal set of data objects, S the set of all data states, and S_d the set of all possible data states for a* *specific data object $d \in D$. For each data object $d \in D$, the LTL formula that captures the mutual exclusion between data states is given by $\bigwedge_{s \in S_d} G(state(d,s) \rightarrow \bigwedge_{s' \in S_d \setminus \{s\}} \neg state(d,s'))$.*

Algorithm 1 describes our approach to check consistency among a given set of compliance rules. The algorithm takes a set of compliance rules and a business context as input. Based thereon, the additional LTL formulas are generated in order to meet the requirements introduced above. Finally, the algorithm decides consistency by analyzing the existence of an accepting run of the resulting Büchi automaton.

Algorithm 1. Consistency Checking for a Set of Compliance Rules

Require: A set of compliance rules R expressed in LTL.
Require: Domain specific knowledge.

Let A be the set of all activities mentioned in compliance rules.
Let $A_{condition} \subseteq A$ be the set of activities mentioned in the condition part of the rules.
Let D be the set of data objects mentioned in the rules.
Let S be the set of data states for the data objects in D.
Let M be the set of LTL formulas that will be conjuncted and checked for consistency.
$M = R$
for all $a \in A_{condition}$ **do**
    $M = M \cup \{F(a)\}$ // Handling activities
end for
for all $a \in A$ **do**
    for all $b \in A$ **do**
        if $a \neq b$ **then**
            $M = M \cup \{G(\neg(a \wedge b))\}$ // Including knowledge about execution environment
        end if
    end for
    Let C_a be the set of contradicting activities to activity a according to the context.
    for all $c \in C_a$ **do**
        $M = M \cup \{G(a \rightarrow G(\neg c))\}$ // Contradictions between activities
    end for
end for
for all $d \in D$ **do**
    Let $S_d \subseteq S$ be the set of states data object d can assume.
    for all $s \in S_d$ **do**
        $M = M \cup \bigcup_{s' \in S_d \wedge s' \neq s} \{G(state(d,s) \rightarrow \neg state(d,s'))\}$ // One data state at a time
        LET $C_{(d,s)}$ be the set of contradicting data states of s.
        $M = M \cup \bigcup_{s' \in C_{(d,s)}} \{G(state(d,s) \rightarrow G(\neg state(d,s')))\}$ // State contradictions
    end for
end for
Let $BA = LTL2BA(\bigwedge_{m \in M} m)$
if BA has accepting run **then**
    return *true*
else
    return *false*
end if

6 Related Work

A large body of research on compliance checking of business process models has already been published. Our primary interest is the work on execution ordering compliance checking. The research in this area can be classified into two groups: compliance by design and compliance checking of existing models. The idea of compliance by design is to enforce process model compliance already at the stage of design [16,17,21, 25,26]. Here, violations to a compliance rule are highlighted while a process model is created.

The other branch of research employs model checking techniques to verify that existing process models satisfy the compliance rules [3, 12, 23, 31]. Based thereon, explanation of how violation could occur [5] has been tackled. Further on, resolution strategies have been presented in order to resolve compliance violations automatically [15,4].

Resolution of violations can be driven by the severity of violations. In this sense an interesting method was introduced in [22]. This formal approach enables measuring the *degree* of compliance. Once a compliance rule is specified, the approach tells the degree of compliance for a given process model on the scale from 0 to 1.

In the above mentioned approaches, the need to check consistency of compliance rules was not addressed. Moreover, the consistency of the requirement of a rule with the way business is conducted, e.g. the business context, was not discussed.

Recently, several requirements frameworks for business process compliance management have been proposed. In [24] the authors formulate requirements for compliance management tools. The requirements address the issues of lifetime compliance. The focus is also on the requirements to languages expressing compliance rules, on the rules priority, and on validation of process models against rules during design time and runtime. Another framework was proposed in [11]. The requirement to check consistency among several rules complements these frameworks. Moreover, the approach we presented in this paper is a realization of this requirement.

The review of related work illustrates that the problem of business process compliance is pressing. However, it reveals that in the area of compliance rules consistency checking not much has been done yet.

Declarative business process modeling is a way to allow flexibility in processes. Processes are modeled by specifying a set of execution ordering constraints on a set of activities [29]. In that approach, constraints are mapped onto LTL formulas; which are used to generate an automaton to both guide the execution and monitor it. Albeit for a different purpose, this approach is similar to our work in terms of mapping LTL formulas to Büchi automata. However, in our approach, we just need to check the resulting automata for accepting states/runs as means to decide about consistency between compliance rules.

7 Conclusion

Consistency checking between compliance rules and the way business is conducted, i.e. the business context, on the one hand and among a set of compliance rules on the other hand, is an integral step in the compliance management lifecycle. In this paper, we demonstrated a formal approach to check such consistency. Checking is done by mapping compliance rules, represented as PLTL formulas, into Büchi automata. In order to correctly decide about consistency, domain knowledge was reflected. Therefore, further PLTL formulas were added to the set of compliance rules. Rules are consistent under the domain knowledge, if and only if the Büchi automaton has accepting runs.

In future, we would consider approaches for managing inconsistencies among rules. One approach could be to prioritize rules. Another would be deriving consistent subsets of rules.

References

1. Sarbanes-Oxley Act of 2002. Public Law 107-204 (116 Statute 745), United States Senate and House of Representatives in Congress (2002)
2. Awad, A., Decker, G., Lohmann, N.: Diagnosing and repairing data anomalies in process models. In: BPD 2009. LNBIP. Springer, Heidelberg (to appear)
3. Awad, A., Decker, G., Weske, M.: Efficient Compliance Checking Using BPMN-Q and Temporal Logic. In: Dumas, M., Reichert, M., Shan, M.-C. (eds.) BPM 2008. LNCS, vol. 5240, pp. 326–341. Springer, Heidelberg (2008)
4. Awad, A., Smirnov, S., Weske, M.: Towards Resolving Compliance Violations in Business Process Models. In: GRCIS, CEUR-WS.org (2009)
5. Awad, A., Weidlich, M., Weske, M.: Specification, verification and explanation of violation for data aware compliance rules. In: Baresi, L. (ed.) ICSOC 2009. LNCS, vol. 5900, pp. 500–515. Springer, Heidelberg (2009)
6. Awad, A., Weske, M.: Visualization of compliance violation in business process models. In: BPI 2009. LNBIP. Springer, Heidelberg (to appear)
7. F. S. Commission: Guidelines on anti-money laundering & counter-financing of terrorism (2007)
8. Dasgupta, P.: A Roadmap for Formal Property Verification. Springer, Heidelberg (2006)
9. Dijkman, R.M., Dumas, M., Ouyang, C.: Semantics and Analysis of Business Process Models in BPMN. Inf. Softw. Technol. 50(12), 1281–1294 (2008)
10. Dwyer, M.B., Avrunin, G.S., Corbett, J.C.: Patterns in property specifications for finite-state verification. In: ICSE, pp. 411–420. ACM, New York (1999)
11. El Kharbili, M., Stein, S., Markovic, I., Pulvermüller, E.: Towards a Framework for Semantic Business Process Compliance Management. In: GRCIS, June 2008, pp. 1–15 (2008)
12. Förster, A., Engels, G., Schattkowsky, T., Van Der Straeten, R.: Verification of Business Process Quality Constraints Based on VisualProcess Patterns. In: TASE, pp. 197–208. IEEE Computer Society, Los Alamitos (2007)
13. Gastin, P., Oddoux, D.: Fast LTL to büchi automata translation. In: Berry, G., Comon, H., Finkel, A. (eds.) CAV 2001. LNCS, vol. 2102, pp. 53–65. Springer, Heidelberg (2001)
14. Gerth, R., Eindhoven, D.D., Peled, D., Vardi, M.Y., Wolper, P.: Simple on-the-fly automatic verification of linear temporal logic. In: Protocol Specification Testing and Verification, pp. 3–18. Chapman & Hall, Boca Raton (1995)
15. Ghose, A., Koliadis, G.: Auditing business process compliance. In: Krämer, B.J., Lin, K.-J., Narasimhan, P. (eds.) ICSOC 2007. LNCS, vol. 4749, pp. 169–180. Springer, Heidelberg (2007)
16. Goedertier, S., Vanthienen, J.: Compliant and Flexible Business Processes with Business Rules. In: BPMDS, CEUR Workshop Proceedings, vol. 236, CEUR-WS.org (2006)

17. Goedertier, S., Vanthienen, J.: Designing Compliant Business Processes from Obligations and Permissions. In: Eder, J., Dustdar, S. (eds.) BPM Workshops 2006. LNCS, vol. 4103, pp. 5–14. Springer, Heidelberg (2006)
18. Kähmer, M., Gilliot, M., Muller, G.: Automating privacy compliance with expdt. In: CEC/EEE, pp. 87–94. IEEE, Los Alamitos (2008)
19. Küster, J.M., Ryndina, K., Gall, H.: Generation of business process models for object life cycle compliance. In: Alonso, G., Dadam, P., Rosemann, M. (eds.) BPM 2007. LNCS, vol. 4714, pp. 165–181. Springer, Heidelberg (2007)
20. Laroussinie, F., Markey, N., Schnoebelen, P.: Temporal logic with forgettable past. In: LICS, pp. 383–392. IEEE Computer Society, Los Alamitos (2002)
21. Lu, R., Sadiq, S., Governatori, G.: Compliance Aware Business Process Design. In: ter Hofstede, A.H.M., Benatallah, B., Paik, H.-Y. (eds.) BPM Workshops 2007. LNCS, vol. 4928, pp. 120–131. Springer, Heidelberg (2008)
22. Lu, R., Sadiq, S., Governatori, G.: Measurement of Compliance Distance in Business Processes. Inf. Sys. Manag. 25(4), 344–355 (2008)
23. Lui, Y., Müller, S., Xu, K.: A Static Compliance-checking Framework for Business Process Models. IBM Systems Journal 46(2), 335–362 (2007)
24. Ly, L.T., Göser, K., Rinderle-Ma, S., Dadam, P.: Compliance of Semantic Constraints – A Requirements Analysis for Process Management Systems. In: GRCIS, pp. 16–30, `CEUR-WS.org` (June 2008)
25. Milosevic, Z., Sadiq, S., Orlowska, M.: Translating Business Contract into Compliant Business Processes. In: EDOC, pp. 211–220. IEEE Computer Society, Los Alamitos (2006)
26. Namiri, K., Stojanovic, N.: Pattern-Based Design and Validation of Business Process Compliance. In: Meersman, R., Tari, Z. (eds.) OTM 2007, Part I. LNCS, vol. 4803, pp. 59–76. Springer, Heidelberg (2007)
27. OASIS. Universal Description Discovery and Integration UDDI (2004)
28. B.C. on Banking Supervision. Basel ii accord (2004)
29. Pesić, M.: Constraint-Based Workflow Management System: Shifting Control to Users. PhD thesis, Technische Universiteit Eindhoven (2008)
30. Pnueli, A.: The temporal logic of programs. In: SFCS, pp. 46–57. IEEE Computer Society, Washington (1977)
31. Yu, J., Manh, T.P., Han, J., Jin, Y., Han, Y., Wang, J.: Pattern Based Property Specification and Verification for Service Composition. In: Aberer, K., Peng, Z., Rundensteiner, E.A., Zhang, Y., Li, X. (eds.) WISE 2006. LNCS, vol. 4255, pp. 156–168. Springer, Heidelberg (2006)
32. Zuck, L.: Past Temporal Logic. PhD thesis, Weizmann Intitute, Israel (August 1986)

From Economic Drivers to B2B Process Models: A Mapping from REA to UMM

Rainer Schuster, Thomas Motal, Christian Huemer, and Hannes Werthner

Institute of Software Technology and Interactive Systems
Vienna University of Technology, Austria
schuster@ec.tuwien.ac.at, motal@ec.tuwien.ac.at,
huemer@big.tuwien.ac.at, werthner@ec.tuwien.ac.at

Abstract. Inter-organizational B2B systems are most likely tending to change their business requirements over time - e.g. establishing new partnerships or change existing ones. The problem is that business analysts design the business processes from scratch, disregarding the economic drivers of the business network. We propose to use business modeling techniques - such as REA (Resource-Event-Agents) - to ensure that business processes beneath do not violate the domain rules, i.e. to fulfill the basic economic principle for every business transaction - the give-and-take convention, called economic reciprocity. This helps us to quickly adapt the B2B processes to changing requirements without the need to change the overall architecture. In this paper we provide a mapping from REA, which represents one of the most prominent ontologies for business modeling, to UMM (UN/CEFACT's Modeling Methodology), a standardized methodology for modeling the global choreography of inter-organizational business processes. We formalize the mapping by the use of the model-to-model transformation language ATL (Atlas Transformation Language).

Keywords: Business modeling, Business Process Modeling, REA, UMM.

1 Introduction

In order to open-up enterprise applications to e-business and make them profitable for a communication with other enterprise applications, a business model is needed showing the business essentials of the business case to be developed. However, most current approaches are limited to the technical process aspects, disregarding the economic drivers [1] [2]. Therefore specific business modeling techniques have been introduced in order to capture the business perspective of an e-commerce information system. Presently, there are three major and well-accepted business modeling techniques - e3-value [3], Resource-Event-Agent (REA) [4] and the Business Modeling Ontology (BMO)[5].

e3-Value was designed for getting a first overview of the economic values exchanged in a business network. Furthermore, e3-Value allows to proof the

W. Abramowicz and R. Tolksdorf (Eds.): BIS 2010, LNBIP 47, pp. 119–131, 2010.

economic sustainability of the business idea by quantifying the net value flow for each actor in the value web. Whereas e3-Value concentrates more on the profitability of the IT system, an REA business model focuses on issues that may be relevant for the implementation and alignment of an IT system from an economical point of view. Thus, we see the e3-Value ontology one layer above REA since it describes the value exchanges on a rather abstract level. In [6] we already published a mapping from e3-Value to REA. The third methodology is BMO, which focuses on the position of a specific business partner in the e-business network and how he can make profit. Due to the fact that BMO concentrates on the business semantics from an internal perspective and e3-Value concentrates on the economic sustainability of an entire exchange system, we propose to use the REA ontology as a starting point for designing business processes. The basic idea of this multi-layered approach, in which we propose to use different ontologies and techniques for the development of maintainable inter-organizational systems has been shown in [7].

As mentioned, REA was initially designed for specifying the domain rules assuring soundness and consistency of business software applications from the business perspective [8]. However, the REA concept found its place in some standardized specifications as well. The ISO Open-edi specification [9] uses REA as an ontological framework for specifying the concepts and relationships involved in business transactions. Furthermore, the REA ontology definitions are part of the work of UN/CEFACT (United Nations Center for Trade Facilitation and Electronic Business), which is an international e-business standardization body known for its work in the area of electronic data interchange(EDI) - UN/EDIFACT and ebXML [10]. This is the reason why we propose a mapping from REA to UMM (UN/CEFACT's Modeling Methodology), which is one of the most promising standards for modeling the global choreography of B2B processes [11]. We, as the authors of this paper, are part of the editing team of the current UMM 2.0 specification [12] as well as for the REA specialization module for UMM [13]. The goal of this REA specialization module project, which is led by the originator of REA, William E. McCarthy, is to provide two types of specific guidance to UMM users as they develop their collaboration models: (1) an ontology-based methodology for developing the class diagrams and (2) state machine life cycles for business entities within the Business Entity View of the UMM Business Requirements View.

Our contribution within this paper is (1) to explore the different perspectives of these two modeling techniques and to find overlaps between them on the meta model layer (2) to define a conceptual mapping between REA and UMM, and (3) to formalize the mapping by the use of a model-to-model transformation.

2 Input and Output Models for Our Transformation

2.1 REA - The Input Model

The concepts of REA originate from business accounting where the needs are to manage businesses through a technique called double-entry bookkeeping [4]. By the help of this technique every business transaction is registered as a double entry (a credit and a debit) in a balance sheet. REA is using this technique in order to fulfill the basic economic principle for every business transaction - the give-and-take convention, called economic reciprocity. The acronym REA comes from the core concepts *Resource*, *Event*, and *Agent*. The intuition behind these concepts is that every business transaction can be seen as an event where exactly two agents exchange resources. An economic resource is a good, right, or service of value, under the control of an economic agent. These basic REA concepts are illustrated in the cutout of the simplified REA meta model using a UML class diagram. Figure 1 illustrates the simple Resource-Event-Agent structure at the meta model layer (MOF M2)[14]. The high level semantic view of the essentials of the REA meta model is the economic exchange (*EconExchange*), where the trading partners engage in the exchange of resources with value. Each economic exchange must have at least two:

- economic agents (*EconAgent*) - one requests (*toParticipte*) the resources from another agent and the other one offers (*fromParticipate*) the resource
- economic events (*EconEvent*) - one *initiates* an economic event and the other one *terminates* it
- economic resources (*EconResource*) - one decreases the inventory of an economic agent by increasing the inventory of the corresponding agent, and the other does it vice versa (*stockFlow*)

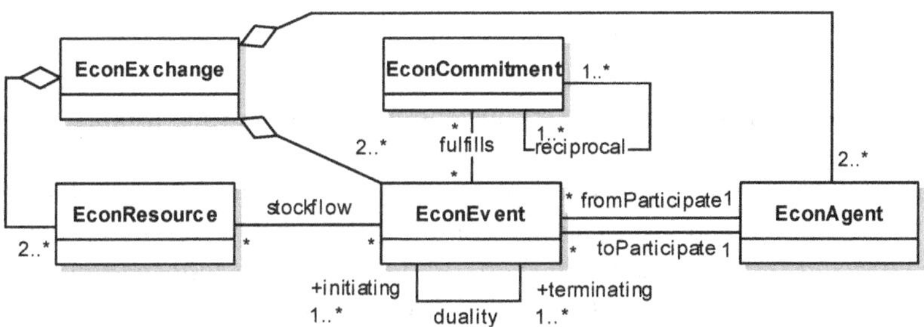

Fig. 1. The base of the conceptual REA meta-model

An economic commitment (*EconCommitment*) is a promise or obligation of economic agents to perform an economic event in the future. Due to space limitations the REA meta model is not depicted in its full version. Concepts such as *typification*, *business locations*, and *economic claims* have been skipped, since they are not relevant for a mapping between REA and UMM. The interested reader is referred to [6], where we explained REA in more detail by means of a mapping between REA and e3-Value. Note, that all REA concepts are based on UML classes at the instance level (see Figure 3 in Section 3.1). A business transaction or exchange has two REA constellations joined together, noting that the two parties of a simple market transfer expect to receive something of value in return when they trade. For example, a seller, who delivers a product to a buyer, expects a requiting cash payment in return. Assuming a simple buyer and seller scenario, REA covers the four fundamental questions of a business collaboration: **Who** is involved in the collaboration? **What** is being exchanged? **When** (and under what trading conditions) do the components of the exchange occur? **Why** are the trading partners engaged in the collaboration? By answering these questions it is possible to specify the economic requirements, which are necessary for developing a B2B process model with UMM.

2.2 UMM - The Output Model

UN/CEFACTs Modeling Methodology is a UML modeling approach to design the business services that each business partner must provide in order to collaborate. It provides the business justification for the service to be implemented in service-oriented architectures (SOA). In other words, UMM enables to capture business knowledge independent of the underlying implementation technology, like Web Services or ebXML. It concentrates on the flow of interactions between collaborating business partners. However, it does not address their private processes. In general, the execution of an inter-organizational business process depends on commitments established between the participating partners. UMM is used to model these procedural and data exchange commitments that must be agreed upon between the business partners at design time of the inter-organizational business process, i.e. before executing the process. UMM is defined as a UML profile [12], i.e. a set of stereotypes, tagged values and constraints, in order to customize the UML meta model to the special purpose of modeling global B2B choreographies.

The UMM follows a well-defined development process that produces a set of well-defined artifacts. Figure 2 depicts a cutout of the simplified UMM meta model. The development process runs through three major phases, which correspond to the three top level packages of UMM: the *business requirements view (A)*, the *business choreography view (B)*, and the *business information view (C)*. The *business requirements view* is used for three reasons: first, to gather the domain knowledge (A.1) and existing process knowledge (A.2) of the business domain under consideration; second, to capture the relationships of the business partners and stakeholders (A.3) participating in the business network, and third, to depict the so-called business entity lifecycle (A.4). A business entity is a real-world thing having business significance that is shared between two or more business partners in a collaborative business process (e.g. order, account, etc.). The *business choreography view (B)* comprises the artifacts for the core parts of UMM, the *business collaboration protocol (B.1)*, which spans over multiple *business transactions (B.2)*. A *business transaction* covers the semantics of a business information exchange between exactly two business partners. It follows that a business collaboration protocol is the sequence of such binary business information exchanges or other nested multi-party business collaborations. The information exchanged within a business transaction is modeled by so-called *information envelopes (C.1)* in the third view - the *business information view*. Since REA captures the business requirements from an economical point of view, it only makes sense to map REA artifacts to the *business requirements view* of UMM. For this reason and due to space limitations we do not go into detail of UMM's *business choreography view* and *business information view*. Furthermore we only discuss UMM on the MOF meta model layer M2. The interested reader will find examples of UMM instances in [11] [12].

The meta model depicted in figure 2 defines only the conceptual view of UMM's business requirements view - i.e. the nomenclature of the stereotypes and the relationships (constraints) between each other. It does not give any information about which stereotype inherits the properties of which UML base class. Thus, we summarize the most important UML artifacts for the requirements view, which are relevant for our mapping: (A.1)UML packages and UML use case diagrams; (A.2)UML activity diagrams; (A.3)UML actors; (A.4)UML classes and UML state machine diagrams;

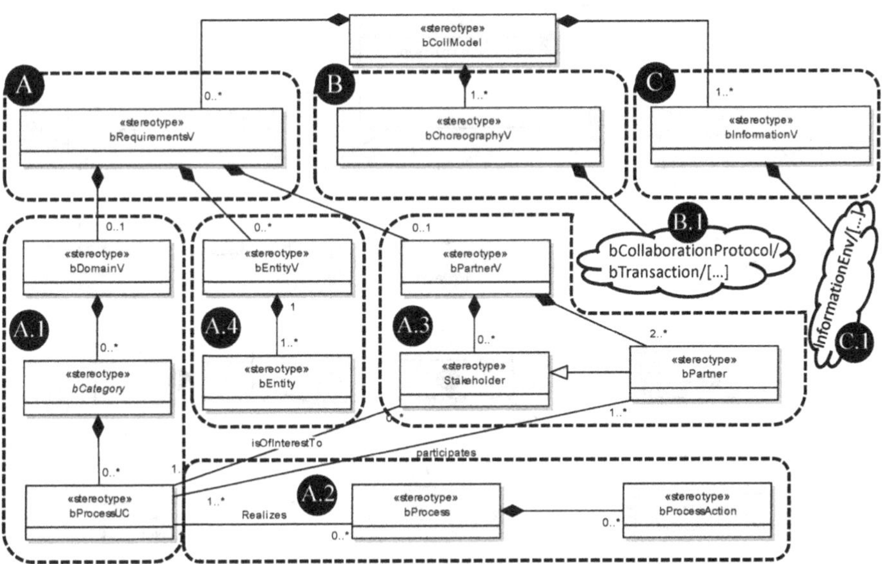

Fig. 2. Simplified UMM Meta Model

3 Mapping REA to UMM

3.1 A Real Life Example from the Print Media Domain

The following example has been taken from the use case scenario of a national funded IT project called BSopt[1] (Business Semantics on Top of Process Technology) in which we applied our business modeling approach and its transformation

[1] `http://www.bsopt.at`

to business process models. We will use this simplified example to show the conceptual mapping between REA and UMM. In the print media domain customer fluctuation is mostly affected by competitors and their aggressive enticement of customers. Thus, it is very important for a newspaper publisher to acquire new test readers in order to keep the customer stock. The customer acquisition is either done in-house (e.g. by mail advertisement) or outsourced (in our case by a call center). Within this use case we have a lot of inter-organizational business processes and information exchanges (e.g. the upload of a set of addresses, the exchange of successfully acquired test subscriptions, or the automated invoicing for the consumed service). For the sake of simplicity we demonstrate only the collaboration between the newspaper publisher and the call center. Following our approach we propose not to start with modeling the B2B processes from scratch, but to capture the requirements from an economic point of view by REA to ensure that the domain rules are not violated.

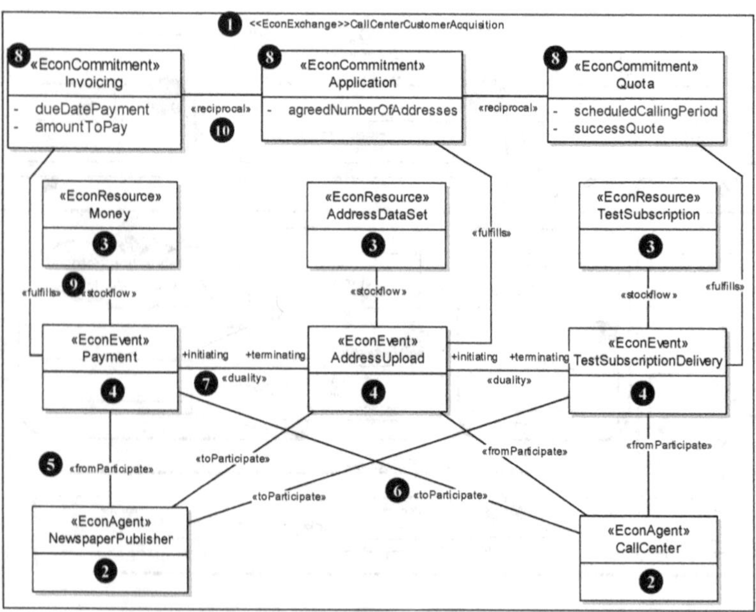

Fig. 3. REA Example

In the following we detail our use case scenario by the help of REA. The REA class diagram in Figure 3 depicts the economic exchange *CallCenterCustomer-Acquisition* (1). As explained above the exchange happens between the economic agents (2) *NewspaperPublisher* and *CallCenter*. Both agents have the intention to exchange economic resources (3), which are furthermore the actual objects of exchange. In our scenario the *NewspaperPublisher* pays the *CallCenter* for the acquisition of new customers. To execute the economic exchange both agents have to participate in adequate events. The economic events denoted by (4) are used to fulfill a resource-flow from one partner to the other. Since a resource-flow is always a directed association, indicating the role of each participant, the involved agents are connected to an event via (5) *fromParticipate* and (6) *toParticipate* associations. The first one points out that one agent gives up the control over a specific resource, whereas the later one defines who receives the resource. The *Payment* event for example provokes that *Money* will be transfered *from* the *NewspaperPublisher to* the *CallCenter*. Since the REA ontology follows the give-and-take principle each event must have at least one opposite event, which will be fulfilled in return. Assigned to our scenario the *CallCenter* has to fulfill two economic events: *AddressUpload* and *TestSubscriptionDelivery*. Both are connected by so called (7) *duality* associations with the *Payment* event. This association denotes that if the *NewspaperPublisher* fulfills a *Payment* event, the *CallCenter* has to fulfill *AddressUPload* and *TestSubscriptionDelivery*, too. The detailed specifications of the economic events are specified by the means of (8) economic commitments. A commitment can be seen as an obligation to (9) fulfill specific events in the future. In the *Invoicing* commitment for example the *NewspaperPublisher* engages to pay a fixed amount of money to the *CallCenter*. The execution of this obligation is done by the *Payment* event. The same concept applies for the other commitments - *Application* and *Quota* and their corresponding events *AddressUpload* and *TestSubscriptionDelivery*. The give-and-take principle, as it has already been used with economic events, also applies for economic commitments. The resulting reciprocity is formalized by (10) *reciprocal* associations.

3.2 Conceptual Mapping

In this section we describe the conceptual mapping from REA artifacts to UMM artifacts. Our approach is twofold: first, we describe the mapping rules from a meta-level perspective to provide a compact overview about the source (REA) and target (UMM) artifacts. Second, we apply these rules to the simplified real world business scenario - the customer acquisition by a call center. As listed in Table 1 we identified seven rules. All of them can be applied to UMM artifacts used within the business requirements view. Each rule is indicated by a number, which is also important for further descriptions (first column). The second column defines the REA artifact that is mapped to a UMM concept specified in column 3. The fourth column refers to the UMM stereotype that is affected by the mapping. The last column indicates whether the rule can be applied fully automated (•) or if the transformation needs additional semantic information (-), which should be provided by the business analyst. In the latter case it is not possible to do a straight forward mapping between the source and the target artifact since both concepts share similar but not equal semantics. This semi-automatic mapping applies to rule R3 and R7. In general, REA concepts, such as events and commitments are mapped to process related UMM artifacts and REA concepts, such as agents and resources are mapped to entities that are involved in business processes. In the following we describe the mapping rules in detail.

Table 1. Mapping table for REA to UMM artifacts

Rule	REA	UMM concept	UMM Stereotype	Auto
R1	EconExchange	Business Process Use Case	≪bProcessUC≫	•
R2	EconAgent	Business Partner	≪bPartner≫	•
R3	EconRessource	Business Entity	≪bEntity≫	-
R4	EconEvent	Business Process Use Case	≪bProcessUC≫	•
R5	EconCommitment	Business Process	≪bProcess≫	•
R6	duality(initiating)	Business Process	≪bProcess≫	•
R7	stockflow	Business Process	≪bESharedState≫	-

Figure 4 is separated into two parts indicated by a dashed line to distinguish between REA (upper part) and UMM (lower part). The annotations in the UMM part refer to the different views of the UMM meta model as depicted in Figure 2 (e.g. [A.4] bEntityV). Note, so far we described the concepts of UMM on the meta model level (by using UML class diagrams). In the mapping figure, UMM is depicted on the instance level by means of UML use case diagrams, activity diagrams, etc. Based on the mapping rules listed in Table 1 we demonstrate how to translate REA concepts to UMM concepts that are used in the business requirements view. The identifiers beside the description follows the annotation in Figure 4 and corresponds to the rule numbers in Table 1.

R1: An *EconExchange* in REA is mapped to UMM's *Business Process Use Case*. In UMM, a business process use case is a set of related activities that together create value for a business partner. Both concepts contain the business transactions, data exchanges, events, and business partners that are necessary to fulfill the business goal.

R2: An *EconAgent* is similar to a *Business Partner* and therefore mapped to *bPartner* in UMM. The mapping is straight forward since both concepts share the same semantics. An economic agent in REA and a business partner in UMM are both independent participants with the intention to join a business collaboration. According to the UMM meta-model (see Figure 2) a *Business Partner* is modeled within (A.3) *bPartnerV*.

R3: *EconResources* in REA are the actual subjects of exchange. Business Entities in UMM have a similar meaning. Both concepts are used to transfer something of interest between participating business partners. However, there is a significant distinction between both stereotypes. In REA, an economic resource is a good, service, or right with economic value that is beeing exchanged between business partners. In UMM such business entities are used to model different states in order to synchronize the interfaces between the business partners (e.g. the *AddressDataSet* is in state `validated`, thus it is ready for an upload). In figure 4 the business entity (denoted by R3 in the *bEntityV*) is a UML class. Its state changes are further on modeled as a state machine diagram. Those states are

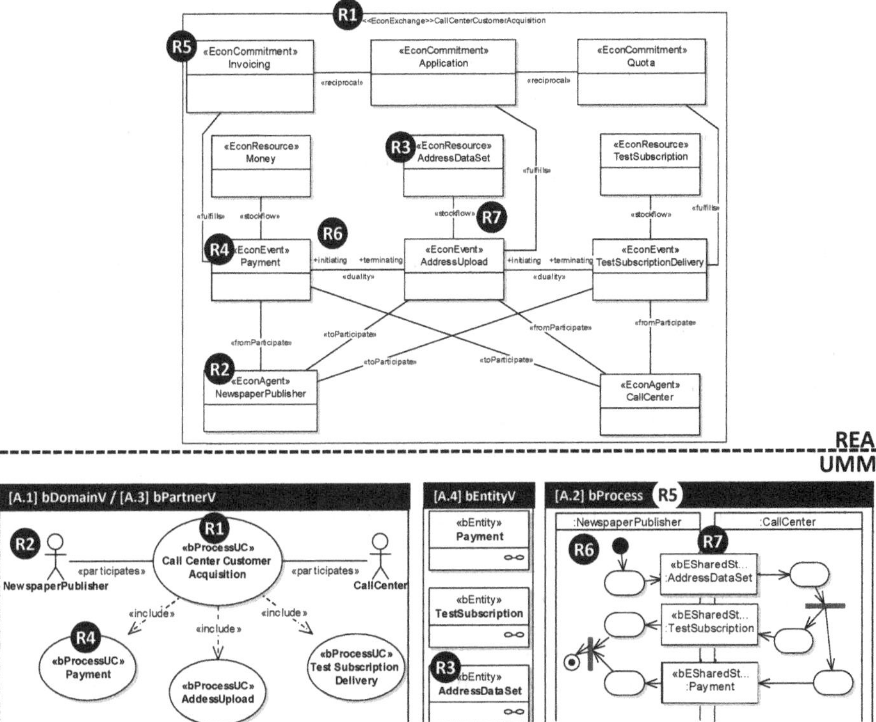

Fig. 4. Applying the REA2UMM mapping

then used as objects in the business process (see R7). Furthermore, a straight forward mapping between both concepts is often not possible, due to the very generic nature of the resource concept in REA. To map a resource to a corresponding business entity we need a detailed domain knowledge. For example the economic resource `Money` can not be mapped 1:1 to a business entity `Money`. Since it is rather likely that a business entity Money does not change its states during a business process we propose to use the term `Invoicing`, which is commonly used for electronic data interchange.

R4: An *EconEvent*, similar to an *EconExchange*, is mapped to the concept of a *Business Process Use Case*. Since an economic event is always nested within an economic exchange the mapped busienss process use case has an include relationship to the *bProcessUC* created by rule R1.

R5: An *EconCommitment* details an *EconEvent*. Therefore we propose to map an *EconCommitment* to the concept of a *Business Process*. A business process in UMM is modeled as a UML activity diagram. An economic commitment comprises the agreements made between business partners involved in an inter-organizational business process. Those agreements are reflected in UMM's business processes as well.

R6: The initiating role of the duality association denotes that the event holding this role initiates an economic exchange. It follows that the involved *Economic Agent* associated via a *from/toParticipate* association plays the initiating role in the business process. Note, it does not necessarily mean, that the terminating role is hold by the opposite business partner. In our use case scenario the initiator is the Newspaper Publisher by starting the business process with an upload of the address data set.

R7: This rule is related to R3. The stockflow association denotes the flow of resources triggered by an economic event. The business entity have already been created by R3. Although we do not know anything about the underlying business entity life cycle, we can already include the objects that are classified by the business entities into the corresponding business process. In UMM, these objects are stereotyped as *Shared Business Entity States*. As soon as the modeler has specified the life cycle state of the business entity (e.g. first, the address data set is in state `validated`, then in state `uploaded`, then `processed`, etc.) he can assign these states manually to the generated *bESharedStates*.

3.3 Transformation Rules

In this section we formalize the conceptual mapping rules described in section 3.2 by using the Atlas Transformation Language (ATL). ATL provides a model-to-model transformation engine which is able to transform any given source model to a specific target model. Before the engine can perform the transformation a proper ATL program specifies the rules that are necessary for a mapping. For a complete description of the abstract syntax of ATL and its execution semantics we refer to the ATL user manual [15]. In order to demonstrate the transformation we use the Eclipse Modeling Framework (EMF). Figure 5 shows the model-to-model transformation pattern for our customer acquisition example.

At the top we define two EMF meta models (Ecore) on the MOF M2 layer - the REA meta model and the UMM meta model. The first one serves as the input for the transformation and the second one for the output. The transformation definition specifies the mapping rules in ATL and refers to both meta models. At the MOF M1 level we specify the REA example model of 3

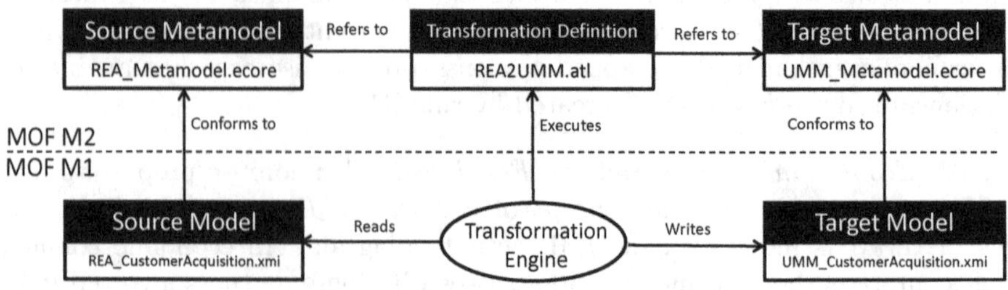

Fig. 5. The transformation pattern for mapping an REA model to a UMM model

```
module REA2UMMTransformation;
create OUT : UMM from IN : REA;

rule EconExchange2bProcessUC(
    from
        r : REA!EconExchange
    to
        u : UMM!UseCase(
            name <- r.name,
            stereotype <- 'bProcessUC'
        )
}

rule EconEvent2IncludedBPUC(
    from
        r : REA!EconEvent
    to
        u : UMM!UseCase (
            name <- r.name,
            stereotype <- 'bProcessUC',
            includes <- r.contains
        )
}

rule EconAgent2BusinessPartner(
    from
        r : REA!EconAgent
    to
        u : UMM!Actor (
            name <- r.name,
            stereotype <- 'bPartner',
            participates <- r.fromParticipates,
            participates <- r.toParticipates
        )
}

rule EconResource2BusinessEntity(
    from
        r : REA!EconResource
    to
        u : UMM!bEntity (
            name <- r.name
        )
}
```

Fig. 6. Excerpt of the REA2UMM.atl file

(REA_CustomerAcquisition.xmi) which is expressed in XMI (XML Metamodel Interchange) - the de-facto standard for formal descriptions of UML based models. In order to transform this example model into a UMM model, the transformation engine reads the source model and generates the stub for a UMM compliant model. The code listing in Figure 6 shows the mapping rules specified in ATL. Due to space limitations we only present a basic transformation example of the ATL file, in order to show the essentials of the formal mapping.

4 Related Work

Two prominent approaches for linking business models and business process models have been introduced by Weigand [16] and Schmitt [17]. Both, define a methodological approach for using business models as a basis for deriving business process models.

Influenced by these approaches, the authors of [18] introduced a reference ontology for business models. As a basis they took concepts from e3-Value[3], REA[4], and BMO[5]. Furthermore, they enriched their reference ontology by additional concepts detailing the resource transfer between participating business partners. A similar approach has been published by the authors in [19].

A more conceptual approach exploiting synergies between goal models and business models (e3-Value) is introduced in [20] and [21]. As a result they were able to complement e3-Value by revealing the strategic reasoning behind the value exchanges. In addition they provide guidelines for the transformation of goal-models to value-models and vice versa. Another ontology-based approach for improving the early requirements engineering phase using goal-models has been proposed in [22]. To incorporate the domain knowledge into their method they incorporated business modeling concepts taken from e3-Value and REA. Thereby the ontological foundations of the business modeling techniques serve as guidelines during the modeling process.

In [23] the authors introduce a transformation approach targeting the interoperability of business process models. The authors argue that in order to gain interoperability on a business process level using business process modeling standards such as UMM or ISO/IEC 15944 [9] both business partners have to use the same business process modeling technique. To overcome this problem they propose to use REA as a shared global knowledge base for transforming model instances from UMM to ISO/IEC 15944.

5 Conclusion

In this paper we introduced our approach about combining two major modeling techniques in the field of B2B. UMM needs to gather business domain knowledge for its business requirements view in an early design phase. REA delivers the requirements from an economical point of view and serves as input for modeling a UMM compliant business process model. In other words, our mapping rules should help the modeler setting up a UMM compliant model without disregarding the give-and-take principles to ensure economic reciprocity. It is not said, that one is able to generate a complete business process model out of an REA model by using our mapping rules. But the modeler can (semi-)automatically generate a stub of a UMM model, which needs to be finalized during further modeling steps. There are still open issues and refinements for future work. In our mapping we propose only a transformation from REA artifacts to UMM artifacts that are relevant in the *business requirements view*. However, the attributes of REA's *economic commitments* capture significant information that may be relevant for further phases in UMM (e.g. the so-called *quality of service* parameters in the *business choreography view*). Furthermore, as a critical reflection we need to say, that we did not consider REA's state machine driven approach [13]. This concept would help us to gather requirements for generating UMM artifacts, which are also used in later modeling steps (e.g. to generate concrete *business transactions* as part of UMM's *business choreography view*). At last, REA's economic resources contain information which can be used to design the information envelopes that are being exchanged in UMM's *business information view*. Integrating those concepts into our approach is a major challenge for future work.

References

1. Dorn, J., Grün, C., Werthner, H., Zapletal, M.: From business to software: a B2B survey. Information Systems and E-Business Management 7(2), 123–142 (2009)
2. Wieringa, R., Pijpers, V., Bodenstaff, L., Gordijn, J.: Value-driven coordination process design using physical delivery models. Conceptual Modeling-ER (2008)
3. Gordijn, J., Akkermans, H.: Value based requirements engineering: Exploring innovative e-commerce idea. Requirements Engineering Journal 8(2), 114–134 (2003)
4. McCarthy, W.E.: The REA accounting model: A generalized framework for accounting systems in a shared data environment. Accounting Review (1982)
5. Osterwalder, A., Pigneur, Y.: An e-Business Model Ontology for Modeling e-Business. In: 15th Bled Electronic Commerce Conf. (2002)

6. Schuster, R., Motal, T.: From e3-value to REA: Modeling Multi-party E-business Collaborations. In: Proceedings of the CEC 2009 (2009)
7. Huemer, C., Liegl, P., Schuster, R., Werthner, H., Zapletal, M.: Inter-organizational systems: From business values over business processes to deployment. In: Digital Ecosystems and Technologies. DEST 2008 (2008)
8. Hruby, P.: Model-Driven Design Using Business Patterns. Springer, Heidelberg (2006)
9. ISO: Information technology - Business Operational View - Part 4: Business transaction scenarios, ISO/IEC, ISO 15944-4 (2007)
10. OASIS, UN/CEFACT: ebXML - Technical Architecture Specification, Version 1.4 (February 2001)
11. Hofreiter, B., Huemer, C., Liegl, P., Schuster, R., Zapletal, M.: UN/CEFACT's Modeling Methodology (UMM): A UML Profile for B2B e-Commerce. In: Roddick, J., Benjamins, V.R., Si-said Cherfi, S., Chiang, R., Claramunt, C., Elmasri, R.A., Grandi, F., Han, H., Hepp, M., Lytras, M.D., Mišić, V.B., Poels, G., Song, I.-Y., Trujillo, J., Vangenot, C. (eds.) ER Workshops 2006. LNCS, vol. 4231, pp. 19–31. Springer, Heidelberg (2006)
12. UN/CEFACT: UN/CEFACT's Modeling Methodology (UMM), UMM Meta Model 2.0, Public Draft V2.0 (2008)
13. UN/CEFACT: REA Specification Module for UN/CEFACT's Modeling Methodology (UMM), Public Draft V1.0 (2008)
14. OMG/MOF: Meta Object Facility (MOF) specification, OMG Document ad/97-08-14 (1997)
15. ATLAS Group, INRIA, and LINA: ATL (Atlas Transformation Language) (2009), `http://www.eclipse.org/m2m/atl/doc/`
16. Weigand, H., Johannesson, P., Andersson, B., Bergholtz, M., Edirisuriya, A., Ilayperuma, T.: On the notion of value object. In: Dubois, E., Pohl, K. (eds.) CAiSE 2006. LNCS, vol. 4001, pp. 321–335. Springer, Heidelberg (2006)
17. Schmitt, M., Grégoire, B.: Risk Mitigation Instruments for Business Models and Process Models. In: Proc. REBNITA, vol. 5 (2005)
18. Andersson, B., Bergholtz, M., Edirisuriya, A., Ilayperuma, T., Johannesson, P., Gordijn, J., Grégoire, B., Schmitt, M., Dubois, E., Abels, S., Hahn, A., Wangler, B., Weigand, H.: Towards a reference ontology for business models. In: Embley, D.W., Olivé, A., Ram, S. (eds.) ER 2006. LNCS, vol. 4215, pp. 482–496. Springer, Heidelberg (2006)
19. Decreus, K., Poels, G.: Putting business into business process models. In: Proceedings of COMPSAC 2008 (2008)
20. Gordijn, J., Yu, E., van der Raadt, B.: e-Service Design Using i* and e3value Modeling. IEEE software 23(3), 26–33 (2006)
21. van der Raadt, B., Gordijn, J., Yu, E.: Exploring Web services from a business value perspective. In: Proc. 13th Int'l Requirements Eng., pp. 53–62 (2005)
22. Gailly, F., España, S., Poels, G., Pastor, O.: Integrating Business Domain Ontologies with Early Requirements Modelling. In: Song, I.-Y., Piattini, M., Chen, Y.-P.P., Hartmann, S., Grandi, F., Trujillo, J., Opdahl, A.L., Ferri, F., Grifoni, P., Caschera, M.C., Rolland, C., Woo, C., Salinesi, C., Zimányi, E., Claramunt, C., Frasincar, F., Houben, G.-J., Thiran, P. (eds.) ER Workshops 2008. LNCS, vol. 5232, pp. 282–291. Springer, Heidelberg (2008)
23. Gailly, F., Poels, G.: Using the REA Ontology to Create Interoperability between E-Collaboration Modeling Standards. In: van Eck, P., Gordijn, J., Wieringa, R. (eds.) CAiSE 2009. LNCS, vol. 5565, pp. 395–409. Springer, Heidelberg (2009)

Using Surveys to Evaluate a Business Rules Based Development Approach*

José L. Martínez-Fernández[1,2], José C. González-Cristóbal[1,3], and Paloma Martínez[2]

[1] DAEDALUS – Data, Decisions and Language S.A.
Avda. de la Albufera, 321
28031 Madrid, Spain
{jmartinez,jgonzalez}@daedalus.es
[2] Advanced Databases Group, Universidad Carlos III de Madrid
Avda. de la Universidad, 30
28911 Leganés, Spain
{joseluis.martinez,paloma.martinez}@uc3m.es
[3] DIT, Universidad Politécnica de Madrid
Avda. Complutense, 30
28040 Madrid, Spain
josecarlos.gonzalez@upm.es

Abstract. Evaluating software engineering artifacts is a difficult task; some empirical methods are available but is a difficult task to measure intangible devices such as methodologies, techniques or software tools [2][12][13] This paper describes the evaluation performed to validate an approach, developed by the authors, for defining standard-based business rules applications. This approach pursues the definition of business rules through standard languages defined by the W3C and OMG organizations to shorten development time in rule based applications and to provide rule engine vendor independence. The approach is the backbone of a tool called K-Site Rules which was developed as a reference implementation for the proposed approach.

Keywords: Business rules, evaluation, software engineering, survey, RIF, MDA, OMG PRR.

1 Introduction

The evaluation of products in the software engineering field is a difficult task. But there is a necessity of measuring quality and other dimensions regarding tools, methodologies and techniques. There have been a lot of efforts in this field, some of them described in [2] and [12], where different methods to carry out these evaluations are

* This paper has been partially supported by the Spanish Center for the Development of Industrial Technology (CDTI, Ministry of Industry, Tourism and Trade), through the project ITECBAN (Architecture for Core Banking Information Systems), INGENIO 2010 Programme.

W. Abramowicz and R. Tolksdorf (Eds.): BIS 2010, LNBIP 47, pp. 132–143, 2010.

identified. The goal of the mentioned methods is to specify mechanisms to objectively say if some tool is better than other or if a technique that is being applied is better than a new proposed alternative. In [12] four instruments are distinguished: *feature analysis*, based on a set of attributes of products or techniques that are going to be subjectively compared; *surveys*, widely applied in social sciences, are used to retrospectively measure people reaction to new artifacts; *case studies*, where key variables are identified and documented and situations are compared where different artifacts are applied; finally, *formal experiments* suppose a complete control on the situations to be studied, so independent variables can be manipulated to measure their effects over dependent variables.

The authors of this paper faced the problem of evaluating a software approach to define business rule based applications following available standards. A software tool was built to support the tasks identified in the aforementioned approach. This tool has been used to evaluate the defined framework by collecting the opinion of developers and non-technical people when interacting with the tool. Surveys have been selected as the most adequate evaluation method in our situation.

The proposed approach is based on standards, which are not supported by commercial rule engines. Evaluations performed on these rule engines are mainly centered on measuring execution performance of business rules, applying some common benchmarks [10] such as Mrs. Manners, where rules to sit around a table guests to a dinner according to some restrictions are given, and Waltz, which deals with lines in a two-dimensional plane that are labeled as three-dimensional objects. From the point of view of functionality, the only comparisons that can be found among commercial rule engines are provided by consultancy firms such as Gartner or Forrester [14]. In the reports produced by these firms the main focus is on market issues so no technical aspects are deeply studied. No previous questionnaires or survey-based evaluation materials have been found.

The rest of the paper is structured as follows; the next section describes the proposed framework, in order to have an idea about the artifact that is going to be evaluated. The third section includes a description of the evaluation process according to literature and available alternatives. The fourth section is devoted to the detailed description of the evaluation carried out to state the quality of the proposed approach. Finally, some conclusions and future works are drawn.

2 Motivation

The research work described in this paper is based on two main hypotheses: business rules technology can improve software development processes by reducing development time; and, on the other hand, people with non-technical knowledge can develop and test business rules without technical support.

The first hypothesis is based on the ability of business rules technology to modify business behavior by changing business rules expressions. No coding is needed, so no development resources have to be devoted to change software applications. Nevertheless, the integration of Business Rules Management Systems (BRMS) with the rest of the information systems available at an organization is still an issue. The approach summarized and evaluated in this paper tries to facilitate this integration process applying semantic web technologies.

The defined approach also uses semantic web technologies in order to reduce the semantic gap between business experts and information systems. For this purpose, the approach introduces ontology based tools allowing links between natural language expressions representing business concepts and software components implementing those business concepts.

The second hypothesis addresses the semantic gap reduction. If business experts (usually people with no technical knowledge) are able to develop and test business rules without technical support, their involvement in business rules development can be deeper and the semantic gap between business experts and information systems will be reduced.

But, as earlier mentioned, evaluation of software engineering artifacts is hard. In order to test the business rules development approach defined in this paper, the two previous hypotheses were stated and a tool to support the development approach was built. It was called K-Site Rules and it was used to validate the mentioned hypotheses.

The following section describes the proposed business rules development approach.

3 Business Rules Development Approach

Business Rules could constitute an efficient development tool when application behavior can be explained through rules. This is the case for financial institutions where there are some well known conditions and processes to decide, for example, if someone can be given a loan. Or, in other situations, government policies must be assured and validated against data managed by some institution. Nowadays, this kind of applications is developed by using commercially available rule engines such as IBML ILOG JRules, Fair Isaac's Blaze Advisor, JBoss Rules and others. Each of these systems uses its own business rules language that developers must know.

Our proposal, described in more detail in [4] and [5], pretends the standardization and automation of the business rules development process, providing rule engine vendor independence and the intervention of non-technical people. The proposed approach is supported by a software tool, called K-Site Rules. Fig. 1 shows the role of K-Site Rules as a broker between business concepts and their implementation.

The proposed framework is based on the combination of Model Driven Architectures [6] and standard business rules languages such as Rule Interchange Format (RIF) [11] and OMG Production Rules Representation (OMG PRR) [8] combined with ontology languages like the Ontology Web Language (OWL).

The approach begins with an expression of a business rule through natural language, using a decision tree or a decision table. These are common tools to define rules that business experts (people with enough knowledge about the business to be able to specify the rules defining business behavior) use in their daily work. These definitions are then expressed in the RIF standard language. RIF has been defined by the W3C consortium and it pretends to specify a standard way to represent business rules allowing their interchange between diverse rule systems. From this point, the K-Site Rules approach gets rid of the implementation of the rule by using a model driven approach. RIF rules are transformed to OMG PRR expressions and, from this point, specific business rule languages interpreted by rule engines selected for implementing business rules are considered. ILOG Rules Language (IRL) and Drools Rule Language (DRL) are some examples of these final languages. On the other hand, these rules must reference business concepts (e.g., clients, providers, employees, etc.) which, in our approach, are represented through an ontology. Concepts to form the ontology are obtained from UML models for the applications supported by the organization IT systems. In this way, there is a clear relationship between business concepts and their implementation in IT systems. So, a transformation from UML class diagrams to OWL ontologies is also considered, using the Ontology Definition Metamodel OMG standard [7].

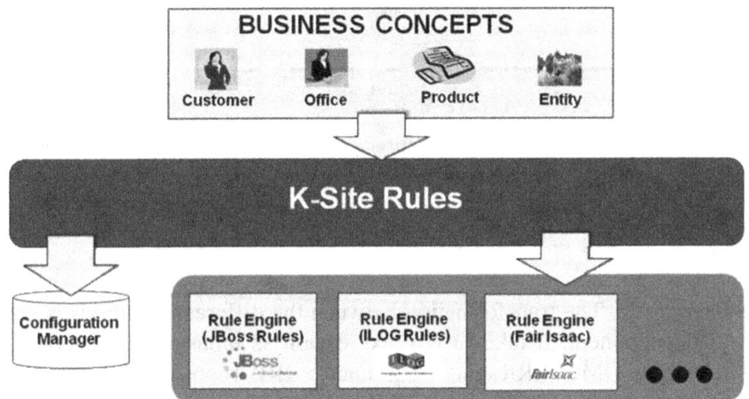

Fig. 1. K-Site Rules as a broker between business concepts and implementations

As mentioned above, a tool, K-Site Rules, has been built to support the proposed framework. It is described in the following section.

3.1 K-Site Rules Business Rules Management System

K-Site Rules constitutes an implementation of the framework explained in [5]. It contains different components, as depicted in Fig. 2, to automate business rules representations transformation between different MDA levels.

The tool is described in depth in [4], so a brief explanation is given in this paper. K-Site Rules is formed by the following main components:

- *Business Expert Editor*. A web accessible user interface specially designed for business experts, i.e., for people without technical background. It covers the whole development process for a business rule, from definition to validation (i.e.: rule testing). Business experts can use natural language, tables or trees to write their rules. They can also test rule behaviour by introducing sample data.
- *Developer Editor*. This editor is integrated with the preferred development environment. K-Site Rules provides an Eclipse based plug-in to define, transform

and test business rules. Developers have more control over business rules, deciding the preferred rule engine to implement them and having access to the final code. In the first K-Site Rules version, IBM ILOG JRules and JBoss Rules can be selected by developers to implement business rules.

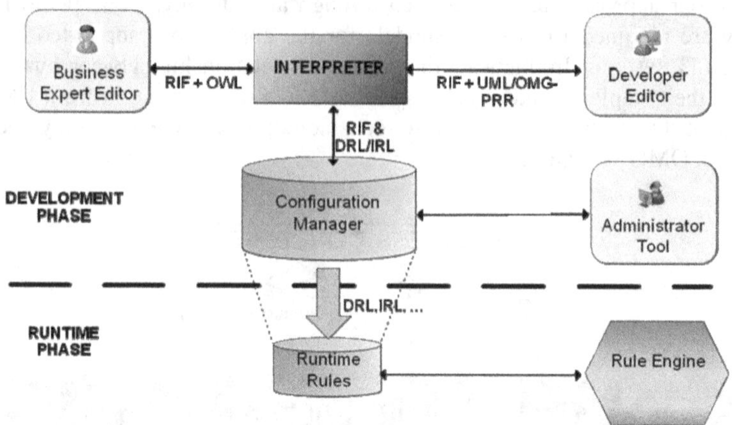

Fig. 2. K-Site Rules software components structure

- *Interpreter*. The transformation between the different standards is coded into this component. It takes a RIF expression as input and produces the corresponding OMG PRR and DRL and/or IRL representations. It is also in charge of transforming the UML class diagrams into OWL ontologies, whose concepts are referenced from the RIF rule expressions.

It is worth mentioning that K-Site Rules does not include an implementation of a rule engine. Any of the available ones can be integrated. Furthermore, the tool does not take part in the application execution phase, so business rules executions does not suffer any delay. The following section is devoted to the description of the characteristics of the evaluation carried out on K-Site Rules.

4 K-Site Rules Expert Editor Evaluation

There are four basic methods to evaluate software engineering processes or techniques: feature analysis, survey, case study and formal experiment. In the situation described in this paper, surveys have been selected. This evaluation method is specially designed for situations in which there is no control over the variables that are relevant for the problem at hand, but it can collect the feelings and thoughts of users retrospectively, once they have interacted with the method or tool that must be evaluated.

The works appearing in [13] specify a method and best practices to construct and apply surveys. In order to successfully carry out a survey, parameters have to be fixed:

- *Survey objectives*. The objectives of the survey were clear, to get users opinion about development speed applying business rules and the necessity of technical knowledge to do so. K-Site Rules usability study was not one of the purposes of the survey, so no questions about usability were included. To minimize the effect of probable usability problems, (a) an use scenario with K-Site Rules, about loans granting, was given at the beginning of the survey, (b) a quick user guide was given to each participant and (c) there were evaluators (i.e., people knowing how to use the tool) available to solve questions about tool usage.
- *Type of study*. The survey was planned as a semi-supervised one. As mentioned above, a person gave a 30 minutes talk, introducing the experiment and developing an example with the tool. The survey construction followed an experimental design, because one of the goals was to measure the impact of the use of business rules in the development of applications. On the other hand, according to [13] it is a *concurrent control study* in which participants are not randomly selected. The professional experience of participants as application developers and their availability has been the discriminatory factor to define groups.
- *Questionnaire building*. The questionnaire has been built taking into account the hypotheses defined in section 2. Questions are intended to collect the thoughts of participants regarding business rules technology and its comparison with traditional programming languages. Twelve closed questions have been defined, using a five point Likert scale (according to [1] several researchers have proved that an odd number of levels reduces biases). On the other hand, 6 open questions have also been posed to participants. Moreover, participant's characterization data was collected, related with professional experience and technical knowledge about programming languages and database or modeling technologies.
- *Questionnaire validation*. Once an initial version of the questionnaire was available, three expert people involved in the design and development of K-Site Rules evaluated it. This way, questions wording, order and relevance were reviewed.
- *Sample selection*. A focus group was defined for the experiment. A focus group is formed by around 10 or 20 people from the researchers' personal contacts. In our case, 20 people were found, all of them with technical knowledge on application programming. This group was divided in another two, one with 6 people and the other one with 14 people. The smaller group was used to test the survey. The work in [13] distinguishes three situations where this kind of sample can be used. One of them concerns situations in which the target population is very specific and with limited availability. This is our case, business experts or people with enough knowledge about the business are not easily available so we have decided to ask for the opinion of people involved in the development of the applications. In this way, we can estimate if developers can implement applications using business rules technology faster than applying programming languages. Of course, we are planning to repeat the survey with people further away from developers and closer to a business expert profile.
- *Sample size*. It comes fixed by the sample selection process carried out. It is clear that the conclusions obtained from the analysis of the collected data are not statistically significant but some light consequences can be stated.

In the following, a short description of the survey is included. Then, data analysis is provided, paying attention to participants' characterization in a first place and to their professional profile in second place. Then the analysis of questions related to the interaction with K-Site Rules is explained.

4.1 Survey Execution Environment

The surveys were carried out in two groups: (a) A 6 people group performed the evaluation at DAEDALUS office, using personal computers with common features, Intel Core 2 processors and 2 GB RAM. All computers had installed Mozilla 3.5. An initial introduction (lasting 30 minutes) was given by one of the researchers in a meeting room, using a big size screen. The total experiment took around two hours, taking into account the time devoted to the introduction. (b) A second group involved in the experiment was formed by 14 people. It was carried out in a room with 20 personal computers and a video projector was available, which was used during the introduction. Personal computers had similar features than the previous ones, with AMD Athlon processors and 1536 Mb RAM, and Mozilla 3.5 installed. The time devoted to the initial presentation was around 40 minutes and the whole experiment took two hours and a half. As can be seen, both environments are very similar so obtained results can be compared.

4.2 Survey Description

The survey began with a short introduction by an evaluator, one of the project researchers. During 30 minutes, the evaluator gave some ideas about BRMSs and the way they work and he developed an example, building three business rules for a simple domain: a textual rule, a decision tree and a decision table. Then, a knowledge model for a car rental company was described to the participants and they were asked to fulfill four tasks, taking note of the time needed in each one. There was one task devoted to the development of some business rules on each of their possible forms, i.e., textual rules, decision tables and decision trees. In the last task they were asked to validate its behavior using the functionality provided by K-Site Rules, annotating the time needed in the whole process. The use case definition distributed to the participants is called ES Rent and is a simplification of the EU Rent use case included in the SBVR standard [9].

In order to test the first hypothesis included in section 2, the ideal situation would have been to ask users implementing the tasks included in the use case using their favorite programming language, then do it again with K-Site Rules and finally to fill the questionnaire comparing both methods. Unfortunately, this evaluation would have taken a lot of time, requiring more than one session. Not enough resources were available to afford this kind of evaluation. For this reason, developers were selected as evaluators because they know about programming languages, being able to estimate the effort required to implement use case tasks. In this way, they can intuitively compare business rules technology with programming languages they already know. Regarding the second hypothesis, developers can only give their opinion about how much technical knowledge is needed to develop business rules, so the survey will be repeated with people with not so deep technical knowledge.

4.3 Time per Task

In the graph shown in Fig. 3 the time (in minutes) taken for each task by each user is depicted.

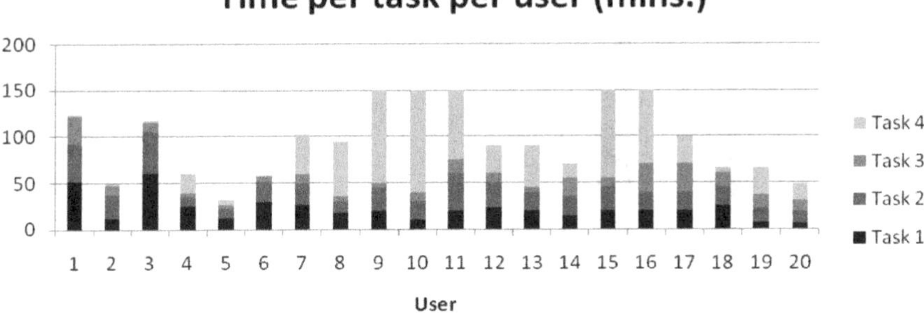

Fig. 3. Time per task per user

Task 1 was devoted to the definition of a textual rule, using the guided natural language editor provided by K-Site Rules. Task 2 asked for the definition of a decision tree; Task 3 includes the development of a decision table and Task 4 is devoted to business rules validation. The 6 first users correspond to the first experimentation group. Fig. 3 shows that this group took less time for the validation task (Task 4) than the second group. This is due to a difference in the procedure followed. The people in the first group, unintentionally, validated each rule at the end of each task, so business rules validation was almost immediate. By contrast, the second group (users 7 to 20) needed a lot of time for validation. This was because validation was postponed to the end of the survey, in Task 4 (as asked) and it was more difficult to find errors in the defined rules because all of them were already built and K-Site Rules had problems in fixing the place where the error occurred. If mean times by group are compared, people in the first group took an average of 73 minutes to finish all tasks. The most time consuming one was Task 1, which took an average of 31 minutes. On the other hand, the second group took an average of 105 minutes to finish the experiment, taking into account that some users could not finish because it was too difficult for them to find the errors they made during rules creation. The most time consuming task for this group was Task 4, validation, which took an average of 30 minutes.

4.4 Participants' Characterization

Fig. 4 and Fig. 5 show the average values regarding professional experience and technical knowledge.

Fig. 4 shows the number of participants having the corresponding years of experience in the given professional role. For example, 10 participants had less than one year experience as developers, while only one of them had more than 10 years of experience as functional analyst.

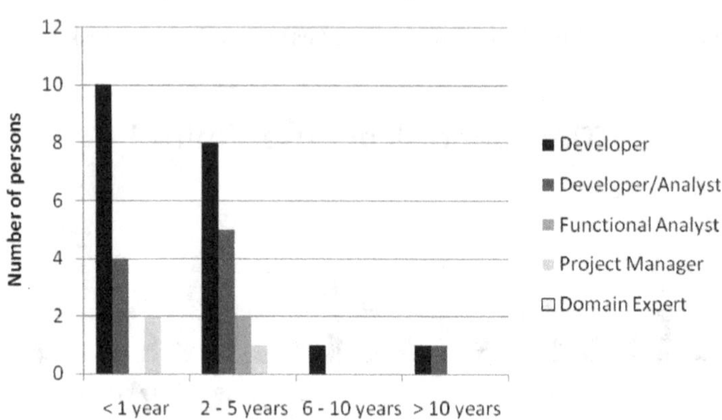

Fig. 4. Participants' professional experience

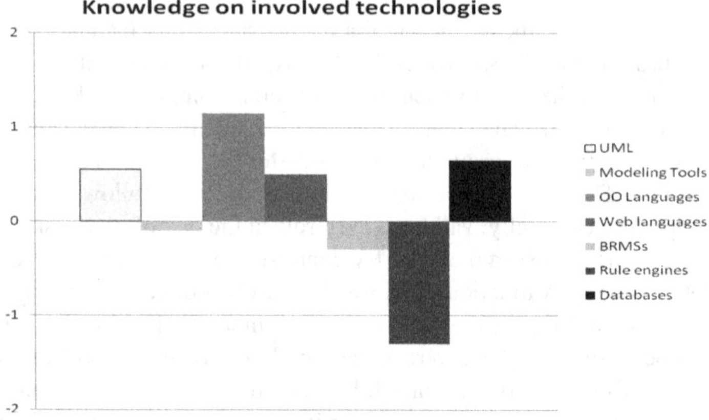

Fig. 5. Participants' knowledge on business rules related technologies

Fig. 5 shows the degree of knowledge (from 'unknown', -2, to 'expert', 2) of the participants in a set of technologies such as UML, modeling tools, object oriented languages, web languages, BRMSs, rule engines and databases.

Both figures evidence that these participants have developer roles, only a few of them have acted as functional analysts and most of them have good knowledge about programming languages and modeling tools (such as Rational Rose). These facts make them more valuable when they are asked to compare traditional programming techniques with the ones applied during the experiment. It is also valuable to point out that, before the experiment was carried out, most of the participants did not know what a rule engine is although they knew a little bit more about BRMSs.

4.5 K-Site Rules Interaction

This section provides results collected for the 12 closed questions and the open ones.

Table 1. Mean answers to closed questions

Q ID	Asseveration	Mean	Deviation
1	I could finish all proposed tasks	**1,15**	**1,35**
2	Available tool to write business rules using natural language facilitate business rule definition	1,55	0,51
3	Available tool to write business rules using decision tables facilitate business rule definition	1,6	0,50
4	Available tool to write business rules using decision trees facilitate business rule definition	**0,7**	**1,03**
5	Programming skills are required to define a business rule	-0,45	1,15
6	Business rules validation requires programming skills	-0,9	1,25
7	The tool clearly shows the business domain for the rule	1,2	0,77
8	I could have developed the same functionality by using a traditional programming language (C, C++, Java, C#, Pascal, etc.)	0,5	0,95
9	I could have developed the same functionality by using a database management system (PL/SQL, stored procedures, triggers, etc.)	-0,4	0,82
10	Using a programming language to implement asked business rules would have been faster	-1,4	0,68
11	Using business rules is a useful alternative in application development	1,45	0,60
12	K-Site Rules is a useful tool to develop business rules	1,4	0,68

Table 1 shows the 12 closed questions posed and the average mean of the punctuations given by participants. The questions follow a Likert scale with 5 levels, from 'Completely disagree' (-2 value) to 'Completely agree' (value 2).

The first thing to mention is that not all participants could finish all the proposed tasks. The same happened for some participants in the second group of users. Some of them could not finish the validation tasks because K-Site Rules failed in pointing out which part of which rule was incorrectly defined. On the other hand, according to question 4, users prefer to use natural language or decision table tools over decision trees. It seems to be more difficult for them to define business rules by tree structures.

Questions 10, 11 and 12 highlight the good opinion users have about the tool and business rules generally speaking. These participants think that using BRMS technology could lead to a cost reduction in development and maintaining tasks. On the other side, questions 5 and 6 remark that, according to this group of users, no programming skills are required to develop business rules.

It is worth mentioning that some users found difficult adapting to the rule development framework. That is to say, the way business rules are applied over facts and elements stored in the working memory is very different from traditional procedural programming.

Open questions have pointed out some lacks appearing in K-Site Rules, specially the lack of error messages in some circumstances.

5 Conclusions and Future Work

This paper has introduced the evaluation carried out using K-Site Rules, an implementation of an approach for business rules development. This approach has been described, pointing out two main goals: reduction of application development time using business rules technology and integration of non-technical people in the development process. Some evaluation methods for software engineering artifacts are mentioned, going deeply into surveys, the selected method applied in K-Site Rules. The implementation of the survey is detailed, from experiment design to questionnaire construction and data analysis.

The survey performed has corroborated the two initial hypotheses: participants believe that the use of business rules technologies can reduce development time; and, on the other hand, programming skills are not needed to take part in the application development process. Obtained figures for questions about skills required and development time needed (questions 5, 6, 10, 11 and 12) are shown in Table 1. Of course, due to the sample selection process followed, these conclusions do not have statistical significance so they cannot be strongly enforced. Nevertheless, given the characteristics of the target population and considering that the evaluation process implemented has been as rigorous as possible, obtained conclusions can be taken as valid.

In order to provide a deeper support to the mentioned conclusions, a new experiment is being planned for people not so close to a development profile. For this purpose, people with project manager or business expert role will be located and the survey will be repeated. Besides, lessons learned will help in the definition of the survey. There will be only three tasks and the rule validation step will be moved to the final part of each task. K-Site Rules will be also modified to provide better information in case of error.

Acknowledgments. Authors would like specially thank the people taking part in the evaluation process, in particular to the members of the Advanced Databases Group at the Universidad Carlos III and our colleagues at DAEDALUS.

References

1. Brown, J.D.: Using surveys in language programs. Cambridge University Press, Cambridge (2000)
2. Dumas, J.S., Redish, J.C.: A Practical Guide to Usability Testing. 1st Intellect Books (1999)
3. Elejabarrieta, F.J., Íñiguez, L.: Construcción de escalas de actitud tipo Thurst y Likert. Universidad Autónoma de Barcelona (1984), `http://antalya.uab.es/liniguez/Materiales/escalas.pdf` (Checked on: November 29, 2009)
4. Martinez-Fernandez, J.L., Gonzalez, J.C., Suarez, P.: K-Site Rules - Integrating Business Rules in the Mainstream Software Engineering Practice. In: ICEIS 2008 - Proceedings of the Tenth International Conference on Enterprise Information Systems, Barcelona, Spain, June 12-16, vol. AIDSS, pp. 446–449 (2008)
5. Martínez-Fernández, J.L., Martínez, P., González-Cristóbal, J.C.: Towards an improvement of software development processes through standard business rules. In: Governatori, G., Hall, J., Paschke, A. (eds.) RuleML 2009. LNCS, vol. 5858, pp. 159–166. Springer, Heidelberg (2009)
6. Miller, J., Mukerji, J.: MDA Guide Version 1.0.1. OMG document omg/03-06-01 (2003), `http://www.omg.org/cgi-bin/doc?omg/03-06-01.pdf` (Checked on: February 2009)
7. OMG; Ontology Definition Metamodel (ODM). Version 1.0. OMG document formal/2009-05-01 (2005), `http://www.omg.org/spec/ODM/1.0/` (Checked on: August 26, 2009)
8. OMG; Object Management Group, Production Rule Representation (PRR) Beta 1. OMG document dtc/2007-11-04 (2007), `http://www.omg.org/spec/PRR/1.0/Beta1/index.htm` (Checked on: October 24, 2009)
9. OMG; Semantics of Business Vocabulary and Business Rules (SBVR), v 1.0. OMG document formal/08-01-02 (2008), `http://www.omg.org/spec/SBVR/1.0` (Checked on: October 24, 2009)
10. Owen, J.: Benchmarking the rules engine. Infoworld (2003), `http://www.infoworld.com/d/developer-world/benchmarking-rules-engine-954` (Checked on: February 3, 2010)
11. Paschke, A., Hirtle, D., Ginsberg, A., Patranjan, P., McCabe, F.: RIF Use Cases and Requirements, Working Draft. W3C (2008), `http://www.w3.org/TR/rif-ucr/` (Checked on: August 31, 2009)
12. Pfleeger, S.L., Atlee, J.M.: Software Engineering: Theory and Practice, 3rd edn. Prentice Hall PTR, Upper Saddle River (2006)
13. Pfleeger, S.L., Kitchenham, B.A.: Principles of survey research (Parts 1 – 6). SIGSOFT Softw. Eng. Notes, First Part `http://doi.acm.org/10.1145/505532.505535` (2001–2003)
14. Rymer, J.R., Gualtieri, M.: The Forrester Wave™: Business Rules Platforms, Q2 2008. Forrester (2008)

Identification of Services through Functional Decomposition of Business Processes

Artur Caetano, António Rito Silva, and José Tribolet

Department of Computer Science and Engineering, Instituto Superior Técnico,
Technical University of Lisbon, 1049-001 Lisboa, Portugal
Centre for Organizational Design and Engineering, INESC INOV,
Rua Alves Redol 9, 1000-029 Lisboa, Portugal
{artur.caetano,rito.silva,jose.tribolet}@ist.utl.pt

Abstract. In a layered service-oriented enterprise architecture, business processes are supported by application services which are, in turn, supported by technological services. Service-orientation promotes the reuse and modular design of information systems. But achieving these design qualities requires the business processes of an organization to be consistently decomposed so that their supporting services can be effectively identified. This paper proposes using the separation of concerns principle to facilitate the consistent decomposition of a business process and the unambiguous identification of its atomic activities thus contributing to the task of identifying the supporting services.

Keywords: Business process modelling, functional decomposition, service identification, separation of concerns, enterprise architecture.

1 Introduction

Service-oriented architecture is an architectural style for constructing systems from a set of universally interconnected and interdependent services. A service is a unit of functionality that some entity makes available to its environment. This style of architecture promotes reuse at a macroscopic service level and can simplify the usage and interconnection the business, application and technological assets within and across organizations [1]. Service orientation promotes a layered view of an enterprise architecture's models. Service layers provide functionality to higher layers and are realized in lower implementation layers. For instance, the ArchiMate enterprise modelling language [2] defines three layers: the business layer defines which products are offered to external customers through business processes; the intermediate application layer supports the business layer with application services which are realised by application components; finally, the technology layer offers infrastructural services needed to run applications.

A business process is a set of interrelated value-adding activities [3]. Activities are often modelled as opaque transformation functions that map inputs to outputs. This abstraction strategy models an activity as a black-box and focus on its external behaviour. The resulting models conceptually divide a business system into a hierarchy of functions [4]. Thus, functionally decomposing a business process entails its recursive separation into a set of more detailed activities.

W. Abramowicz and R. Tolksdorf (Eds.): BIS 2010, LNBIP 47, pp. 144–157, 2010.

Business process models translate the knowledge about how an organization operates. These models are fundamental to enterprise architecture as they support the communication, analysis, implementation and execution of the organization's structure, business, systems and technology [2, 5]. Process models also provide the means to analyze alternative designs intended to align the business with the information systems and technology. However, the process modelling must cope with the multiple views and goals of the different organizational stakeholders. Moreover, the elicitation, modelling and analysis of the processes of an organization is often the result of merging the partial contributions of different teams, probably with different backgrounds and experience. Put together, these factors lead to models that lack consistency. Examples of inconsistency include using different levels of modelling detail and the incoherent naming of the activities and entities of a process. Inconsistent process models are not only hard for their users to understand but also hamper the tasks of process analysis and redesign as they may leave out relevant information or lead to erroneous or ambiguous interpretations of the process content. Such inconsistency also negatively contributes to the identification and the specification of the services that are required to support the process.

Consistent business process decomposition can significantly improve the clarity and the overall model integrity as well as minimizing the omission of relevant information [6]. Decomposition is also a means to modularize large systems and to facilitate the reuse of partial models and favours the compactness of a specification as it allows multiple levels of detail to co-exist and coupling to be reduced [7]. As a consequence of abstraction, models become easier to understand and communicate, which, in turn, make their validation, redesign and optimization easier.

This paper proposes using the separation of concerns principle to facilitate the consistent decomposition of a business process and the unambiguous identification of its atomic activities thus contributing to the task of identifying the supporting services. To do so, we present a method that specifies how to decompose a business process according to the concerns that are involved in the specification of its activities.

The remainder of this paper is structured as follows. The next section reviews related work. Section 3 introduces the concepts of natural type, role type and activity. Sections 4 and 5 describe the functional decomposition method and the underlying role ontology along with a running example. Finally, section 6 summarizes the research methodology and section 7 summarizes the proposal and provides an outlook on future work.

2 Related Work

Functional decomposition is supported at language level by most process modelling languages, including ArchiMate [2], BPMN [8], EPC [9] and IDEF-0 and IDEF-3 [10]. The decomposition of subsystems through the hierarchic classification of process models has also been applied to Petri nets [11] and BPEL [12]. Although these approaches make possible creating a hierarchical representation of a process, their intent is not the definition of techniques for consistent activity decomposition but, instead, the representation of generic decomposition structures. Nevertheless, the shortcomings of the lack of consistency in process decomposition and in the identification of its atomic activities are pointed out by several authors [13, 14].

Several top-down decomposition approaches exploit reference models to describe how a process is structured as a hierarchy of activities. For instance, the Supply-Chain Operations Reference model describes three levels of detail to assist the definition and configuration of an organization's supply chain [15]. The Process Clarification Framework defines a hierarchical (and static) decomposition of business processes which is 3 to 4 levels deep and crosses 12 operating and management categories [16]. Other approaches, such as the ARIS framework [9], describe processes as chains of events and tasks and prescribe the levels of detail for decomposition. The first two decomposition levels address the business viewpoint of the model, the next 3 to 4 levels focus on the structure of process operation and the lower level describes the procedural details of the tasks. However, the contents of these levels of detail are actually arbitrary.

An alternative avenue of research relies on algorithmic methods to analyse the process specification and assess its consistency. One of these methods uses similarity measures derived from the syntactic and structural features of the process to detect inconsistencies between its activities [17]. These measures make use of a linguistic ontology to evaluate the similarity between the names of the activities thus assisting the detection of decomposition anomalies. Process mining techniques extract information from existing event logs and enable the discovery of business processes [18]. These bottom-up mining techniques support the verification of the conformance of a model derived from an event log against an existing model as well as identifying the atomic activities of a process [19]. Other approaches that use ontologies to specify business processes (e.g. [20-22]) also lack the means to identify atomic activities and to consistently decompose a process.

Altogether, and to the best of our knowledge, existing approaches do not define the necessary means to consistently decompose a business process and to unambiguously identify the atomic activities that constitute it. The primary goal of this paper is therefore to provide a contribution to this research subject.

3 Fundamental Concepts

Role modelling is a separation of concerns technique that is used in multiple areas of knowledge such as data modelling [23], object-oriented and conceptual modelling [24-26], framework design [27], business process modelling [28, 29] and enterprise architecture [20, 30-34].

With role-based business process, modelling an activity (a business verb) is abstracted as a set of collaborations between entities (business nouns). The entities represent the things that are of interest within a specific modelling context. Each unit of behaviour of an entity is abstracted as a role and, as a result, activities are defined by a role collaboration pattern. If no roles are being played within the system then there are no collaborations and, therefore, no activities to be modelled.

Figure 1 shows the relationships and cardinalities between four entities involved in the assemble product process which we will use as a running example to illustrate the concepts outlined above. The activity assemble product is defined by the collaboration pattern between the roles being played by the entities part, assembling machine, product and person. The activity describes how a product is assembled from a number of parts by means of an assembling machine. The activity is semi-automated as the machine is operated by a person.

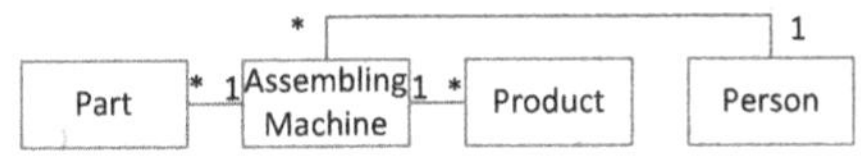

Fig. 1. Relationships between entities

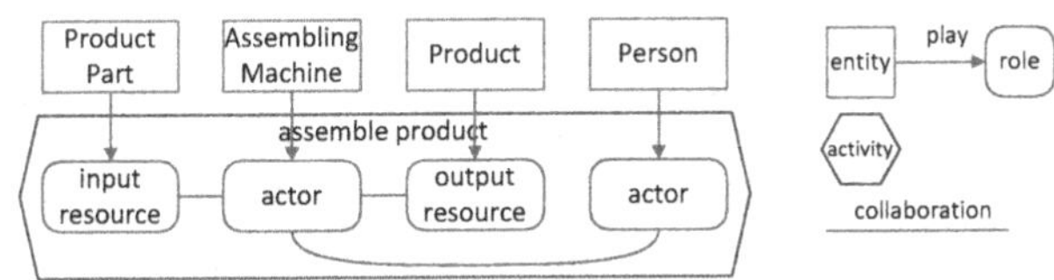

Fig. 2. Role-based specification of the assemble product activity

Figure 2 shows the relationships between the entities result in one collaboration context where a natural type displays a specific behaviour [33, 34]. Such behaviour is abstracted as a role type. Thus, in the first collaboration context each part plays the role of input resource in their relationship with the assembling machine which, in its turn, is playing the actor role. In other context the assembling machine produces the assembled product, i.e. the product is the output resource of this actor. Finally, the person relates to the machine as its actor. The collaboration between these four roles uniquely defines the assemble product activity as depicted in Figure 2. The actor role states that an entity is able to perform some action in the context of an activity. The resource role states that an entity which is playing it can be used or consumed (input resource) or created (output resource) during the performance of an activity.

The remainder of this section details the concept of entity (or natural type), role (or role type) and activity.

3.1 Natural Types and Role Types

Sowa [35] distinguished between *natural types* "that relate to the essence of the entities" and *role types* "that depend on an accidental relationship to some other entity". By developing Sowa's ideas further, Guarino presented an ontological distinction between these two types [36]. This distinction is based on the concepts of *foundedness* and *semantic rigidness*. A type is considered *founded* if its specification implies a dependency or relation to some other individual. A type is *semantically rigid* if the identity of an individual depends on the type assigned to it. If the type is removed from the individual then it cannot be further identified nor classified. Thus, a type is *not semantically rigid* if it can be assigned to and removed from an individual without changing its identity.

Based on the above, a type that is both *founded* and not *semantically rigid* is a *role type*. In contrast, a natural type is characterized by being *semantically rigid* and *not founded*.

To illustrate the above classification properties, let us take the example of Figure 2 and classify the concepts of `person` and `actor` as either natural or role types. First, let us focus on the "foundedness" of these concepts. `Actor` is a founded type since for something or someone to be assigned the `actor` type there must be something being acted upon. Conversely, the `person` type is not founded since it exists on its own terms. It defines the identity of the individual to which it is assigned to, regardless of its relationships with any other individual. Thus, the `person` type is not founded whereas the `actor` type is founded.

Regarding "semantic rigidness", the `actor` type is not semantically rigid because its identity is independent of the individual to whom the type is assigned to. This means the `actor` type is not able to identify the individual by itself. On the other hand, the `person` type is semantically rigid as its identity is directly coupled to the individual's identity. Therefore, `actor` is a role type (founded and not semantically rigid) whereas `person` is a natural type (not founded and semantically rigid).

3.1.1 Natural Types

Entities are natural types. In enterprise modelling, an entity describes a thing that an organization deems relevant to specify in order to fulfil the purpose of a model. Entities model concepts such as persons, places, machines, resources, contracts and products. According to the definition of natural type, an entity can be unambiguously identified and defined in isolation, i.e. without any relationship with other types. Entities can be classified according to its intrinsic features. Entities may relate structurally to other entities (e.g. an order is composed of items).

3.1.2 Role Types

A role type, or role for short, is the observable behaviour of an entity in the scope of a specific collaboration. Different roles separate the different concerns that arise from the collaborations between entities. Hence, a role represents the external visible features of that entity when it collaborates with another entity in the context of an activity. An entity relates to other roles through the *play* relationship. An entity that plays no roles is not participating in any activity since it is not able to produce actual behaviour. An entity enters the role when it starts playing it and leaves the role when the specific behaviour specified by the role is concluded. Each role adds a set of external features to an entity in the context of that collaboration. This effectively separates the entity's feature space since its intrinsic features are differentiated from each of the external features that transiently relate to an entity through the roles it plays.

3.2 Activities

A business process is an ordered execution of activities that produces goods or provides services that add value to the organization's environment or to the organization itself. Thus, modelling a business process involves specifying the set of activities that define its operation and the flow that defines how the activities are coordinated.

An activity is specified by a collaboration of role types. It is a behaviour element that describes part of the functionality available to the organization. Since a role type separates the description of the intrinsic features of an entity from the features that derive from the collaborations it participates in, the specification of an activity itself is independent of the specification of the entities playing the roles.

Figure 2 depicts the `assemble product` activity as a unit of functionality that result from the collaboration between a set of roles. However, this activity model is conceptual as it may have been specified from a different perspective or with a different level of detail, which would have implied using a different role ontology. The granularity level of the activities is also arbitrary as it is always possible to add more detail to its specification. Hence, the naming of an activity is actually irrelevant for the purpose of its specification as the role collaboration pattern is the only means to specify it unambiguously. Therefore, an activity is uniquely identified by the collaboration of roles that are involved in its specification. Two activities are deemed *equivalent* if and only if they share the same set of role collaborations.

4 Functional Decomposition

The functional decomposition of a business process yields a set of sub-activities, each of which can be further decomposed. The behaviour of a whole process can then be constructed upwards from the lowest level of decomposition towards the top-level activity. The lowest level of decomposition describes primitive or atomic activities that cannot be further divided. The related literature (cf. section 2) describes different approaches to the functional decomposition of processes but, to the best of our knowledge, existing approaches do not provide the means to unambiguously identify what makes an atomic activity nor the mechanisms that provide consistent decomposition results.

The approach proposed in this paper is to use role types as the criteria for process decomposition. This means each decomposition step separates a different concern (i.e. a role type) from the other concerns that specify the activity. An activity is deemed atomic, meaning it cannot be further decomposed, when all of its concerns are effectively separated. This translates to having no overlapping role types in the activity's specification. It also implies that the classification of an activity as atomic actually depends on the role ontology that is being utilized to generate the process model. So, different role ontologies yield different decomposition criteria and, thus, different process models.

```
decompose(S, R)
    D ← Ø
    decompose' (S, R, D, 1)
    decompose ← D
end
decompose' (S, R, D, level)
    if R ≠ Ø then
        R0 ← firstElementOf(R)
        Dlevel ← Ø
        if numInstancesOfType(R0, S) > 1 then
            for all r ∈ R0 do
                Sd ← (S - R0) ∪ r
                Dlevel ← Dlevel ∪ Sd
                decompose' (Sd, R - R0, D, level +1)
            end for
        else
            decompose' (S, R - R0, D, level +1)
        end if
        D ← D ∪ { Dlevel }
    end if
end
```

The algorithm `decompose(S, R)` recursively separates an activity into sub-activities as long as there are overlapping concerns. `S` is the ordered set of all the roles type instances used in activity to be decomposed. The set `R` (which is a subset of the types of `S`) contains the role types that define the domain to be used to decompose the activity. If all the role types in `S` are included in `R` then all roles will be separated. The role types not included in `R` will remain overlapped after the decomposition. The output of `decompose(S, R)` is a set of sets. Each of these sets represents an activity, with the outer set representing the first level of decomposition. The symbol `level` identifies the current decomposition level with 0 representing the top level activity. The symbol `D` represents the output set of the decomposition and D_{level} is the set of decomposed activities pertaining to a given `level` of depth. The algorithm makes use of two additional functions not detailed here: `firstElementOf(X)` returns the first element of the set X; `countInstancesOfType(t, X)` counts the number of instances of the type `t` within the set `X`.

Figure 3 illustrates an application of the `decompose` function to activity `A1`. `A1` is defined by the collaboration of role types `R1, R2, R3`. Let us consider that `A1` is specified by `S = {a:R1, b:R1, c:R2, d:R3, e:R3}` and that `S` maps to three role types, `R = {R1, R2, R3}`. Using `decompose(S, R)` to decompose `A1` according to `(R1, R2, R3)`, results in `D = {D1, D2}`. `D1` is the first level of decomposition and divides A1 into `{(a:R1, c:R2, d:R3, e:R3), (b:R1, c:R2, d:R3, e:R3)}`. `D2` is the lowest level of decomposition and comprises four atomic activities: `{(a:R1, c:R2, d:R3), (a:R1, c:R2, e:R3), (b:R1, c:R2, d:R3), (b:R1, c:R2, e:R3)}`.

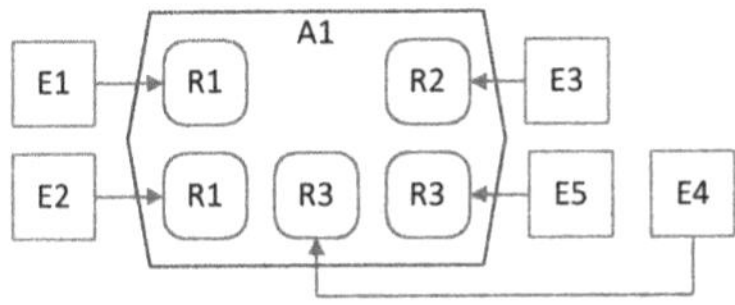

Fig. 3. Activity A1 according to roles R1, R2, R3

If we define the role ontology `R1, R2, R3 to` describe locations, goals and actors, so that `R1` stands for the `Locator` role, which describes a geographical location, `R2` is the `Goal` role, that models the intended state of the affairs to be achieved after executing the activity, and that `R3` is the `Actor` role, which describes the action of someone of something operating in the context of the activity `A1`, we would get the model depicted on Figure 4.

Decomposing `A1` according to the `Locator` role (`R1`) yields two activities, `A1.1` and `A1.2`, as shown in Figure 5. Each of these functionally separate `A1` according to geographical location concern. Decomposing `A1` according to the `Actor` role (`R3`) produces two activities, each focusing on the specific operations of the actor involved in `A1`. Note that `A1` cannot be decomposed according to the `Goal` role (`R2`) as this concern does not overlap with any other role of the same type. Activities `A1.1` and `A1.2` can be further separated as shown in Figure 6.

The decomposition of `A1` according to the role tuple `(Locator, Actor, Goal)` results in four atomic activities, each focusing on a different concern: `A1.1.1 (Office:Locator, Person:Actor, Goal:Goal), A1.1.2 (Factory:Locator, Person:Actor, Goal:Goal), A1.2.1 (Office:Locator, Machine:Actor, Goal:Goal), A1.2.2 (Factory:Locator, Machine:Actor, Goal:Goal)`. Note that `A1` cannot be further decomposed according to these three roles. Further decomposition is only possible if new roles are added to the ontology or additional overlapping concerns are included in the specification of `A1`.

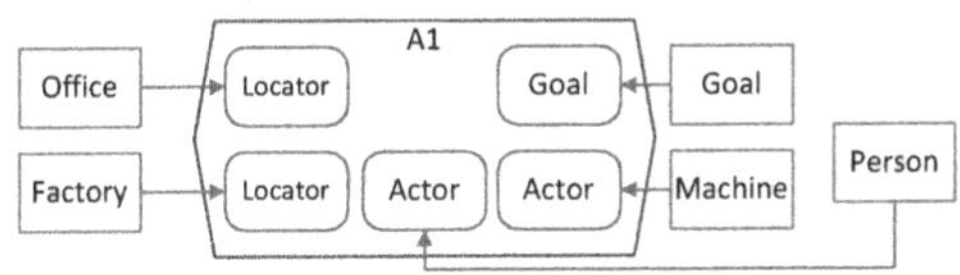

Fig. 4. Activity A1 and Actor, Locator and Goal role types

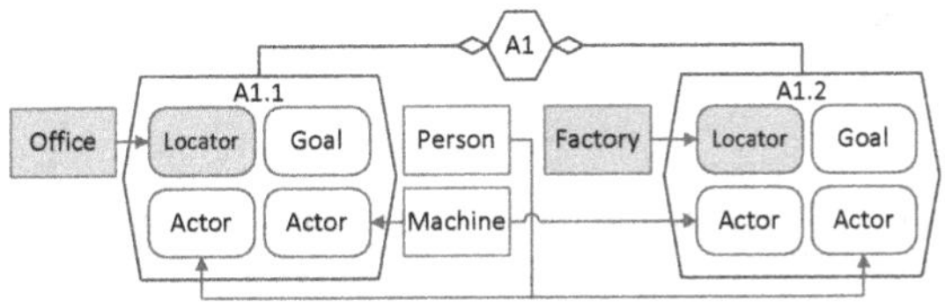

Fig. 5. Decomposition of activity A1 on role R1 (Locator)

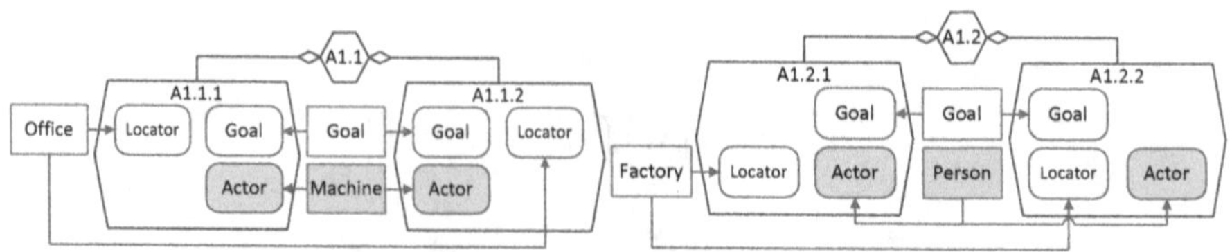

Fig. 6. Left: decomposition of A1.1 on role R. Right: decomposition of A1.2 on role R.

This approach is unambiguous as each level of decomposition can be systematically reproduced. A business process can always be consistently separated into its constituent atomic activities and the corresponding supporting services identified. Additionally, the condition for activity decomposition is explicit as the procedure stops whenever the concerns of an activity are effectively separated. Thus, consistent process decomposition promotes service identification and reuse.

5 Role Ontology

The decomposition method relies on the specification of a role type ontology. An ontology is a formal representation of a set of concepts within a domain and the relationships between those concepts. In this particular case, the ontology represents the set of role types required to model a specific domain and the possible collaborations between these role types.

A business process can be modelled from different perspectives according to the model's goals and purpose as defined by its stakeholders. Although there are multiple classification schemes to categorize the modelling perspectives, these often crosscut the six orthogonal linguistic interrogatives (how, what, where, who, when, why). These interrogatives can be used to construct four basic modelling perspectives [37, 38]. The functional perspective represents *what* activities are being performed in the context of a given process. The informational perspective represents *what* informational entities (i.e. data or resources) are being manipulated by the activities of a process. The behavioural perspective represents *when* activities are performed and *how* they are performed, usually through the specification of the process orchestration. Finally, the organizational perspective represents *why* an activity is being performed, *where* it is performed and *by whom*.

The remainder of this section exemplifies a set of roles types that addresses the above concerns according to the six interrogatives. We emphasize that the role ontology should be specified according to the requirements of the stakeholders and to the specific domain being modelled.

5.1 Actor (Who)

The `actor` role represents the action of an entity that does some task in the context of an activity. Actors are played by entities which represent people, computer systems, mechanical tools or any other devices that produce active change within an organization. A specialization scheme of the `actor` role type focuses on its nature, such as: `social actor` (people or organizations), `application actor` (computational or non-computational applications that are used to perform a task) and infrastructure actor (computer hardware, machines and other devices that support the application and social actors). Another specialization scheme, which is orthogonal to the actor's nature, includes roles such as operator, auditor and supervisor. Using the actor role as the criterion for decomposition identifies atomic that describe the actions of each individual actor. The decomposition of the assemble product activity in Figure 2 according to the actor role identifies two activities: one for the actions being performed by the person and other for the actions of the machine.

5.2 Resource (What)

A resource is the role played by an entity when manipulated by an actor in the context of an activity. A resource specialization scheme that focus on how a resource is transformed within an activity consists of two roles: input resource role and output resource role. The former can be further specialized as consumed resource role and used resource role, whereas the latter can be specialized as created resource role and refined resource role. Other orthogonal schemes are possible, such as classifying a resource according to its existence (e.g. tangible, intangible, etc.)

5.3 Locator (Where)

The locator role captures the geographical or the logical location of an entity. The sub-activities of an activity that is decomposed according to the locator role are operated in different locations.

5.4 Goal, Rule (Why)

A goal represents a measurable state of affairs that the organization intends to achieve. The entity plays the goal specifier role which relates to the goal fulfiller role. Goals are usually achieved by the entities playing the actor or resource role. A rule asserts conditions or operating parameters that an activity must comply with. The entity that specifies the constraint plays the rule specifier role which relates to the rule complier role.

5.5 Starter, Finisher (How, When)

The behavioural perspective can be captured through the starter and finisher roles. The first models the event that triggers the start of an activity while the second signals its completion. These two roles can be used to describe how the activities of a process are orchestrated, as described in the next section.

6 Research Methodology

The methodology behind the results reported in this paper is grounded on design science [39, 40]. Design science focuses on the development of solutions for practical problems. This contrasts with the development and the verification of theories as in behavioural science methodologies.

Research on enterprise architecture, modelling and engineering fits the design science paradigm as its focal goal is not building information systems but creating methods and techniques to analyze, model, and understand the horizontal and vertical interfaces between the business, systems and technology [41]. The essential tangible result of a design science project consists in creating an artefact that addresses a particular issue that is relevant to a certain group of stakeholders. In this context, Hevner et al. proposed a set of guidelines to conducting design science projects [40]. The following points briefly summarize how these were applied to this work.

- **Design as an artefact.** This project deals with applying the principle of separation of concerns to business process modelling. This paper describes an artefact that deals with business process decomposition role modelling as a separation of concerns mechanism.
- **Problem relevance.** The artefact enables the consistent decomposition of a business process. By doing so, it addresses several problems that are relevant in enterprise engineering in general and business process modelling in particular. We emphasize the following problems: (1) how to systematically identify the atomic activities of a process; (2) how to make explicit the principles behind process decomposition; (3) how to make decomposition dependent on the specification of the process and not on the modelling team experience
- **Design evaluation.** This paper makes use of a *scenario* [40] built around the artefact to demonstrate its application and utility.
- **Research contributions.** The paper describes an algorithm for consistent business process decomposition and its applicability to the identification of business services.
- **Research rigour.** The artefact addresses a problem identified in the enterprise engineering and business process modelling literature. The solution is grounded on the principles of role modelling, separation of concerns and business process modelling.
- **Communication of research.** The research is reported through publications aimed at the practitioners and researchers within the enterprise engineering area and mainly targets business process modellers.

7 Conclusion and Future Work

Activity decomposition is an abstraction technique that enables the modularization of business processes. A decomposed process is easier to understand as each decomposition step incrementally reduces the number of overlapping concerns. This fosters the reuse and identification of the supporting services and increases the ability to communicate and analyze them. Each decomposition step provides a consistent level of detail so that the set of atomic activities comprising the lowest level of decomposition are always coherent, regardless of the stakeholder's requirements and the modelling team's experience.

The aim of the project is to guide the procedure of process decomposition so that decompositions are explicit and consistent. The proposed method supports the decomposition of business processes according to the separation of overlapping concerns. Business processes are modelled as the collaboration of natural types that play role types in the context of activities. A role ontology is used to specify the domain of role types and constrains the decomposition space. This approach facilitates the consistent decomposition of a process and the identification of the atomic activities, which contributes to service identification. However, the scenario presented in this paper does not evaluate the impact of the specification of the ontology and the overhead introduced by role-modelling in business process modelling. To overcome this limitation, we are currently developing a set of case studies intended to evaluate the applicability of the method to large-scale business processes.

References

[1] Bieberstein, N., Bose, S., Fiammante, M., Jones, K., Shah, R.: Service-Oriented Architecture (SOA) Compass: Business Value, Planning, and Enterprise Roadmap. IBM Press, New York (2005)
[2] Lankhorst, M.: Enterprise Architecture at Work: Modelling, Communication and Analysis. Springer, Berlin/Heidelberg (2006)
[3] Davenport, T.: Process Innovation: Reengineering Work Through Information Technology. Harvard Business School Press, Boston (1993)
[4] Dietz, J.L.G.: Enterprise Ontology: Theory and Methodology. Springer, Berlin (2006)
[5] Op't Land, M., Proper, E., Waage, M., Cloo, J., Steghuis, C.: Enterprise Archi-tecture: Creating Value by Informed Governance. Springer, Heidelberg (2009)
[6] Huber, P., Jensen, K., Shapiro, R.M.: Hierarchies in Coloured Petri Nets. In: Rozenberg, G. (ed.) APN 1990. LNCS, vol. 483, pp. 313–341. Springer, Heidelberg (1991)
[7] Bass, L., Clements, P., Kazman, R.: Software Architecture in Practice. Addison-Wesley, Reading (1998)
[8] OMG, Business Process Modeling Notation Specification. v 1.1 (formal/2008-01-17) (2008)
[9] Scheer, A.-W.: Business Process Modeling, 3rd edn. Springer, Berlin (2000)
[10] Mayer, R.J., Menzel, C.P., Painter, M.K., de Witte, P.S., Blinn, T., Perakath, B.: Perakath, Information Integration for Concurrent Engineering - IDEF3. Knowledge Based Systems Inc. (1995)
[11] Reisig, W., Rozenberg, G.: APN 1998. LNCS, vol. 1491. Springer, Heidelberg (1998)
[12] Kloppmann, M., Koenig, D., Leymann, F., Pfau, G., Rickayzen, A., Riegen, C.v., Schmidt, P., Trickovic, I.: WS-BPEL Extension for Subprocesses BPEL-SPE. IBM and SAP Joint White Paper (2005)
[13] Davis, R., Brabdänder, E.: ARIS Design Platform. Springer, London (2007)
[14] Ingvaldsen, J.E., Gulla, J.A.: Model Based Business Process Mining. Journal of Information Systems Management 23 (2006)
[15] Bolstorff, P., Rosenbaum, R.: Supply Chain Excellence: A Handbook for Dra-matic Improvement Using the SCOR Model, 2nd edn. Springer, Berlin (2008)
[16] APQC, APQC Process Clarification Framework - Consumer Products, version 5.0.2 (10/04/2008)
[17] Hornung, T., Koschmider, A., Lausen, G.: Recommendation based process modeling support: Method and user experience. In: Li, Q., Spaccapietra, S., Yu, E., Olivé, A. (eds.) ER 2008. LNCS, vol. 5231, pp. 265–278. Springer, Heidelberg (2008)

[18] van der Aalst, W.M.P., de Beer, H.T., van Dongen, B.F.: Process mining and verification of properties: An approach based on temporal logic. In: Meersman, R., Tari, Z. (eds.) OTM 2005. LNCS, vol. 3760, pp. 130–147. Springer, Heidelberg (2005)
[19] van der Aalst, W.M.P., Reijers, H., Weijters, A., van Dongen, B., Medeiros, A.A.d., Song, M., Verbeek, H.: Business Process Mining: An Industrial Application. Information Systems Journal 32, 713–732 (2007)
[20] Uschold, M., King, M., Moralee, S., Zorgios, Y.: The Enterprise Ontology. The Knowledge Engineering Review 13, 31–89 (2000)
[21] Greco, G., Guzzo, A., Pontieri, L., Sacca, D.: An ontology-driven process modeling framework. In: Galindo, F., Takizawa, M., Traunmuller, R. (eds.) 15th International Conference on Database and Expert Systems Applications, pp. 13–23. IEEE Computer Society, Zaragoza (2004)
[22] Albani, A., Dietz, J.L.G., Zaha, J.: Identifying Business Components on the basis of an Enterprise Ontology. In: Interoperability of Enterprise Software and Applications, pp. 335–347. Springer, Heidelberg (2006)
[23] Bachman, C.W.: The role data model approach to data structures. In: Deen, S.M., Hammersley, P. (eds.) International Conference on Databases, pp. 1–18. Heyden & Son (1980)
[24] Kristensen, B.: Object-Oriented Modeling with Roles. In: 2nd International Conference on Object-Oriented Information Systems (1995)
[25] Reenskaug, T., Wold, P., Lehn, O.: Working With Objects: The OOram Software Engineering Method. Manning Publication Co., Greenwhich (1996)
[26] Steimann, F.: On the representation of roles in object-oriented and conceptual modelling. Data & Knowledge Engineering 35, 83–106 (2000)
[27] Riehle, D.: Framework Design: A Role Modeling Approach, Zurich, vol. PhD, p. 229. Swiss Federal Institute of Technology, Switzerland (2000)
[28] Ould, M.: Business Processes: Modeling and analysis for re-engineering and improvement. John Wiley & Sons, Chichester (1995)
[29] Krogstie, J., Carlsen, S., Consulting, A., Chicago, I.L.: An integrated model-ling approach for process support. In: 30th Hawaii International Conference on System Sciences, HICSS 1997, vol. 2 (1997)
[30] Wegmann, A.: On the systemic enterprise architecture methodology. In: International Conference on Enterprise Information Systems (ICEIS 2003) Angers, France (2003)
[31] Lê, L.-S., Wegmann, A.: SeamCAD: Object-Oriented Modeling Tool for Hierarchical Systems in Enterprise Architecture. In: 39th Hawaii International Conference on System Sciences, Hawaii, USA (2006)
[32] Zacarias, M., Caetano, A., Magalhães, R., Pinto, H.S., Tribolet, J.: Towards Organizational Self-Awareness. In: Rittgen, P. (ed.) Ontologies for Business Interactions. Idea Group Inc., USA (2007)
[33] Caetano, A., Rito Silva, A., Tribolet, J.: A Role-Based Enterprise Architecture Framework. In: 24th Annual ACM Symposium on Applied Computing, ACM SAC 2009, Hawaii, USA (2009)
[34] Zacarias, M., Magalhães, R., Pinto, H.S., Tribolet, J.: An agent-centric and 'context-aware' perspective for the alignment between individuals and organizations. In: Information Systems (2009.03.014) (2009)
[35] Sowa, J.: Conceptual Structures: Information Processing in Mind and Machine. Addison-Wesley, New York (1984)
[36] Guarino, N., Carrara, M., Giaretta, P.: An Ontology of Meta-Level Categories. In: Principles of Knowledge Representation and Reasoning: Proceedings of the Fourth International Conference (KR 1994), pp. 270–280. Morgan Kaufmann, San Mateo (1994)

[37] Carlsen, S.: Comprehensible Business Process Models for Process Improvement and Process Support. In: Constantopoulos, P., Vassiliou, Y., Mylopoulos, J. (eds.) CAiSE 1996. LNCS, vol. 1080. Springer, Heidelberg (1996)
[38] Giaglis, G.M.: A Taxonomy of Business Process Modeling and Information Systems Modeling Techniques. International Journal of Flexible Manufacturing Systems 13, 209–228 (2001)
[39] March, S., Smith, G.: Design and natural science research on information technology. Decision Support Systems 15, 251–266 (1995)
[40] Hevner, A.R., March, S.T., Park, J., Ram, S.: Design science in information systems research. MIS Quarterly 28, 75–105 (2004)
[41] Braun, C., Wortmann, F., Hafner, M., Winter, R.: Method construction - a core approach to organizational engineering. In: ACM Symposium on Applied Computing, USA, pp. 1295–1299 (2005)

Requirements for a Business Process Model Repository: A Stakeholders' Perspective

Khurram Shahzad, Mturi Elias, and Paul Johannesson

Department of Computer and Systems Science (DSV),
Royal Institute of Technology (KTH) / Stockholm University, Sweden
{mks,mturi,pajo}@dsv.su.se

Abstract. Reuse of business process models is the act of designing business processes by using existing process models. Reuse of business process models has been considered as a way to reduce the cost of modeling business processes from scratch. In order to support reuse a critical mass of process models is required which justifies the effort of maintaining a process model repository. However, recent studies show that complete repositories which can support reuse are not yet available. One of the reasons is that stakeholder requirements for process model repositories have not been sufficiently investigated. Therefore, the purpose of this work is to define requirements of a process model repository from stakeholders' (researchers and practitioners) perspective. In this study, we start by eliciting preliminary requirements (defined as propositions) through an exploratory study followed by an empirical validation of the propositions. Based on the analysis of the results we define as a set of requirements for a process model repository.

1 Introduction

Business Process Management (BPM) has become one of the most important management instruments that help organizations meet their business goals and achieve competitive advantage. One of the most important aspects of BPM is business process modelling. Modelling of business processes is a complex, error prone and time consuming task [1, 2, 3]. However, the efforts made to develop business process models are seldom reused beyond their original purpose. Reuse of business process models can help business users and researchers simplify the work of modelling business processes [2], improve efficiency and substantially reduce the cost of modelling business processes [3, 4]. In order to support reuse a critical mass of process models is required which justifies the effort of maintaining a process model repository.

A process model repository offers a space for storing, maintaining and changing process knowledge (business rules, relationships, process elements, etc.) for future reuse. In addition to that, a repository enables stakeholders to retrieve process models for various purposes like understanding, updating, simulating and analyzing process models. While there exists a number of process model repositories [5, 6, 7, 8], recent studies show that the existing repositories do not adequately support reuse of process models [9, 12]. One of the reasons is that stakeholder requirements for process model

W. Abramowicz and R. Tolksdorf (Eds.): BIS 2010, LNBIP 47, pp. 158–170, 2010.

repositories have not been sufficiently investigated. Stakeholders of process model repository are researchers, practitioners, process owners, process participants etc.

The aim of this study is to establish a set of requirements for a process model repository (the primarily for the reuse of process models) from stakeholders' perspective. However, for acquisition of requirements we specifically focus on two large groups (researchers and practitioners) that are directly involved in reusing process models from the repository. This is done by eliciting preliminary requirements (defined as propositions) through an exploratory study and then validating the propositions through an empirical study. Finally, based on the analysis of the empirical study, a set of requirements for a process model repository are suggested.

The remainder of the paper is organized as follows. Section 2 presents the research approach used to define the requirements. Section 3 presents the exploratory study used for collecting opinions from users (called propositions). Section 4 presents an empirical study for validating the propositions. In Section 5 requirements for a process model repository are defined. Finally, conclusions and future research directions are presented in Section 6.

2 Research Approach

In this section we present the research approach for defining requirements for a process model repository. The approach consists of three phases as shown in figure 1: exploratory study, empirical study and requirements definition.

The exploratory study aimed at eliciting comments, opinions, suggestions and ideas on process model repositories from both researchers and practitioners. The study was designed to collect as many ideas and suggestions as possible encouraging the participants not to restrict their responses. Therefore, this exploratory study consisted of an open ended questionnaire used in an oral interview. The responses were collected and reformulated into propositions that expressed suggestions for requirements on a process model repository. As the purpose was to identify propositions so we limited the participants to a small number of experts.

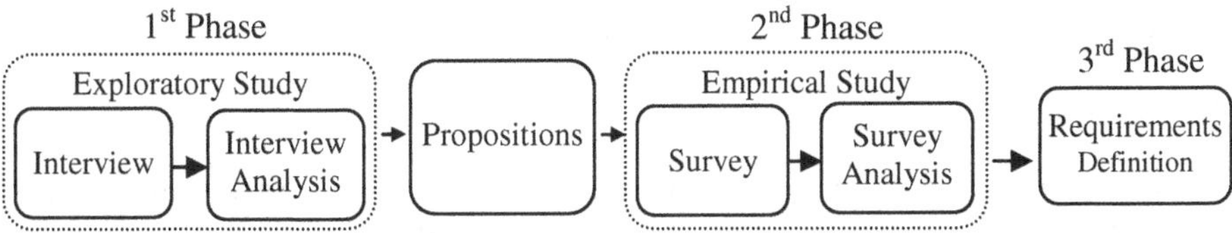

Fig. 1. The Research Approach

In order to validate the propositions an empirical study was conducted. For that, a larger set of participants was considered with precise questions (called propositions). A total of 30 participants participated in the study while responses from 25 participants (16 researchers and 9 practitioners) were used for the study (see table 1). Finally, based on the analysis of the data collected from the empirical study, requirements for a process model repository are suggested. The purpose of this study was to

Table 1. The Study Participants

Study type	Method	Total Participants	Participant type	No of participants
Exploratory Study	Interviews	5	Practitioners	2
			Researchers	3
Validation Study	Survey	25	Practitioners	9
			Researchers	16

validate the propositions by letting a number of participants judge the validity of the propositions. Therefore, a larger number of experts were involved in the validation.

3 Exploratory Study

In this section we describe how the exploratory study was conducted. Furthermore, the analysis of interviews is discussed in order to define a set of propositions.

- *Selection of Participants:* In order to include both industrial and academic perspectives a total of five participants were interviewed. Out of the five interviewees, three were researchers and two were practitioners. Researchers are academics who are doing research in enterprise modeling in general and process modeling in specific. Practitioners are experts who have worked for more than a decade in business process management industry and have worked on various projects as business analysts or modeling experts.
- *Questionnaire Preparation:* The questionnaire was prepared using information gathered from the literature study, personal experiences and our previous research work. The questions were open-ended so that the interviewees could discuss their experiences, important issues and problems faced when modeling and reusing process models.
- *Conducting the Study:* Each respondent was given a copy of the questionnaire to enhance understanding of questions during the interview. Each interview lasted for approximately one hour and all the interviews were recorded. Based on the answer of the participants some follow-up questions were asked to pursue interesting issues that came up during the conversation.

3.1 Analysis

The interviews indicate that modeling business processes from scratch is difficult and time consuming. This has also been affirmed in existing studies [1, 2, 3]. Another challenge indicated by the respondents is getting information from the people working in a business flow. They agreed that reuse of process models may reduce these challenges, which justifies the need for a process model repository. However, practitioners pointed out that the reuse of process models heavily depends on the quality of the content stored in the repository.

The analysis of the collected data showed that the features and characteristics most desirable for a process model repository to support reuse of process models can be grouped into: *business domain perspective, modeling languages support, business process representation, business goals association* and *business environment.*

Business domain perspective. Reuse of process models imply taking a process model from the repository and using it as a starting point for modeling organization specific processes. The response from interviews indicates that a process model that is specific to a particular domain may require a lot of customization effort before it can be reused in a different domain. Therefore, a repository that is not limited to domain specific process models may increase the flexibility of sharing, modifying and therefore reusing process models.

Modeling language support. A number of process modeling languages (e.g. BPMN, EPC, and YAWL) are used for modeling business processes. These languages have different elements and control structures, therefore, specifications of a business process may vary from one language to another [16]. The interviews confirm that users of one language may not understand a process model written in another language. Therefore, the chance of process model reuse will be increased if a repository supports different modeling languages.

Business process representation. The description of a business may exist in two forms, graphical representation and textual representation. The responses from the interviews show that while it is easier to store and share processes in textual form, it is much easier for users to understand a business process in graphical representation. Therefore, providing graphical representations of business processes will increase the likelihood of understanding and reusing them.

Business goals association. The purpose of a business process is to achieve one or more goals, where a goal is a condition or state of affairs that some actor wants to hold [10]. The interviews indicate that one of the most important aspects users consider when searching for a business process is whether it can achieve a certain goal or not. Therefore, relating process models with goals can help users in understanding and thereby reusing process models.

Business process evolution. The dynamic and competitive nature of most business environments requires organizations to often change and adapt their business processes to meet specific business demands [11]. The respondents indicated that the original and adapted process should be maintained in the repository for future reuse. In addition to that, the importance of representing a business process at different levels of detail in a repository was discussed by respondents.

Business environment. The respondents indicated that in order to reuse process models it should be possible to easily locate the required process, i.e. through navigating, searching, querying, etc. In addition, it is important to know the *environment* in which a process can or is intended to work. This environment consists of the business context in which the business process can be applied, the goals of the process, and the actors of the process.

3.2 Propositions

Proposition are the suggestions for requirements on a process model repository that are derived from the analysis of the interviews. The interviews were carefully transcribed and all the issues discussed by the interviewees were listed, i.e. we were exhaustive in our approach to include all the suggestions gathered from the experts. Following that, the conflicting statements were omitted and similar statements were

Table 2. The derived propositions

ID	Propositions
P1	A domain expert can understand a process related to its domain written in any process modeling language.
P2	Experts of a process modeling language with common knowledge of a domain can understand any process model in that domain written in a language of his/her expertise.
P3	Reuse of process models can simplify the work of modeling business processes, improve modeling efficiency, and reduce the cost of modeling business processes.
P4	A process model written in one process modeling language is difficult to reuse by users of another language.
P5	Domain independent process models can be reused for modeling specific business processes in an enterprise.
P6	A graphical representation of a business process is easier to understand than a textual representation.
P7	Communication gaps between business experts and IT designers often cause problems in understanding process models.
P8	A process model repository can help reduce the gap between business experts and IT designers.
P9	A process model repository can play an important role in reusing process models.
P10	A repository can support reuse even if only fundamental elements (activities, agents, control flow) of process models are stored, i.e. composite tasks, intermediate events etc. are omitted.
P11	In a repository, it is useful to represent the same process using several process models with different levels of detail.
P12	A repository should maintain multiple versions of all its process models.
P13	The following are important to search, navigate and interpret process models in a repository. *a) Process description* *b)Business Context* *c) Business Goals* *d) Domain specific classification schemes* *e) Generic Classification Schemes* *f) Properties of processes* *g) Resources* *h) Actors* *i) Relationship between Processes*

grouped and rephrased in such a way that redundancy could be avoided. Table 2 provides the list of propositions.

4 Empirical Study

In the exploratory study only a small number of participants (five) were involved. Therefore, in order to affirm the propositions (elicited from the exploratory study), an empirical study was conducted. In this section, a brief overview of the criteria used for selection of the participants and the study procedure is presented followed by an analysis of the data collected through the empirical study.

- *Questionnaire Preparation:* For validating the propositions elicited from the interviews a questionnaire was prepared. In order to check the consistency of the questionnaire, a pilot study was conducted in which the questionnaire was sent to six participants and responses of four participants (67%) were received. Based on the feedback of the pilot study, the questionnaire was revised, i.e. the language of some questions was improved and one question was removed from the questionnaire. In addition to that, the questionnaire was divided into two sections, one related to the content of the repository and another on the repository. The questionnaire had a set of propositions and an evaluation scale from 1 to 5. 1 is for *strongly disagree*, 2 is for *disagree*, 3 is for *not sure*, 4 is for *agree* and 5 is for *strongly agree*. The design of the questionnaire allowed participants to provide additional comments on each question.
- *Conducting the Study:* The participants of the study were researchers and practitioners who attended the 2nd IFIP WG 8.1 Working Conference on The Practice of Enterprise Modeling, (PoEM'09) Stockholm, Sweden [18]. A total of 37 copies of the questionnaire were distributed and participants were asked to answer the questions. 30 participants submitted their filled questionnaire making the response rate 81%.

  During the study, participant information was kept partially anonymous i.e. personal information (name, email, etc) about participants was not collected. However, information about area of expertise was collected in order to ensure that only data from process or enterprise modeling experts was collected. Furthermore, role information (researcher / practitioner) was collected in order to distinguish between the responses from researchers and practitioners.

- *Selection of Participants:* Only the responses from participants who met the following criteria were included, a) area of expertise is process and/or enterprise modeling, b) for researchers the minimum qualification is PhD student, c) . Furthermore, incomplete responses and participants who had not marked their profession (researcher and/or practitioner) were omitted. Therefore, the empirical study includes data from 25 participants (9 practitioners and 16 researchers) i.e. 83% of the response.

4.1 Empirical Analysis

In order to validate the propositions, the data collected from the empirical study is analyzed and discussed. Furthermore, the analysis of the differences between responses from practitioners and researchers is discussed.

Propositions Analysis: For analyzing the propositions, a *frequency distribution analysis* has been used in order to identify the distribution of responses over a scale of 1 to 5 (strongly disagree to strongly agree). Graph 1 (a) shows the frequency distribution of the propositions from P1 to P12. The y-axis represents the propositions whereas the x-axis represents the percentage of the response. Different colors of the bars represent different values (1 to 5) as shown in the graph key. From the graph it is evident that a large number of participants agree (either agree or strongly agree) with

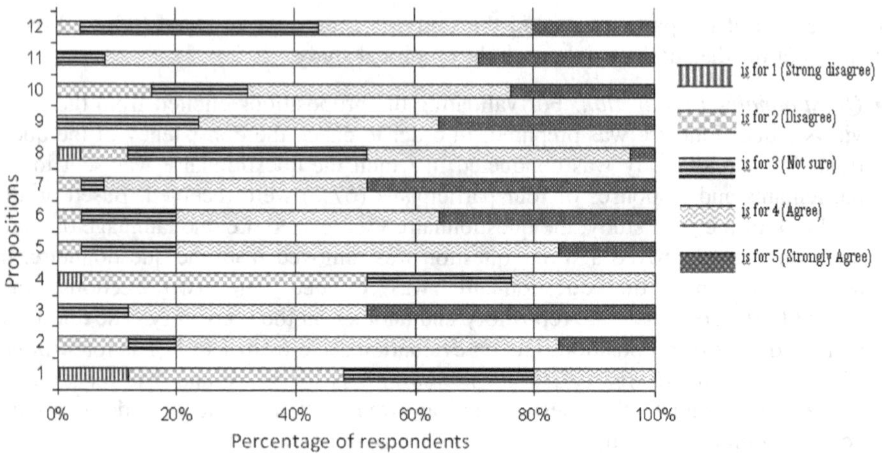

Graph 1 (a). Frequency Distributions of Propositions (P1-P12)

most of the propositions. The detailed results of the frequency distribution of each proposition are given in table 3 and important results are discussed below.

From table 3 it can be seen that a large percentage (80%) of participants agrees (either *agree* or *strongly agree*) with P2 (Experts of a process modeling language with common knowledge of a domain can understand any process model in that domain written in a language of his/her expertise). The results indicate that the understanding of a business process depends upon the knowledge of the process modeling language rather than the knowledge of the domain to which the process belongs.

88% of the participants agree with P3 (reuse of process models can simplify the work of modeling business processes, improve modeling efficiency, and reduce the cost of modeling business processes). These results are consistent with the results acquired from our exploratory study (interviews). Furthermore, some participants added that in their experience '*once modeling time of processes is reduced the saved time can be used for optimization of processes*'.

Table 3. Propositions Analysis (P1-P12)

Propositions	Strongly Disagree%	Disagree %	Not Sure %	Agree %	Strongly Agree %
P1	12	36	32	20	0
P2	0	12	8	64	16
P3	0	0	12	40	48
P4	4	48	24	24	0
P5	0	4	16	64	16
P6	0	4	16	44	36
P7	0	4	4	44	48
P8	4	8	40	44	4
P9	0	0	24	40	36
P10	0	16	16	44	24
P11	0	0	8	63	29
P12	0	4	40	36	20

More than 50% of the participants disagree with P4 (a process model written in one process modeling language is difficult to reuse by users of another language) and another 24% are not sure about P4. It means that, a process model written in one language is not difficult to reuse by users of another language. Therefore, a process model repository may support reuse for a large percentage of users even if multiple process modeling languages are not supported by the repository.

A large percentage of participants (92%) agreed with P11 (In a repository, it is useful to represent the same process using several process models with different levels of detail), whereas the remaining 8% were not sure. Therefore, the repository should support multiple views of a process (with different levels of details). The view management functionality for process repositories has also been discussed in existing studies e.g. Yan et. al. [12].

Similar to graph 1 (a), that shows the results from propositions 1 to 12, graph 1(b) shows the frequency distribution of the proposition P13 from *a* to *i*. The y-axis represents the elements of proposition 13, while the x-axis represents the percentage of the response. Different colors of the bars represent different values (1 to 5) as shown in the graph key. Graph 1 (b) reveals that a large number of participants agree (either agree or strongly agree) with most of the elements of P13. Due to space limitations the discussion on each element is not included.

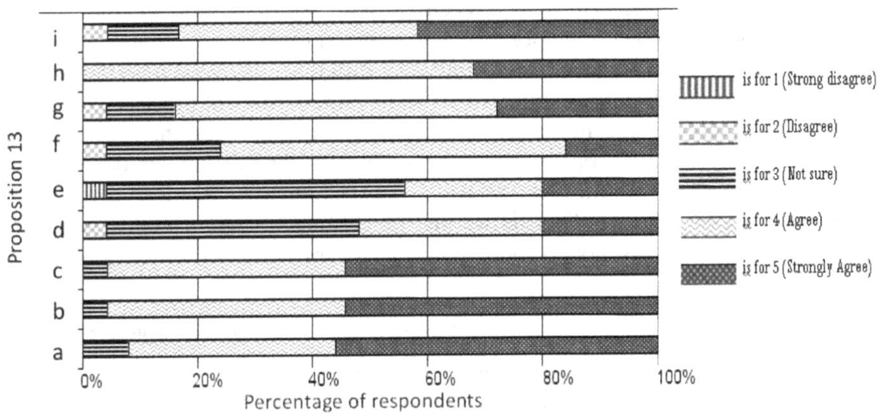

Graph 1 (b). Frequency Distributions of Proposition P13 (*a* - *i*)

Practitioners and researchers comparison: In this subsection we compare the data collected from practitioners and researchers to determine significant differences (if any). This is done by analyzing the variance between the responses from practitioners and researchers by using ANOVA test with the help of an online calculator (available at [14]). The ANOVA for unequal sample size is used for the comparison because the number of practitioners is not equal to the number of researchers. The results of the analysis are given in table 4 and the main findings are discussed below.

Table 4. Analysis of variance between practitioners & researchers

Propositions	Mean	StDev	P-Value
P1	P = 2.78, R = 2.5	P = 1.09, R = 0.89	0.263
P2	P = 3.89, R = 3.81	P = 0.78, R = 0.91	0.4143
P3	P = 4, R = 4.56	P = 0.87, R = 0.51	0.0511
P4	*P = 2.56, R = 2.75*	*P = 0.73, R = 1*	*0.2916*
P5	P = 4.11, R = 3.81	P = 0.33, R = 0.83	0.1106
P6	*P = 4.11, R = 4.13*	*P = 0.78, R = 0.89*	*0.4839*
P7	P = 4.33, R = 4.38	P = 1, R = 0.62	0.4555
P8	*P = 3.22, R = 3.44*	*P = 0.67, R = 0.96*	*0.2586*
P9	P = 3.78, R = 4.31	P = 0.83, R = 0.70	0.0631
P10	*P = 3.78, R = 3.75*	*P = 1.09, R = 1*	*0.4751*
P11	P = 3.89, R = 4.12	P = 0.33, R = 1.26	0.2442
P12	*P = 3.78, R = 3.69*	*P = 0.67, R = 0.95*	*0.3921*

Where, *P is for practitioners* *R is for researchers.*

Graph 2 shows that a significant difference exists between practitioners and researchers in supporting P3 (reuse of process models can simplify the work of modeling processes, improve efficiency and reduce modeling cost). Furthermore, from table 4 it can be seen that the deviation in response between practitioners (StDev = 0.87) is less than that of researchers (StDev = 0.51), which implies that researchers are more confident about P3. Therefore, it is likely that the reuse of process models is more accepted by the research community than among practitioners.

From graph 3, it can be seen that a significant difference between practitioners and researchers exists on the acceptability of P5 (domain independent process models can be reused for modeling specific processes). i.e. in contrast to researchers all practitioners affirm the proposition. Furthermore, from table 4 it can be seen that the deviation in response between practitioners (StDev = 0.33) is significantly less than that of researchers (StDev = 0.83). This shows that practitioners are prepared to adapt domain independent process models more than researchers.

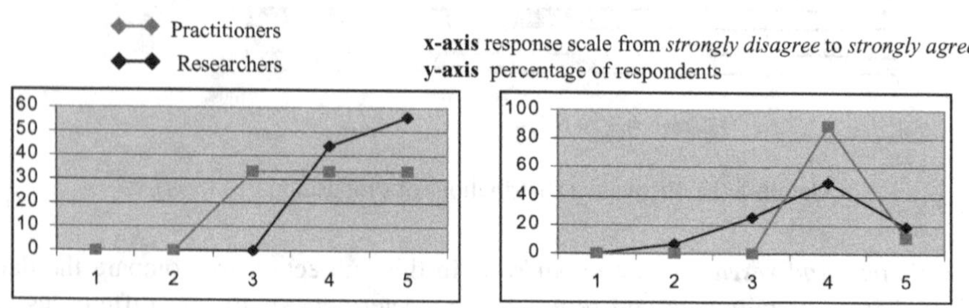

Graph 2. Researchers & Practitioners Comparison on P3

Graph 3. Researchers & Practitioners Comparison on P5

Another point of significant difference between researchers and practitioners is the ability of repository to search, navigate and interpret process models based on generic classification schemes (P13). *Open EDI phases* and *Porter value chain* are the examples of generic classification schemes. Graph 4 reveals that researchers support the use of generic classification schemes more strongly than practitioners. However, from the literature the use of classification schemes for categorizing business processes is advocated [9, 13, 17] as a mean to facilitate navigation.

Graph 5 reveals that, while both practitioners and researchers accept the use of relationship between processes for supporting navigation, practitioners strongly agree as compared to researchers.

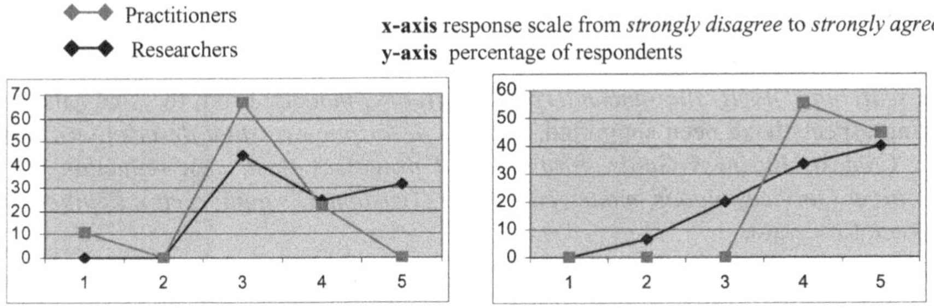

Graph 4. Researchers & Practitioners Comparison P17

Graph 5. Researchers & Practitioners Comparison P21

5 Requirements of Process Model Repository

Primarily based on the analysis of the empirical study and secondarily on the exploratory study, we define the following requirements for a process model repository. It is notable that the presented requirements can be extended and adapted based on the primary purpose of the repository.

Requirement 1: The repository should be able to store process models in at least one process modeling language. In other words, to provide reusable process models it is not necessary for a repository to store process models in more than one language. This requirement is based on the response to P4 (A process model written in one process modelling language is difficult to reuse by users of another language).

Requirement 2: The repository should allow storing process models regardless of their domain, i.e. both domain specific and generic process models. This requirement is based on the response to P5 (Domain independent process models can be reused for modeling specific business processes in an enterprise).

Requirement 3: Process models in the repository should be represented in both graphical and textual form. This requirement is based on the response to P6 (a graphical representation of a business process is easier to understand than a textual representation) and the comments (see section 4.1).

Requirement 4: The repository should store both business and process models. The proposition P7 (Communication gap between business experts and IT designers often cause problems in understanding process models), has been affirmed by the empirical study. Furthermore, it has been supported by half of the participants that a repository may bridge the gap.

Requirement 5: In the repository a business process should be represented by several process models having different levels of detail. This requirement is based on the response to P11 (In a repository, it is useful to represent the same process using several process models having different levels of detail).

Requirement 6: The repository should allow maintaining multiple variants of a process model. This requirement is based on the response to P12 (A repository should maintain multiple versions of all its process models). This requirement may also hold for other types of repositories.

Requirement 7: A process model should be annotated with information that can facilitate searching, navigating and interpreting process models. From the study the following aspects have been supported, *Process description (textual description), Business Context, Business Goals, Properties of processes (fast, cost reduction, etc.), Resources (services, goods, money etc), Actors (customer, supplier, etc), Relationship between Processes.*

Requirement 8: Process models in the repository should be categorized based on different classification schemes to facilitate navigation. This requirement is based on the literature study, exploratory study, and it has been partially affirmed by the empirical study.

There also exist several generic requirements for any repository, for example, multiuser environment, consistency management, content management, configuration management, check-in and check-out, interoperability with other repositories etc. However, in this study only the specific requirements for a process model repository were addressed.

6 Conclusion

The aim of this paper was to collect a set of requirements for a business process model repository based on stakeholders needs. This was done by collecting initial results from an exploratory study (interviews) and validating the results through an empirical study (survey). In addition, the differences and commonalities between practitioners and researchers were discussed. Based on the analysis of the empirical and the exploratory study, a set of requirements for process model repositories were suggested.

From the study the following can be concluded, a) support of several modeling languages by the repository is not a major requirement in reusing process models, b) reuse of process models can simplify the work of modeling business processes, c) as the requirements are collected and discussed from practitioners perspective a repository that fulfills these requirements can be used by both researchers and practitioners, d) the presented requirements are not necessarily complete and can be extended based on the aim of a repository.

Future research aims at identifying principles for populating, maintaining and using a process model repository. More work is also required, a) to validate the collected requirements from a large number of users, b) to collect requirements from the remaining stakeholders of the repository, c) to identify the aspects needed for characterizing processes in a repository. Using metadata for annotating process models that can be used for searching, understanding and navigating process models in the repository is another future research direction.

References

[1] Markovic, I.: Towards a Formal Framework for Reuse in Business Process Modeling. In: ter Hofstede, A.H.M., Benatallah, B., Paik, H.-Y. (eds.) BPM Workshops 2007. LNCS, vol. 4928, pp. 484–495. Springer, Heidelberg (2008)

[2] Hornung, T., Koschmider, A., Oberweis, A.: A Recommender System for Business Process Models. In: Proceedings of the 17th Annual Workshop on Information Technology and Systems (WITS 2007), Montreal, Canada, pp. 127–132 (2007)

[3] Rodrigues, J.A., Souza, J.M., Zimbrao, G., Xexeo, G., Neves, E., Pinheiro, W.A.: A P2P Approach for Business Process Modelling and Reuse. In: Eder, J., Dustdar, S. (eds.) BPM Workshops 2006. LNCS, vol. 4103, pp. 297–307. Springer, Heidelberg (2006)

[4] Ma, Z., Leymann, F.: A Lifecycle Model for Using Process Fragment in Business Process Modeling. In: Proceedings of the 9th International Workshop on Business Process Modeling, Development and Support (BPMDS 2008), held in conjunction with CAiSE 2008, Montpellier, France (2008)

[5] MIT Process Handbook, `http://process.mit.edu/Directory.asp?ID=114&Expand=92` (last accessed December 14, 2009)

[6] Phios Process Repository for Supply Chain Management, `http://repository.phios.com/SCOR/Activity.asp?ID=5316` (last accessed December 14, 2009)

[7] SAP Business Map, `http://help.sap.com/saphelp_sm40/helpdata/EN/5e/c8145e3a9d93 40913099159d80fc87/frameset.htm` (last accessed December 14, 2009)

[8] IBM Process Repository, `http://publib.boulder.ibm.com/infocenter/wchelp/v5r6m1/ index.jsp?topic=/com.ibm.commerce.business_process.doc/ concepts/processPrice_order.htm` (last accessed December 14, 2009)

[9] Shahzad, K., Andersson, B., Bergholtz, M., Edirisuriya, A., Illayperuma, T., Jayaweera, P., Johannesson, P.: Elicitation of Requirements for a Business process Model Repository. In: Ardagna, D., et al. (eds.) BPM 2008 Workshops. LNBIP, vol. 17, pp. 42–53. Springer, Heidelberg (2009)

[10] Edirisuriya, A.: Design Support for e-Commerce Information Systems using Goal, Business and Process Modelling. PhD Thesis, at the Department of Computer and Systems Science, Stockholm University (September 2009) ISSN 1101-8526

[11] Zhao, X., Liu, C.: Version Management in the Business Process Change Context. In: Alonso, G., Dadam, P., Rosemann, M. (eds.) BPM 2007. LNCS, vol. 4714, pp. 198–213. Springer, Heidelberg (2007)

[12] Yan, Z., Dijkman, R., Grefen, P.: Business Process Model Repositories - Framework and Survey. In: Beta Working Papers, vol. 292. Eindhoven University of Technology (2009)

[13] The UN/CEFACT Common Business Process Catalog (CBPC). Technical Specification, Version 1.0. (2009), `http://www.uncefactforum.org/TBG/TBG14/TBG14Documents/ cbpc-technical-specification-v1_0-300905-11.pdf` (last accessed December 14, 2009)

[14] ANAOVA Calculator (2009), `http://www.usablestats.com/calcs/2samplet` (last accessed December 14, 2009)

[15] Peck, R., Olsen, C., Devore, J.: Introduction to Statistics and Data Analysis, 3rd edn. Cengage Learning, Inc., USA (2008)

[16] List, B., Korherr, B.: An Evaluation of Conceptual Business Process Modelling Languages. In: Proceedings of the 21st ACM Symposium on Applied Computing (SAC 2006), Dijon, France, pp. 1532–1539 (2006)

[17] Shang, G., Krogstie, J.: A Combined Framework for Development of Business Process Support. In: Persson, A., Stirna, J. (eds.) Proceedings of the 2nd IFIP WG8.1 Working Conference on the Practice of Enterprise Modeling (PoEM 2009), Stockholm, Sweden. LNBIP, vol. 39, pp. 115–129. Springer, Heidelberg (2009)

[18] `http://poem.dsv.su.se/` (last accessed December 14, 2009)

Supporting Complex Business Information Systems
A Case Study Focusing on Incidents, Recovery and Evolution

Oliver Daute[1] and Stefan Conrad[2]

[1] SAP Deutschland AG & Co. KG
oliver.daute@sap.com
[2] Heinrich Heine University Düsseldorf
conrad@cs.uni-duesseldorf.de

Abstract. Maintainability is fundamental to keeping business information systems alive and making evolution possible. Steadily increasing functionalities lead to giant networked application landscapes which need to be maintained. A failure in one part can rapidly impair the whole landscape and harm the business. Maintainability is a critical issue and new approaches are required to keep complex landscapes under control. Lack of information together with unknown dependencies is only one problem to be named. Missing control is another one. We present a framework for monitoring and controlling process execution, which allows the prevention of a new process from being started when the applications needed are not available; it also allows the identification of the best recovery point.

Keywords: RT-BCDB, PAC, Incident, Landscape Recovery, Evolution.

1 Introduction

Maintainability is an important quality aspect for availability, reliability and evolution of enterprise solutions [11, 18]. Hence, the interests of system maintenance must be given more weight in all phases of the software lifecycle management, starting from the blueprint to the obsolescence and replacement of applications. Right now these are neglected and most frameworks are focused on business requirements. They have been used to improve the design of enterprise solutions significantly. But too little information can be found about how to run business solutions and maintain them in operation. Our concepts and ideas [5] [3] [4] provide useful knowledge for the entire software lifecycle of deployed applications. The focus lies on the support of system administration and maintenance of large enterprise solutions.

Maintainability requires transparency and control of activities within application landscapes [3, 9, 13]. We introduced '*Real-Time Business Case Database*' (RT-BCDB) [5] and '*Process Activity Control*' (PAC) [4] to gain more details and more control. RT-BCDB is a knowledge base which concentrates on information about business process activities, run-state information and dependencies between processing units or applications. PAC controls processes activities which are running on an application landscape. The control instance uses the information of RT-BCDB and collects run-states of processes. We will give a short description next.

W. Abramowicz and R. Tolksdorf (Eds.): BIS 2010, LNBIP 47, pp. 171–182, 2010.

This case study is a proof of concepts. We choose two challenging support scenarios, landscape recovery and avoidance of incidents. Incidents can cause further faults, impair other processes and are able to harm the business tremendously. Users are hindered in their work, causing less productivity. Faults can lead to indeterminate and unclear processing states. Landscape recovery is always an exceptional situation and therefore it considers the side effects of faults for an application landscape. The system administration has to react purposefully to identify swiftly the cause of an incident, their dependencies, impaired business processes or faulty processing units. On the basis of chosen scenarios, we will show how *'RT-BCDB & PAC'* improve maintainability of enterprise landscapes.

2 Related Work

Complexity of application landscapes is driven by business requirements, integrated and distributed software as well as lack of information. Complexity is of interest for enterprise architectures or service frameworks, like SOA [17], IT Service Management [9] or TOGAF [20]. The design and implementation process of solutions has improved [12, 16] but administration issues have been neglected. Business scenarios can be created easily by combining different functionalities of the landscape, but little information is given about how to support them in operation.

	Focus	Status	Process Control	Optimization	Landscape Recovery	Evolution
ITIL	Services Management	Services	Services	Yes	No	Yes
SOA	Service Architecture	No	No	Yes	No	Yes
TOGAF	Architecture Framework	No	No	Yes	No	Yes
PAC	Process Control	No	Yes	Yes	Yes / No	No
RT-BCDB	Transparency Maintenance	Yes	Yes / No	Yes	Yes	Yes

Fig. 1. Complementary Concepts for Enterprise Solutions Design & Support

Figure 1 depicts a summary of complementary concepts and frameworks, whereas the first three are focused on the design of IT architectures or service management. The last two focus on process control, transparency and maintenance of enterprise solutions. RT-BCDB provides a repository of business processes running in distributed application environments. It contains also information on activities and dependencies and creates a virtual image of a landscape's business processing but is not restricted to standards. Business processes or activities can be of different types. It is not of interest what a specific activity does. RT-BCDB delivers information to support different kinds of maintenance scenarios, for instance landscape recovery. Control applications like

PAC can make use of this information as well. The communication between processes and PAC & RT-BCDB is based on simple mechanisms.

Other repositories like SOA provide standardized services. Complex services can be created by orchestration. Often standardized data types, process components and business objects are used. Communication or data exchange run over open standards like WDSL, SOAP and XML. The aim of SOA repository is to provide reusable, structured and easily callable services for business usage.

Landscape recovery differs from database recovery. The aim is to reset a landscape on business process level to a consistent state after a failure. This ensures logical data integrity with possibly many databases being involved. Activities of landscape recovery can enclose database recoveries and restart of faulty or halting processes.

To improve maintainability and reliability of application landscapes researchers investigate issues regarding availability [1], evolvability [2, 14, 15], longevity [1, 3] and maintenance [10, 11, 18]. The challenge is to find better mechanisms to manage business application solutions and reduce the operation costs [8].

3 Terminology

Real-Time Business Case Database is an approach to collecting and providing information about business processes and applications in large heterogeneous application landscapes in order to improve transparency and visibility of activities. An instance of RT-BCDB is depicted in Fig. 2. RT-BCDB is an open knowledge base reflecting the need to support and improve maintenance scenarios for large environments. RT-BCDB stores information about business scenarios, processes, process owners, run-states, history of previous processing, frequency of executions, run-time, landscape dependencies and availabilities of processing units and applications. Information about run-states is important for determining the current state of processes activities within an environment. The knowledge acquired is also of interest to the business designers and application supporters. Data of RT-BCDB supports system updates, landscape recovery or optimization of deployed resources.

Business processes are seen as objects. It is not of interest what a specific business process does within a landscape. This view to business processes reduces the need to know what a single process does. RT-BCDB contains process run-states like *active*, *successful* or *failed*.

System failures must be investigated in detail regarding the impact beore a landscape recovery can take place for it to be possible to set back the application landscape to a consistent state. Processes which were impaired must be identified and have to be included into the recovery procedures. Here, the data of RT-BCDB is essential for the analysis and restoration phase. It is also indispensable for reporting and changing a landscape. Above all, business processes with user interaction and those which change data are focused by the concept. In general, this could be extended to support any processing types. But the effort will increase significantly and may have an impact on the overall processing time. For the moment it should be restricted to business process of core type.

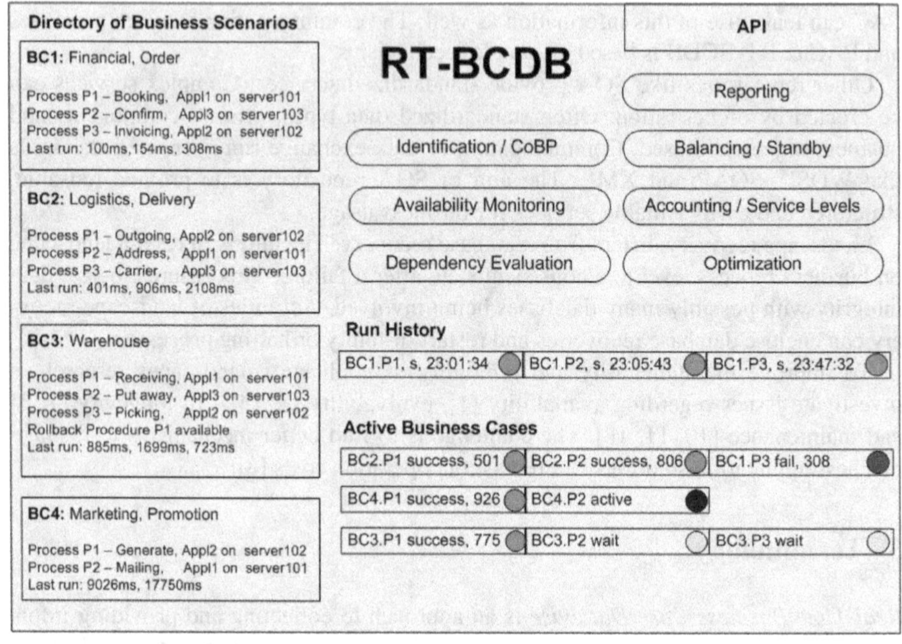

Fig. 2. RT-BCDB: Source of information on current and past process activities

Agents are part of RT-BCDB architecture (Fig. 3). They inspect different sources and try to identify run-states and availabilities of applications and processing units. The information is stored synchronously and reflects the current states.

Process Activity Control [4] is an approach to having power over processes in order to reduce incidents and to gain better control of application landscapes activities. PAC steers processes which are currently active. This is necessary to avoid indeterminate processing states which can impair the entire enterprise solution. PAC avoids the start of business scenarios when problems of applications in use are known. To interact with application processes, PAC uses '*RunControl*' commands. PAC receives a message or '*Request to Run*', RtR from a process whenever it changes its run-state. The message contains process-ID and run-state. After receiving, PAC decides about further processing and sends a '*Commit to Run*', CtR to proceed.

Minimum requirements for business processes communication are summarized in the C*ode of Business Processes, CoBP* [4]. Various situations arise in distributed application environments because of a missing form of identification. These situations are difficult to handle in case of faults. The code contains general rules and requirements for processes when running within an application environment. Besides unique identification, CoBP requires process documentation and a recovery procedure for it. A rule of CoBP, for instance, demands that communication between processes must always take place along traceable ways.

Used terms: An *application landscape* can consist of solitary and integrated applications, like legacy systems, ERPs, data warehouses and middleware for exchanging data and connecting applications. A *business scenario* is a sequence of process activities to fulfill specific tasks, for instance storage inventory. Business scenarios are subdivided into different parts or (sub)*-activities and make use of different applications and databases across an entire landscape. A *business process* encapsulates a single task that, for example, reads data or supplies results to users or other processes. Processes should have an easily identifiable structure [19], see CoBP [3]. Processes with a high significance for an enterprise are called *core business processes.* An *enterprise solution* is an application landscape, built up of several software components and databases. It is designed on the basis of business requirements. All business scenarios determine the purpose of an enterprise solution.

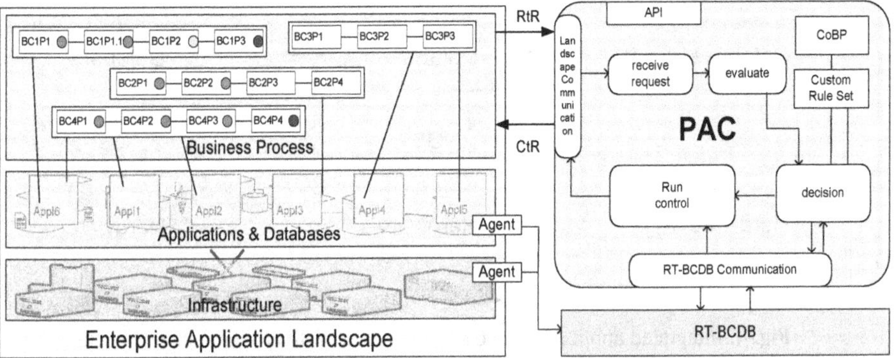

Fig. 3. PAC controls execution of business processes in distributed application environments

4 Maintainability

In distributed environments applications are often installed on stacks with their own operating, database systems and additional software packages. Business scenarios, as shown in figure 4, make use of these application stacks, by starting processes across the landscape and changing data. Due to the scenarios, the stacks are linked together on the business process level. Maintenance scenarios are more complex and *multi-dimensional* in these environments. The picture shows two dimensions, *vertical* and *horizontal.* And there is one more, *time.* Dependencies between application stacks are not always obvious, but support scenarios have to consider them.

Vertical dimension is related to the maintenance of a single stack from the level of hardware to its applications. In general, this dimension is easier to maintain. *Horizontal* dimension needs to be considered whenever applications must be changed in their version or behavior. Then, linked stacks may need to be adapted too. The reason, a change can alter run prerequisites of business scenarios. Therefore details about interdependencies between stacks and using processes are needed before maintenance scenarios can be performed. *Time* dimension: In general, it is not possible to implement changes all at once. Changes are done one by one while the enterprise landscape is in operation. Users might try to access these applications consciously or unconsciously. A control mechanism is required to protect parts of an application landscape which are currently under construction or maintenance.

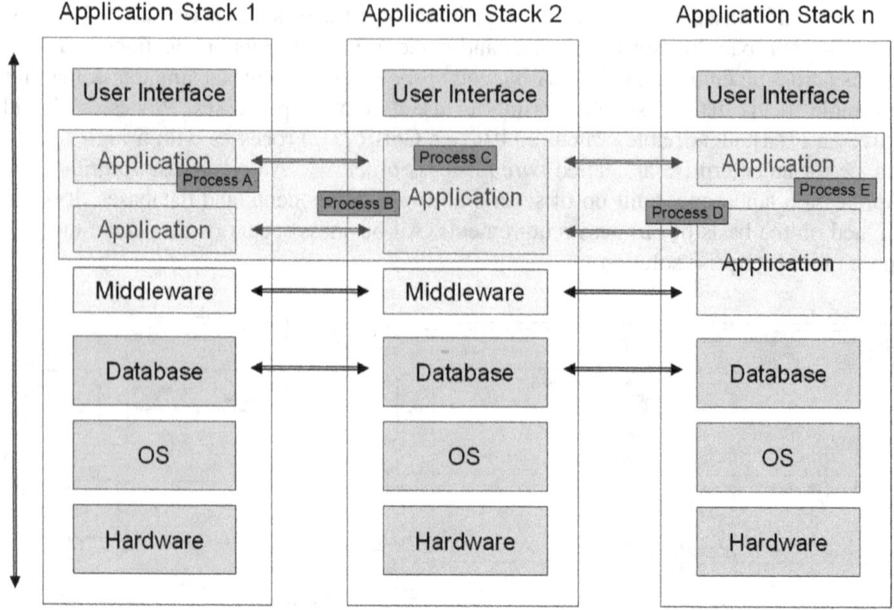

Fig. 4. Integrated application landscape consists of diverse application stacks

RT-BCDB monitors constantly business scenarios and archives the information of past activities. Dependencies can be derived, creating a virtual image of interdependencies between applications, processing units and business processes. Next, we will show how RT-BCDB & PAC improve maintenance scenarios in the horizontal and time dimensions.

5 Case Study's Scenario

The case study's example consists of three heterogeneous applications, their databases and four business scenarios of an imaginary enterprise solution. Each business scenario makes use of one or more applications and consists of several processes. Details about processes are provided by RT-BCDB (Fig. 2). The showcase (Fig. 5) is a visualization of this data. It reflects the current run-states of business processes and applications. Without RT-BCDB, the current circumstances of the assumed failure would be really difficult to determine.

$BC1, BC2, BC3, BC4 \in \overline{BC}$ $\qquad \overline{BC}$, domain of all business scenarios

$Appl1, Appl2, Appl3 \in \overline{AP}$ $\qquad \overline{AP}$, domain of all business scenarios

$BCn := \{BCnP1, .., BCnPm\}$ $\qquad n, m \in \overline{N}$, definition of a business scenario

We assume that following situation has occurred in the landscape when *Appl3* has stopped processing due to a fault. Here are the facts:

i. Application *Appl3* failed, no further use of this application is possible, database recovery is required
ii. *BC2-P3* was active on *Appl3* when failure occurred and fails too
iii. *BC3* starts a process *BC3-P1* on application *Appl1* and tries to trigger a successor process *BC3-P2* on application *Appl3*
iv. *BC3-P2* failed when trying to process on application *Appl3*
v. *BC4-P1* finished successfully its processing on application *Appl3*
vi. *BC4-P2* is currently active on application *Appl2*

To discuss the benefits of RT-BCDB & PAC we will use diverse criteria to evaluate aspects regarding: *data consistency* on business process level (data integrity), *user wait* (hindered or can proceed), *process state* is determined and known, *run options* are available (e.g. alternate processing path), *landscape recovery* is supported, *reaction time* of system administration, *cost for a single incident* to repair (effort for fault identification, concept implementation) and *cost for multiple incidents* (return of investments). To estimate each aspect, values are *No*, *Yes*, *Low* and *High*.

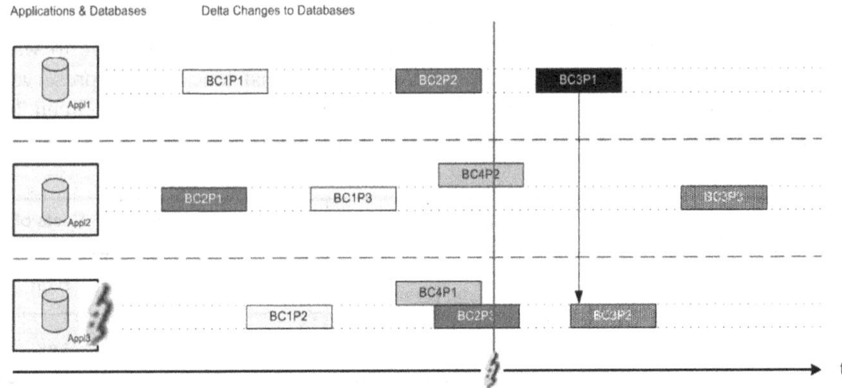

Fig. 5. Showcase: A failure of application Appl3 and its implications (source: RT-BCDB)

6 Avoiding Incidents

Frequently, incidents within an enterprise solution interrupt the business and derogate productivity. Incidents can be avoided by use of control mechanisms. Business scenarios trying to access unavailable applications must fail. A malfunction of just one processing unit can cause many additional incidents which can result in uncompleted business processes and unclear processing states. Execution of previous processes have possibly modified data or invoked communication processes. These changes must be identified and eventually set back to retain data consistency on business process level. To prove our concepts we have to distinguish between two cases. One case describes what would happen in application environments without the use of the concepts and the other when concepts are connected and in operation. Finally, we will emphasize the benefits by valuation the aforementioned criteria. Relating to our showcase (Fig. 5), at t_0 the application *Appl3* terminates with a failure.

Case A), the following will happen when PAC & RT-BCDB is not in use:

- At t_1 *BC3* starts processing on application *Appl1* (Fig.5, iii).
- At t_2 a successor process of *BC3* tries to start a task on application *Appl3* and must fail (Fig.5, iv).
- **Summary:** Business scenario *BC3* cannot be completed and users have to wait. *BC3* hangs in an uncompleted processing state with changes already made on of *Appl1*. The business scenario must wait until application *Appl3* is recovered and changes to *Appl1* are set back. Only after that can users of *BC3* proceed with their work.

Case B), PAC & RT-BCDB are connected and in use:

- At t_1 *BC3* send a '*Request to Run*' to PAC. PAC reads RT-BCDB whether any problems are known which could hinder *BC3* performing its tasks.
- RT-BCDB verifies applications used by *BC3* and dependencies. RT-BCDB discovers that *Appl3* is not available and returns this information to PAC immediately.
- PAC will prevent *BC3* from performing processing on *Appl1*.
- **Summary:** The business scenario is stopped by PAC and users have to wait. No changes have been made on *Appl1* and data consistency is still preserved. If an alternate sequence of applications for processing exists then *BC3* can "*be redirect along another path*" and users do not have to wait.

PAC & RT-BCDB	Data Consistent	User Waits	Process State	Run Options	Recovery Support	Costs of Single Inc.	Costs of Multi Inc.
without	No	Yes	No	No	No	Low	High
using	Yes	Yes / No	Yes	Yes	Yes	High	Low

Fig. 6. Evaluation 1: Avoiding Incidents using PAC & RT-BCDB

PAC acts proactively and is able to minimize aftereffects due to an incident. The advantages are obvious. (a) Data integrity is given. No changes of *Appl1's* data have been made and data consistency remains. (b) *BC3* was not allowed to start processing and further user interaction was prevented. When using PAC, run options like an alternate processing path can be offered (d). Otherwise users have to wait until *Appl3* is recovered or changes to *Appl1* have been restored.

Process states are known (c) when RT-BCDB is connected. This makes it much easier for system administration to react purposefully to the aggravating circumstances of an error. Otherwise, process states have to be determined at the time when problems are occurring. This is time consuming and prevents reacting swiftly to overcome the incidents. More difficulties to be mentioned are the diverse applications' monitoring tools which often provide different, not always comparable views on business processing and make the determination of process run-states complicated.

PAC supports the recovery process (e). While restoration of the landscape takes place, further processes may try to access application *Appl3*. PAC protects those parts of the landscape meanwhile and so supports maintainability on the time dimension. Without PAC users or processes would try to access *Appl3* and risk their own failure.

Implementation expenses for PAC & RT-BCDB are high for single incidents (f). And for uncritical business systems these concepts are also too expensive. But critical business scenarios, especially in large business information systems, have to be available and supported permanently. The avoidance of each single failure saves time and money for identification and resolving inconsistencies.

PAC benefits from detailed information collected by RT-BCDB. This information provides an image of process activities and dependencies. PAC supports maintenance tasks on the horizontal dimension. Additional information can be given to PAC as a criterion for the decision. The *Custom Rule Set* offers an option to announce events or to change the behavior of business processing. Timeframes for maintenance can be specified or the provisioning of additional resources, like standby systems, can be given notice of. The way to steer processing varies according to priorities or the naming of business processes which are to have a special preference. PAC works as an outer control mechanism and is especially useful for the control of core business processes. PAC can also support the start-up or shut-down procedure of application landscapes or parts of it.

7 Landscape Recovery

Landscape recovery is the second challenging support scenario to check. The main focus is put on data integrity on business process level of a distributed decentralized application environments. From the perspective of a business scenario, a consistent state requires more than data integrity of each application database involved. A single business process is able to trigger process activities across the landscape, uses diverse applications, databases and servers. If a failure occurs in the environment, then this process and several other business processes might be impaired. Those can halt anywhere in an application environment in an inconsistent state. These need to be discovered and considered before landscape recovery with all its dependencies can take place. Landscape recovery encapsulates the identification of impaired business processes, the consideration of dependencies, the restart of single business processes and the recovery of single databases, if necessary. As shown in figure 4, landscape recovery aims at the horizontal maintenance level in contrast to database recovery, which focuses on the vertical level. After the determination of faulty applications and affected processes, landscape recovery resets data of related applications to a logically consistent state. Knowledge provided by RT-BCDB is required once again. Initial situation: Application *Appl3* failed, database and landscape recovery is required.

Case A), without support of PAC & RT-BCDB:

- No detailed information about the current state of processes and applications is available. Dependencies between applications or processes are probably unknown.
- Impaired business scenarios have to be identified due to the failure of *Appl3*
- Meanwhile *BC3* starts processing on application *Appl1* (Fig.5, iii)
- A process of *BC3* tries to start a task on *Appl3* and fails (iv).

- **Summary:** The determination of the current circumstances is time consuming. Meanwhile avoidable aftereffects are occurring. System administration has to collect information about impaired processes. Users are hindered and have to wait until *Appl3* is restored. *BC4-P1 has* finished shortly before failure and triggered a successor process on *Appl2*. This information is not visible. The right point-in-time for recovery of *Appl3* is difficult to determine.

Case B), PAC & RT-BCDB are connected and in use:

- Information about process activities and dependencies is available
- At t_1 *BC3* sends a '*Request to Run*' to PAC (Fig 3).
- PAC evaluates the request and checks if any faults are known and if necessary applications are available. Because *Appl3* is unavailable, PAC will refuse to send a '*Commit to Run*' (Fig 3). The start of *BC3* is prevented (see avoiding incidents).
- The best point-in-time has to be determined for the database recovery of *Appl3*. The impaired business scenarios need to be considered. A look at RT-BCDB provides the following information:
    - *BC4-P1 has* finished recently and its successor *BC4-P2* has started on *Appl2*. To preserve data integrity, the best time for recovery is right after the termination of *BC4-P1*.
    - *BC2-P3* was active (ii) and must be restarted after database recovery
- **Summary:** States of business processes are available. Impaired business scenarios can be identified easily due to the visualization of RT-BCDB. Only *Appl3* must be restored and *BC2-P3* needs to be restarted. PAC ensures that no business scenarios will access *Appl3* while it is under reconstruction. This prevents further incidents.

PAC & RT-BCDB	React swiftly	State Overview	Ensure Integrity	Landscape Recovery	Cost of Single Inc.	Cost of Multi Incidents
without	No	No	No	No	Low	High
using	Yes	Yes	Yes	Yes	High	Low

Fig. 7. Evaluation 2: Landscape Recovery using PAC & RT-BCDB

System administration can react swiftly (a) right after the fault has occurred. Without RT-BCDB & PAC, administration has to determine in a costly manner the current conditions. State overview (b) is known and enables the determination of affected processes. RT-BCDB and PAC allow performing landscape recovery and ensure data integrity on the horizontal level (c, d). The evaluation of the criterion "cost of implementation and introducing" (e, f) is the same as mentioned above.

8 Evolution

Further development and maintainability are important features of business information systems. Once again information about versions of deployed software, their usage and dependencies, is a prerequisites. To describe roughly the theme of further development, we will give some examples.

The update of an application may result in the updating of dependent applications. To find dependencies, business scenarios making use that application need to be investigated. Applications that exchange data or communicate with it must be checked if an update has an impact on the functionality of business scenarios. If so, then dependent applications need to be updated too or the original update must be canceled. If no dependencies exist, the update is feasible without any additional effort.

Optimization is another example of accelerating processing, reducing costs or identifying *Single-Point of Failures, SPoF*. Weaknesses in the communication between processes are also focused on. SPoF and weaknesses can be derived easily by evaluating dependencies between applications, processes and processing units. If an application *Applx* is used by most business scenarios then this can become a potential SPoF. In particular, if the application is accessed by many business scenarios at the same time, then this can paralyze the whole enterprise landscape.

PAC & RT-BCDB provide mechanisms for landscape evolution. The detection of dependencies is only one important feature of RT-BCDB to be mentioned (Fig. 2). The protection and control are further advantages.

9 Conclusion

We demonstrated that RT-BCDB & PAC are able to improve landscape maintainability significantly. The reasons why those concepts are only partially implemented vary. Communication and implementation of business processes differ greatly from manufacturer to manufacturer. Their products are only partially applicable to heterogeneous application environments, like Clouds [22].

Landscape recovery, unlike database recovery, requires more details about the activities on a more comparable level, no matter who developed an application. Standardization of communication of business scenarios and control mechanisms must to be strengthened. They will have an impact on software design and also on development. CoBP is a small step forward in defining a frame for those requirements. The constantly growing complexity of enterprise landscapes is the number one cause of failure today [7] and requires better mechanisms for the future design and support of applications. The real challenge is gaining control and preventing a single failure from being able to halt the whole thing.

SAP AG has started investigations into the design and implementation of these concepts and tools.

References

1. Alonso, J., Torres, J., Gavaldà, R.: Predicting web server crashes: A case study in comparing prediction algorithms. In: ICAS The Fifth International Conference on Autonomic and Autonomous Systems (2009)
2. Côté, I., Heisel, M.: Supporting Evolution by Models, Components and Patterns. In: 1. Workshop des GI-Arbeitskreises Langlebige Softwaresysteme (L2S2), vol. 537 (2009) ISSN 1613-0073, `http://CEUR-WS.org`

3. Daute, O., Conrad, S.: Maintainability and control of long-lived enterprise solutions. In: 1. Workshop des GI-Arbeitskreises Langlebige Softwaresysteme (L2S2), vol. 537 (2009) ISSN 1613-0073, http://CEUR-WS.org
4. Daute, O., Conrad, S.: Activity Control in Application Landscapes. In: 1st Intl. Conference on Cloud Computing. Cloudcomp 2009. LNICST, vol. 34, pp. 83–92. Springer, Heidelberg (2009)
5. Daute, O.: Introducing Real-Time Business CASE Database, Approach to improving system maintenance of complex application landscapes. In: ICEIS 11th Conference on Enterprise Information Systems (2009)
6. Daute, O.: Representation of Business Information Flow with an Extension for UML. In: ICEIS 6th Conference on Enterprise Information Systems (2004)
7. Economist Intelligence Unit: Coming to grips with IT risk, A report from the Economist Intelligence Unit, White Paper (2007)
8. Gartner Research Group: TCO, Total Cost of Ownership, Information Technology Research (1987), http://www.gartner.com
9. ITIL, IT Infrastructure Library, ITSMF, Information Technology Service Management Forum, http://www.itsmf.net
10. Kobbacy, Khairy, A.H., Murthy, Prabhakar, D.N.: Complex System Maintenance Handbook. Springer Series in Reliability Engineering (2008)
11. O'Neill, G.: Maintainability: Theory and Practice. In: NASA ISHEM Conference (2005)
12. Papazoglou, M., Heuvel, J.: Service oriented architectures: approaches, technologies and research issues. In: International Journal on Very Large Data Bases (2007)
13. Rosemann, M.: Process-oriented Administration of Enterprise Systems, ARC SPIRT project, Queensland University of Technology (2003)
14. Riebisch, M., Bode, S.: Software-Evolvability. In: GI Informatik Spektrum, Technische Universität Ilmenau, vol. 32 4 (2009)
15. Riebisch, M., Brcina, R., Bode, S.: Optimisation Process for Maintaining Evolvability during Software Evolution. In: ECBS (2009)
16. Schelp, J.: Winter, Robert: Business Application Design and Enterprise Service Design: A Comparison. Int. J. Service Sciences 3(4) (2008)
17. SOA: Reference Model for Service Oriented Architecture Committee Specification (2006), http://www.oasis-open.org
18. Stammel, J., Reussner, R.: Karlsruhe Architectural Maintainability Prediction. In: 1. Workshop des GI-Arbeitskreises Langlebige Softwaresysteme, L2S2, vol. 537 (2009), http://CEUR-WS.org ISSN 1613-0073
19. Svatoš, O.: Conceptual Process Modeling Language: Regulative Approach, Department of Information Technologies, University of Economics, Czech Republic (2007)
20. TOGAF, 9.0: The Open Group Architecture Framework, Vendor- and technology-neutral consortium, The Open GROUP (2009), http://www.togaf.org
21. UML: Unified Modeling Language, Not-for-profit computer industry consortium, Object Management Group, http://www.omg.org
22. Vouk, M.: Cloud Computing – Issues, Research and Implementations. In: Proceedings of the 30th International Conference on Information Technology Interfaces (2008)

On Integrating Data Mining into Business Processes

Dennis Wegener and Stefan Rüping

Fraunhofer IAIS, Schloss Birlinghoven, 53754 Sankt Augustin, Germany
{dennis.wegener,stefan.rueping}@iais.fraunhofer.de

Abstract. Integrating data mining into business processes becomes crucial for business today. Modern business process management frameworks provide great support for flexible design, deployment and management of business processes. However, integrating complex data mining services into such frameworks is not trivial due to unclear definitions of user roles and missing flexible data mining services as well as missing standards and methods for the deployment of data mining solutions. This work contributes an integrated view on the definition of user roles for business, IT and data mining and discusses the integration of data mining in business processes and its evaluation in the context of BPR.

Keywords: Data Mining, Business Processes, Integration, BPM, CRISP.

1 Introduction

The capability of data analysis is a crucial factor of success for business today. Main parts of the business world are based on IT and deal with huge amounts of electronic data. Conventional approaches of modelling data mining in business contexts are limited in addressing a major current trend: Data Mining becomes more and more an integral part of executing a business. Tasks like placing advertisements, recommending products, or detecting fraud have become standard application fields of data mining, and have a serious implication for business profits. A frequent re-engineering of business processes is a consequence of this development. For example, as soon as data mining discovers that one advertisement channel performs much better for a certain group of customers, the delivery mode of advertisements is changed. When fraud detection discovers that a certain mode of payment is associated with a high fraud rate, this mode of payment is no longer allowed. In effect, every change in the deployed process immediately changes the incoming data: users cannot be analyzed for their response to one type of advertisement, if they are targeted with another type of campaign. A fraud detection rule makes one type of fraud disappear (but may in turn cause fraudster to shift to other types of fraud). For a process modelling of data mining this means that the steps of defining the data mining goal and understanding the data on the one hand, and deployment on the other hand, are much more connected and dependent on each other than it appears in traditional approaches such as CRISP [1].

W. Abramowicz and R. Tolksdorf (Eds.): BIS 2010, LNBIP 47, pp. 183–194, 2010.

From an organizational perspective, the growing integration of data mining also calls for a much stronger role of a data analyst, who needs not only to transport business requirements to the data mining, but also to bring data mining input into a business reengineering process. In contrast to traditional role definitions, which do not address the process of data mining specifically, we argue that the definition and execution of any data mining process which brings significant innovation to the business needs to have a balanced view of the business perspective and the data mining perspective. It is necessary to not only answer the question of what should be done by data mining (e.g., detect fraud), but also of what can be done to allow for a better data mining (e.g., record additional information), and of what significant new input data mining can be expected to offer (e.g., from the use of a novel data mining approach).

Current research progress in business process management (BPM) is based on defining and managing business processes in BPEL- and BPMN-based [2,3] service-oriented environments. Such modern BPM environments provide flexible design, management and deployment of business processes. Given that these powerful BPM environments and the CRISP model exist, one could assume that it is very straightforward to efficiently integrate data mining in business processes. But is this really the case? In this paper we make the point that in practice still many redundancies and inefficiencies exist. We believe that the integration of data mining into business processes in such environments can be simplified by developing an integrated approach. We aim at a concept for the integration that facilitates the modelling of the data mining process within the business process as well as the technical deployment into the business IT environment. This includes an integrated view on the interfaces between data mining and the business, as well as additional specifications, standards and definitions.

This work contributes an integrated role model for business, IT and data mining roles, an analysis on how the integration of data mining matches with business process reengineering best practices, and an approach for the evaluation of the integration of data mining processes into business processes.

The remainder of the paper is as follows: Sec. 2 introduces the field of BPM and gives details on BPR and role definitions that are related to the problem of integrating data mining in business processes. Sec. 3 gives an overview on data mining, including data mining problems, methods and the CRISP-DM process. In Sec. 4 we go into details on integrating data mining in business processes. Sec. 5 discusses related work. Sec. 6 concludes and gives an outlook on future work.

2 Business Process Management

2.1 Business Processes and User Groups

A business process is a series of steps designed to produce a product or a service which includes all the activities that deliver particular results for a given customer [4]. Business process management (BPM) is a discipline combining software capabilities and business expertise to accelerate business process improvement and to facilitate business innovation [5]. Integrating data mining in business processes involves different groups of users with different responsibilities, knowledge and background. Naively speaking, this will include the roles of business experts, who are in charge of the business but do not have knowledge in the implementation and in data mining, data miners, who are experts in data mining and who are in charge of designing and implementing the data mining process, and the IT experts, who manage the hardware and software resources of the business and who are in charge of implementing and integrating the business process in the IT environment.

In literature, a lot of classifications of roles in the context of BPM is available. In [6], a detailed study on employee competencies is given based on the following classification of roles and their relations: The *Project Leader*, the *Process Consultant*, the *Process Coordinator*, the *Process Owner*, the *Process Controller*, and the *Process Staff*. However, this definition lacks in describing the IT roles that are involved in the scenario and thus is not suitable for discussion the integration problems. In [5], four key groups that have to work together in BPM projects are defined, namely the *Workforce*, the *IT*, the *Management*, and the *Business Analysts*, including a lot of sub-groups among these.

2.2 Business Process Reengineering and Its Evaluation

Current research on business process management (BPM) outlines the importance of business process reengineering (BPR) and its role in improving business processes [7], e.g., in terms of improving efficiency and effectiveness of an existing business. BPR regards business processes from a "clean slate" perspective to determine how to best construct these processes to improve how the business is conducted. Reengineering is the fundamental rethinking and radical redesign of business processes to achieve dramatic improvements in critical, contemporary measures of performance [8]. In literature, BPR is often evaluated according to a set of dimensions in the effects of redesign measures, e.g. time, cost, quality and flexibility [9], cost, quality, service and speed [8] or cycle time, cost, quality, asset utilization and revenue generated [4]. Ideally, a redesign or modification of a business process decreases the time required to handle incidents, it decreases the required cost of executing the business process, it improves the quality of the service that is delivered and it improves the ability of the business process to react flexible to variation [7]. However, a property of such an evaluation is that trade-off effects become visible, which means that in general, improving upon one dimension may have a weakening effect on another.

In [9], a set of best practice heuristic rules on business process (re)design is evaluated according to the metric cost, time, flexibility and quality. In total, 29 rules are described which are classified according to their orientation towards customers, business process operation, business process behaviour, organization, information, technology and external environment. Later, we will discuss which rules are involved in the integration of data mining in business processes.

3 Data Mining

3.1 Data Mining Problems, Goals and Methods

Data mining, also called knowledge discovery in databases (KDD), is the process of extracting (unknown) patterns from data. In general, a data mining process includes several iterations of single data mining steps (algorithm executions). The goals of the data mining process are defined by the intended use of the system from the user perspective and can be classified into two types: *verification*, where the system is limited to verifying the user's hypothesis, and *discovery*, where the system autonomously finds new patterns. The discovery goal can be further subdivided into *prediction*, where the system finds patterns for predicting the future behavior of some entities, and *description*, where the system finds patterns for presentation to a user in a human-understandable form [10].

A variety of data-mining methods exists which help in achieving the goal of prediction and description. According to [11], data mining methods commonly involve the following classes of tasks: Inferring rudimentary rules, statistical modeling, constructing decision trees, constructing rules, mining association rules, linear models, instance-based learning, and clustering. For each of these methods a variety of data mining algorithms exist that incorporate these methods. We refer to [11] for an updated reference on data mining methods and algorithms.

3.2 The Data Mining Process

The data mining process is an interactive and iterative process that involves numerous steps with many decisions made by the data miner. CRISP-DM [1] is a standard process model for data mining that depicts corresponding phases of a project, their respective tasks, and relationships between these tasks. According to CRISP-DM, the lifecycle of a data mining project consists of the following six different phases: *Business Understanding* - understanding the project objectives and requirements from a business perspective and converting this knowledge into a data mining problem definition; *Data Understanding* - getting to know the data and to identify data quality problems; *Data Preparation* - construct the final dataset from the initial raw data as input for the modelling; *Modeling* - various modeling techniques are selected and applied, including the calibration of their specific settings; *Evaluation* - assess how well the built model achieves the business objectives; *Deployment* - the results of the data mining and the knowledge gained are delivered to the user, reaching from generating a simple report up to a complex implementation of a repeatable data mining process. The process in general is iterative, but also foresees stepping back between certain phases to adjust some of the decisions made. From the data mining perspective, the (business) user is mainly involved in the phases Business Understanding and Deployment, while the other phases are mostly performed only by the data miner. In terms of integration, it has to be distinguished between the (technical) deployment of the data mining solution as a whole, which might be done only once for a given business process, and the deployment of new data mining models, which might be done frequently.

3.3 Evaluating Data Mining

At the end of the modeling step of the data mining process, the data mining model is evaluated in order to determine its quality. Model-evaluation criteria are quantitative statements of how well a particular data mining model meets the goals of the KDD process [10] and the business objectives [12]. The criteria differ according to the data mining goal. For each of the goals verification, prediction and description a number of performance measures exist for the evaluation. E.g., predictive models are often evaluated by the empirical prediction accuracy on some test data and descriptive models can be evaluated along the dimensions of predictive accuracy, novelty, utility, and understandability of the fitted model [10]. Other measures include, e.g., precision, recall and f-measure. In addition, techniques like cross-validation or bootstrap [11] are applied in order to ensure the representativeness of the evaluation. Despite these metrics for evaluating the result of the data mining process, other important factors like the time spent for the process, the resources that were used, etc., can be included in the evaluation. In the evaluation phase of the data mining process, the model as well as the way it was constructed is evaluated according to the business objectives.

4 Integration of BPM and Data Mining

Data mining is often integrated with a business process to provide value [12]. However, data mining needs a lot of domain knowledge and thus is difficult to handle for non-experts. On the other hand, continuous data mining and flexible adaption of the data mining and the business process plays a crucial role in the context of modern data mining solutions as part of business applications, e.g. online advertisement or fraud detection. From the business point of view, the data mining results have to be frequently evaluated according to relevance for the business and respective actions have to be taken, e.g. adapting the business process due to new emerging fraud patterns or adapting the data mining to provide more detailed results. This means, that the CRISP-DM phases deployment and business understanding are much more connected than before. Thus, there is a clear need for approaches for the integration of data mining into business processes which need to be compatible with modern business process management environments. In particular, they need to cover flexibility w.r.t. adapting the data mining process as well as the business process itself in an online environment, which they do not provide so far. While CRISP-DM includes longer process cycles, modern data mining needs for fast development and quick experiment setup and evaluation (also on live systems). Motivating examples for integrating a data mining process into a business process in order to improve the business are, e.g., the EC-funded projects RACWeB[1] and iWebCare [13]. RACWeB aimed at improving the Western Balkans and EU countries' customs efficiency and transparency in risk assessment by enhancing the identification of risk profiles through the utilisation of data mining techniques. In iWebCare, a flexible fraud detection platform was developed in order to ensure quality

[1] http://www.racweb.org/

and accuracy and minimise loss of health care funds in the Healthcare business. The basic idea behind both projects was to develop a web service platform where participating organizations can upload datasets and semi-automatically select an appropriate data mining process. Based on the analysis of the business processes of participating organizations, it was possible to develop generic data mining solutions that can be re-used in similar business processes. Because of the detailed business process modelling it is not necessary to follow the CRISP-DM process step by step again a second time, as much of the relevant business knowledge is already contained in the business process model. In other words, redundancies exist between the business perspective and the data mining perspective.

4.1 An Integrated Role Model

Data mining is typically performed by a specialist with lots of expertise in data mining (the data miner) who is responsible for the steps of the data mining project as, e.g., described by CRISP-DM. The client (from the data miner's perspective) is involved in the first phase (Business Understanding) and the last phase (Deployment); all phases in-between are solely carried out by the data miner. The data miner is not yet described by one of the roles in BPM. He is not responsible for the full process, but as data mining consists of several steps, also not just for a single task. There are tasks and responsibilities of the data miner which are not yet described in the area of BPM. From the data mining point of view, a lot of domain knowledge is needed to set up a high quality process. Typically, the setup of a data mining process requires a lot of interaction with other roles, e.g. the business user and the IT experts. So, important in the context of integrating data mining in business processes are the groups of business roles and of IT roles. In addition to the existing interaction between these roles, new interactions with the group of data mining roles appear (see Fig. 1).

Persons who are responsible for the data mining can also be classified into different roles, e.g. as follows: *Data Mining Senior* - responsible for the conceptual design; *Data Mining Experimenter* - responsible for the experiments; and *Data Mining Architect* - responsible for the integration, deployment and integration. The typical approach is to let the data mining senior define the problem and the general procedure, to let the experimenter conduct experiments with a data mining toolkit, and to let the data mining architect implement, deploy and integrate the solution into a bigger context.

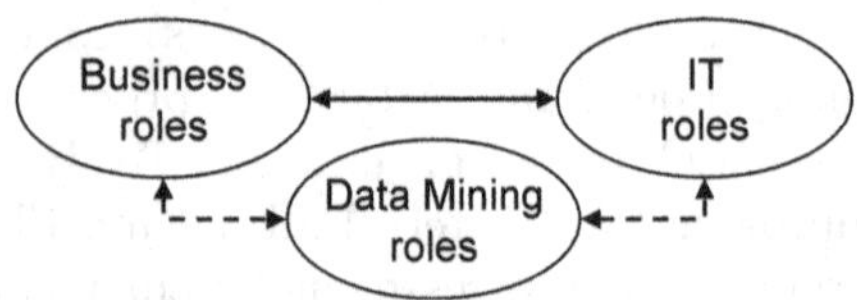

Fig. 1. Interaction of the different groups of roles - existing interaction between business and IT roles and new interactions with data mining roles

4.2 Integration of Data Mining Processes into Business Processes

For the integration, we assume that there is an existing business process. The goal is to integrate a data mining process into this business process in order to improve the business. A data mining process cannot be seen as normal business process. The necessary domain knowledge for the setup of data mining and the resources needed for the implementation justify the special role for the data miner.

CRISP-DM [1] describes a standard process model for data mining processes, but lacks in defining detailed concepts, definitions and standards for a deployment of the data mining solution as well as the integration of the whole data mining process. Often, only the integration of the data mining results is discussed, but not the integration of the data mining process as a whole. Business processes and data mining processes interface at the CRISP-DM phases Business Understanding and Deployment. The other CRISP-DM phases are mainly data mining specific with small or no involvement of the user. As there is already a business process defined, many of the decisions that need to be taken in the CRISP-DM phases Business Understanding and Deployment are already fixed in advance. Such decisions include, e.g., which task to replace or to add to the original business process, which data mining problem to solve, the definition of the data mining constraints in terms of quality, time, etc., and how to integrate things technically in the IT environment. On the other hand, results of data mining might suggest taking decisions in a different way. Hence, there exist redundancies when not carefully coordinating CRISP-DM and the revision of the business process.

Workflows involving data mining introduce additional dependencies among tasks as well as a combination of automated and manual tasks [12]. Thus, data mining cannot be described by a single task or box inside a business process. As described above, data mining itself can be seen a complex process. In addition, the data mining services (modelling part) can be quite complex or can have totally different functionality. There exist solutions for distributed and grid based data mining, including highly parameterized generic services as GridR [14], where the algorithm itself could be passed as a parameter.

Integrating data mining in business processes means to change the business processes. Thus, the integration has to follow the rules, standards and practices for BPR. In the following, we give details on which rules from [9] apply or explicitly apply not for the integration:

- Task elimination: 'eliminate unnecessary tasks from a business process' - a typical goal of integrating data mining is to replace (manual) tasks. However, new tasks for the data mining itself appear.
- Order-based work: 'consider removing batch-processing and periodic activities from a business process' - the model building step will not be executed once per order but rather as batch job (a periodic activity that is started according to some conditions).
- Parallelism: 'consider whether tasks may be executed in parallel' - if data mining replaces a manual task, it can, once it is deployed in a business

process, be executed automatically. Thus, this might give an option for parallelization of preceding or subsequent tasks.

- Split responsibilities: 'avoid assignment of task responsibilities to people from different functional units' - the data miner will be involved in the data mining tasks, so responsibilities are distributed to a larger number of persons. However, we aim at a minimal involvement.
- Numerical involvement: 'minimize the number of departments, groups and persons involved in a business process' - see split responsibilities.
- Extra resources: 'if capacity is not sufficient, consider increasing the number of resources' - by the integration of data mining, resources in terms of people (the data miner) and hardware (computing and storage) are extended. If data mining replaces a manual task, previously used human resources become free.
- Control addition: 'check the completeness and correctness of incoming materials and check the output before it is send to customers' - by data mining, completeness and correctness of data can be checked more extensively.
- Task automation: 'consider automating tasks' - with the help of data mining, some manual tasks could be replaced.
- Integral technology: 'try to elevate physical constraints in a business process by applying new technology' - data mining represents a new technology that can help improving the business process.
- Outsourcing: 'consider outsourcing a business process in whole or parts of it' - parts of the business process are outsourced in the way that a new group, the data miner, is responsible.

The details on the integration of the data mining into business processes also depend on the data mining problem to solve. E.g., we distinguish between supervised and unsupervised data mining, as different characteristics raise different requirements in terms of modeling. In the context of supervised learning, labeled datasets are needed for training a model (which, e.g., specify if a dataset is fraud or not), whereas in the context of unsupervised learning no labels are needed. Thus, a different set of components is needed for the integration.

Instead of deciding on the kind of integration each time anew and of integrating these steps manually, we propose to define a standard set of data mining services that can interface with modern BPM environments. For the adaption of the business process models, templates could be developed that define on how exactly the data mining can be integrated. Our approach is generic, but works especially well in certain scenarios. These include scenarios with an objective, automatically computable measure of quality, and with standardised structured data with limited volume. This allows for automating many decisions in the data mining process and working with existing standardised solutions.

4.3 Evaluating the Integration

In order to determine if the integration of data mining into a business process makes sense and is valuable, we have to prove that the new integrated solution is better. In addition, as data mining has special requirements for IT [12], there is the need for a metric that helps to decide on if and how to adapt the IT environment. As integrating data mining in business processes means to apply the rules and standards of BPR, we propose to evaluate the integration including the metrics for BPR, taking into account the evaluation of data mining related BPR best practices as described above. The evaluation has to be two-fold. Both, the new operational business processes as well as the effort for the integration itself have to be evaluated.

For the former, there is a need to find a metric that covers both, available performance measures of business process redesign and data mining processes. In principle, the integration of a data mining process can be evaluated in the same way as standard BPR according to the key performance indicators time, cost, quality and flexibility that have been described earlier. The measures can be mapped as follows: The (IT-) resources that are needed by the data mining map to the cost measure; The runtime of the data mining process maps to the time measure; The model-evaluation criteria that describe the quality of the data mining result map to the quality measure; The level of generality of the integrated data mining solution maps to the flexibility measure. In addition, this can incorporate, e.g., how many data mining processes (e.g. classifications) can be performed simultaneously. It has to be noted that in the context of data mining not all of these measures are always fix. E.g., the time needed for learning a model is hard to predict. In addition, there is a non-trivial correlation between resources denoted to the data mining process and the quality of the result.

For the evaluation of the integration the time needed for the redesign and integration can be measured. E.g., one solution can be realized very fast, but the quality of the data mining result is not best. There is a solution with a better result quality (e.g. based on distributed computing), but the realization takes a lot longer. So, there is a trade-off that has to be taken into account. Thus, the speed-up of integration and development is also an important measure that has to be considered.

In modern frameworks incorporating BPEL and BPMN, a simple design, setup and deployment of business processes is possible. But, it is not clear how to model an integrated process in detail, meaning how much detail of the data mining process has to be visible in order to integrate it conceptually and technically. In the end, all technical steps have to be integrated. But, for instance it has to be answered which parts of the data mining process have to be integrated into the business process at minimum and which can be aggregated or hidden from the user. Thus, the complexity of the modeling of the business process can serve as metric. This could include, e.g., the number of additional components and tasks that have to be added to the original business process, the number of services that have to be implemented or used by the data miner, etc.

5 Related Work

In [10] the integration of data mining with other systems, e.g. database management systems or spreadsheet and visualization tools, is described as a research and application challenge. As applications today are getting more and more complex due to larger amounts of data or the distribution of data or resources, the problem of integration is also getting harder. Most important benefits of data mining for the business are achieved when the data mining results are deployed into a business process in a repeatable manner, which, e.g., involves the ability to rebuild, assess and apply models automatically [12]. [15] gives a survey on data mining techniques and business applications in the context of mining data from the business. There even exists some literature on integrating data mining in business processes from the end of the 90s [16]. They describe their experience on integration of data mining and observe open issues, but do not incorporate modern concepts and techniques for BPM yet.

According to CRISP-DM, "in many cases it will be the customer, not the data analyst, who will carry out the deployment steps". "Even if the analyst will not carry out the deployment effort it is important for the customer to understand up front what actions will need to be carried out in order to actually make use of the created models" [1]. Thus, the CRISP-DM model lacks in the deployment phase [17] and misses phases important for engineering projects [18]. There is no specification or support for standards on how to deploy the data mining results into the business. In addition, problems on integrating the data mining process into a business process in praxis are not addressed.

In [17] a methodology for the implementation of data mining into operational business processes is proposed, consisting of the phases Exploratory Data Mining, Deployment of IT into the Business Process, and Operational Data Mining. The first phase consists of performing a CRISP-DM process and evaluating the readiness for an integration of the data mining solution. In the second phase, the data mining solution is deployed into the business environment, including changes in design and implementation of the business process (which means to perform BPR) and associated applications. The third phase describes the steps of the operational solution, including all CRISP-DM phases but business understanding and an additional phase for model updating. They do not specify a general concept for the technical integration and the re-design of the process and its evaluation. In their example of integrating data mining into a direct marketing business process, the data mining is nearly modeled as black box.

Based on experience in software engineering, [18] proposes a model for data mining engineering that includes engineering-related phases which are missing in CRISP-DM. They identify as open issue, that available process models specify what to do, but not how to do it. This is a point that we start addressing with this work. [19] also identifies the lack of guidance towards implementing particular tasks of data mining methodologies and introduces a framework for the implementation of the business understanding phase of data mining projects. However, they do not focus on business integration and deployment of data mining solutions into business processes.

Scheduling and workflow environments are slowly being addressed by business process environments [12], e.g., with frameworks like BPEL, that allow and facilitate the inclusion of (external) web-services within business processes. JDM [12] provides web service interfaces for such a kind of integration on API level that can be used in modern BPEL based frameworks. In addition, a use case is presented on how to integrate data mining based on JDM into a business process based on BPEL in a Bank scenario. The authors use a role model with the groups Business Analysts, Data Analysts and IT. However, they do not specify in general how to adapt a business processes in detail, how to evaluate the integration and which requirements for the modelling of the business process when including data mining exist.

6 Conclusion

Both areas of BPM and data mining are very complex and require a lot of human resources. In response, many approaches for BPM and data mining have been proposed in the literature. In many practical applications, e.g. integrating fraud detection in an e-commerce system, these approaches work out fine. However, in this paper we showed that following the CRISP-DM model in parallel to standard BPR approaches results in many redundancies. In the context of integrating data mining into business processes we have to deal with two different processes that work together at two defined steps - the Business Understanding and the Deployment phase according to CRISP. Business processes can be quite different, but the adaption and redesign for the integration of data mining is often similar. Hence, there is a clear need for a coordinated approach. From the data mining point of view, the deployment in terms of business process design is similar (e.g., exchange one BP-step by another), but with respect to deployment on the IT infrastructure it can differ a lot. Thus, additional DM-process steps (w.r.t. deployment) and a standard set of services are needed. This motivates the development of flexible services such as those from the context of GridR.

This work contributed an integrated role model for business, IT and data mining roles, an analysis on how the integration of data mining matches with business process reengineering best practices, and an approach for the evaluation of the integration of data mining processes into business processes. It represents a further step towards an integrated environment which allows for flexible adding, exchanging or adapting data mining and business process tasks and fast experimenting, even on live systems, which is needed by modern data mining solutions in business applications.

As future work we foresee improvement on the concepts and techniques for an easy deployment of flexible data mining solutions into business processes in the context of modern BPM frameworks based on BPEL and BPMN, based on a uniform concept for both modelling and technical integration. This will include work on data mining services that support an easy integration as well as process templates for the business processes.

References

1. Shearer, C.: The CRISP-DM model: the new blueprint for data mining. Journal of Data Warehousing 5(4), 13–22 (2000)
2. Jordan, D., Evdemon, J.: Web Services Business Process Execution Language Version 2.0. Technical report, OASIS Standard (2007)

3. White, S.A., Miers, D.: BPMN Modeling and Reference Guide Understanding and Using BPMN. Future Strategies Inc., Lighthouse Pt (2008)
4. Mayer, R.J., Dewitte, P.S.: Delivering Results: Evolving BPR from art to engineering. In: Elzinga, D.J., Gulledge, T.R., Lee, C.Y. (eds.) Business process engineering: advancing the state of the art (1998)
5. Peisl, R.: The Process Architect: The Smart Role in Business Process Management. IBM Red Paper (2009)
6. Eicker, S., Kochbeck, J., Schuler, P.M.: Employee Competencies for Business Process Management. In: Abramowicz, W., Fensel, D. (eds.) Proc. of 11th International Conference on Business Information Systems. LNBIP, vol. 7, pp. 251–262. Springer, Berlin (2008)
7. Bessai, K., Claudepierre, B., Saidani, O., Nurcan, S.: Context-aware Business Process Evaluation and Redesign. In: Int. Workshop on Business Process Management, Design and Support, at Int. Conference on Advanced Information Systems, Montpellier, France (2008)
8. Hammer. M, Champy, J.: Reengineering the Corporation: A Manifesto for Business Revolution. Harper Collins, London (1993)
9. Reijers, H.A., Liman Mansar, S.: Best practices in business process redesign: an overview and qualitative evaluation of successful redesign heuristics. Omega - The International Journal of Management Science 33(4), 283–306 (2005)
10. Fayyad, U., Piatetsky-Shapiro, G., Smyth, P.: From Data Mining to Knowledge Discovery in Databases. AI Magazine 17, 37–54 (1996)
11. Witten, I.H., Frank, E.: Data Mining: Practical machine learning tools and techniques, 2nd edn. Morgan Kaufmann, San Francisco (2005)
12. Hornick, M.F., Marcadé, E., Venkayala, S.: Java Data Mining: Strategy, Standard, and Practice. Morgan Kaufmann, San Francisco (2006)
13. Tagaris, A., Konnis, G., Benetou, X., Dimakopoulos, T., Kassis, K., Athanasiadis, N., Rüping, S., Grosskreutz, H., Koutsouris, D.: Integrated Web Services Platform for the facilitation of fraud detection in health care e-government services. In: Proc. ITAB 2009, Lacarna, Cyprus (2009)
14. Wegener, D., Sengstag, T., Sfakianakis, S., Rüping, S., Assi, A.: GridR: An R-based tool for scientific data analysis in grid environments. Future Generation Computer Systems 25(4), 481–488 (2009)
15. Bose, I., Mahapatra, R.K.: Business data mining - a machine learning perspective. Information and Management 39(3), 211–225 (2001)
16. Holsheimer, M.: Data mining by business users: integrating data mining in business processes. In: Han, J. (ed.) Tutorial Notes of the 5th ACM International Conference on Knowledge Discovery and Data Mining, pp. 266–291. ACM, New York (1999)
17. Rupnik, R., Jaklic, J.: The Deployment of Data Mining into Operational Business Processes. In: Ponce, J., Karahoca, A. (eds.) Data Mining and Knowledge Discovery in Real Life Applications, I-Tech, Vienna, Austria (2009)
18. Marbán, O., Segovia, J., Menasalvas, E., Fernández-Baizán, C.: Toward data mining engineering: A software engineering approach. Information Systems 34(1) (2009)
19. Sharma, S., Osei-Bryson, K.: Framework for formal implementation of the business understanding phase of data mining projects. Expert Systems with Applications 36(2) (2009)

From Process Execution towards a Business Process Intelligence

Carsten Felden[1], Peter Chamoni[2], and Markus Linden[2]

[1] University for Mining and Technology of Freiberg
Faculty of Business Administration
Chair of Information Systems and Information Management
Lessingstraße 45, 09599 Freiberg, Germany
[2] University of Duisburg-Essen, Mercator School of Management
Department of Technology and Operations Management
Chair of Information Systems and Operations Research
Lotharstraße 63, 47057 Duisburg, Germany
Carsten.Felden@bwl.tu-freiberg.de,
Peter.Chamoni@uni-due.de,
Markus.Linden@uni-due.de

Abstract. There exist some approaches to support decision making in the context of business processes. Most of them are not systemized. The aim of this paper is to evaluate and differentiate existing approaches of Business Process Intelligence and to detect further research activities in this field to propose a holistic concept. This is done by a literature review to identify related concepts and to be able to constitute further research by doing an empirical study and a case study. The results are a morphological box and a definition to clarify potentials of a Business Process Intelligence. Additionally, propositions based on selected theories are formulated which provide a basis for further research.

Keywords: Business Process Intelligence, Business Process Management, Operational Business Intelligence, Process Mining.

1 Introduction

Business publications usually contain a reference to dynamic market conditions in the last decades. This enforces adaptation strategies in order to allow for changes. The financial crisis in 2008 has shown that companies have to adapt changing conditions fast, in order to ensure the company's existence. Academic literature and practical experiences show developments, which focus on analytical information systems regarding an economic process control - but this with neither any clear systematization nor concept in sense of a tool box. The necessary real time decision making is described as *latency* and leads to concepts like real time / near time Data-Warehousing, Operational Business Intelligence or Process Intelligence. This paper evaluates and differentiates existing Business Process Intelligence (BPI) approaches and detects further research activities.

W. Abramowicz and R. Tolksdorf (Eds.): BIS 2010, LNBIP 47, pp. 195–206, 2010.

The coincidence of Business Process Management (BPM) and Business Intelligence (BI) has been predictable, because their intersection deals with analysis and design of economic processes. However, a literature research shows that publications concerning the concepts named above focus on operations rather than strategic value proposition or a process development. Primarily, the inspection of individual processes is discussed in the approaches, while the dependency analysis between processes is usually not focused. On this initial stage of the research, this paper contributes to the fields of Business Intelligence and Business Process Management in providing a literature based classification of Business Intelligence and its potentials in the Business Process Management. It serves as a basis for the overall research goal to improve the process landscape within companies on a holistic level. The following research framework is used in order to conduct the analyses.

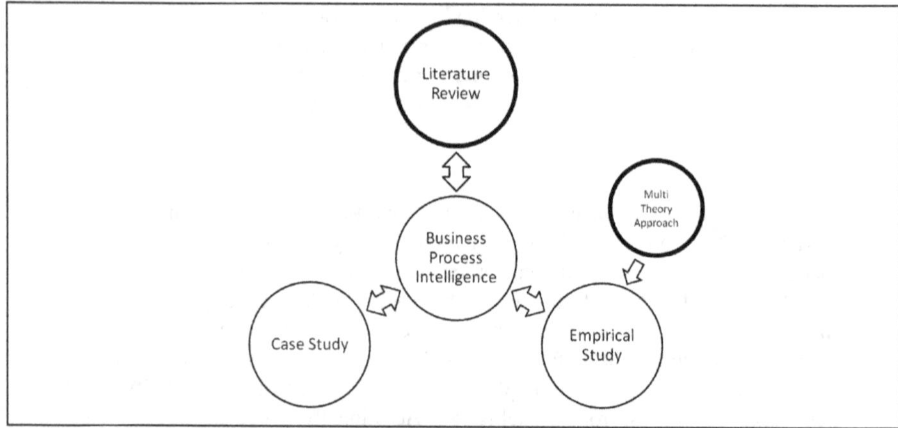

Fig. 1. Research Framework

The research method is divided into a literature review to differentiate process orientated Business Intelligence approaches, an empirical study based on a multi theory approach to analyze the fundamentals of a Business Process Intelligence, and a case study to be able to analyze the usability and benefits of a Business Process Intelligence. In the sense of a research in progress, this paper focuses on the literature review and based on this the definition of the multi theory approach (as highlighted in Figure 1) in favor of the empirical study. Finally, the paper provides conclusions and defines the constitution for further research.

2 Process Orientation and Concepts of Process Analyses

Process orientated approaches offer a possibility for an efficient result achievement [6]. This section discusses Business Process Management and concepts of process analyses to build up a fundament for the following systematization and the multi theory approach.

2.1 Business Process Management

The term *process* can be applied in different ways, because it assumes an intuitive knowledge of the temporal-logical development of activities. Depending on the perspective, a consideration of technical, physical/chemical or economic processes can be taken either. A generally accepted definition of the term *process* is: "A set of activities, which are interrelated and transform input in results." [6] On the one hand, results are the output, e.g. a product for the costumer. On the other hand, entries make up the input, e.g. the claiming of resources evaluated by cost [15]. As additional step, business processes shall be taken into consideration as well. They can describe clustered sub-processes and offer a specialized perception of process orientated approaches considering economic questions [22].

The Strategic Porterain Framework serves as a foundation for business process inspection in this context [20]. The underlying principle is the value chain, which divides company's activities into technical and economic operations. The value reflects the costumers' willingness to pay for a specific commodity. Due to this reason, a company should organize its activities in a cost-efficient way. The activities must be categorized into central and supporting activities. Moreover, an activity must not be pictured as a single activity. There are interdependencies between internal and external activities. The activities form a so called value system. Each activity exhibits a cost driver, which has to be identified and managed, in order to achieve cost advantages. Such advantages may be identified with the help of the competitive scope, which is divided into the four dimensions segment, vertical integration, geographic and sectoral factors. The inspection of activities includes a physical and exploratory component. The exploratory component enables the company to identify variables, generate models and picture scenarios. This supports a shortening of the activities as well as the enhancement of products with information and decreasing costs [20].

So, the Strategic Porterain Framework describes the utilization of a Business Process Intelligence to identify value and cost drivers and to define dependencies in order to support flexibility regarding changing environmental condition.

2.2 Current Concepts of Process Analyses

Several approaches referring to process analyses models are discussed in the Business Intelligence oriented literature. These approaches are presented in the following to clarify the point of view on analyzing processes from a BI perspective.

Operational Business Intelligence (OpBI) focuses on the analyses of business processes and their connections with further information. The results of the application of OpBI are suggestions for many users in order to improve the control of business processes. Additionally, BLASUM [3] proposes that OpBI is a collection of methods, aiming controlling and optimization of key processes within a company.

Moreover, OpBI tries to improve operative processes during progress [2, 6]. Connected to this, ECKERSON [7] states a merger of operative and analytical processes into one integrated whole. The increase of user values of Business Intelligence will be generated throughout integrated information and business insides. Furthermore, OpBI transfers experience values into business rules. As a result, a company can use automated decisions and answers in time-consuming processes without the need of human interaction [7].

Furthermore, BAUER and SCHMID [2] differentiate between classical Business Intelligence and Operational Business Intelligence regarding process state and process result. Strategic and tactical Business Intelligence focus on process results, while OpBI is rather concerned with the process state. Stepping into the process might improve the result [2]. A decision support regarding analytical information can only be made reactively, which means that latencies mostly exceeded reaction time. Therefore, process adaptations could only be made for the future. GLUCHOWSKI et al. [11] take up this question as well. According to them, OpBI represents business process orientated systems, which use classical Business Intelligence methods to produce real time decision support on the basis of process data and historical data.

Because of its focus on process control, OpBI is directly related to existing approaches like Business Activity Monitoring (BAM) as well as Business Performance Management. Moreover, GLUCHOWSKI et al. [10] recognize a connection and approximation of OpBI and Process Performance Management (PPM). Therefore, OpBI can be understood as a method for fast and flexible process control and decision support [3].

The term *Business Process Intelligence* appeared almost at the same time like OpBI. This dilution has been supported by software providers, who used BPI as a buzz word for management dashboards in order to stimulate their business [14]. As a result, the boundaries between these terms are considered to be indeterminate. That is why BPI and OpBI are often used as synonyms especially in the Anglo-Saxon area [13].

CASTELLANOS and WEIJTERS [5] point out the confusion of ideas and the different aspects of BPI and their relation. According to them, BPI aims at the improvement of processes, which focus on process identification, process analyses, process simulation and static and dynamic process improvement. HOSNY [16] states, that the aim of BPI is a better understanding and support of business processes at the time of construction and during progress. According to KANNAN [17], BPI represents an objective measure of different activities within a company that gives indication of current efficiency and bottlenecks of business processes.

PEREZ and MOELLER also come up with a distinction consisting of many degrees of freedom. According to them, Business Process Management offers the central concept, while BPI is just a method which reflects this concept [19]. Discussing the usage of BPI, GRIGORI et al. [12] point out a selection of tools. These tools support companies´ IT and include the domains *analyses*, *prediction*, *control* and *improvement of business processes*. On the one hand, those methods are supposed to allow an integrated approach regarding networks and electronic business platforms. On the other hand, they are supposed to identify, analyze and forecast a process, in order to improve the whole process [10, 14]. The definition of quality bases on the specialists and the IT as well as the selection of methods. The IT is also responsible for the characteristics, which have to be analyzed [12]. These analyses are executed by use of data mining methods and statistical proceedings. According to GENRICH et al. [9], the methods have to be assimilated to specific demands of Business Process Management.

The introduced concepts show, that there remains a need for an analytical approach in order to concentrate on process analyses on a higher management level which is discussed in the following sections.

3 Systematization of Business Process Intelligence

This section presents the characteristics of the morphological box. A morphological box classifies and systematize the above mentioned distinctions. The Business Process Management steps: process identification, process implementation, process execution, and process improvement [4] constitute as a core of BPI. The following morphological box is based on the result of the literature review. Morphological boxes are used in the literature to arrange and visualize concept characteristics [21]. Task and process oriented descriptions were taken and mapped to each other to identify characteristics and types to structure Business Process Intelligence.

Table 1. Morphological Box of Business Process Intelligence

Characteristics	Types			
Focus	Process design	Process redesign	Process execution	
Direction	Business		Technology	
Management level	Operational	Tactical	Strategic	
Data level	Instance level	Model level	Meta model level	Meta meta model level
Process phase	Identification / Definition / Modelling	Implementation / Execution	Monitoring / Controlling	Continuous improvement
Kind of process	Business processes		Technical processes	
Time relevance	Real-time		Historic	
Range of users	Small	Middle	Broad	
Technology	Business Activity Monitoring	Service-oriented Architecture	Complex Event Processing	Process Warehouse
Information sources	Internal data		External data	
Kind of information	Unstructured data		Structured data	

OpBI concerns a process oriented decision support including process control. In contrast to this approach, BPI tries to offer decision support regarding process design. Against this background, BPI focuses on process design and process redesign with a business orientation. For this purpose, ratios are used to implement measurements, structure analyses and efficiency of business processes. This leads to a process improvement beyond IT and organizational boundaries. Therefore, automated techniques find conspicuous events and determine potentials regarding core and supporting processes.

In the context of BPI, simulations and what-if-analyses investigate processes, generate guidance and support decisions made by the tactical and strategic management. The tactical and the strategic management level receive process information, because the information does not only describe indicators for the creation of value but also an addition to a periodic description of business performance. Accordingly, the user group stays functional focused and small, especially in contrast to operative process control. Due to this, BPI works as well as classical Business Intelligence. This relies on the inspection of historical data. According to the time relevance, a Process Warehouse (PWH) plays an important role, because process logs which have to be analyzed are stored within a PWH. The Process Warehouse receives structured and unstructured data from internal and external data sources. In this context, an application of Process Mining (PM) [24] is necessary, concentrating on the identification of process structures. Thus, the result of such analyses and simulations is an improvement of whole process landscapes and not of single processes. The following definition can be stated on the basis of this systematization and the existing distinctions in the academic literature:

Business Process Intelligence (BPI) is the analytical process of identifying, defining, modelling and improving value creating business processes in order to support the tactic and strategic management.

In conclusion, the data and information concerning business processes within the concept of OpBI can be used in favor of a BPI, in order to develop a valid process design for management purposes. Business Process Intelligence is understood as a generic term, which includes areas like the shown data storage and data analysis and brings it on a holistic level.

4 Research Framework

The existing approaches mentioned above and the paper's definition lead to a multi theory approach, in order to investigate the use of BPI. Based on the Strategic Porterain Framework, theories with different perspectives on business processes are chosen. Of course, the usage of four theories seems to be oversized. But the initial classification and definition of a BPI should be reflected from different perspectives.

The following theories are the basis for the next steps of the research agenda. As mentioned before, the experiment design consists of a literature review, an empirical study and a case study (cf. Figure 1). In this context, these different approaches will be used for validating the theory-based assertions, because each cause-effect-relation has various requirements. Within the first step to verify the assertion H1 of Figure 2, branches have to be identified to demonstrate the need and benefit for a Business Process Intelligence in the stated context. Especially the energy sector seems to be an industry, where BPI meets its challenges regarding rapidly-changing environments (e.g. unbundling). The verification of the assertion H2 are going to be analyzed within a case study. Against this background the process landscape with the whole computer-aided production data acquisition and process models (business and support processes) of a utility company has to be analyzed. To prove assertion H3, the research approach is based on non-standardized expert interviews with representatives of the energy branch. The main purpose is to figure out different decision processes, influences of unbundling guidelines and the potential of BPI in this context. To evaluate the assertion H4, the research step is to inspect the organizational and technical concepts (on demand / near real time systems) of a utility company within the scope of a case study. The following Figure 2 aggregates the theories and illustrates insofar the multi theory approach.

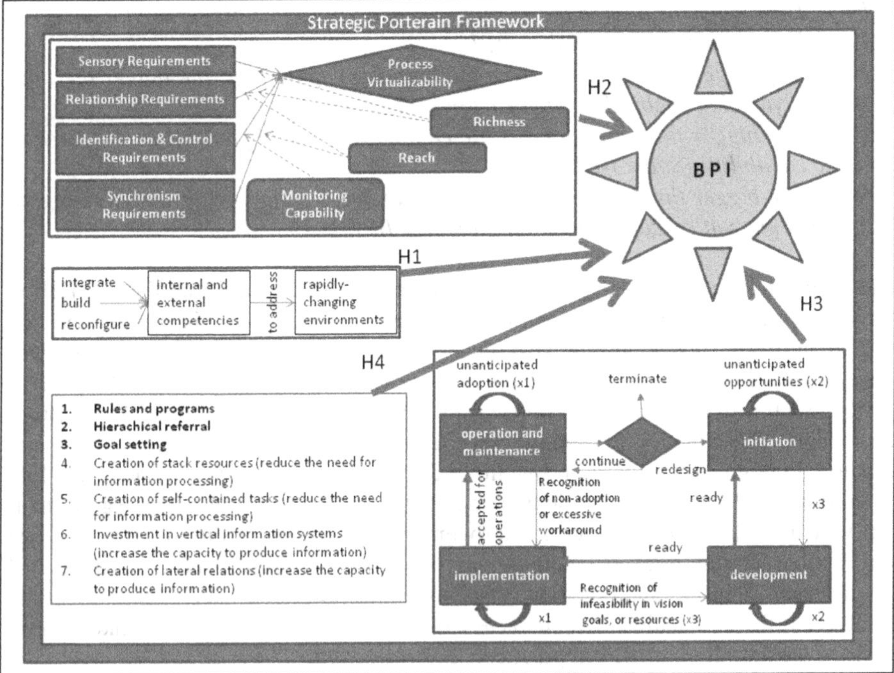

Fig. 2. Multi Theory Approach

The formation of the propositions is based on the fundamental acceptance that BPI affects positively on the company's performance. Figure 2 gives an overview about the underlying theories and their influence to BPI, which are surrounded by the Strategic Porterain Framework. The propositions are theoretically founded as far as possible on the basis of the existing literature. But there exist, however, many relations to date without any empirical foundations. This leads to specific employed considerations and references from existing theories to be able to analyze the relevant parameters.

Propositions of *dynamic capabilities* [Figure 2, H1]

TEECE et al. [23] define dynamic capabilities as the ability to integrate, create and reconfigure internal and external competences in order to concentrate on changing framework conditions. This theory extends the Resource Based View (RBV) of the firm, because it ignores environmental influences. Dynamic capabilities shall act as a buffer between business resources and changing framework conditions, so that the companies` ability to ensure the competitive advantage can be used. Accordingly, it comes to an evaluation of the companies´ competitive advantage within an instable environment. Therefore, the first assumption is: the bigger the support of dynamic capabilities by Business Process Intelligence is, the higher the business related outcome is. This leads to the following propositions:

P1.1: The bigger the degree of information capabilities, the bigger the total degree of dynamic capabilities supported by BPI.

P1.2: The bigger the degree of dynamic learning capabilities, the bigger the total degree of dynamic capabilities supported by BPI.

P1.3: The bigger the degree of flexible capabilities, the bigger the total degree of dynamic capabilities supported by BPI.

P1.4: The bigger the degree of innovation capabilities, the bigger the total degree of dynamic innovation capabilities supported by BPI.

The propositions of dynamic capabilities can be validated concerning the connection between strategic planning and operative business processes. In this context and due to a strength-weakness-opportunity-threads-analysis [20], internal resources are identified and environmental factors are considered, which strongly influence the process design. Such a strategy conform process design is implemented by information process models. These models are the basis for fitting the processes to a specific company strategy. In contrast with BPI and within the concept of OpBI, there is no direct link to strategic goals. Only value-oriented approaches show those ambitions, e.g. a financial view for a continuous process improvement. Finally, the ability to react in a fast and flexible way in terms of changing environment conditions is the goal which BPI has to reach. The presented method is one aspect to point out, which general method could be utilized to achieve the characteristics of the morphological box and to demonstrate the definition of BPI in practice.

Propositions of *process virtualization* [Figure 2, H2]
A lot of processes change from physical to virtual ones, e.g. electronic commerce. Electronic commerce functions well for some processes, but this cannot be seen as a general rule. This of course, leads to the question, which factors influence process virtualization. BPI shall support process flexibility with the help of an IT-based approach. In doing so, it may also act in the sense of cost efficiency.

The process virtualization theory uses four important constructs (sensor requirements, relationship requirements, synchronism requirements and identification & control requirements), in order to point out the significance of information systems explicitly [18]. Therefore, the second assumption is that the usage of information systems as a secondary process in the Strategic Porterain Framework offers a fast and cost efficient process assimilation for businesses.

P2.1: The greater (lower) the sensory requirements of a process, the less (more) applicable is the process for a BPI.

P2.2: The greater (lower) the relationship requirements of a process, the less (more) applicable is the process for a BPI.

P2.3: The greater (lower) the synchronism requirements of a process, the less (more) applicable is the process for a BPI.

P2.4: The greater (lower) the identification and control requirements of a process, the less (more) applicable is the process for a BPI.

Not individual sub-processes are focused and improved, but a view on the whole value-creating process is established. This becomes more visible, if the presented strategic specification will be involved. This is modelled as a meta-process. The potential information system can be used to adapt core processes semi-automatically.

Operational Business Intelligence can also create a contribution to company's performance. For instance, technological components like Business Activity Monitoring can inform about errors during the process enabling a direct correction. Accordingly these systems are able to control a process real or right time.

Proposition of *work systems* [Figure 2, H3]

A work system is a system, in which human and/or mechanical components use information, techniques and other resources, in order to produce goods and services for internal and external customers [1]. The work system shown in Figure 2 illustrates the IT-dependency in organizations with the help of nine elements. Processes and activities, participants, information and techniques describe the work system. Further elements are a semantic enrichment, which help to increase the understanding. A complete work system has to include the customer view which requires an iterative inspection of processes. Thus, the third assumption says that unplanned changes of processes belong to process evolution. BPI supports this in order to reveal dependencies and accomplish assimilations/redesigns.

P3.1: Business Process Intelligence generates a sociotechnical work system, which is more useful than traditional focal points including information technology, the information system itself, the organization, or the firm.

This proposition has to be validated with the usage of BPI. In this context, BPI uncovers dependencies between strategic and operational management by using key performance indicator systems and information process models. The latter provide information about goal conflicts and internal and external modifications. The internal and external perspectives are checked regularly and build up the framework for changes to achieve process improvements. As mentioned before, the main focus of OpBI is not on continuous process development. A strategic change has no high impact unless the core processes are changed. Equally, BPM acts on operational level and has only a weak connection to strategic level.

Propositions of *organizational information processing* [Figure 2, H4]

This theory identifies concepts of information processing needs and information processing capability [8]. It shows a relation between them enabling an achievement of an optimal process performance. In order to narrow decision finding's uncertainty, which is based on dynamic framework conditions, businesses can choose between two strategies. On the one hand, buffers may be included, in order to reduce the effect of uncertainty. On the other hand, structural mechanisms can be implicated, so that the information flow can be improved. Especially two strategies lead to the assumption that BPI provides a framework for the design of IT-architectures, in order to improve information flow. This creates transparency along process chains and reduces uncertainty effects.

P4.1: BPI will result in relative increases in information processing capacity associated with decision centralization and coordination.

P4.2: BPI will result in relative increases in information processing capacity associated with formalization.

P4.3: BPI will result in relative increases in information processing capacity associated with internal/external communication.

The organizational information processing concerns the design of new business processes depending on Business Intelligence as an integrated information system. In doing so, measuring points in process instances are analyzed and provided to the process owner. The description of measuring points and process instances creates transparency in business processes, which is supported and improved due to OpBI. According to this, the BPI approach is a holistic/integrated concept, because it uses on one hand operational data from classical BPM/OpBI and on the other hand strategic planning information from information process models. This closed loop generates events for process design.

The literature review and the deduced assertions from the multi theory approach constitute the first steps. An empirical study is the next intention within the BPI research. The examination of this first study objective is the analysis whether the benefits and the demands of a BPI. This is done by a regression based explanation model. This supports the analysis and discussion about the stated propositions. The empirical study focuses international and local companies to prove their employment concerning the propositions of dynamic capabilities (cf. P1.1 – P1.4). After market liberalization and process unbundling, the utility sector seems to be a candidate for the usage of a BPI. Especially the challenges of the rapidly-changing environment will be one main topic of this research type. Against this background, the results of this sample should be an objective and validate indicator for the relevance of a BPI. Moreover, a non-standardized expert interview with representatives of the energy branch will be conduct to prove the propositions of work systems (cf. P3.1). The main goal of these interviews is to find out the set of different decision and business processes with all their dependencies as well as the influences of unbundling guidelines. In addition to this, a first impression about the derived potential economic benefit of BPI is possible. An economic evaluation based on return other ratios seems to be meaningful at this point. Additionally, we are examining a target return and target variance portfolio to investigate the economic value of BPI more deeply. Based on this portfolio, the impact on the economic desirability can be seen and the adaption interval of decision making with BPI can be determined.

Further investigations are done with a case study method to prove the propositions of process virtualization (cf. P2.1 – P2.4). As part of this work, an explanatory case study is used. One of the largest German utility companies made his unbundled company-wide process models (event-driven-process chains) available. Thus, dependencies between different process types and potentials of process virtualization could be exposed. Finally, the propositions of organizational information processing (cf. P4.1 – P4.3) are proved within the case study. Hereby, the organizational and technical concepts of an utility company are inspected and monitored. The evaluation concentrates on business units, on process organization as well as on the use of integrated

IT-concepts for process execution (e.g. near real time systems). The result of this research step is in conclusion a placement within a business maturity model.

5 Conclusion

The paper provides a framework of conditions and guidance implications in favor of a Business Process Intelligence. It is the aim of BPI to advice analytical activities and the dynamic assimilation of business processes. It is determined that it is important that BPI supports not only the adaptation, but also the construction of business processes. In this sense a strategic/tactic connection between Business Process Management and Business Intelligence offers new concepts for a management support.

The paper serves with a literature review, too, facilitating a differentiation of process oriented Business Intelligence approaches. This has led to a morphological box to place the relevant concept differences and to be able to propose a BPI definition. Based on this, a multi theory approach is defined to serve as a basis for further research activities. The formulated propositions are a fundament for an empirical study to verify the need for a BPI. Additionally, a case study has to be done to be able to analyze the usability and benefits of a BPI.

References

1. Alter, S.: The Work System Method: Connecting People, Processes, and IT for Business Results. Work System Press, Larkspur (2006)
2. Bauer, A., Schmid, T.: Was macht Operational BI aus? BI-Spektrum 4(1), 13–14 (2009)
3. Blasum, R.: Operational BI, 1–8 (2006), `http://www.businesscode.de/cms/uploads/media/BCD_Operational_BI_01.pdf` (November 28, 2009)
4. Bucher, T., Dinter, B.: Anwendungsfälle der Nutzung analytischer Informationen im operativen Kontext. In: Bichler, M., Hess, T., Krcmar, H., Lechner, U., Matthes, F., Picot, A., Speitkamp, B., Wolf, P. (eds.) Multikonferenz Wirtschaftsinformatik 2008 (MKWI 2008), München, GITO, Berlin, pp. 1–13 (2008)
5. Castellanos, M., Weijters, T.: Preface (BPI 2005). In: Bussler, C.J., Haller, A., et al. (eds.) BPM 2005. LNCS, vol. 3812, pp. 159–161. Springer, Heidelberg (2006)
6. Deutsches Institut, D.I.N.: für Normung e.V.: DIN EN ISO 9000 (2005): Qualitätsmanagementsysteme - Grundlagen und Begriffe (ISO 9000:2005), EN ISO 9000:2005 (2005)
7. Eckerson, W.: Best Practices in Operational BI: Converging Analytical and Operational Processes, TDWI Best Practices Report, 1–32 (2007)
8. Galbraith, J.R.: Organization design: An information processing view. Interfaces 4(3), 28–36 (1974)
9. Genrich, M., Kokkonen, A., Moormann, J., et al.: Challenges for Business Process Intelligence: Discussions at the BPI Workshop 2007. In: ter Hofstede, A.H.M., Benatallah, B., Paik, H.-Y. (eds.) BPM Workshops 2007. LNCS, vol. 4928, pp. 5–10. Springer, Heidelberg (2008)
10. Gluchowski, P., Gabriel, R., Dittmar, C.: Management Support Systeme und Business Intelligence: Computergestützte Informationssysteme für Führungskräfte und Entscheidungsträger. Springer, Heidelberg (2008)

11. Gluchowski, P., Kemper, H., Seufert, A.: Innovative Prozess-Steuerung. BI-Spektrum 4(1), 8–12 (2009)
12. Grigori, D., Casati, F., Castellanos, M., et al.: Business Process Intelligence. Computers in Industry 53(3), 321–343 (2004)
13. Hall, C.: Business Process Intelligence. Business Process Trends 2(6), 1–11 (2004)
14. Harmon, P.: Business Performance Management: The Other BPM. Business Process Trends 2(7), 1–12 (2004)
15. Horváth, P., Mayer, R.: Prozeßkostenrechnung - Konzeption und Entwicklungen. Physica, Wiesbaden (1993)
16. Hosny, H.: Business Process Intelligence. In: ATIT 2009, Cairo (2009)
17. Kannan, N.: BPI: What is it and how does it help (2008), `http://www.businessprocesstrends.com/deliver_file.cfm?fileType=publication&fileName=07%2D05%20%` (December 11, 2009)
18. Overby, E.M.: Process Virtualization Theory and the Impact of Information Technology. Organization Science 19(2), 277–291 (2008)
19. Pérez, M., Möller, C.: The Predictive Aspect of Business Process Intelligence: Lessons Learned on Bridging IT and Business. In: ter Hofstede, A.H.M., Benatallah, B., Paik, H.-Y. (eds.) BPM Workshops 2007. LNCS, vol. 4928, pp. 11–16. Springer, Heidelberg (2008)
20. Porter, M., Millar, V.E.: How information gives you competitive advantage. Harvard Business Review 63(4), 149–160 (1985)
21. Ritchey, T.: Modeling Complex Socio-Technical Systems using Morphological Analysis (2010), `http://www.swemorph.com/it-art.html` (February 5, 2010)
22. Schmelzer, H., Sesselmann, W.: Geschäftsprozessmanagement in der Praxis: Kunden zufrieden stellen, Produktivität steigern, Wert erhöhen. Hanser, Munich (2008)
23. Teece, D., Pisano, G., Shuen, A.: Dynamic capabilities and strategic management. Strategic Management Journal 7(18), 509–533 (1997)
24. Weijters, A.J.M.M., van der Aalst, W.M.P.: Process Mining: Discovering Workflow Models from Event-Based Data. In: Kröse, B., De Rijke, M., Schreiber, G., van Someren, M. (eds.) Proceedings of the 13th Belgium-Netherlands Conference on Artificial Intelligence (BNAIC 2001), pp. 283–290. BNVKI, Maastricht (2001)

Auditing Workflow Executions against Dataflow Policies

Rafael Accorsi and Claus Wonnemann

Department of Telematics
Albert-Ludwigs-Universität Freiburg, Germany
{accorsi,wonnemann}@iig.uni-freiburg.de

Abstract. This paper presents IFAudit, an approach for the audit of dataflow policies in workflow models. IFAudit encompasses three steps. First, propagation graphs are generated from workflows' log data. They represent the explicit information flows caused, e.g., by data access and message-passing, that have occurred during the execution of the workflow. Second, dataflow policies expressing security and compliance requirements are formalized in a system-independent manner as a binary relation on the workflow principals. Third, an audit algorithm analyzes the propagation graphs against the policies and delivers evidence with regard to whether the workflow complies with them. Besides presenting the corresponding algorithms, the paper discusses possible extensions to address more general types of information flows.

Keywords: Dataflow, audit, policy, workflow and business process.

1 Introduction

With workflows becoming omnipresent in the realization of automated business processes, their security and dependability aspects have been gaining on momentum. While a plethora of approaches exists which address the construction of workflows that meet functional and non-functional requirements "by design" [5,15,18], there is no work tackling a-posteriori analysis of workflow logs for the automated detection of policy violations [16]. In consequence, audits are manual and, thereby, time-intensive, costly and error-prone [4,7].

This paper presents IFAudit, a novel approach for the audit of workflow models against dataflow policies. The key idea of IFAudit is the use log files as a basis for the detection of dataflow violations. Given a log file containing the execution traces of a workflow, IFAudit reconstructs a set of *propagation graphs* that formalize the flow of information between the subjects in the workflow. Besides representing models of the execution used for auditing, propagation graphs are also useful as a graphic cue to demonstrate the flow of information and possible attacks.

Within the context of IFAudit, dataflow policies are formalized as constraints on the possible and undesirable relations among system subjects, independently from the concrete implementation. This formalization is stronger than access

W. Abramowicz and R. Tolksdorf (Eds.): BIS 2010, LNBIP 47, pp. 207–217, 2010.

Instance ID	Timestamp	Activity Name	Originator	Input	Output
1	2009-04-23 08:08:00	Retrieve_Data	Subject1	Msg1 (EXT)	File1
1	2009-04-23 08:09:00	Retrieve_Data	Subject1	Msg2 (EXT)	File2
1	2009-04-23 08:12:00	Create_Report	User_Accounting	File1, File2	Report1
1	2009-04-23 08:12:00	Publish_Report	User_IR	Report1	Public_Report09

Fig. 1. An exemplary workflow log file

control policies, such as XACML and EPAL, because it captures information propagation throughout the system (*end-to-end*) rather than access at certain access points and channels.

With a set of models and the corresponding policies at hand, IFAudit encompasses algorithms for auditing the models and generating evidence with regard to whether the dataflow policies are complied with. Technically, this means traversing the propagation graphs and detecting either unallowed or missing transitions prescribed by the policies.

The contributions of this paper are the following:

- A meta-language for the expression of dataflow and, more generally, information flow requirements (Section 3).
- An algorithm to generate propagation graphs from log files (Section 4).
- An audit algorithm for the automated analysis of propagation graphs against policies and the generation of evidence of adherence (Section 4).

The overall goal of IFAudit is to design methods for the reconstruction of workflow models and their properties from execution traces, and to determine whether these models comply with security policies. While this paper focuses on dataflow properties and, hence, on a subset of information flow properties, preliminary results show that the approach can be generalized for other information flow policies, such as Chinese-Wall and Biba [6], whose instantiations are relevant in enterprise settings, and *implicit* information flow, through covert channels [13].

2 Workflows and Log Data

Workflows formally describe business processes as structured sequences of activities that must be performed in order to reach a certain business goal. The activities in a workflow can be a mixture of automated tasks (i.e. programs/services) and human interaction (e.g. the creation of documents). All the different formalisms that are used for workflow specification (such as BPEL, BPMN, Event-driven Process Chains) share a "core" of basic control constructs, including parallelism, conditionals and synchronization, making them in essence equally powerful (Turing-complete). The execution of a workflow is coordinated by an execution engine which, e.g., triggers activities, synchronizes their interaction

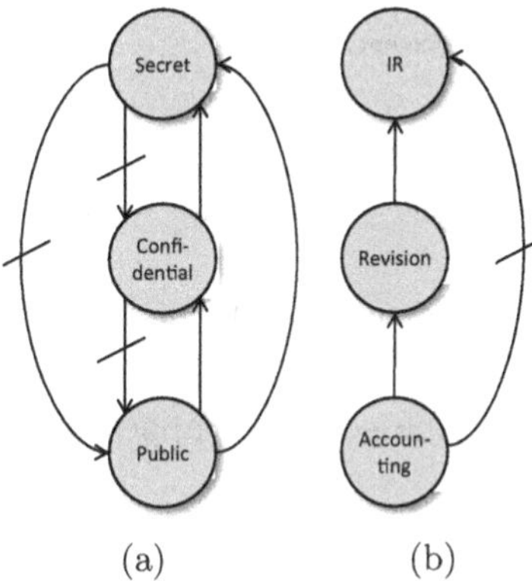

Fig. 2. Examplary flow policies

and communication, and writes log data. The latter builds the basis for the audits considered in this paper.

An excerpt of a log file with the required attributes is depicted in

Log files of workflow systems are structured as sequences of entries, as depicted in Fig. 1. An entry comprises attributes of the activity, such as the particular workflow instance, the timestamp, and the data items that were processed. The IFAudit system uses the MXML log format, that originated as a log format for process mining [20]. We assume that a log file has the following properties:

- An entry can be attributed to an activitiy and to a workflow instance.
- An entry contains the originator (i.e. the subject on which behalf the corresponding activity was performed) and the data items that were read (input) and written (output) by the activity.
- The events are chronologically ordered by a timestamp.
- The log data is authentic, i.e. it has not been tampered with. Mechanisms to ensure authenticity exist [2].

Formally, $\mathcal{L}_\mathcal{W}$ denotes the log file for a workflow $\mathcal{W}$. The execution of $\mathcal{W}$ produces a log file $\mathcal{L}_\mathcal{W}$ with the aforementioned properties. $\mathcal{L}_\mathcal{W}$ is in $\mathcal{A}^*$, where $\mathcal{A}$ is the universe of all log file entries. $\mathcal{L}_\mathcal{W}$ can be partitioned into a set $\{i_0^\mathcal{W}, i_1^\mathcal{W}, ..., i_n^\mathcal{W}\}$ where $i_i^\mathcal{W}$ denotes the trace (ordered sequence of log entries) for the ith execution of $\mathcal{W}$ $(0 \leq i \leq n)$. An entry a has the attributes *orig* (the originator), *input* (the set of input data items) and *output* (the set of output data items). The attributes of an entry are projected with a dot, e.g. *a.orig* for the originator.

For conciseness' sake, below the term *activity* is also used to denote the *log entry* of an activity.

3 Policies

An information flow policy $\mathcal{P} = \{r_1, ..., r_n\}$ is a set of rules that specify which groups of principals in a system may or may not exchange information. The

```
<Policy>      ::= <Rule> | <Rule>, <Policy>
<Rule>        ::= <Restriction> ⇒ <Exception>
<Restriction> ::= true | <FlowRel>
<Exception>   ::= false | <FR-DNF>
<FR-DNF>      ::= (<ConClause>) | (<ConClause>) ∨ <FR-DNF>
<ConClause>   ::= <FlowRel> | <FlowRel> ∧ <ConClause>
<FlowRel>     ::= <Domain>⇝<Domain>
<Domain>      ::= d ∈ 𝒟
```

Fig. 3. BNF grammar of the policy language

principals are the originators (subjects) that appear in a log file $\mathcal{L}_\mathcal{W}$, denoted as $\mathcal{S}_\mathcal{W} = \bigcup_{a \in \mathcal{L}_\mathcal{W}} a.orig$.

Principals are assigned security classifications from a set $\mathcal{D}$ of security domains. A security domain denotes the rights and privileges of principals to obtain or manipulate information. The actual information flow policy specifies among which security domains information may or must not be exchanged, respectively. The function $sc : \mathcal{S} \rightarrow \mathcal{D}$ assigns principals to security domains.

Fig. 2(a) shows an example of a multi-level-security policy with three domains that are arranged according to a lattice $Secret \succ Confidential \succ Public$. A crossed arrow indicates that there must not flow information. Information may flow only upwards this lattice and thus cannot leak to principals with a lower clearance.

However, it is insufficient to state that some information may or may not flow from one principal to another. Rather, the exact path that some information has to take through the organization must be prescribed, for instance, to ensure that financial statements are cleared by the revision department before being published to investors. A corresponding information flow policy is depicted in Fig. 2(b): information coming from the *Accounting* domain must not flow directly to the *IR* department, but has to pass through *Revision*.

3.1 Syntax

A policy rule has the form $Restriction \Rightarrow Exception$. *Restriction* is a flow relation $source \leadsto target$, which specifies that information must not flow from domain *source* to domain *target* ($source, target \in \mathcal{D}$). *Exception* is a logical combination of flow relations in disjunctive normal form which defines legitimate flows that might contradict *Restriction* (as in the example in Fig. 2(b)). Fig. 3 gives the grammar for these policies in Backus-Naur-Form (BNF).

Using this grammar, the policies in Fig. 2 have the form

```
Secret⇝Confidential ⇒ false,
Confidential⇝Public ⇒ false,
Secret⇝Public ⇒ false
```

and

```
Accounting⇝IR ⇒
  (Accounting⇝Revision ∧ Revision⇝IR).
```

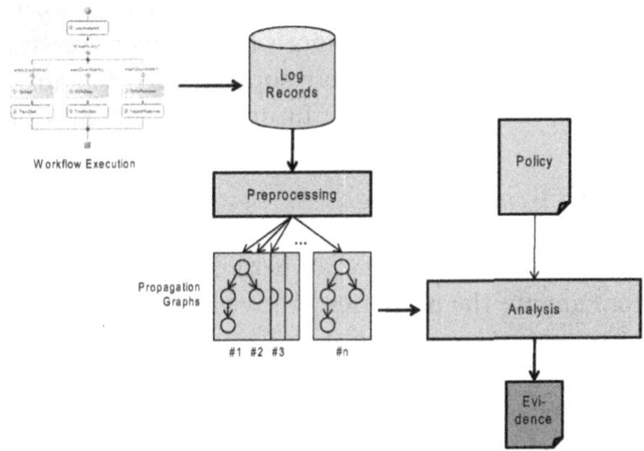

Fig. 4. Outline of the IFAudit system

This rule format has been integrated in the ExPDT policy language to build a fully-fledged language for information flow policies. ExPDT is an expressive policy language designed for formalizing privacy and compliance policies [12]. An ExPDT policy and the target system share a common ontology, which maps the policy entities to those of the system. Ontologies are expressed in OWL-DL, which is the maximum subset of the Web Ontology Language (OWL) that is computationally complete and decidable.

3.2 Semantics

Besides the extensional specification of flow relations, which denote whether data may flow between domains, an information flow policy defines which patterns of system actions constitute information transmission. We refer to this part of the policy as *flow semantics*.

The IFAudit system currently supports the specification and verification of dataflow requirements, i.e. constraints on the explicit information flow. Here, the flow semantics is trace-based and fairly straightforward: there is an dataflow from domain d_1 to domain d_2, if, and only if, there is a data item which has been modified by an activity from d_1 and is subsequently read by an activity from d_2. Formally:

$$\begin{aligned}
&\forall d_1, d_2 \in \mathcal{D} : d_1 \rightsquigarrow d_2 \Leftrightarrow \\
&\qquad \exists (a_1, a_2 \in \mathcal{A}), \exists (p_1, p_2 \in \mathcal{S}) : \\
&\qquad (a_1.orig = p_1) \wedge (a_2.orig = p_2) \wedge \\
&\qquad (sc(p_1) = d_1) \wedge (sc(p_2) = d_2) \wedge \\
&\qquad ((d_1.out \cap d_2.in) \neq \{\}) \wedge (a_1 < a_2),
\end{aligned}$$

where $<$ is the temporal ordering according to the timestamp. This approach is similar to the tainting mode in the Perl programming language. It is sufficiently expressive to capture violations, such as failure to "clear" information or illicit propagation of some data item. For a more fine-grained analysis and to capture other kinds of information flows, more sophisticated semantics and analysis algorithms are needed and are subject of future work (see Section 6).

4 Audit Algorithm

The IFAudit system analyzes dataflow at workflow level, i.e. the information transfer that occurs among the activities. Activities are regarded as black boxes of whose internal operation is not necessarily visible, but only their I/O. At this level of abstraction, IFAudit allows to check whether a workflow instance has exhibited illicit information flows with regard to a policy, e.g. whether some datum was possibly read by a non-authorized party or whether a document has been double-checked before being published (four-eye rule).

The structure of IFAudit is outlined in Fig. 4. In the first phase of the audit process, the log entries are mapped into a graph-based representation. For each workflow instance, a *propagation graph* (PG) is created to denote the dataflows between the involved subjects that have occurred in the corresponding instance. The PGs are subsequently analyzed for illicit information flows according to the given policy. In the case of policy violations, the IFAudit system issues evidence specifying the dataflow that caused the violation.

The PG for a trace $i_n^{\mathcal{W}} \subseteq \mathcal{L}_{\mathcal{W}}$ is denoted $PG_n^{\mathcal{W}}$. It is defined as a graph (V, E), where $V = \{a \in \mathcal{A} \,|\, a \in i_n^{\mathcal{W}}\}$ is a set of activities (representing the graph's vertices), and $E = \{(a,b) \in (\mathcal{A} \times \mathcal{A}) \,|\, a < b \wedge a.output \cap b.input \neq \{\}\}$ is an asymmetric relation representing the graph's (directed) edges. An edge (a, b) in a PG indicates that there was a dataflow from activity a to activity b.

Constructing Propagation Graphs. Fig. 5 shows the pseudo-code for the CONSTRUCT-procedure, which constructs the propagation graph $PG_n^{\mathcal{W}}$ for a trace $i_n^{\mathcal{W}}$. During the construction process, the procedure maintains a mapping MOD that maps a data item to the activity that last modified it. Starting with the initial activity, every activity from $i_n^{\mathcal{W}}$ is added as a vertex to $PG_n^{\mathcal{W}}$. It is checked whether an input datum of the activity that is currently under consideration has been modified by previous activities. This is done by comparing the activities' *input*-attributes with the domain DOM(MOD) of mapping MOD. If a data item d is found, an edge from the activity that last modified d to the current activity is inserted into $PG_n^{\mathcal{W}}$. Afterwards, the mapping for each data item that is modified by the current activity is updated or added to MOD. The result of the CONSTRUCT procedure is a propagation graph $PG_n^{\mathcal{W}}$ which contains every activity in $i_n^{\mathcal{W}}$ as a vertex. Not every activity in $PG_n^{\mathcal{W}}$ can necessarily be reached from the initial activity, if there has not been a corresponding dataflow. Therefore, $PG_n^{\mathcal{W}}$ might have multiple nodes with an indegree of zero (i.e. there are no inbound dataflows). All dataflows originating from these nodes have to be checked separately (see below).

```
CONSTRUCT(i_n^W):
MOD := {};
for each (a in i_n^W) do
    Add a as a vertex to PG_n^W;
    for each (d in (a.input ∩ DOM(MOD))) do
        Add edge (MOD(d), a) to PG_n^W;
    for each (o in a.output) do
        MOD := MOD ∪ o⟶a;
```

Fig. 5. Pseudo-code for the CONSTRUCT-procedure

The CONSTRUCT procedure is applied consecutively to every trace $i_n^{\mathcal{W}}$ from a logfile $\mathcal{L}_{\mathcal{W}}$. If a propagation graph is identical to another that has been generated before, it is discarded in order to minimize the effort of the audit algorithm.[1]

Audit. To check whether a workflow instance adheres to a given policy, its PG is traversed in a depth-first fashion. The starting points for the traversal are those activities with no incoming dataflow (nodes with an indegree of zero). During traversal, it is checked whether an activity marks the starting point of an illicit information flow (i.e. if it is assigned a security domain that is the source of a rule's restriction). Such rules are kept in a set of "open" rules and checked whether they are "closed" (i.e. violated) by a subsequent activity. An activity closes a rule, if its assigned security class corresponds to the end point of that rule's restriction, and if the rule's *exception*-clause evaluates to *false*. Fig. 6 shows the pseudo-code for the procedures CHECK and VISIT. The CHECK procedure is the main procedure which initializes the data structures and triggers the traversals. The VISIT procedure checks whether an activity closes or opens a rule before recursively applying itself to each of the activity's successors. The field *OpenRules* contains the set of rules that have been opened by one or many activities residing above the current activity in the PG.

The mapping SRC maps each rule from *OpenRules* to the set of activities that have opened that rule. At the beginning, VISIT checks whether the current activity u closes any rules and reports a violation along with corresponding evidence (see below). Afterwards, *OpenRules* and SRC are updated with the rules that are opened by u itself. The successors of u are subsequently processed according to their chronological appearance in the log file (otherwise, if some activity a_2 would be visited before a_1, and $a_1 < a_2$, a dataflow from a_1 to a_2 might be missed). Before VISIT finishes the processing of activity u and returns to its predecessor in the PG, SRC and *OpenRules* are adjusted: for every rule r that is opened by u, u is removed from the set SRC(r). If u is the only activity that currently opens r, r is removed from the set of open rules.

The evidence that is created when a violation occurs contains the corresponding rule and a subgraph from the PG in which the violation was detected. This subgraph denotes the dataflow that caused the violation and thus serves as a

[1] Because a PG abstracts from the concrete value of a transferred datum, log traces with the same sequence of activities (and identical I/O) will result in identical PGs. In consequence, the audit algorithm will identical results.

```
CHECK(PG_n^W, P):
for each (Vertex a in PG_n^W with INDEGREE(a) = 0) do
    OpenRules := {};
    for each (Rule r ∈ P) do
        SRC(r) := {};
    VISIT(a);

VISIT(u):
for each (Rule r ∈ OpenRules that is closed by u) do
    Report violation of r through flow(s) from SRC(r) to u;
for each (Rule r ∈ P that is opened by u) do
    OpenRules := OpenRules ∪ r;
    SRC(r) = SRC(r) ∪ u;
Mark u as visited;
Successors := Direct successors of u;
Sort Successors in ascending order;
for each (v in Successors) do
    if (v is not marked as visited) then
        VISIT(v);
for each (Rule r ∈ P that is opened by u) do
    SRC(r) = SRC(r) \ u;
    if (SRC(r) = {}) then
        OpenRules := OpenRules \ r;
```

Fig. 6. Pseudo-code for the CHECK and VISIT procedures

counterexample for the workflow's adherence to the corresponding rule. Fig. 7 depicts an example of a PG that violates the policy rule from Fig. 2(b), along with the corresponding evidence generated by the audit algorithm.

5 Related Work

A number of approaches to the a-posteriori checking of security policies have been proposed that are related to IFAudit. The ExaMINA system allows the formalization and checking of privacy policies [1]. ExaMINA formulates policies in terms of access rules that can be augmented with conditions and obligations (e.g. requiring the deletion of a datum after a certain period). APPLE is geared towards controlling the use and propagation of documents in distributed environments [9]. It consists of a logical framework, which uses logs to verify whether actions were authorized, and a trust management system which ensures that data items are only provided to users on an auditable system. Cedequist et al. present a policy language that allows the specification of conditions, obligations and the refinement of policies [8]. The associated proof checking system can verify whether data that is distributed in a decentralized architecture has been used according to a usage policy that is passed along with the data. IFAudit differs from these approaches as it uses an explicit notion of information flow, which allows to track information over several data items without having to specify the precise actions that may or must not be performed by the subjects.

Process mining is a discipline from business process management which addresses the reconstruction of workflow models from log data [19]. Process mining is driven by organizational problems and delivers models of a workflow's functionality which are used, for instance, to check the structural conformance of

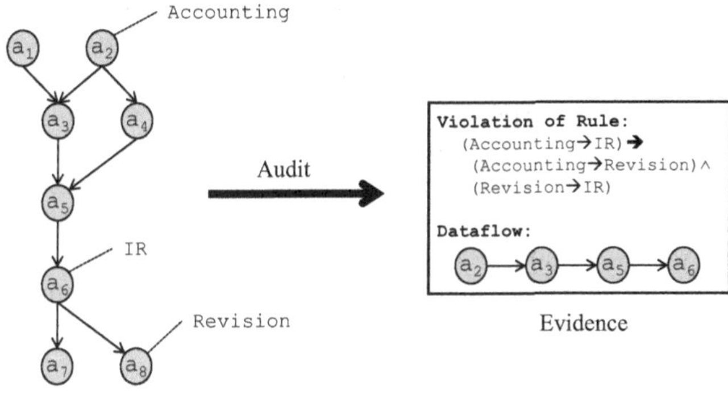

Fig. 7. Generation of evidence

the implemented workflow with the intended business process or to identify performance bottlenecks. In contrast to the propgation graphs used by IFAudit, reconstructed workflow models do not account for information flows. Propagation graphs as they are used in this paper build on a similar concept proposed in [14].

A plethora of research exists on the prevention of illicit information flows in programs through static or dynamic analyses (for an overview see [17]). Its a-posteriori detection has previously been addressed by the authors [3,21]. A hybrid approach is proposed by Hammer et al. which combine static program analysis with log information of the corresponding program in order to increase the precision of the analysis [10].

6 Conclusion and Ongoing Work

In its current state, IFAudit is restricted to checking dataflow policies constraining the path of unspecified data items. Therefore, IFAudit is capable of expressing and checking elementary security requirements (in essence those depicted in the example in Fig. 2). However, as it does not disinguish between data items, more fine-grained security requirements are currently not supported. A further limitation regards the detection of implicit information flows, i.e. information transmission through channels that are not intended for that purpose [13]. These and other issues are currently addressed in the realm of a more comprehensive research project on secure workflows.

We currently evaluate the efficiency of IFAudit with a proof-of-concept implementation. For this purpose, a simulation environment was built, which executes workflows and writes the corresponding log files. Workflow models are taken from a collection of industrial business processes and parametrized to exhibit illicit dataflows with respect to policies that were derived from common compliance frameworks (such as Hipaa [11]).

Ongoing Work. IFAudit is part of an ongoing project on the forensic generation of formal security certificates for workflows. Central to the project is a formal meta-model for workflows which subsumes the propagation graphs used in this paper and allows to express both dataflows and implicit information flows. Corresponding models are generated either from static workflow descriptions (for instance in BPEL or BPMN) which are complemented with runtime information from log traces, or solely from log data, using reconstruction algorithms. For the analysis of the workflow model, we aim to employ existing techniques for information flow analysis which are adapted correspondingly. The issued certificates shall formally circumscribe the security guarantees provided by the workflow.

References

1. Accorsi, R.: Automated Privacy Audits to Complement the Notion of Control for Identity Management. In: de Leeuw, E., Fischer-Hübner, S., Tseng, J., Borking, J. (eds.) Policies and Research in Identity Management, IFIP, vol. 261. Springer, Heidelberg (2008)
2. Accorsi, R.: Safe-Keeping Digital Evidence with Secure Logging Protocols: State of the Art and Challenges. In: Proceedings IMF 2009, September 2009, pp. 94–110 (2009)
3. Accorsi, R., Wonnemann, C.: Detective information flow analysis for business processes. In: BPSC, pp. 223–224 (2009)
4. Bace, J., Rozwell, C., Feiman, J., Kirwin, B.: Understanding the costs of compliance. Technical report, Gartner Research (July 2006)
5. Barletta, M., Ranise, S., Viganò, L.: Verifying the Interplay of Authorization Policies and Workflow in Service-Oriented Architectures. In: CSE (3), pp. 289–296 (2009)
6. Benantar, M.: Access Control Systems. Springer, Heidelberg (2006)
7. Bussmann, K.-D., Krieg, O., Nestler, C., Salvenmoser, S., Schroth, A., Theile, A., Trunk, D.: Wirtschaftskriminalität, – Sicherheitslage in deutschen Großunternehmen. Report by Martin-Luther-Universität Halle-Wittenberg and PricewaterhouseCoopers AG (2009) (in German)
8. Cederquist, J.G., Corin, R., Dekker, M.A.C., Etalle, S., den Hartog, J.I.: An Audit Logic for Accountability. In: Proceedings of the Sixth IEEE International Workshop on Policies for Distributed Systems and Networks, pp. 34–43. IEEE Computer Society, Los Alamitos (2005)
9. Etalle, S., Winsborough, W.: A posteriori compliance control. In: Proceedings of the 12th ACM symposium on Access control models and technologies, pp. 11–20 (2007)
10. Hammer, C., Grimme, M., Krinke, J.: Dynamic path conditions in dependence graphs. In: Proceedings PEPM 2006, pp. 58–67. ACM, New York (2006)
11. HIPAA: Health Insurance Portability and Accountability Act (2006), `http://www.cms.hhs.gov/HIPAAGenInfo/`
12. Kähmer, M., Gilliot, M., Müller, G.: Automating Privacy Compliance with ExPDT. In: CEC/EEE, pp. 87–94 (2008)
13. Lampson, B.W.: A note on the confinement problem. Communications of the ACM 16(10), 613–615 (1973)
14. Livshits, B., Nori, A.V., Rajamani, S.K., Banerjee, A.: Merlin: Specification inference for explicit information flow problems

15. Lohmann, N., Massuthe, P., Stahl, C., Weinberg, D.: Analyzing Interacting BPEL Processes. In: Dustdar, S., Fiadeiro, J.L., Sheth, A.P. (eds.) BPM 2006. LNCS, vol. 4102, pp. 17–32. Springer, Heidelberg (2006)
16. Müller, G., Accorsi, R., Höhn, S., Sackmann, S.: Secure usage control for transparency in financial markets. Informatik Spektrum 33(1), 3–13 (2010)
17. Sabelfeld, A., Myers, A.C.: Language-based information-flow security. IEEE Journal on Selected Areas in Communications 21(1), 5–19 (2003)
18. Sun, S.X., Zhao, J.L., Nunamaker, J.F., Sheng, O.R.L.: Formulating the Data-Flow Perspective for Business Process Management. Information Systems Research 17(4), 374–391 (2006)
19. van der Aalst, W., Weijters, T., Maruster, L.: Workflow Mining: Discovering Process Models from Event Logs. IEEE Transactions on Knowledge and Data Engineering 16(9), 1128–1142 (2004)
20. van Dongen, B.F., van der Aalst, W.M.P.: A Meta Model for Process Mining Data. In: EMOI-INTEROP, vol. 160 (2005)
21. Wonnemann, C., Accorsi, R., Müller, G.: On Information Flow Forensics in Business Application Scenarios. In: Proceedings Compsac 2009, vol. 2, pp. 324–328. IEEE Computer Society, Los Alamitos (2009)

Workflow Data Footprints

Nikola Trčka

Department of Mathematics and Computer Science
Eindhoven University of Technology
P.O. Box 513, 5600 MB Eindhoven, The Netherlands
n.trcka@tue.nl

Abstract. Traditional business workflows are activity-centric, i.e., they focus mostly on specifying the control-flow aspect of business processes. The data aspect, although equally relevant, is attached to the control-flow later, as a second rate citizen, making the actual document sharing and exchange much less transparent and harder to verify. In this paper we introduce the notion of a data footprint, a directed graph representing the flow of some (user-specified) data elements, abstracting, as much as possible, from all the other aspects. We show how data footprints can be obtained automatically and efficiently from every activity-centric workflow that includes some conceptual data information. We also show how a footprint can be used to discover data-flow errors, or to compare the modeled object life-cycle with the required one.

Keywords: Business process management, Workflow verification, Data-Flow, Data Life-Cycle.

1 Introduction

A business workflow typically specifies three perspectives of a business process: control-flow (ordering of business tasks), data-flow (document sharing and exchange) and resources (people and/or machines for performing the tasks). In the initial design phase the resource information is often omitted, being somehow orthogonal to the process. Moreover, in the traditional way of modeling, the control-flow is specified first, and the data information is added on top of it. Despite the many promising data-centric approaches [6], this so-called activity-centric approach remains dominant.

Data-flow, although also fully specified, is still a second rate citizen of a workflow. While it is clear which tasks will be executed in a sequence or in parallel, the actual flow of data at execution time is not at all obvious. This can lead to several problems. First, workflows are often used for documentation, and for communication between business partners and legal authorities. Looking only at the specified order in which the tasks are executed often provides insufficient information, and a much better insight into the whole process is obtained if the most important documents of the process are identified and their stages are studied in isolation. In addition, two processes that seem different from the outside, might manipulate their common data in almost the same way. Second problem

W. Abramowicz and R. Tolksdorf (Eds.): BIS 2010, LNBIP 47, pp. 218–229, 2010.

is that the data-flow can be incorrectly specified, or simply not comply with the control-flow. The common data-related modeling errors, like missing or redundant data [12,13], should be detected and repaired at design time. Third, every data object is expected to follow a certain life-cycle, that is, either implicitly or explicitly, known to the workflow designer. The control-flow based approach makes it difficult for the designer to ensure that the modeled data-flow indeed complies to this required life-cycle.

To enable workflow designers to have a better insight over the data, and to enable them to diagnose data-related problems at design time, this paper introduces the concept of *data-footprint.* Given a set of data elements, such as e.g. an insurance claim or client details, the data footprint is a directed graph in which the nodes represent states of these data elements, and the labels on arcs represent tasks that manipulate these elements and cause them to change their state. Task labels can correspond to task names in the process, but the user is also given an option to define suitable representations/abstractions for these labels. In addition, not every arc is required to have a label; arcs without labels are *internal*, meaning that their actual content is irrelevant for the considered analysis. For example, the data footprint of the *insurance claim* document in a claim-handling process would typically contain a transition from the state *claim.registered* to the state *claim.checked.* If tasks *Check by manager* and *Check by clerk* both cause the claim to change its state in this way, we could, depending on the analysis objective, choose to keep both task names as labels (when the actual executor of the task is relevant), replace both names by one label *Check* (when only the task type is relevant), or simply omit the labels, assuming that there is already enough information in the states.

We use the model of *workflow nets with data* (*WFD-nets*) [13] for the modeling of business workflows. A WFD-net is basically a workflow net [1] (a Petri net tailored towards the modeling of control-flow in workflows), extended with conceptual read/write/delete data operations and data dependent guards (cf. Figure 2). The model has been successfully used for specifying business workflows (as an abstraction from notations deployed by popular modeling tools like *Protos* of Pallas Athena), and for detecting data- and control-flow problems [13]. Given a WFD-net and a set of data elements, the process of obtaining the data-footprint for these elements is threefold (cf. Figure 4). First, the statespace of a WFD-net is generated, capturing all reachable states of the modeled process (cf. Figure 3). The information related to those data elements that are not in the input set is next hidden, and the user can specify a desired labeling for the remaining tasks (cf. Figures 5 and 8). Then, standard minimization modulo branching bisimulation equivalence [4,5] is applied, efficiently producing the minimal graph in which (almost) all internal behavior has been removed (cf. Figures 6 and 9). This graph is the *footprint* of the considered data elements.

Although data footprints can be used for various kinds of analysis, this paper focuses on the following two applications:

1. *Verification of data-flow errors* – In [13] we formalized nine typical data-flow errors in business workflows. These errors are per data element, so they can be efficiently checked on data footprints, very often by visual inspection only. We give one example of this technique in the paper.
2. *Checking data life-cycle compliance* – A data footprint can be seen as a graph describing the states of some data objects in the workflow. We show how simulation relations [9] can be used to compare the data footprints of these objects with their expected life-cycles.

All the results in this paper are illustrated on a small but realistic model of a shipment handling process.

The paper is structured as follows. In the reminder of the introduction we discuss some related work. In Section 2 we introduce WFD-nets and explain the method for generating their statespaces. Section 3 is the main section of the paper; it describes the actual data footprint generation process with some examples of its use. The last section gives some conclusions and directions for future work.

Related work. The work closest to ours is [11], where the authors devise a procedure for generating object life-cycles from UML activity diagrams (without guards and data removal). While we base our work on a well established behavioral equivalence, namely branching bisimulation, their procedure is based on a set of ad-hoc rules, and is not placed in any known abstraction framework. Moreover, their focus is entirely on compliance checks, and they do not support task-label abstractions. As related work we also mention [2], where branching bismulation is used as a correctness criterion for refining object life-cycles.

Several authors have worked in the direction opposite to us [10,8,7]; they develop methods to automatically assemble workflows from the existing life-cycles of their data elements.

2 WFD-Nets for the Modeling of (Business) Workflows

In this section we introduce *workflow nets with data* (WFD-nets). WFD-nets are based on Petri nets and workflow nets, so we define these two models first. The style of this section is rather informal; for a formal definition of WFD-nets please see [13].

Petri nets. Petri nets are directed graphs with two types of nodes: *places* (drawn as circles) and *transitions* (drawn as rectangles). Places can only be connected to transitions and transitions can only be connected to places. Figure 1 shows a Petri net with places $p_1, \ldots, p_7$ and transitions $t_1, \ldots, t_5$.

If there is an ingoing arc from a place to a transition t, then this place is an *input place* of t. Output places are defined accordingly. For example, in the Petri net depicted in Figure 1, p_2 is the input place of both t_2 and t_3, and p_6 and p_7 are the only output places of t_5.

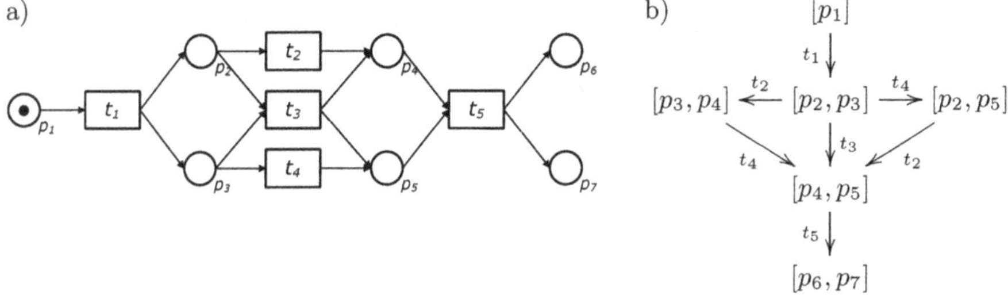

Fig. 1. a) A Petri net and b) its reachability graph

At any time a place contains zero or more *tokens*, drawn as black dots. The *state* of the Petri net, often referred to as *marking*, is the distribution of tokens over its places. A Petri net with a marking is called a *marked* Petri net. In Figure 1 only one place is initially marked (p_1). Note that more places could be marked in the initial state and that places can be marked with multiple tokens. A transition is said to be *enabled* in some marking if all its input places contain at least one token. An enabled transition may *fire*, consuming one token from each input place and producing one token for each output place. In Figure 1, t_1 is enabled and its firing will result in the state that marks places p_2 and p_3 with one token. In this state, t_2, t_3, and t_4 are enabled. If, e.g., t_2 fires now, t_3 becomes disabled, but t_4 remains enabled. Similarly, if t_4 fires, t_3 becomes disabled, but t_2 remains enabled, etc.

The *reachability graph* (or the *statespace*) of a marked Petri net shows its dynamic behavior. Every node in this graph represents a reachable marking, and every labeled arc indicates the firing of a transition. Figure 1b shows the reachability graph of the Petri net from Figure 1a.

Workflow nets. The assumption that typical workflows have a well-defined starting point and a well-defined ending point has led to the notion of *workflow nets* [1]. A workflow net is a Petri net in which: 1) there is a single *source* place *start* (no transition has this place as output); 2) there is a single *sink* place *end* (no transition has this place as input); and 3) every node, i.e. place or transition, is on a path from *start* to *end*.

The Petri net from Figure 1 is not a workflow net because it has two sink places, p_6 and p_7. If these two places are merged into one place p_{67}, the net becomes a workflow net, with one source place p_1 and one sink place p_{67}.

Transitions in workflow nets are also called *tasks*. A *case* is an instance of a workflow, formally defined as a marked workflow net in which the start place is marked with one token and all the other places are empty (this marking is called the *initial marking*). Several cases of a workflow may coexist but we assume that they are completely independent from each other. Therefore, we can refer to the properties of a case as the properties of the workflow net itself.

The *final marking* of a case (and of the workflow net) is the marking in which the end place is marked with one token and all the other places are empty.

All workflow nets in this paper are assumed to be sound [1], i.e. that the final marking can be reached from any marking reachable from the initial one. The soundness criterion ensures that the workflow is free of deadlocks and livelocks, and that its reachability graph is finite.

Workflow nets with data. A workflow net with data (WFD-net) is a workflow net in which tasks can *read* from, *write* to, or *delete* data elements. A task can also have a *guard*, a boolean expression over atomic data-dependant *predicates*, that can block its execution. The actual values of data elements are not considered, so the WFD-net model is a conceptual model, or a schema for characterizing several executable workflows. Note that most industrial workflow languages also support this type of underspecification.

We illustrate the idea of WFD-nets by showing the model of a shipment handling process in Figure 2. The first task in this process is Receive goods. This task creates (writing without reading corresponds to data creation) three documents: *cl* containing the client details, *ads* containing the destination address, and *gds.R* describing the actual goods to be shipped. The dot symbol has no special meaning here; its only purpose is to indicate that goods are initially in state R (*registered*). In the next task, Perform check, the goods are checked and their status is changed from R to C (*checked*). This state-change is modeled using the (semantical) fact that inside a task reading always precedes writing, and writing always precedes destroying. If either the type of goods or the destination is not supported by the company, the shipment is rejected (*gds* moves to state RJ), and the case ends. If the goods are ok to be shipped, but the destination address is not complete, the client is contacted for additional information (task Request more info). When this info is received (task Info received), the document *ads* is updated (reading + writing corresponds to data updating) and the *gds* document is moved back to its initial state R. It is also possible for the client to never respond to the request, in which case a timeout occurs and the case ends again. When the address is completed, the price for the shipment is determined (task Calculate price). If this price is high (i.e., if isHigh(*price*) evaluates to true), the express post is used (task Ship express); otherwise, the cheaper standard post is used (task Ship normal). Both of these tasks require the destination address and checked goods, and they change the status of goods to S (*shipped*). The client is informed about the shipment only in the case of high price (task Inform client). In parallel to the shipping process, but using the same condition on price, the customer support division calculates the bonus (task Calculate bonus) for the client, or decides that no bonus is given (task No bonus). If the bonus is granted, the information about it is added to the *cl* object by task Register bonus. Finally, the last task in the process is to file the case; the client data is updated to include the details of the shipment, and the *gds* document is moved to its *final* state F.

The state space of a WFD-net is not simply the state space of its underlying workflow net. First, without looking at the guards an otherwise deterministic behavior can only be treated as non-deterministic. Second, a task can be blocked if its input data is not (yet) available, a behavior that cannot be observed if data is ignored. The semantics of WFD-nets thus needs to incorporate the data information somehow.

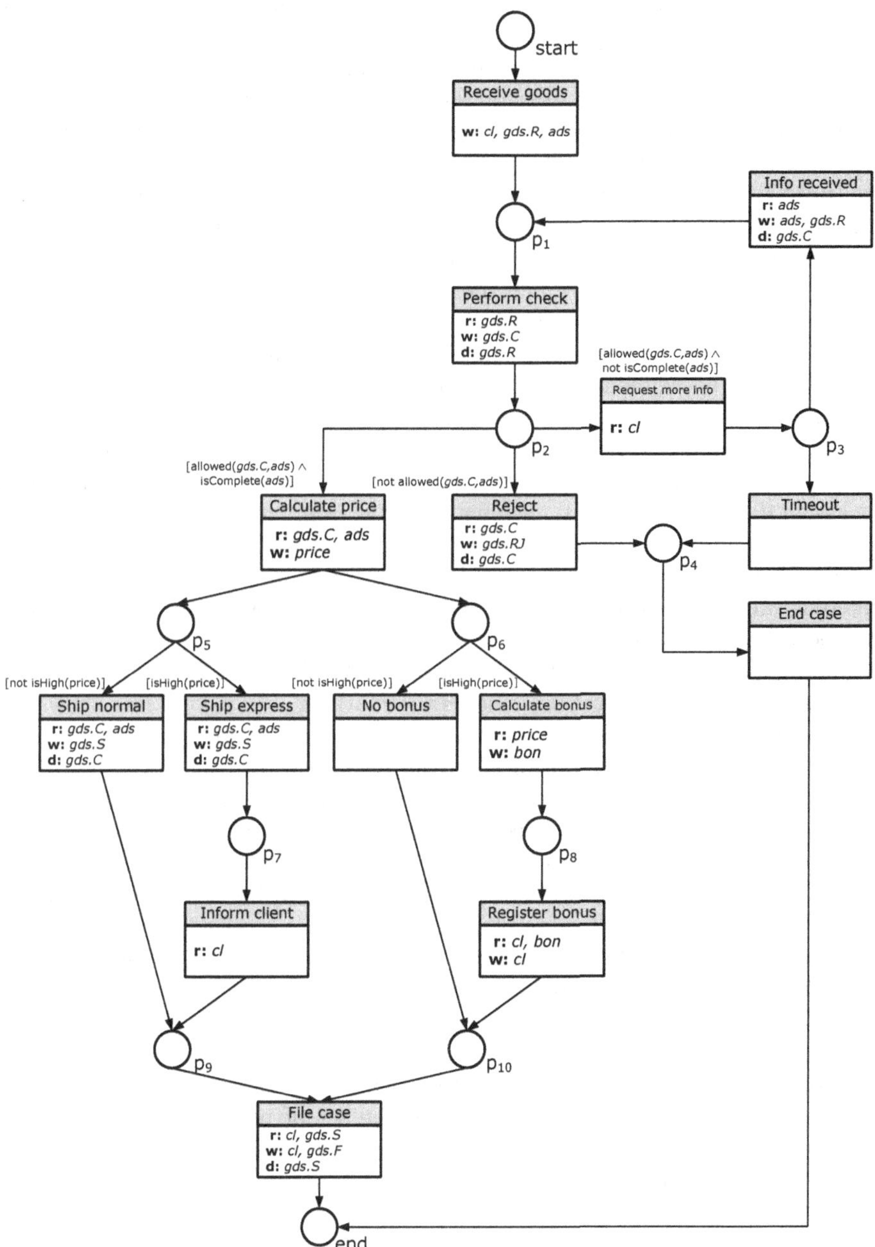

Fig. 2. WFD-net modeling a shipment handling process

Although data values are not specified in a WFD-net, non-created data values can be distinguished from created ones, and this information is added to the marking first. We choose to keep the exact values of the predicates, i.e. evaluate predicates and guards to true, false or undefined (the latter only if some data element assigned to them does not have a value). This information is then also added to the marking. The combination of a marking, data elements that are (un)defined in this marking, and evaluation of predicates in this marking, is called a *configuration.* The *start configuration* contains the initial marking only; every data element and every predicate is initially undefined. A *final configuration* is any configuration of which the marking is the final marking.

The information in a configuration is enough to determine whether some task in a WFD-net can be executed or not: all data elements required for reading in the task must be defined, the guard must be true, and the standard condition that there are enough tokens in the input places should be fulfilled. The firing of a task, however, yields a *set* of successor configurations. Each of these configurations has the same marking, the one induced by the firing. On the data level, we assign *defined* to each data element that has been created (i.e., written), and we assign *undefined* to each data element that has been deleted. Every predicate that contains a data element that has been written or updated is given a possibly different value, and every predicate that contains a data element that has been deleted becomes *undefined.*

Figure 3 shows (a part of) the statespace of the WFD-net from Figure 2. The first line of every configuration denotes the marking, the second line shows the defined data elements and the third line indicates which predicates are true in this configuration. Configuration c_0 is the initial configuration; configurations c_{13}, c_{16} and c_{19} are the final ones and are drawn using dashed lines. Initially, only task Receive goods is enabled. As this task creates the element *ads*, which fully determines the predicate isComplete, it has two outcomes, one for each truth value for this predicate. The next enabled task, Perform check, produces *gds.C* and determines the value of allowed. Task Info received, enabled in c_8 in which p_3 is marked and *ads* is defined, deletes the element *gds.C*, subsequently making the value of the predicate allowed undefined. The same task, however, also updates *ads*, and can turn the predicate isComplete to true (outcome c_1) or leave it false (outcome c_2).

The statespace of a WFD-net is finite if the underlying workflow net is sound, and if both the set of data elements and the set of predicates are finite. Although the statespace can in principle be exponentially larger than the net, our experience shows that the situations where it cannot be constructed are rare.

3 Generation of Data Footprints

In this section we explain how data footprints are generated from WFD-nets. We do not explicitly give a formal definition of a data footprint, but rather explain the algorithmic procedure for its generation. We also give two examples for the use of footprints.

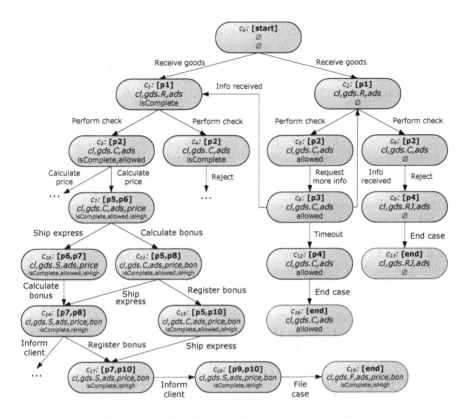

Fig. 3. Statespace of the shipment handling process - An excerpt

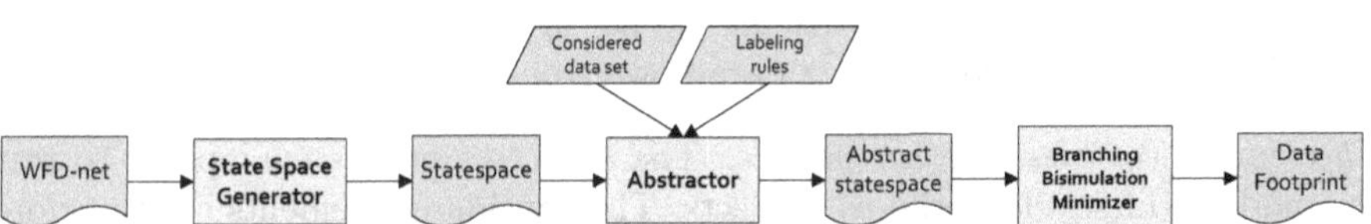

Fig. 4. Procedure for generating data footprints

To generate a data footprint from a given WFD-net two ingredients are needed: a set of data elements for which the footprint is to be generated (the so-called *considered set*), and a set of renaming rules saying how tasks that use (i.e., read, write, delete or have in the guard) a data element from this data set are to be represented in the footprint. In these rules one can also specify that certain tasks should be internal, i.e. not have a label in the footprint. The actual generation process is depicted in Figure 4 and we explain it in detail now.

The first task in the procedure is to generate the complete statespace by the means explained in the previous section. This is done regardless of the data set in consideration and of the renaming rules. When the state space is obtained, the abstraction process starts in which the following elements are removed from every configuration: the marking, the predicates, and the data elements that are not in the considered set. In addition, tasks that do not use any of the data elements from the input set are made internal (no label is given), while the other tasks are renamed according to the relabeling rules (some of them possibly made internal as well). Note that the renaming can, in principle, also be done prior to statespace generation, but that the same does not hold for data removal: *every* data element that is read, or appears in some guard, can potentially have an influence on the behavior. In the last phase, reduction modulo branching bisimulation is performed, to remove irrelevant and redundant behavior.

Branching bisimulation [4] is a well established equivalence relation that requires two systems to agree on every *visible* step they make, while allowing them to differ on their *invisible* steps, respecting, however, always the options being offered and keeping the moment of choice unchanged. The relation is known to preserve and reflect all the properties that can be expressed in the powerful temporal logic CTL^*_{-X} [3], meaning that no real behavior is lost when a system is replaced by another system branching bisimilar to it. There exists efficient algorithms for minimizing systems modulo branching bisimulation [5], with several tools supporting them.

In our setting, invisible steps are defined to be exactly those that have no label and that do not change the state of any considered data element. These steps are removed in the reduction phase, when configurations are combined into equivalence classes, leaving the abstract state space with the minimal amount of information required to observe the full behavior of the considered data elements. The resulting *minimal* graph is called the footprint of these elements.

To illustrate the method we generate two footprints from our shipper example, one for the *gds* documents and one for the *ads* object. In the first example we show how the footprint can be used to test whether the modeled life-cycle of *gds* corresponds to the intended (predefined) one. In the second example we use the footprint to test the process for a data-flow error related to the *ads* element.

Checking object life-cycle compliance. The objective in this example is to test the modeled life-cycle of the *gds* objects. The considered elements are therefore *gds.R*, *gds.C*, *gds.S*, *gds.F* and *gds.RJ*. We are not interested in the actual tasks performed, so we make them all internal. Figure 5 illustrates, on a part of the statespace, the abstraction phase and the subsequent minimization. Configurations in the abstract statespace (the middle graph) that cannot be distinguished modulo branching bisimulation are colored using the same pattern. The rightmost graph is the final reduced version, where branching bisimilar configurations are merged and redundant arcs are removed. The full data footprint for the *gds* objects is given in Figure 6.

Now, suppose that the reference model for goods is given by the graph in Figure 7. It is, therefore, required that goods are first *registered* (R), and then they can alternate between being registered and being *checked* (C). Checked goods can also be *rejected* (RJ) or *shipped* (S). From these two states goods can only move to state *final* (F). States C, RJ and F are all allowed to be the ending states.

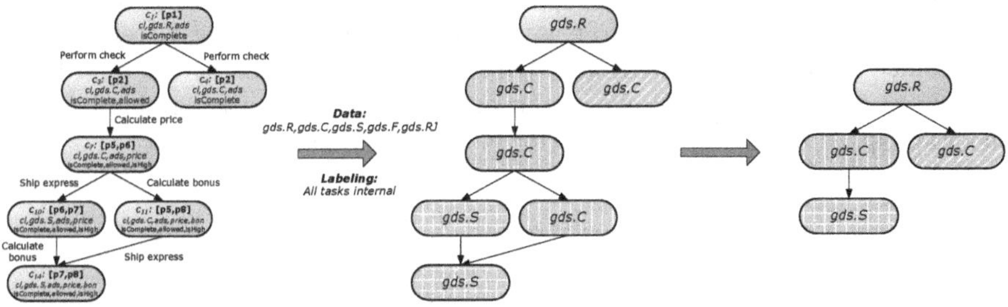

Fig. 5. Generation of the footprint for goods-related documents - An excerpt

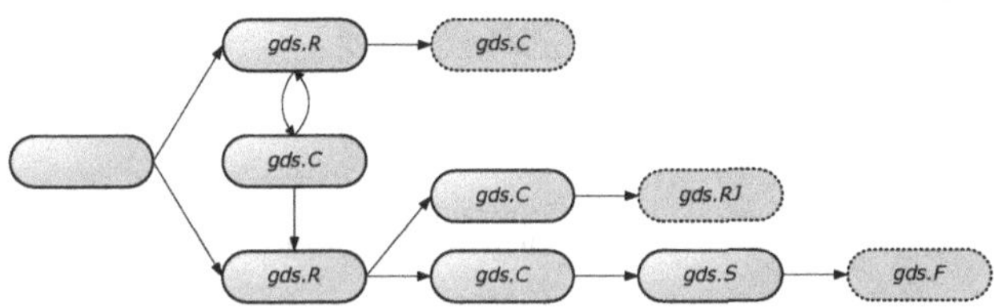

Fig. 6. Full data footprint of the *gds* objects

To check that the modeled behavior of the *gds* objects complies with their intended behavior, we need to show that, staring from the initial configuration, every step in the footprint can be mimicked by its corresponding step in the required life-cycle, and the same must hold for termination. This amounts to establishing a *simulation relation* [9] between the two graphs, and relating their initial states. In our example such relation is directly obtained by connecting states of the life-cycle with configurations that have the same label (i.e., relating C with *gds.C*, etc.). Note that the life-cycle still allows for more behavior than what is supported by the model; it is, e.g., never possible to finalize rejected claims in the model.

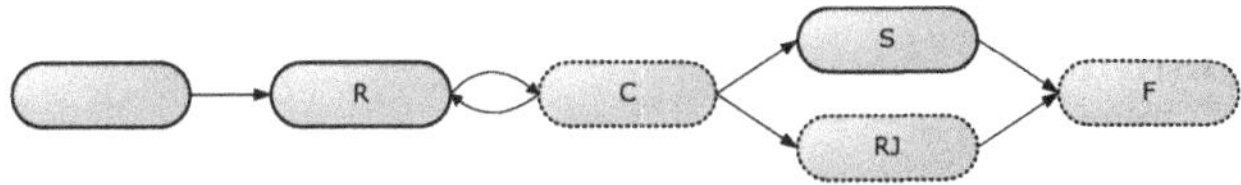

Fig. 7. Reference life cycle of the *gds* objects

Checking for data-flow errors. In the second example we test the address object *ads* against the *(weakly) redundant data* anti-pattern introduced in [13]. According to this anti-pattern, we must check that it is not possible for an execution path to create or update *ads* and not read it afterwards. For this purpose, we only consider the *ads* object, and we rename every task that manipulates this element appropriately, to directly indicate its effect on *ads*. For example, task Info received updates *ads*, and so it is renamed to RW. Similarly, Received goods is renamed to W as it creates *ads*. We consider a presence in the guard as a reading operation. Figure 8 shows the footprint generation on a small part of the state space; the complete footprint is given in Figure 9.

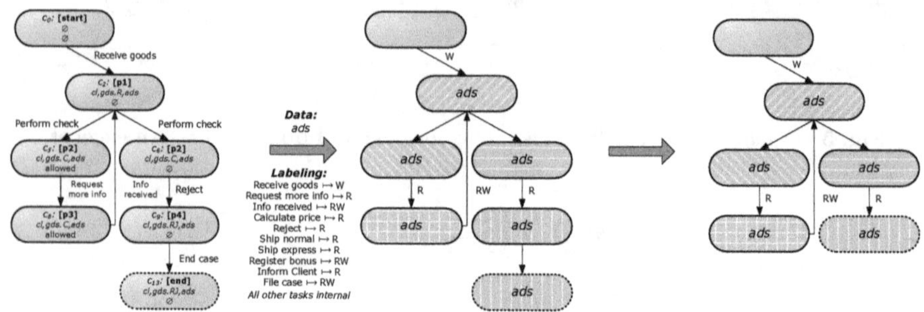

Fig. 8. Generation of the data footprint for the *ads* object - An excerpt

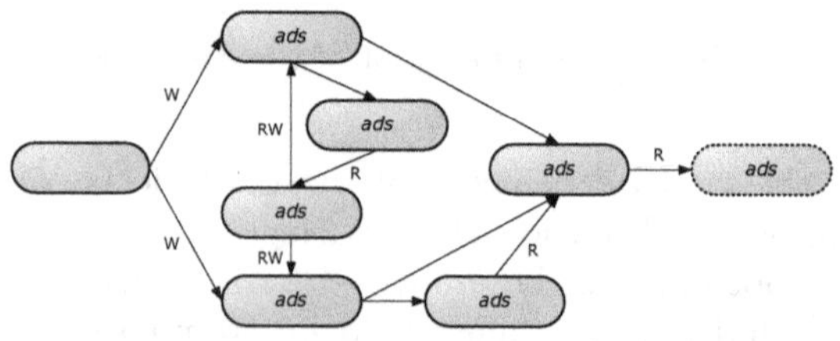

Fig. 9. Full data footprint for the *ads* document

As [13] suggests, redundant data errors can be found by the well established model-checking techniques. However, as the footprint in Figure 9 is rather simple, a simple visual inspection suffices to show that a writing to *ads* is never redundant. The final state is always reached via some reading task.

4 Conclusions

We introduced the notion of a data footprint, a labeled directed graph in which the nodes represent possible states of some data elements, and the labels on arcs are user-defined representations of tasks that cause these elements to change their state. We presented a procedure that, given a set of data elements in a WFD-net, automatically extracts the data footprint for these elements. The procedure is based on the notions of branching bisimulation, ensuring the soundness of our approach. Using a realistic shipment handling process we showed how data footprints can be used to show that a process is free of data-flow errors, or that the actual object life-cycles comply with those defined in reference models.

For future work we plan to implement the proposed approach and to find more applications of data footprints. We will also try to transform data footprints into Petri nets, to explicitly show parallelism whenever possible.

References

1. van der Aalst, W.M.P.: The Application of Petri Nets to Workflow Management. The Journal of Circuits, Systems and Computers 8(1), 21–66 (1998)
2. van der Aalst, W.M.P., Basten, T.: Identifying Commonalities and Differences in Object Life Cycles using Behavioral Inheritance. In: Colom, J.-M., Koutny, M. (eds.) ICATPN 2001. LNCS, vol. 2075, pp. 32–52. Springer, Heidelberg (2001)
3. Clarke, E.M., Grumberg, O., Peled, D.A.: Model Checking. The MIT Press, Cambridge (1999)
4. van Glabbeek, R.J., Weijland, W.P.: Branching Time and Abstraction in Bisimulation Semantics. Journal of the ACM 43(3), 555–600 (1996)
5. Groote, J.F., Vaandrager, F.: An efficient algorithm for branching bisimulation and stuttering equivalence. In: Proceedings of the seventeenth international colloquium on Automata, languages and programming, pp. 626–638. Springer, New York (1990)
6. Hull, R.: Artifact-Centric Business Process Models: Brief Survey of Research Results and Challenges. In: Meersman, R., Tari, Z. (eds.) OTM 2008, Part II. LNCS, vol. 5332, pp. 1152–1163. Springer, Heidelberg (2008)
7. Küster, J.M., Ryndina, K., Gall, H.: Generation of business process models for object life cycle compliance. In: Alonso, G., Dadam, P., Rosemann, M. (eds.) BPM 2007. LNCS, vol. 4714, pp. 165–181. Springer, Heidelberg (2007)
8. Liu, R., Bhattacharya, K., Wu, F.Y.: Modeling Business Contexture and Behavior Using Business Artifacts. In: Krogstie, J., Opdahl, A.L., Sindre, G. (eds.) CAiSE 2007 and WES 2007. LNCS, vol. 4495, pp. 324–339. Springer, Heidelberg (2007)
9. Park, D.: Concurrency and automata on infinite sequences. In: Deussen, P. (ed.) GI-TCS 1981. LNCS, vol. 104, pp. 167–183. Springer, Heidelberg (1981)
10. Preuner, G., Schrefl, M.: Observation Consistent Integration of Views of Object Life-Cycles. In: Embury, S.M., Fiddian, N.J., Gray, W.A., Jones, A.C. (eds.) BNCOD 1998. LNCS, vol. 1405, pp. 32–48. Springer, Heidelberg (1998)
11. Ryndina, K., Küster, J.M., Gall, H.: Consistency of business process models and object life cycles. In: Kühne, T. (ed.) MoDELS 2006. LNCS, vol. 4364, pp. 80–90. Springer, Heidelberg (2007)
12. Sadiq, S.W., Orlowska, M.E., Sadiq, W., Foulger, C.: Data Flow and Validation in Workflow Modelling. In: 15th Australaian Database Conference (ADC), Dunedin, New Zealand, CRPIT, vol. 27, pp. 207–214. Australian Computer Society (2004)
13. Trčka, N., van der Aalst, W.M.P., Sidorova, N.: Data-flow anti-patterns: Discovering data-flow errors in workflows. In: van Eck, P., Gordijn, J., Wieringa, R. (eds.) CAiSE 2009. LNCS, vol. 5565, pp. 425–439. Springer, Heidelberg (2009)

On the Cognitive Effectiveness of Routing Symbols in Process Modeling Languages

Kathrin Figl[1], Jan Mendling[2], Mark Strembeck[1], and Jan Recker[3]

[1] Vienna University of Economics and Business, 1090 Vienna, Austria
{kathrin.figl,mark.strembeck}@wu.ac.at
[2] Humboldt-Universität zu Berlin, 10099 Berlin, Germany
jan.mendling@wiwi.hu-berlin.de
[3] Queensland University of Technology, Brisbane QLD 4000, Australia
j.recker@qut.edu.au

Abstract. Process models provide visual support for analyzing and improving complex organizational processes. In this paper, we discuss differences of process modeling languages using cognitive effectiveness considerations, to make statements about the ease of use and quality of user experience. Aspects of cognitive effectiveness are of importance for learning a modeling language, creating models, and understanding models. We identify the criteria representational clarity, perceptual discriminability, perceptual immediacy, visual expressiveness, and graphic parsimony to compare and assess the cognitive effectiveness of different modeling languages. We apply these criteria in an analysis of the routing elements of UML Activity Diagrams, YAWL, BPMN, and EPCs, to uncover their relative strengths and weaknesses from a quality of user experience perspective. We draw conclusions that are relevant to the usability of these languages in business process modeling projects.

Keywords: Process modeling, cognitive analysis, UML, YAWL, BPMN, EPCs.

1 Introduction

Business process models play an important role for the documentation of organizational processes and for the specification of information systems requirements. These models are specified using graphical modeling languages, such as EPCs [7], UML Activity Diagrams [22], YAWL [1], or BPMN [21]. These languages provide sets of graphical constructs, together with rules for how to combine these constructs, to express graphically relevant aspects of business processes, such as the tasks that have to be performed, the actors that are involved in the execution of these tasks, relevant data, and, notably, the control flow logic that describes the logical and temporal order in which tasks are to be performed. One important aspect in the control flow logic of a business process is that processes often contain points where parallel or alternative paths might be taken, or where such paths merge. Such points characterize the convergence or divergence of process flows [9]. In process models, points of convergence or divergence

W. Abramowicz and R. Tolksdorf (Eds.): BIS 2010, LNBIP 47, pp. 230–241, 2010.

are typically expressed through *routing elements* such as "Gateways", "Connectors, or "Splits" and "Joins" [29]. While these routing elements are sometimes well-defined formally [9], they remain a key reason for modeling errors such as violation of deadlock and synchronization rules [16], and may further lead to understandability problems with practitioners [15].

In this paper, we discuss the representation of routing elements in different process modeling languages from a usability perspective. An important reference discipline to discuss usability issues of process modeling languages is cognitive psychology. This area deals with insights on how humans process information, create knowledge, and solve problems. A central property of the human brain is that it works with specialized areas. *Visual perception* enables understanding of sensory information, which is transmitted to the *sensory memory*, which holds an after-image of that information for a moment. This after-image is analyzed and key concepts are held in *short-term memory* for some minutes. Those aspects that can be linked to other prior knowledge can become part of *long-term memory*. All these three different memory parts have different characteristics, which are the foundation of various theories of comprehension, learning, and problem solving. In this paper, we argue correspondingly that these characteristics inform useful perspectives that can also be considered for discussing relative advantages and drawbacks of process modeling languages.

There are many orthogonal characteristics of process modeling languages that may be subject to a cognitive investigation. In this paper we draw on a recent framework proposed by Moody and Van Hillegersberg [18] that describes desirable properties of notation elements from a perceptual perspective. The aim of our paper is to discuss how the principles in [18] can be used to identify strengths and weaknesses of process modeling languages. Furthermore, we synthesize them in terms of propositions, which speculate on the cognitive effects of these strength and weaknesses. In this way, we pave the way towards an empirical investigation of their arguments in an experimental setting. Our research further identifies normative principles that can assist practitioners in the selection decision for a particular process modeling language.

We proceed as follows. In Section 2, we summarize the major arguments on usability of modeling languages and discuss cognitive theories which are relevant for understanding process modeling languages. Section 3 then turns to the work by Moody and Van Hillegersberg, which we utilize in Section 4 to discuss strengths and weaknesses of process modeling languages and identifies a number of propositions from this analysis. Finally, Section 5 concludes the paper and gives an outlook on future research.

2 The Cognitive Side to Process Modeling

Usability in general can be described as the measure of the ease of use and quality of the user experience when interacting with a device the user can operate in some way or another [19]. There are at least two areas in which these considerations also pertain to process modeling (see [6]):

- **Creating models:** Usability aspects of creating models with a given process modeling language include the effort (e.g. time) required to construct models, the subjective ease-of-use of doing so, and the ease-of-learning a language. The result of such a modeling process is a model, which can be assessed concerning different quality aspects (such as correctness, accuracy, detail, completeness, quality, type of errors).
- **Interpreting models:** In the process of model understanding, much cognitive activity is involved. The outcome of understanding is cognitive per se, i.e. it is created in the viewer's cognition and may only be measured by observing a viewer's problem-solving capacity, the level of process understanding generated from reading a process model or different recall capacities. Models from different modeling languages are likely to differ according to the effort required to interpret them and develop understanding, as well as in the perceived difficulty of obtaining information about a process through the visual representation chosen in a model.

Both model creation and model interpretation tasks highlight the complex interplay between human cognitive models and the visual models used to convey process information. The ability of a language to support appropriate translations between cognitive and visual models, therefore, is an essential criterion for determining the usability of any given modeling language.

We believe that Cognitive theories are central to our understanding of the usability of different modeling languages. Mental processes such as visual perception, information processing, reasoning and problem solving, attention, as well as short and long term memory are affected in learning how to use specific modeling languages, creating models, and understanding models. Our research, therefore rests on the assumption that there are specific aspects attributable to process modeling language that are likely to have an impact on the cognitive processes of the individual working the language.

Process models represent complex organizational relationships in a visual diagram; yet, humans have limited information processing capabilities (see [30]). Therefore, a main goal in the design of process modeling languages is to reduce *cognitive load* for users to enable more effective problem solving. Low cognitive effort is positively related to a variety of quality aspects of models, such as perceived ease of understanding [12]. Cognitive load is determined by the amount of elements needed to be paid attention to at a point of time. There is a natural limit of the capacity of short-term memory of humans of approximately 7 +/- 2 elements [17], which, in consequence, should be a criterion for selecting an appropriately parsimonious symbol set in any process modeling language.

Dual coding theory further suggests that humans' short-term (or working) memory [3] includes a phonological loop and a visuo-spatial sketchpad. The theory postulates that visual information (e.g. graphical elements in process models) and verbal information (e.g. textual labels) are stored and processed differently via separate mental channels that do not compete with each other [23]. The cognitive multimedia learning theory [13] proposes that, as per the *contiguity principle*, understanding of graphical material (such as a process model) is better, when text and pictures are presented spatially near each other. In consequence, text and icons belonging together should be placed near each other in process models. We note that such a situation is only partially, and inconsistently, given in process modeling, where graphical elements (e.g., routing elements) may be, but don't have to be, annotated with textual labels to convey additional semantics about the elements.

The cognitive load theory [28] further details how the working memory load influences learning and knowledge acquisition. The theory differs between three types of cognitive load: *intrinsic*, *extraneous* and *germane cognitive load*. In contrast to *intrinsic cognitive load* (which is determined by the complexity of information, i.e. the amount of elements, and their relations and interactions), the *extraneous cognitive* load is influenced by the way the information is represented [10]. While the cognitive load devoted to learning and understanding (*germane cognitive load*) should be promoted, *extraneous cognitive load* should be held low. This can, for example, be achieved by reducing additional, irrelevant information.

By mapping the cognitive load theory to the context of process modeling, it becomes clear why modeling languages might vary in their cognitive effectiveness. If the same information is modeled in different modeling languages, the resulting models should, to a large extend, have a similar *intrinsic cognitive load*, but they differ in their *extraneous cognitive load*. The amount of *extraneous cognitive load* caused by the modeling languages leads to differences in learning and understanding (see, e.g., [5]).

Due to the complex control flow logic attributed to organizational processes, the creation and understanding of process models is likely to demand high cognitive reasoning and effort for logical thinking for human users. Visual models not only demand, but also support users in their reasoning processes because they convey cues to the next logical step in reasoning about a process-related problem by representing process information (e.g., tasks to be performed) in the context of adjacent locations (e.g., in the context of the routing elements that describe important business rules pertinent to the execution of the task).

Research has shown that there are systematic fallacies (so called 'illusory inferences') when individuals internally construct, or interpret mental models on premises including modeling-level connectives (like conjunctions, inclusive, or exclusive disjunctions) [8]. This situation may also be present for externalized visual process models. The body of literature on error analysis of process models suggests the existence of systematic reasoning fallacies concerning routing elements [15]. Since correct interpretation of routing elements in process models is inevitable for overall understanding of the process depicted, we thus conjecture that different visualisations of routing elements in different process modeling languages determine, at least partly, to which extent different process model languages support understandability and the quality of the user experience.

3 Evaluating the Cognitive Effectiveness of Modeling Languages

The form of visual information representation can have a significant impact on the efficiency of information search, explicitness of information, and problem solving (see [11]). One of the key goals for the visual design of a model is that viewers draw attention to those components crucial for understanding and cognitive inferencing [27]. According to Moody and Hillersberg [18] there are 5 principles that inform our understanding of the cognitive effectiveness of visual modeling languages: representational clarity, perceptual discriminability, perceptual immediacy, visual expressiveness and graphic parsimony:

- **Representational Clarity:** This principle points out the importance of a good fit between the graphical symbols used in a modeling notation and the semantic concepts they refer to. Anomalies like symbol redundancy (more than one symbol represents the same concept), overload (one symbol represents more than one concept), symbol excess and deficit (there are graphical symbols without a correspondence to a semantic construct or vice versa) should be avoided, since they lead to ambiguity and additional unnecessary cognitive load for the user [18]. A recent comparative analysis [25] compared the modeling languages EPC and BPMN concerning their representational completeness and clarity. The results of this comparison revealed numerous differences between process modeling languages that the authors expect to have an effect on the cognitive efficiency of the languages considered.
- **Perceptual Discriminability:** Perceptual discriminability of symbols determines how easy it is for a user to distinguish between and visually recognize different symbols in a graphical artefact such a model. It is highly influenced by the amount of visual variables in which symbols differ (referred to as visual distance). If visual symbols are highly unique on a visual variable, they are likely to 'pop out' and are easy to locate in a model [18]. Low perceptual discriminability can lead to misunderstandings. Research showed that for instance rectangles and diamonds in ER diagrams are easily confused (see [20]). On the other hand, if different symbols in a notation have similar attributes as color or shape, they are likely to be recognized as belonging together. In consequence, symbols in a modeling language should differ sufficiently by visual variables to be perceptual discriminable. However, sometimes it is intended that symbols share visual variables if they should be recognized as related to each other.
- **Perceptual Immediacy:** Perceptual immediacy supports the user's understanding of the meaning of graphical symbols and representations, and describes whether symbols and their corresponding concepts are easily associated. Icons, for example, are easily associated with their referent real-world concepts. Iconic representations for classes of activities could improve the understandability of process models [14], but are not yet commonly used. Additionally, spatial relationships of symbols can help to induce specific desired interpretations by a user (e.g. left-to-right implies sequence). Even a

small layout change in the same graph may transport a different meaning (e.g. centrality vs. hierarchy) (see [2]). Modeling languages are likely to differ according to the intuitiveness of the visual metaphors they use for expressing real-world concepts. Specifically, modeling effectiveness and efficiency will be higher if the symbols used in a modeling notation are more similar to the concept of node-relationship arc depiction of information [4]. Therefore, it can be hypothesised that process modeling languages with higher levels of nodes and edges are likely to be intuitively understandable because of their compatibility with internal mental representations.

- **Visual Expressiveness:** Modeling notations which fully exploit the range of visual variables (spatial dimensions like horizontal and vertical, as well as shape, size, colour, brightness, orientation, and texture) have higher visual expressiveness. In comparison to a textual representation (words), which are encoded verbally in their reading direction, visual symbols are internally encoded in their spatial arrangement (see [26]). Therefore, it is of importance to assess spatial dimensions of modeling notations. Using swimlanes in activity diagrams, for example, includes both planar variables for depicting information on who is working on an activity (see [18]).
- **Graphic Parsimony:** Parsimony is an indicator of graphical model complexity and is determined by the use of embedded symbols and distinct graphic symbols [20]. High graphic complexity of a modeling language, e.g., the use of too many constructs and routing elements in one model, may impair understanding and therefore should be avoided [15].

4 Language Differences

4.1 Basic Elements of Process Modeling Languages

In general, process modeling languages include a number of basic, generic, and consensual elements that allow to define process flows. Typically, these languages provide symbols for different variants of task nodes, events, or start and end of the process. A task node models a clearly defined action or process step. Tasks can be conducted by human users or software agents. Below we briefly introduce the routing elements, before the subsequent sections discuss how different process modeling languages define these generic elements.

Split: A split node models parallel branches in a process. Thus, sub-processes started by the same split node are performed simultaneously.

Join: A join node synchronizes parallel sub-processes. Typically, a join node synchronizes sub-processes resulting from a split node.

Decision: A decision node models choices in a process flow. Decision nodes thereby define alternative routing options in a certain process.

Merge: A merge node consolidates different (optional) paths that result from a choice made by a decision node.

Figure 1 shows four symbol sets of routing elements of EPCs, UML, YAWL, and BPMN, respectively. The figure shows splits and joins as well as decision and merge from left to right.

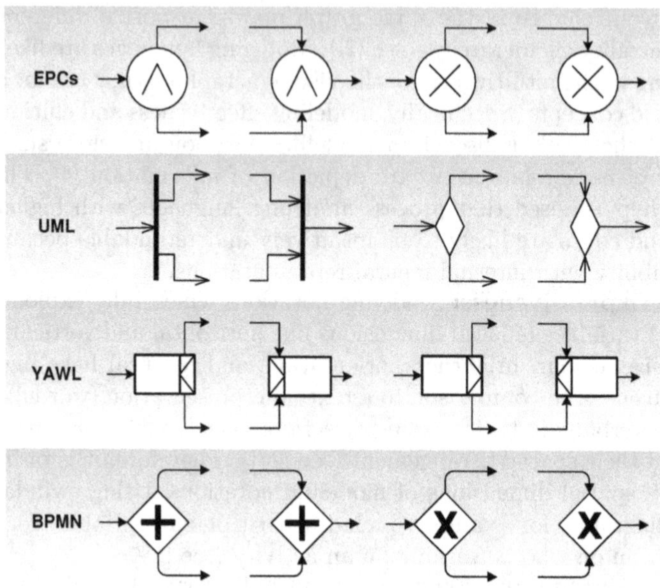

Fig. 1. The routing elements of EPCs, UML, YAWL, and BPMN

4.2 Event-Driven Process Chains (EPCs)

The EPC notation contains three types of symbols: circles for connectors, rounded rectangles of functions, and hexagons for events. Different connectors can be distinguished by their symbol, $\times$ for XOR, $\wedge$ for AND, and $\vee$ for OR.

As per our cognitive effectiveness criteria introduced above, we observe that the use of EPCs may incur usability problems for the users working with the language. Specifically, we identify a problem to easily discriminate AND and OR connectors. They share the same symbol, albeit mirrored vertically. Altogether, the symbol set of EPCs is very abstract, such that there is little immediacy and intuition of the symbols. Visual expressiveness is also limited. Some tools depict events and functions in red and green color, which helps to distinguish them. The notation is also parsimonious by using only a small symbol set, yet, the parsimony of the language limits its representational clarity as many of the symbols are overloaded from an ontological perspective [25].

4.3 UML Activity Models

The main element of an activity model is an Activity. The Activity represents a process that consists of Actions and different types of control nodes. Actions thereby define the tasks (steps) that are performed when executing the corresponding Activity. To model the (synchronous or asynchronous) invocation of other processes from an Activity, one may use an action symbol (round-cornered rectangle) including a small rake symbol. In essence, this modeling element defines that the corresponding step in a process is itself a process that is modeled via an own Activity model.

Activity models have a token semantics, similar (but not equal) to Petri nets. A Decision node (a routing element) is represented by a diamond-shaped symbol that has one incoming and multiple outgoing edges. A Merge node is represented by a diamond-shaped symbol and has multiple incoming and one outgoing edge. A Fork node is represented via a thick line and has one incoming and multiple outgoing edges. A Join node is represented via a thick line and has multiple incoming and one outgoing edge.

The UML notation partially violates some of the criteria we consider in our evaluation. There is some gap of representational clarity with different end symbols (activity final and flow final). On the other hand, the different end symbols have clearly defined and distinct semantics. A strong point of UML is the clear discrimination between decisions and concurrency - two important aspects of routing elements. Indeed, both routing elements are significantly different. Visual expressiveness is used to distinguish concurrent from alternative branching. Altogether, the notation set is quite parsimonious whilst being reasonably expressive.

4.4 Yet Another Workflow Language (YAWL)

YAWL uses a unique start and end condition to mark the beginning and termination of a process. Conditions are used to separate tasks (similar to places in Petri nets), yet they do not need to be explicitly drawn. Tasks are depicted as rectangles. Routing behavior is defined by thin blocks on the left-hand and right-hand side of tasks. Both XOR and AND splits and joins use triangle symbols.

On the basis of our criteria, we can point to a number of areas with potential usability concerns pertaining to the YAWL language. Representational clarity is violated, because a decision and a simple merge can be described either by conditions with multiple incoming and outgoing arcs, or with XOR joins and splits, thereby affording the problem of ontological redundancy. We further identify a problem with the visual discrimination of AND and XOR splits and joins as these routing elements share the same visual symbol. The semantics have to be identified based on the position on the split/join block relative to and alongside with the number of incoming and outgoing arcs to the respective task. YAWL further offers only limited visual expressiveness due to little variation in shape and size. On the other hand, we note the language to be relatively parsimonious, at least when compared to more recent languages such as BPMN.

4.5 Business Process Modeling Notation (BPMN)

Aside from a variety of elements to depict tasks and events in a process model, BPMN offers a set of gateways for specifying routing constraints. Splits and joins both use a diamond shape. XOR gateways can be drawn without a symbol or with an X inside. AND gateways contain a plus sign.

The BPMN language exhibits different weaknesses from a cognitive expressiveness perspective. Representational clarity is partially violated [24]. XOR gateways can be described with different symbols (blank diamond and X diamond). This may be confusing to model readers. Also, XOR gateways as X diamonds are difficult to distinguish from AND gateways with a plus. Intermediacy is rather low with the blank set of symbols. We further note a somewhat limited visual expressiveness for the standard set of symbols: tasks and gateways are both quadrangles and gateways are circles. Texture and color is not used in the standard symbol set, but is often introduced by modeling tools like ARIS, e.g., to highlight different types of tasks. Finally, there is hardly any graphic parsimony. BPMN uses an extensive set of symbols and subtype symbols. This might make it difficult to learn the language.

4.6 Evaluation and Discussion

Based on the number and types of issues identified above we can hypothesize about understanding and learning performance depending on the process modeling language. In Table 1 we conceptualize our analysis above by highlighting relatively good ("+"), average ("+/-") and weak support ("-")of the languages considered, in terms of their cognitive expressiveness of routing elements in process models.

Table 1. Relative strengths and weakness of routing element visualizations in different process modeling languages

	EPCs	UML	YAWL	BPMN
Representational Clarity	-	+/-	-	-
Perceptual Discriminability	-	+	-	-
Perceptual Immediacy	-	-	-	-
Visual Expressiveness	+/-	+	-	+/-
Graphic Parsimony	+	-	-	-

Representational Clarity: A lack of clarity is likely to result in two problems when creating a model based on redundant, overloaded or excess symbols. With representational redundancy, modelers may require more time to decide which among several alternative elements to use for representing routing elements relevant to a real-world process. Models created by different modelers may further vary significantly in terms of the symbols they use for the same routing decisions taken in a process. These problems are likely to show up with BPMN and YAWL. On the other hand, symbol overload may result in corresponding ambiguity for somebody who is reading the model. This issue seems to be more relevant to EPCs and Petri nets, due to the parsimony of the symbol set offered. Overall, we note that UML activity diagrams appear to be attributed the highest degree of clarity across the languages discussed.

Perceptual Discriminability: Good discrimination should support fast visual perception and good recall in short term memory. From our analysis, it appears that YAWL is very weak in discriminating routing elements. This is also partially the case for EPCs (OR versus AND) and BPMN (X versus +). UML very clearly distinguishes concurrency and alternative branching with significantly different symbols.

Perceptual Immediacy: Many language elements in the languages considered are very abstract such that no intuition is provided. We note that some languages (e.g. EPCs and BPMN) offer perceptual immediacy for events and tasks, yet the graphical representation of routing elements is a weakness inherent in all languages we consider in this paper.

Visual Expressiveness: The visual expressiveness of process modeling languages is limited. BPMN and EPCs offer markers to distinguish different types of routing behaviors, and UML uses two distinct graphical shapes albeit with no explicit markers, to distinguish concurrency from alternative routing.

Graphic Parsimony: BPMN is by far the richest language in terms of its symbol set. Therefore, it should also be the most time consuming to learn. YAWL and UML also provide a rather large set of symbols. EPCs are lean in terms of symbols, such that they should be easy to learn notation-wise. On the other hand, they are the most abstract notations such that they should be the most difficult ones to be applied correctly.

Forthcoming from this synthesis of our evaluation, we can uncover a set of dimensions that can be used for a comparative empirical evaluation of the different process modeling languages. A particular aspect that is strongly supported by one language and weakly by another should directly materialize in a difference in understanding or learning performance. For example, one may hypothesize that the superiority of UML in terms of perceptual discriminability may result in better interpretation or comprehension performance of individuals confronted with UML models, when compared to, say, EPCs or BPMN. A comparative empirical evaluation on basis of the evaluation presented may further identify the relative importance of the different cognitive effectiveness criteria, to explaining or predicting interpretation effectiveness or efficiency of different process modeling languages. It could turn out, for instance, that graphic parsimony is a more relevant criterion to establish interpretational efficiency, than, say, perceptual immediacy. At this stage of our research, we note that a respective empirical experiment is missing; however, we note the potential of our research to inform a research agenda for a series of controlled studies to test the predictions made.

5 Conclusion

Despite increasing consciousness about the need to consider the (non-technical) user's point of view in the area of information systems engineering, little research has been undertaken in order to improve and understand the usability of modeling languages. In this paper, we contribute to this emerging stream of research by presenting a set of cognitive effectiveness criteria informed by cognitive theories, such that we can identify differences in four process modeling languages in terms of the suspected usability of these languages for modeling processes. The main contribution of this paper is an analysis of the symbol sets of four prominent process modeling languages for the modeling of routing elements to depict the control flow logic of business processes. Our evaluation results uncovers differences between the languages according to representational clarity, perceptual discriminability, and graphic parsimony. Our research informs a series of experimental studies that may test the predictions made. Further, we can extrapolate our analysis to the symbol sets in the process modeling languages that are used to graphically express tasks, events, actors, data or other process-relevant facts.

We expect that our research contributes to our understanding of process modeling languages, and assists the development and selection of process modeling languages likewise.

References

1. van der Aalst, W.M.P., ter Hofstede, A.H.M.: YAWL: Yet Another Workflow Language. Information Systems 30(4) (June 2005)
2. Aranda, J., Ernst, N., Horkoff, J., Easterbrook, S.M.: A framework for empirical evaluation of model comprehensibility. In: 29th International Conference on Software Engineering (ICSE 2007), Minneapolis, USA (2007)
3. Baddeley, A.D., Hitch, G.: Working memory. In: The psychology of learning and motivation: Advances in research and theory, vol. 8, pp. 47–89. Academic Press, New York (1974)
4. Bajaj, A., Rockwell, S.: COGEVAL: A Propositional Framework Based on Cognitive Theories To Evaluate Conceptual Models. In: Siau, K. (ed.) Advanced Topics in Database Research, pp. 255–282. Idea Group Publishing, USA (2005)
5. Chandler, P., Sweller, J.: Cognitive load while learning to use a computer program. Applied Cognitive Psychology 10(2), 151–170 (1996)
6. Gemino, A., Wand, Y.: A framework for empirical evaluation of conceptual modeling techniques. Requirements Engineering 9(4), 248–260 (2004)
7. Keller, G., Nüttgens, M., Scheer, A.-W.: Semantische Prozessmodellierung auf der Grundlage Ereignisgesteuerter Prozessketten (EPK) (1992)
8. Khemlani, S., Johnson-Laird, P.N.: Disjunctive illusory inferences and how to eliminate them. Memory & Cognition 37(5), 615–623 (2009)
9. Kiepuszewski, B., ter Hofstede, A.H.M., van der Aalst, W.M.P.: Fundamentals of control flow in workflows. Acta Informatica 39(3), 143–209 (2003)
10. Kirschner, P.A.: Cognitive load theory: implications of cognitive load theory on the design of learning. Learning and Instruction 12(1), 1–10 (2002)
11. Larkin, J.H., Simon, H.A.: Why a diagram is (sometimes) worth ten thousand words. Cognitive Science 11(1), 65–100 (1987)
12. Maes, A., Poels, G.: Evaluating quality of conceptual modelling scripts based on user perceptions. Data & Knowledge Engineering 63(3), 701–724 (2007)
13. Mayer, R.E.: Multimedia Learning. Cambridge University Press, Cambridge (2001)
14. Mendling, J., Recker, J., Reijers, H.A.: On the usage of labels and icons in business process modeling. International Journal of Information System Modeling and Design 1(2) (2010)

15. Mendling, J., Reijers, H., van der Aalst, W.M.P.: Seven process modeling guidelines (7pmg). Information and Software Technology (2) (2010)
16. Mendling, J., van Dongen, B.F., van der Aalst, W.M.P.: Getting rid of or-joins and multiple start events in business process models. Enterprise Information Systems 2(4), 403–419 (2008)
17. Miller, G.A.: The magical number seven, plus or minus two: some limits on our capacity for processing information. Psychological Review 63, 81–97 (1956)
18. Moody, D., Hillegersberg, J.: Evaluating the Visual Syntax of UML: An Analysis of the Cognitive Effectiveness of the UML Family of Diagrams. In: Gašević, D., Lämmel, R., Van Wyk, E. (eds.) SLE 2008. LNCS, vol. 5452, pp. 16–34. Springer, Heidelberg (2009)
19. Nielsen, J.: Usability 101: Introduction to usability (2009)
20. Nordbotten, J.C., Crosby, M.E.: The effect of graphic style on data model interpretation. Information Systems Journal 9(2), 139–155 (1999)
21. OMG. Business Process Modeling Notation (BPMN), Version 1.2, formal 2009-01-03, The Object Management Group (January 2009), `http://www.omg.org/spec/BPMN/1.2/`
22. OMG Unified Modeling Language (OMG UML): Superstructure, Version 2.2, formal 2009-02-02, The Object Management Group (February 2009), `http://www.omg.org/technology/documents/formal/uml.htm`
23. Paivio, A.: Dual coding theory: Retrospect and current status. Canadian Journal of Psychology 45(3), 255–287 (1991)
24. Recker, J., Indulska, M., Rosemann, M., Green, P.: How good is bpmn really? insights from theory and practice. In: Ljungberg, J., Andersson, M. (eds.) 14th European Conference on Information Systems, Goeteborg, Sweden, pp. 1582–1593. Association for Information Systems (2006)
25. Recker, J., Rosemann, M., Indulska, M., Green, P.: Business process modeling- a comparative analysis. Journal of the Association for Information Systems 10(4), 333–363 (2009)
26. Santa, J.L.: Spatial transformations of words and pictures. Journal of Experimental Psychology: Human Learning & Memory 3, 418–427 (1977)
27. Scaife, M., Rogers, Y.: External cognition: how do graphical representations work? Int. J. Hum.-Comput. Stud. 45(2), 185–213 (1996)
28. Sweller, J.: Cognitive load during problem solving: Effects on learning. Cognitive Science: A Multidisciplinary Journal 12(2), 257–285 (1988)
29. Verbeek, H.M.V., van der Aalst, W.M.P., ter Hofstede, A.H.M.: Verifying workflows with cancellation regions and or-joins: An approach based on relaxed soundness and invariants. The Computer Journal 50(3), 294–314 (2007)
30. Vessey, I.: Cognitive Fit: A Theory-Based Analysis of the Graphs Versus Tables Literature*. Decision Sciences 22(2), 219–240 (1991)

Visualising Business Capabilities in the Context of Business Analysis

Christopher Klinkmüller, André Ludwig, Bogdan Franczyk, and Rolf Kluge

University of Leipzig, Information Systems Institute, Grimmaische Straße 12, 04109 Leipzig, Germany
{klinkmueller,ludwig,franczyk,kluge}@wifa.uni-leipzig.de

Abstract. Business capabilities represent potentials of an organisation to reach a specific goal or outcome. Business capabilities abstract from processes, resources and people that are required to provide the potential and are connected with a role model of provider and customer, both, internally and externally to an organisation. While related work provides fundamental concepts and usage descriptions of the business capability approach, so far the aspect of visualisation of business capabilities in the context of business analysis was only rudimentary addressed. In this paper, a three-dimensional business capability visualisation metaphor for business analyses is outlined which supports the visualisation of business capabilities and their qualifying dimensions but also the representation of their complex multi-dimensional interrelations.

Keywords: Business Capability, Visualisation, Business Analysis, Business Potential.

1 Introduction

Due to increasing competition on globalised markets companies are faced with growing time, cost and flexibility pressures. In order to respond to these pressures companies outsource parts of their business processes to external business partners what leads to a better exploitation of specialisation advantages and concentration on core competencies. However, business process outsourcing decisions should only be made on the basis of a stable view of the business and its constitutional, logical capabilities. The concept of *business capabilities* is a promising approach to gain visibility of potentials of an organisation to reach a specific goal or outcome [1, 2]. Business capabilities reflect the structure of a business and abstract from processes, resources and people that are required to provide the capability. Furthermore business capabilities are connected with a role model of provider and customer and specific business capability instances can be compared on the base of their attributes.

An important part of the concept of business capabilities is their usage in a business analysis. The goal of a business capability-based business analysis is to model a business, identify its business units and the dependencies between them and assess

W. Abramowicz and R. Tolksdorf (Eds.): BIS 2010, LNBIP 47, pp. 242–253, 2010.

their performance and contribution to the overall business value. However, conducting a business analysis leads to an enormous amount of information about the complex structure of the identified business units, their interdependencies and attributes. While related work provides fundamental concepts and usage descriptions of the business capability approach and its associated business analysis process, so far the aspect of visualisation of business capabilities in the context of business analysis was only rudimentary addressed. In this paper, a three-dimensional business capability visualisation metaphor for business analyses is outlined which supports the visualisation of business capabilities and their qualifying dimensions but also the representation of their complex multi-dimensional interrelations. The visualisation metaphor helps to identify business capabilities that are poorly implemented and need to be changed. Instead of presenting plain text, lists and tables the visualisation metaphor allows a business analyst to review an organisation and browse the overall business in an appropriate way. Therefore the assessment of one capability can be mapped to values reflecting different aspects. To evaluate a capability based on the aggregated values it is also helpful to understand the capability's context and to know how this context is assessed. By scanning data in tables it is difficult to keep track of both issues at the same time, whereas a metaphor can largely simplify this. Hence, the visual support must be able to illustrate the assessments and the dependencies between the capabilities. Furthermore the visualisation metaphor for business capability analysis can also be used in a virtual reality laboratory, what allows a business analyst to virtually explore the analysed business.

The paper is structured as follows; section 2 summarises the concept of business capabilities and business analysis as a basis for the presentation of the business capability visualisation metaphor which is outlined in section 3. The application of the metaphor on an exemplary business is presented in section 4. Section 5 discusses related work and is followed by section 6 which gives final remarks and outlines next steps.

2 Business Capabilities and Business Analysis

2.1 Business Capabilities

Business capabilities represent potentials of an organisation and outline what an organisation is able to accomplish. They are connected to a role model, i.e. business capabilities are offered by providers and consumed by customers, i.e. departments or persons, internal or external to a company [3]. Business capabilities abstract from processes, resources and people that are required to use the potential [4]. Figure 1 presents the business capability information model.

An example for a business capability is the capability *activation of customer telephone connection* of a telecommunication company. In the past, telecommunication companies had to send a technician to customers installing the connection on site. Abstracting from its implementation, resources, processes etc. the same business capability can nowadays be provided remotely by configuring the connection with a special software product [5]. The example outlines the potential character by showing that the capability is realised by two different processes. Moreover it shows that capabilities

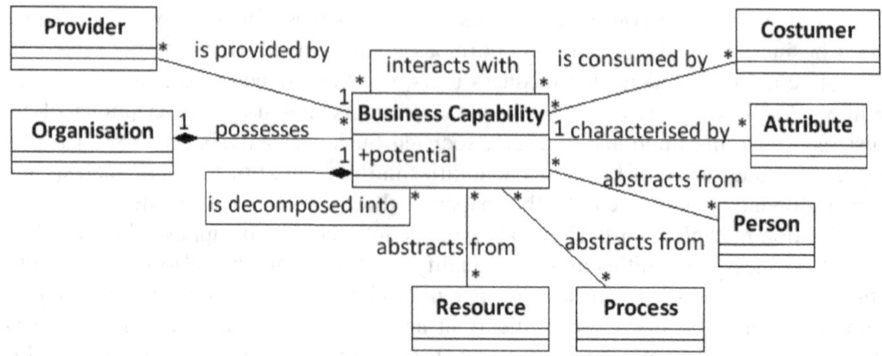

Fig. 1. The business capabilities information model

provide a stable view on the business because the processes of the activation may change over time but the capability remains the same.

Business capabilities are hierarchically structured and can be decomposed into fine grained sub-capabilities [6]. Due to the top-down character these relations are referred to as vertical relations. Horizontal relations on the other hand describe how business capabilities interact with each other [7]. With vertical and horizontal relations between business capabilities the structure of a business can be modelled.

Business capabilities are characterised by a defined set of attributes which can be quantified during a business analysis (examples of attributes and their application are presented in 2.2). Using the same set of attributes for each business capability makes it possible to compare them [6].

2.2 Business Analysis Based on Business Capabilities

The goal of a business analysis is to discover the structure of a business, identify business units and quantify business capability attributes as a basis for their assessment. The business analysis serves as a foundation for conducting improvement projects and for deciding on potential business capability outsourcing candidates. A business analysis consists of four steps as illustrated in figure 2.

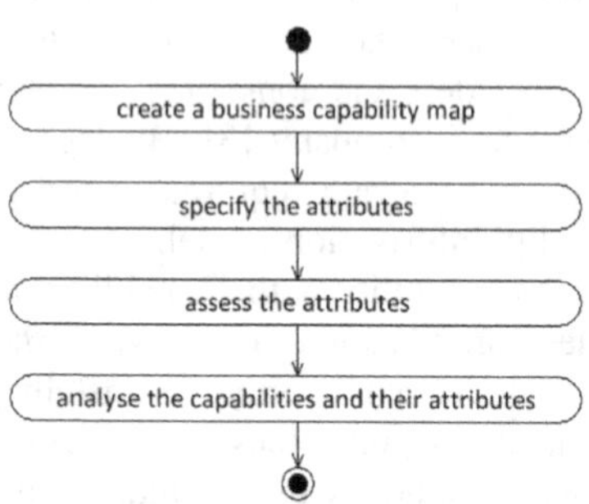

Fig. 2. The business analysis process

Step 1: During the creation of a business capability map knowledge about the business structure is gained. A business capability map contains business capabilities as well as their vertical and horizontal relations. Useful information sources in this step are interviews with the organisation that is examined, interviews with organisations that possess domain knowledge and business capability maps that were created in past projects. A tool which supports the creation of a business capability map is described in [8]. According to [7], five top level capabilities can be identified in almost every organisation:

- Develop products and/or services,
- Generate demand for those products and/or services,
- Produce and/or deliver the products and/or services,
- Plan and manage the business and,
- Collaborate with constituencies.

After coarse-grained capabilities are identified they are decomposed into more fine-grained capabilities. The decomposition usually stops between the third and the fifth level. The results of the decomposition are the business capabilities and their vertical relations. Still the horizontal relations are missing which have to be added through careful inspection of the business capabilities. The resulting business capability map outlines the structure of the business.

Step 2: The second step is to specify the attributes which help to compare the capabilities. The attributes are not fixed to a default scheme. Instead they can be defined individually for each analysis with regard to the aspects of interest. After determining the attributes, an ordinal scale needs to be specified for each attribute. Each of the objects of a scale is assigned to a numerical value that is unique inside the scale and helps to order the objects. The objects that signal interesting capabilities should be assigned to high values whereas those signalling irrelevant capabilities should be represented by small values. This is important for the aggregation of values during the analysis. Having this done the step of specifying the attributes is done.

Step 3: The tree of capabilities on the one hand and the attributes on the other span a table whereby the tree of capabilities is transformed into a list of capabilities by assigning position numbers. This list builds the vertical axis while the attributes build the horizontal one. During the assessment, the cells are set to the appropriate level for the attribute given by the column and the capability indicated by the row. The object a capability is assigned to for one attribute is determined by analysing gathered information or conducting interviews.

Step 4: Once, this is done the last step is to analyse the results by aggregating the attributes to reduce the dimensions of space in which the decision is made. The basis for the aggregation are weighted additive indices [9] leading to high values for interesting capabilities. Therefore the attributes are given a weight. Afterwards the value of a capability is calculated by summing up the product of the weight and the value of the assigned object for each attribute. Of course there can be attributes with a weight set to zero. The number of values calculated to reduce the dimension of the assessment is not restricted to one. However, it should be smaller than the dimension itself.

After finishing the aggregation of the assessment the foundation for identifying problem regions inside an organisation is laid. To identify such regions the capabilities need to be compared according to the aggregated values. If there was more than one aggregated value calculated for each capability this cannot be done by simply ordering the capabilities by one value. Instead the decision must be based on all of the aggregated values. The dependencies (vertical and horizontal) also add complexity to this problem because by them the context of the capabilities is given. One way to help persons analysing is to visualise the capabilities and their assessment. But before a metaphor addressing these two problems is introduced, future work on the analysis is explained.

One of the next steps in our future work is that the aggregation of the attributes is restricted to additive indices. Whenever the viewpoint onto an attribute changes the whole scale of objects of this attributes must be changed. The following example underlines this. If capabilities for which the software support should be improved must be identified, capabilities with a low *IT support* level are relevant. In the case of identifying capabilities for inter-organisational collaboration, capabilities with a high *IT support* level become more interesting. A solution that is more flexible than changing the numerical values is therefore to let the user determine a formula by which the aggregated values are calculated. This problem lines up with the fact that the whole business analysis lacks formal methods supporting the steps outlined in figure 2. Instead, the steps often follow an intuitive approach quickly leading to biased data. Therefore questions that need to be asked in the future should include the gathering of capabilities, their assessment and aggregation.

An example of the analysis is given in section 4. This section also shows how the gathered data is visualised using the metaphor introduced in the next section.

3 Visualisation of Business Capabilities

A picture is worth a thousand words; as the saying suggests, by relying on visualisation rather than plain text descriptions and tables, the complexity of a business can be illustrated much more intuitive and can help to build a mental image. Hence, by introducing a visualisation metaphor supports a business analyst "*[... to interpret] the visual representation of the data and [to] build [...] mental images from which knowledge of the domain is gained.*" [10].

There are two aspects that need to be addressed by the visualisation metaphor in order to support a business analyst in exploring the business. On the one hand a business analyst should be able to gain knowledge of the business structure on the other hand it should be possible to identify business units that are interesting with regard to a special topic. According to these aspects there are two objectives that need to be accomplished by developing a visualisation metaphor.

To visualise the business structure the metaphor must consider the business capabilities and their vertical and horizontal relations. The vertical relations between the business capabilities describe the logical composition of a business while the horizontal relations express dependencies between the business capabilities. Thus, the first objective is to draw the business structure in a way that the logical composition of capabilities can be understood easily. Furthermore, it must be possible to add the dependencies among capabilities in a way that it allows the viewer to keep track of dependencies and compositions at the same time.

From a mathematical viewpoint, business capabilities can be seen as nodes and their relations as edges forming a graph. As long as only the vertical relations are considered, business capabilities form a tree with the organisation at the root. By adding the horizontal relations or by taking only the horizontal relations into account the capabilities span the more general structure of a graph. Referring to the first objective of the visualisation metaphor the layout must be determined by the tree structure formed through the vertical relations, but the horizontal relations must still be added in a clear way.

On this basis, the developed visualisation metaphor for business capabilities has to meet two criteria which adopt aesthetic rules for drawing trees, described in [11] and [12]. According to these rules, it has to be recognizable which nodes are on the same level and the arrangement of descendants with regard to their ancestor must always follow the same principle. With regard to the horizontal relations the metaphor has to avoid the crossing of edges and nodes or at least minimise the crossing of edges [13]. Having these criteria in mind, a metaphor was developed which is based on the projection of business capabilities to a hemisphere. First, a tree is drawn in two dimensions. Afterwards, it is projected to a hemisphere in a way that the root of the tree which is in case of business capabilities the organisation itself is put to the pole of the hemisphere. Then each capability level is drawn on a circle on the surface of the hemisphere that is parallel to the equator whereas the highest level is drawn next to the pole and the lowest level on the equator. In this way all nodes are positioned but still the edges need to be added. The edges representing vertical relations are drawn on the surface of the hemisphere, whereas the horizontal relations are drawn inside the hemisphere. Thus, the use of the third dimension ensures a separation between both relation types. Figure 3 shows an example of this metaphor.

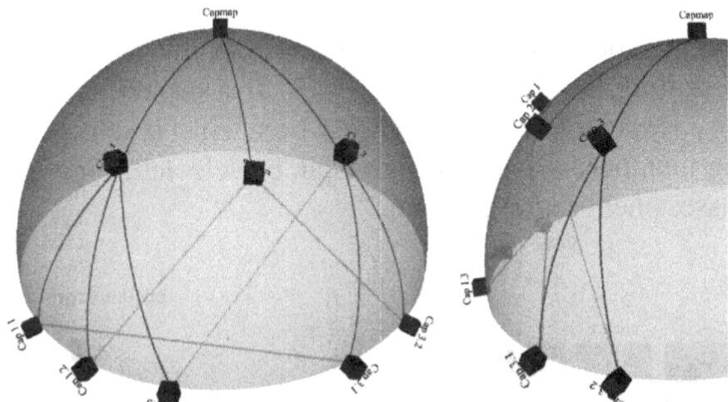

Fig. 3. Projection of business capabilities onto a hemisphere

The developed metaphor meets all introduced criteria. By placing each level on a circle parallel to the equator it is easy to comprehend which nodes are located on the same level. By centring the parent above its direct descendants the requirement that a node's descendants are always drawn following the same principle is met, too. Furthermore, edges will never cross nodes because the edges for vertical relations are always drawn on the surface between two neighbouring circles. Additionally, all nodes are on the surface and the edges for the horizontal relations are secants that touch the surface only in two points. These points are the boundary points of the connected nodes. Finally, the crossing of edges with each other is minimised because edges for vertical relations do not cross each other due to a common tree layout. Due to the separation of edges for vertical and horizontal relations, an edge for a horizontal relation will never cross an edge for a vertical relation. Only edges for horizontal relations can cross each other.

The second objective of the visualisation metaphor deals with integrating the capability assessment. As mentioned in the previous section the attributes which qualify the capabilities can be aggregated. By aggregating values the dimension of the assessment is reduced, leading to a less complex space in which decisions need to be made. That is why the visualisation fulfils the statement of Weber that "*Data visualisation is about comprehension [...]*" [14] per se. Nevertheless the number of aggregations can differ and be defined by the analyst. Hence, four options for the assessment visualisation were identified which support an analyst to represent the assessment in a configurable way. Thereby it is assumed that the aggregated values follow the rule introduced in section 2.2 that low values indicate uninteresting capabilities and vice versa.

The first option is to visualise one of the aggregated values by the colour of the node. Therefore, nodes with the lowest value will be set to blue and with the highest to red. Values in between are coloured from the spectrum of colours between blue and red. A further option is to modify the height of a node. This is done by following a simple rule, the higher the value that is visualised the higher the node. Another option is deforming the shape of the node's base. Here the lowest value is represented by a circle and the highest value by a triangle. Again values in between are projected to polygons with a decreasing number of corners. The last option is to group the capabilities respective to their values. The range between the highest and the lowest value is cut into pieces of the same length and of a configurable number. Every capability is than put into the class that corresponds to the value of the capability. This grouping is integrated into the metaphor in an interactive way. For this, an axis is integrated along with boxes representing the different categories. If a capability is selected its corresponding category respectively the integrated box will be selected. Additionally, all capabilities being member of the same class can be selected. Figure 4 summarizes the four options of assessment representation.

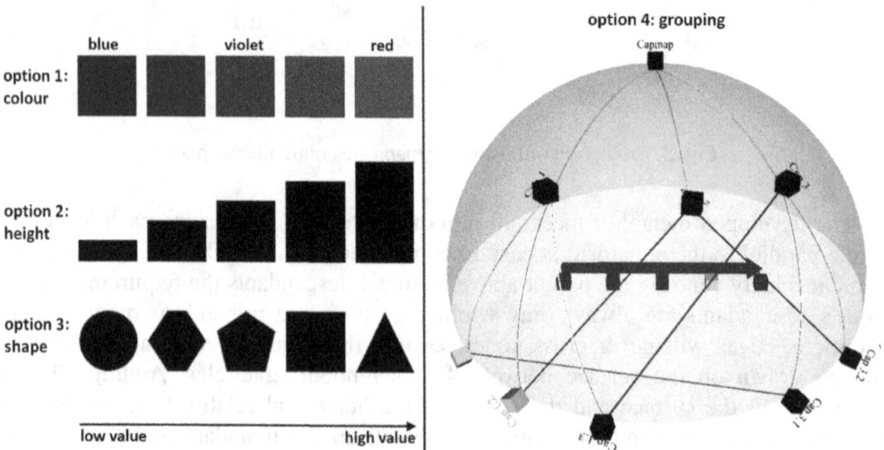

Fig. 4. Options of representing business capability assessments

So far, both aspects of exploring the business mentioned at the beginning of this section are covered by the metaphor. What was also promised is that visualising data helps a user to gain knowledge of the domain more easily. A further step to boost this requirement is presenting this metaphor in the virtual reality because it provides the viewer with an "*[...] increased ability to identify patterns, anomalies, and trends in data that is visualised.*" [15]. Therefore the developed tool is able to generate artefacts that can be interactively explored in a virtual reality laboratory. The option of integrating the assessment by grouping also goes along with using a virtual reality. Yet the metaphor is not evaluated referring to support the viewer. Therefore, future work will have to include tests with business analysts and real world scenarios evaluating whether the metaphor really clarifies the view on the business.

4 Example Visualisation

In this section a short example of the introduced metaphor on the basis of a civil engineering corporation (CEC) is presented. The example is based on realised business analysis case studies. The first step was to create the business capability map including all business capabilities together with their vertical and horizontal relations. This was done by studying literature to gain knowledge of the civil engineering industry and conducting interviews. Step by step the top level business capabilities were decomposed into more fine-grained capabilities. After having recorded the logical structure of the business this way the horizontal relations reflecting dependencies were added based on carefully inspecting the business units and processes.

Before the business capabilities were assessed the attributes were defined. In order to do so the goal of the analysis was taken as the starting point which was to identify business capabilities that suffer from poor IT support. This goal in mind led to the three attributes *business value*, *IT support* and *monthly usage*. The attribute *IT support* and *business value* consist of the objectives *very low*, *low*, *medium*, *high* and *very high.* According to the analysis goal the objectives of both attributes have a contrary meaning. In the case of *IT support* the objectives *very low* and *low* are most interesting and therefore assigned to high numerical values. The same objectives of *business value* are instead assigned to small numerical values because business capabilities with a high impact on the business are more critical. *Monthly usage* was split into the objects *very seldom*, *seldom*, *often* and *very often* with *very often* having the highest numerical value.

The next step was to assess all business capabilities with regard to these attributes based on a further inspection of the business units and business processes. The result of this step was a spreadsheet with the business capabilities at the vertical axis and the attributes at the horizontal. Table 1 shows an excerpt of this spreadsheet which further includes the horizontal relations and their description as a separate column while the vertical relations are reflected by positioning numbers in front of the capability names. As this excerpt already shows the data to be reviewed is complex and unclear. Besides, the example includes only three attributes while in real world scenarios there can be up to 20 attributes. In order to identify the capabilities which will be object of further improvement projects the attributes were aggregated and then visualised using the introduced metaphor.

Table 1. An excerpt of CEC's business capabilities and their assessment

Business Capability	Horizontal related Business Capabilities		Business Value	IT support	Monthly usage
	Business Capability	**Description**			
5.1. monitor finances			High	High	Often
5.1.1. accomplish accounting	5.1.2. create tax declaration	The accounting information is the basis for the tax declaration.	High	High	Often
	5.2.2. conduct operational project tasks	The accounting must consider a project's finances.			
	…				
5.1.1.1. manage revenues	5.1.1.3. set up balance	Revenues have to be integrated in the balance.	Medium	High	Often
5.1.1.2. manage expenses	5.1.1.3. set up balance	Expenses have to be integrated in the balance.	High	High	Often
5.1.1.3 set up balance	5.1.1.2. manage revenues	Revenues have to be integrated in the balance.	High	High	Seldom
	5.1.1.2. manage expenses	Expenses have to be integrated in the balance.			

To aggregate the values the attributes were cumulated whereas each attribute was multiplied with a weight before. The weights were set in a way that the influence of *IT support* was twice as high as the one of each of the other attributes because *IT support* reflects the goal of the analyses. The other attributes only reflect the value of the capability and therefore signal how improving a capability reacts upon the overall business.

The data was then visualised using the option height of the nodes for representing the assessment. Figure 5 shows the result. The figure illustrates that the capabilities on the left side are higher than the ones at the right and therefore need to be improved. By comparing the heights the complex dependencies of the business capabilities are not considered but they influence the choice as well because capabilities with many dependencies should be preferred to those with fewer dependencies. As shown in figure 5 the visualisation metaphor addresses this issue and therefore can be taken as an analysis tool.

In the example all attributes were aggregated to one value. Instead they could have been separated by two aspects the *impact on the business* and the *IT support*. Visualising these two aspects would still enable the viewer to identify poor supported capabilities. It would also enable the viewer to compare badly supported capabilities with regard to their dependencies to capabilities with a high impact on the business.

In the future tests with users need to be done that address different aspects. At first it should be determined that the metaphor really enables analysts to explore a business. Further objectives should be to which extend the application of virtual reality supports this and which combinations of assessment visualisation options suit which goals best.

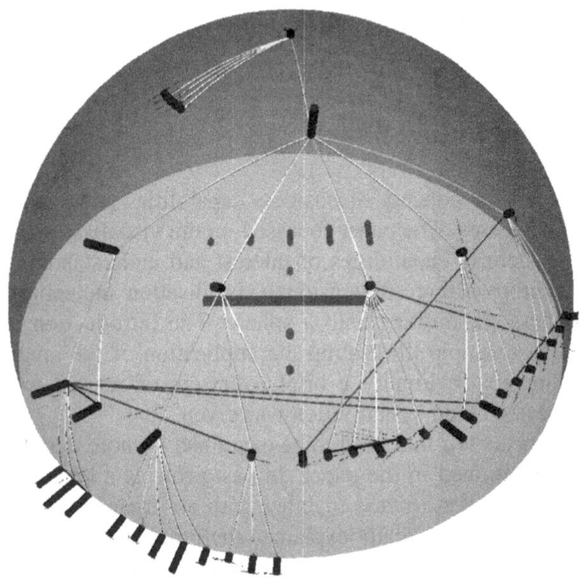

Fig. 5. Visualisation of CEC's business capabilities and their assessment

5 Related Work

There are different contributions that address different aspects of business capabilities. This includes for instance, approaches for selection of commercial off the shelf software solutions [1], for modelling service-oriented architectures on the basis of business capabilities [3], or for supporting strategic management decisions [16], [17]. All of these approaches are relevant for the conceptual model of business capabilities but only few address their visualisation aspect.

One of the few ones dealing with visualisation is the Microsoft Service Business Architecture formerly Microsoft Motion [6,18]. In this approach a tool supporting the analysis is provided by visualising business capabilities using so called heat maps [19]. A heat map is a two-dimensional representation of a business capability map. It is mainly used for comparing business capabilities and identifying poor implementations. A heat map is limited to the visualisation of two aggregated attribute values. It also lacks horizontal relations.

In [20] a method for configuring value added networks is described. This method is supported by an online platform called WerNer [21] enabling the graphical modelling and configuration of value added networks based on business capabilities. It provides first ideas for visualising dependencies between capabilities and processes but leaves the aspect of capability attribute assessment visualisation open.

Business capabilities are also visualised in the enterprise architecture tool *planningIT* developed by Alfabet(TM). The tool visualises the assessment of business capabilities by representing attribute levels via colours. It also provides ideas for visualising the relation to processes [22] and can therefore together with WerNer serve as a starting point when integrating the processes into the business analysis and also into the visualisation metaphor.

6 Conclusion and Future Work

The paper introduced the concept of business capabilities and showed a way to use them to analyse businesses. The paper focussed on the visualisation of business capabilities in order to identify capabilities of interest and understanding the structure of the business. Therefore a three-dimensional visualisation metaphor was introduced that projects business capabilities onto a sphere. The introduction of this metaphor was followed by an example illustrating the application of the analysis process and the visualisation metaphor. Finally a brief overview of related work dealing with business capabilities and their visualisation was given.

There are still aspects left that need to be examined in more detail in the future and that were already mentioned in the paper. In past projects a business capability map and its assessment were constructed together with an organisation during interviews or by studying literature. As already explained the problem arising here is that this is an intuitive work that is not based on formal methods. Because the analysis depends on the quality of the collected data future work will address this issue.

Business capabilities are only one way to view an organisation. Of course, there are more related ways to view different capabilities such as processes and services. In future work integration of such views needs to be addressed.

The visualisation metaphor itself needs further improvement, too. Here testing the use of this metaphor is one big issue. On this basis limitations of the metaphor need to be revealed and solved. Further questions are if the metaphor really helps to understand the business and how the metaphor can support focusing regions of capabilities. It also needs to be examined which combinations of assessment representation styles ensure the best support for comparison. Furthermore the integration of additional information like the detailed assessment description of a capability should be integrated.

References

1. Polikoff, I., Coyne, R., Hodgson, R.: Capability Cases - A Solution Envisioning Approach. Personal Education, Inc., Boston (2006)
2. Winter, S.: Understanding Dynamic Capabilities. Strategic Management Journal 24, 991 (2003)
3. Karakostas, B., Zorgios, Y.: Engineering Service Oriented System: A Model Driven Approach. IGI Global, Hershey (2008)
4. Malan, R., Bredemeyer, D., Krishnan, R., Lafrenz, A.: Enterprise Architecture as Business Capabilities Architecture, `http://www.ewita.com/newsletters/10025_files/EnterpriseArchitectureAsCapabilitiesArchSlides.PDF` (accessed July 21, 2009)
5. Cook, D.: Business-Capability Mapping: Staying Ahead of the Joneses, `http://msdn.microsoft.com/en-us/library/bb402954.aspx` (accessed July 23, 2009)

6. Homann, U.: A Business-Oriented Foundation for Service Orientation, http://msdn.microsoft.com/en-us/library/aa479368.aspx (accessed July 24, 2009)
7. Merrifield, R., Tobey, J.: Motion Lite: A Rapid Application of the Business Architecture Techniques Used by Microsoft Motion, http://www.microsoft.com/indonesia/msdn/motionlite.aspx (accessed July 23, 2009)
8. Kluge, R., Hering, T., Klinkmüller, C.: Geschäftsanalyse mit CMTools - Geschäftsanalyse auf der Basis von Geschäftsfähigkeiten mit Unterstützung von CMTools. Technischer Bericht der Universität Leipzig, Leipzig (2009)
9. Bortz, J., Döring, N.: Forschungsmethoden und Evaluation für Human- und Sozialwissenschaftler. Springer, Heidelberg (2006)
10. Faisal, S., Paul, C., Ann, B.: Paper Presented at the 21st British HCI Group Annual Conference on HCI, Lancaster. Großbritannien (2007)
11. Wetherwell, C., Shannon, A.: Tidy Drawings of Trees. IEEE Transactions on Software Engineering 5, 514 (1979)
12. Reingold, E.M., Tilford, J.S.: Tidier Drawings of Trees. IEEE Transactions on Software Engineering 7, 223 (1981)
13. Davidson, R., Harel, D.: Drawing graphs nicely using simulated annealing. ACM Transactions on Graphics 15, 301 (1996)
14. Weber, J.: Visualization: Seeing is Believing - Grasp and analyze the meaning of your data by displaying it graphically. Byte Magazin 18, 121 (1993)
15. Bowen Loftin, R., Chen, J.X., Rosenblum, L.: In: Hansen, C.D., Johnson, C.R. (eds.) The Visualization Handbook, pp. 479–489. Elsevier Butterworth–Heinemann, Oxford (2005)
16. Collis, D.J.: Research Note: How Valuable Are Organizational Capabilities? Strategic Management Journal 15, 143 (1994)
17. Hungenberg, H.: Strategisches Management in Unternehmen. Betriebswirtschaftlicher Verlag Dr. Th. Gabler GmbH, Wiesbaden (2001)
18. Homann, U., Tobey, J.: From Capabilities to Services: Moving from a Business Architecture to an IT Implementation, http://msdn.microsoft.com/en-us/library/aa479075.aspx (accessed July 23, 2009)
19. Microsoft: Microsoft Motion Heat Mapping Tool, http://blogs.microsoft.co.il/files/folders/2034/download.aspx (accessed December 4, 2009)
20. Lanza, G., Ude, J.: Configuration of dynamic value added networks. Proceedings of the Institution of Mechanical Engineers, Part B: Journal of Engineering Manufacture 223, 561 (2009)
21. Herm, M.: Konfiguration globaler Wertschöpfungsnetzwerke auf Basis von Business Capabilities. Shaker Verlag, Aachen (2006)
22. alfabet: Business Capability Management Demo, http://www.alfabet.de/var/files/html/de/produkte/produkt_demo/bcm_small.html (accessed December 4, 2009)

A Model Driven Engineering Approach for Modelling Versions of Business Processes using BPMN

Imen Ben Said[1], Mohamed Amine Chaabane[1,2], and Eric Andonoff[2]

[1] MIRACL / University of Sfax,
Route de l'aéroport, BP 1088, 3018 Sfax, Tunisia
bensaid.imen@gmail.com, ma.chaabane@fsegs.rnu.tn
[2] IRIT/UT1, 2 rue du Doyen Gabriel Marty, 31042 Toulouse Cedex, France
andonoff@univ-tlse1.fr

Abstract. This paper presents a solution to model and specify flexible business processes using the version concept. This solution advocates a driven engineering approach considering at the CIM level, a specific meta-model, the Version Business Process (VBP) meta-model for modelling versions of Business Processes (BP), and at the PIM level, an extension of the BPMN meta-model for visualizing and user validating the modelled BP versions. This paper introduces the VBP meta-model, presents the extension of BPMN we propose to specify versions of BPs, and illustrates how we automatically map, using QVT rules, BP versions modelled using the VBP meta-model onto corresponding extended BPMN ones. This solution is intended to business process designers: it supports them for modelling and specifying flexible business processes using the version concept.

Keywords: Flexible Business Process; Version; VBP meta-model; BPMN; QVT rules; MDE.

1 Introduction

In order to fully achieve the effectiveness of Business Processes (BPs) in Information Systems, the Business Process Community has still to address some open research issues. Flexibility of BPs is probably one of the most important issues to be addressed [1], and several tracks or keynotes in workshops [2] or conferences [3] are dedicated to it. Indeed, the very fast changing environment in which enterprises are involved nowadays leads them to often change their BPs in order to meet as quickly and efficiently as possible new customer or organizational requirements [4]. Thus, the ability to rapidly adapt their BPs is essential for enterprises that want to continue to be competitive in today's economic context.

Even though there is not yet an agreement on flexibility of business processes, the following definition provided in [5] clearly indicates the goal to reach to deal with this issue: *flexibility is the ability to deal with both foreseen and unforeseen changes in the environment in which business processes operate.* In addition to this definition, [5] also defines types of flexibility in order to really characterize flexibility

W. Abramowicz and R. Tolksdorf (Eds.): BIS 2010, LNBIP 47, pp. 254–267, 2010.

and evaluate the ability of models and systems to support it. More precisely, [5] identifies four types of flexibility: *flexibility by design*, for handling foreseen changes in BP where strategies can be defined at design-time to face these changes, *flexibility by deviation*, for handling occasional unforeseen changes and where the differences with initial BP are minimal, *flexibility by under-specification*, for handling foreseen changes in BP where strategies cannot be defined at design-time but rather at run-time, and *flexibility by change*, for handling unforeseen changes in BP, which require occasional or permanent modifications in BP schemas. Finally, [5] concludes that none of the considered systems support all BP flexibility types.

VerFlexFlow project[1] aims to deal with this issue, and to implement a system supporting these types of flexibility. Versions play a central role in VerFlexFlow. Indeed, and as defended in [6] for instance, the version notion is an appropriate concept to face the very important issue of BP flexibility and more precisely, flexibility by design, flexibility by under-specification and flexibility by change.

VerFlexFlow distinguishes $\text{VerFlexFlow}_{\text{design}}$ for flexible BP modelling, specification and implementation, from $\text{VerFlexFlow}_{\text{run}}$ for flexible BP execution. $\text{VerFlexFlow}_{\text{design}}$ supports a process designer for modelling and specifying versions of BPs using a MDE approach and considering (i) at the CIM level, a specific meta-model, the Version Business Process (VBP) meta-model for modelling versions of BPs, (ii) at the PIM level, an extension of the BPMN meta-model for visualizing and user validating the modelled versions of BPs, and finally, (iii) at the PSM level, several meta models for implementing business process versions (e.g. XPDL and BPEL meta models). $\text{VerFlexFlow}_{\text{run}}$ is responsible for specified BP versions execution. It integrates an agile engine able to deal with the previous types of flexibility, through the notions of versions, checkpoints and guidelines [7].

This paper focuses on $\text{VerFlexFlow}_{\text{design}}$, and more precisely deals with the automatic mapping from the VBP meta-model onto the extended BPMN meta-model. In section 2, the paper indicates how we model versions of BPs using the VBP meta-model considering five main perspectives of BPs (i.e. the process, functional, operational, information and organizational perspectives). Section 3 presents the extension of BPMN we provide to model versions of BPs at the CIM level. Section 4 is dedicated to the automatic mapping of BP versions modelled using VBP, onto versions of BPs modelled using the proposed extension of BPMN, and according to QVT rules. Section 5 illustrates this mapping through screenshots of $\text{VerFlexFlow}_{\text{design}}$. Finally, section 6 recaps our proposition, discusses it according related works, and gives some directions for future works.

2 Modelling Versions of BPs: The VBP Meta-model

This section briefly introduces the Version Business Process (VBP) meta-model we propose to model versions of business processes. This section only focuses on the main concepts of the meta-model first introducing the notion of version, and then presenting the VBP meta-model for BP versioning.

---

[1] Project partners are MIRACL laboratory from Sfax, Tunisia, and IRIT laboratory from Toulouse, France.

2.1 Notion of Version

As illustrated in figure 1 below, a real world entity has characteristics that may evolve during its lifecycle: it has different successive states. A version corresponds to one of the significant entity states. So, it is possible to manage several entity states (neither only the last one nor all the states). The entity versions are linked by a derivation link; they form a version derivation hierarchy. When created, an entity is described by only one version. The definition of every new entity version is done by derivation from a previous one. Such versions are called derived versions. Several versions may be derived from the same previous one. They are called alternative versions.

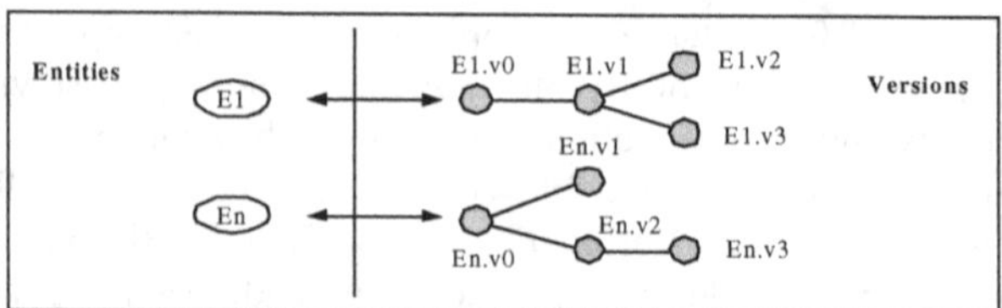

Fig. 1. Versions to describe Entity Evolution

A version is either frozen or working. A frozen version describes a significant and final state of an entity. A frozen version may be deleted but not updated. To describe a new state of this entity, we have to derive a new version (from the frozen one). A working version is a version that temporarily describes one of the entity states. It may be deleted or updated to describe a next entity state. The previous state is lost to the benefit of the next one.

2.2 VBP Meta-model

The VBP meta-model results from the merging of two layers: a Business Process (BP) meta-model for classical business process modelling, and a versioning kit to make classes of the BP meta-model versionable, i.e. classes for which we would like to handle versions. Because of space limitation, we directly focus on the VBP meta-model. Interested readers can consult [6] to have additional information about these two layers and the way we merge them to define the VBP meta-model.

Figure 2 below presents this meta-model in terms of classes and relationships between classes. This figure visualizes in blue versionable classes (i.e. classes for which we handle versions), from non-versionable classes (i.e. classes for which we do not handle versions). An example illustrating the definition of a BP version will be given in section 5.

Mains concepts of the meta-model. The main concepts of the meta-model are the Process, Activity, Control Pattern, Operation, Informational Resource, and Role concepts. A process performs activities, which can be atomic or composite. Only the first of these activities is explicitly indicated in the meta-model. If an activity is composite, we keep its component activities, which are coordinated by control patterns.

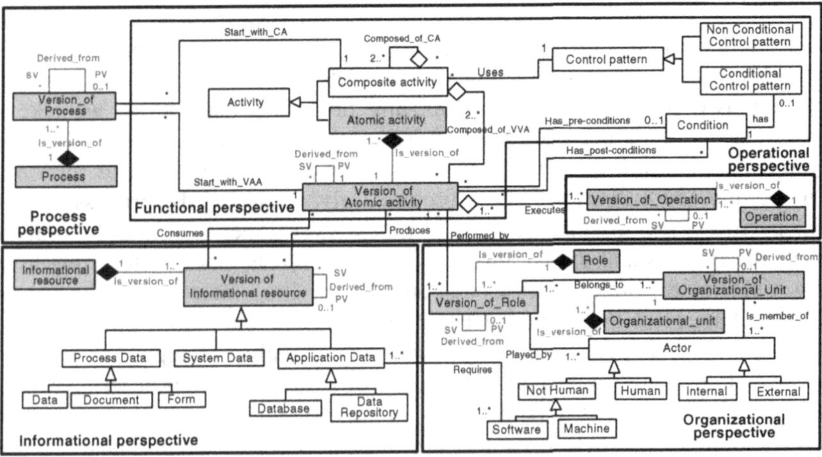

Fig. 2. VBP Meta-Model in UML

In our meta-model, the main control patterns described in the literature are provided. Some of them are conditional (e.g. if, while…), while others are not (e.g. sequence, fork…).

An atomic activity can have pre-condition (or start condition), post-conditions and executes one or several operations. It is performed by a role, which can be played by several actors belonging to organizational units (organizational perspective). An actor can be (i) human or not human (i.e. software or machine), and (ii) internal or external. Moreover, an atomic activity consumes and/or produces informational resources (informational perspective). An informational resource is a system data, an application data (i.e. data repository or database), or a process data (i.e. form, document, data).

Taking into account versions. The underlying idea of our proposition to take into account versions of business processes is to describe, for each versionable class, both entities and their corresponding versions as indicated in figure 1. As a consequence, each versionable class is described using two classes: a first class, called "…", to model entities and a second one, called "Version_ of_…", whose instances are the corresponding versions. For instance, versions of processes are modelled within two classes: the *Process* class gathers the different modelled business process while the *Version_Of_Process* class gathers the different versions of the modelled processes. These classes are linked together by two relationships: the "Is_version_of" relationship links a versionable class with its corresponding "Version of…" class and the "Derived_from" relationship describes version derivation hierarchies between versions of a same entity. This latter relationship is reflexive and the semantic of both sides of this relationship are: (i) a version (SV) succeeds another one in the derivation hierarchy and, (ii) a version (PV) precedes another one in the derivation hierarchy. Moreover, we introduce in the "Version of…" classes, classical properties for versions i.e. version number, creator name, creation date and status [8].

Versionable classes. Finally, it is possible to manage versions both at the schema and the instance levels. In our opinion, in the Business Process context, it is only interesting to consider versions at the schema level (i.e. versions of BP schemas), and the notion of version must be applied to all the perspectives defined at the schema level. In our proposition, and unlike related works (e.g. [9,10]), which consider only two perspectives (functional and process perspectives), we take into account the five main perspectives of BPs, i.e. the process, functional, operational, organizational and informational perspectives, which are considered as relevant for BP modelling and execution [11]. More precisely, regarding the process and functional perspectives, we think that it is necessary to keep versions for only two classes: the Process and the Atomic activity classes. It is indeed interesting to keep changes history for both processes and atomic activities since these changes correspond to changes in the way that business is carried out. More precisely, at the process level, versions are useful to describe the possible strategies for organizing activities while, at the activity level, versions of atomic activities describe evolution in activity execution. We defend the idea that versioning of processes and atomic activities is enough to help organizations to face the fast changing environment in which they are involved nowadays. Regarding the other perspectives, it is necessary to handle versions for the Operation class of the operational perspective, for the Informational resource class of the informational perspective, and for the Role and Organizational Unit classes of the organizational perspective.

3 Extending BPMN to Model Versions of BPs

The general framework we propose for supporting a process designer in modelling and specifying versions of BPs advocates a model driven engineering approach considering at the CIM level, a specific meta-model, the Version Business Process (VBP) meta-model for modelling versions of business processes, and at the PIM level, an extension of BPMN (Business Process Modelling Notation). In fact, we use two models at the PIM level: the first one (Petri net with Objects) for formalizing, simulating and validating modelled versions of BPs, and the second one (BPMN) for a graphic representation of modelled versions of BPs. On the one hand, Petri net with objects formalism, which is well fitted to take into account the different dimensions of BPs through the notion of object, is used for formal specifications of BP versions [12], and the Renew platform [13] supports their simulation and validation. On the other hand, BPMN [14] is used for graphic representation of modelled BP versions. Indeed, BPMN is a notation, defined by the Business Process Management Initiative, readily understandable by business users (business analysts, business developers and business managers) and it is recognized as a standard.

Our goal is to translate versions of BPs modelled according to the VBP meta-model onto BPMN business process diagrams. As BPMN does not support the version notion, we have extended it. This section briefly presents BPMN and explains how we extend it for business process version modelling.

3.1 Core BPMN Concepts

We present here a core set of BPMN concepts, which are useful in the context of the paper that only considers intra-organisational business processes.

According to [15], BPMN distinguishes two types of elements: *graphical* elements and *supporting* elements. Graphical elements are elements involved in a Business Process Diagram (BPD) and they have a specific notation for their representation. (e.g. a task is represented as a rectangle). These graphical elements correspond to Swimlanes, Flow objects, Connecting Flow objects and Artifacts (see figure 3 below).

Swimlanes allows grouping elements of BPDs. A Swimlane can be a Pool or a Lane. A *Pool* represents a participant in a business process. A *Participant* can be a specific business entity (e.g. a company) or a business role (e.g. a buyer, a seller). A *Lane* represents a sub-partition within a pool that is used to organize and categorize activities.

Flow objects are the main graphical elements used to define BPs behaviour. A Flow object can be an Activity, a Gateway or an Event. An *Activity* is a generic term for work that a company performs. It can be atomic, i.e. a *Task*, when the work in the process is not broken down into a finer level of detail. A *Gateway* is used to control the divergence and the convergence of Sequence Flows. BPMN proposes different types of gateways, but nevertheless, in the context of the paper, we only consider Exclusive (XOR), Inclusive (OR) and Parallel (AND) gateways. An *Event* is something that happens during the course a business process. It affects the flow of the process, and usually has a cause or an impact. In the context of the paper, we only consider two types of events: *start* and *end* events.

Connecting Flow objects are used to connect Flow objects. In the context of the paper, we only consider two connecting flow objects: Sequence Flows and Associations. A *Sequence Flow* is used to show the order that activities are performed in a business process, while an *Association* is used to link Flow objects with Artifacts.

Finally, *Artifacts* are used to provide additional information about the process. In the context of the paper, we only consider Data Object that provides information about what activities require and/or produce.

In addition to these graphical elements, BPMN also integrates supporting elements, which correspond to BPMN types involved in the definition of graphical elements or other supporting elements. For instance the supporting element Process is referenced by the graphical element Pool: it means that a Pool represents a Process in a BPD. The main supporting elements considered in this paper are the following:

- *Process*, which is represented within a Pool and depicted as a graph of Flow objects and the control that sequence them.
- *Participant*, that defines a role or an entity invoked to achieve process activities.
- *Entity*, that represents the organization' structure in which a process performs.
- *Role*, which corresponds to a business role that executes a process.
- *Condition*, representing a text or an expression that must be evaluated.
- *InputSet* and *OutputSet*, which define the data requirements for input to and output from activities.
- *ArtifactInput* and *ArtifactOutput*, referring to artifacts that will be used as input to and output from an activity.

3.2 BPMN Extensions

We propose to extend BPMN in order to take into account the version notion and to also integrate the VBP-M concepts that are not supported in BPMN. This extension consists in both adding new BPMN supporting elements (i.e. new BPMN types), and new attributes in the existing graphical and supporting elements. Figure 3 below presents the obtained BPMN meta-model. It distinguishes already existing elements from new added attributes and elements, which are visualised in blue.

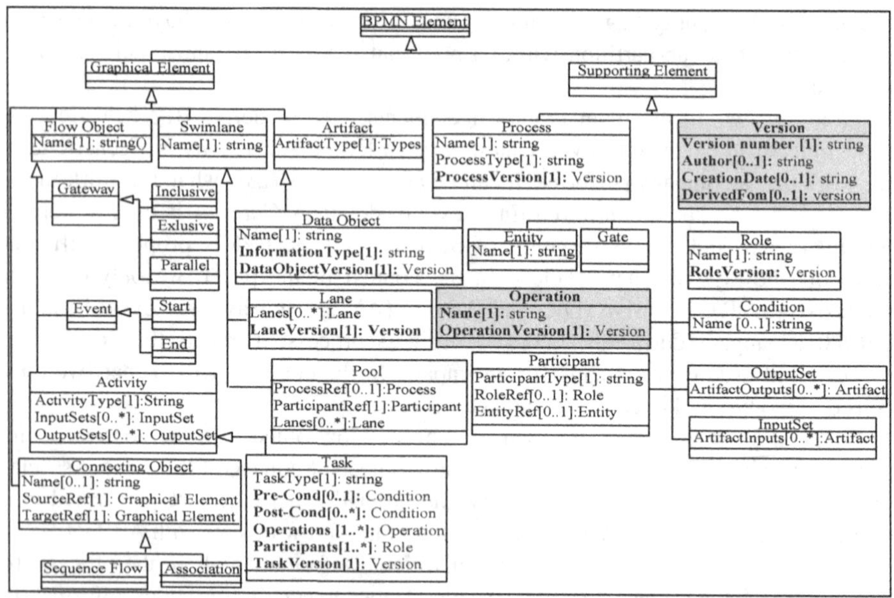

Fig. 3. Extended BPMN Meta-model in UML

First, we add two new supporting elements: Version and Operation. *Version* allows the description of versions of BPMN elements, such as Process, Lane, Data Object, Task and Role. These elements correspond to versionnable classes of the VBP meta model. The Version supporting element contains the following attributes: *Version-Number*, *Author* and *CreationDate*. Regarding *Operation*, it allows the description of operations performed within a Task. Second, we add the following attributes to existing elements:

- *Version* attribute. We add the Version attribute referencing the new supporting element Version to each BPMN element, which corresponds to a versionnable class in the VBP meta-model. For instance, considering the Process element, we add the *ProcessVersion:Version* attribute to describe versions of processes.
- *InformationalResouceType* attribute. In the business process context, information can be a Process Data, System Data or Application Data. So, to consider these information types, we add the *InformationalResouceType* attribute in the Data Object Element.

- *Pre-condition, Post-Conditions, Participant* and *Operations* attributes. We add the Pre-condition, Post-condition, Participant and Operations attributes in the graphical element *Task* in order to be able to describe its starting and ending conditions, the operations to be executed within it and the invoked role to achieve it.

4 Mapping VBP onto Extended BPMN

This section first introduces the mapping rules from VBP onto extended BPMN considering both concepts and patterns. Then, it gives an example of a mapping rule description using the MOF QVT (Query/View/Transformation) standard [16].

4.1 Concepts and Pattern Mapping

In order to ensure the mapping from versions of BPs modelled according to the VBP meta-model to their corresponding BPD designed according to the extended BPMN meta-model, we specify the correspondence between concepts and patterns of these two meta-models. Figure 4 illustrates this concept correspondence specifying in the left side of the figure concepts of the source meta-model (i.e. VBP meta-model), in the right part of the figure concepts of the target meta-model (BPMN meta-model), and in the middle of the figure, rules supporting the correspondence (in red circles). Table 1 explains the mapping from VBP patterns to our extension of BPMN.

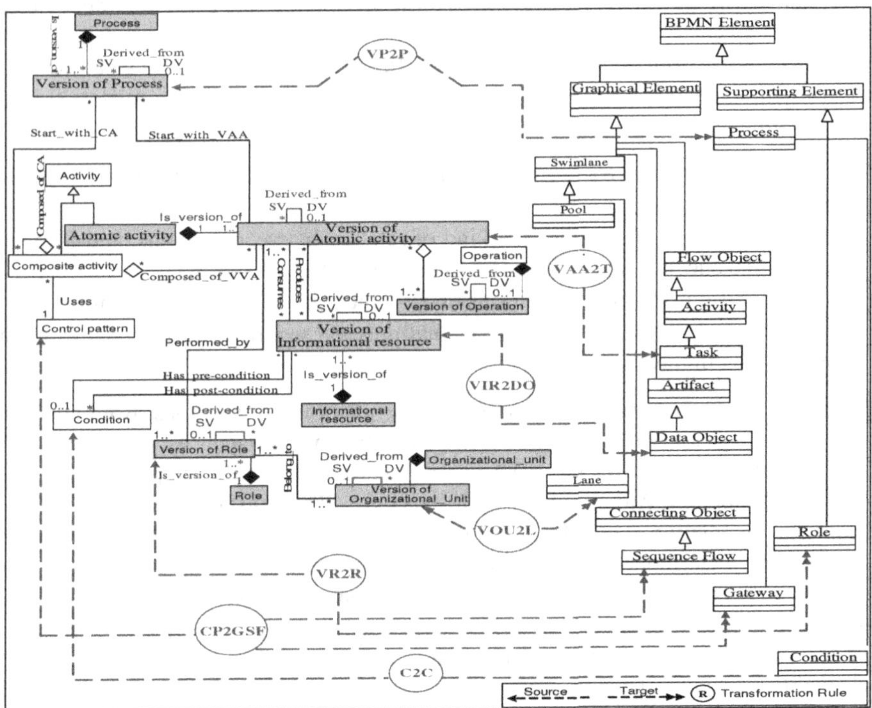

Fig. 4. Mapping between VBP and extended BPMN meta-models

Table 1. Mapping rules for control pattern

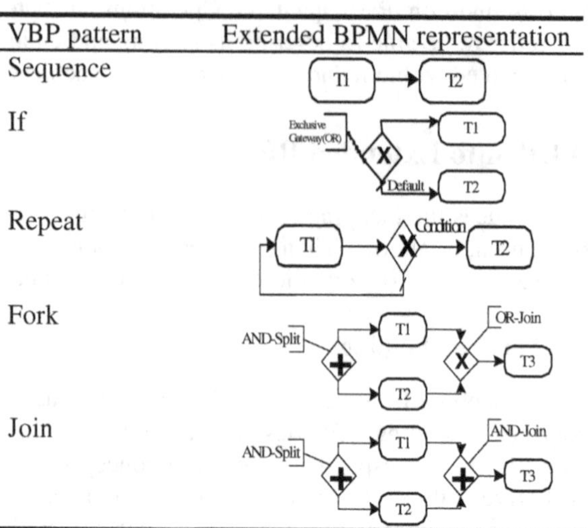

VBP pattern	Extended BPMN representation
Sequence	
If	
Repeat	
Fork	
Join	

4.2 QVT Transformation Rule

In order to illustrate the mapping between concepts of VBP and extended BPMN meta-models, we give here an example of a transformation rule using the Meta Object Facility QVT. QVT [16] is an Object Management Group standard for defining and formalizing transformations between models. In QVT, a transformation is defined as a list of relations. A relation defines a mapping between two candidate models (source and target models) specifying:

- two or more *domains*: each domain is a distinguished set of elements of a candidature model;
- a *relation domain*: it specifies the kind of relation between domains, and it can be marked like checkonly (labelled as C) or enforced (labelled as E).
- a *when clause*: it specifies conditions under which the relation needs to hold;
- a *where clause*: it specifies conditions that must be satisfied by all model elements participating in the relation.

Moreover, QVT supports textual and graphical notations for relations. Both notations can be used to declaratively define transformations. In this paper, we only present the QVT graphical notation for the VAA2T relation i.e. the relation supporting the mapping of Version_Of_Atomic_Activity instances to Task instances. Figure 5 below illustrates this relation. The left side of the figure shows concepts of the source model (i.e. the VBP meta-model) while its right side shows concepts of the target model (i.e. the extended BPMN meta-model). This relation makes explicit the transformation as follows: the C arrow allows selection of an instance from the source model (i.e. a version of an atomic activity and its related classes) while the E arrow inserts the selected instance into the appropriate elements of the target model (task and its related elements). Once this relation holds, the relations *C2C*, *VR2R*, *VIR2DO* and *VOP2OP* must also hold (according to the *where* clause).

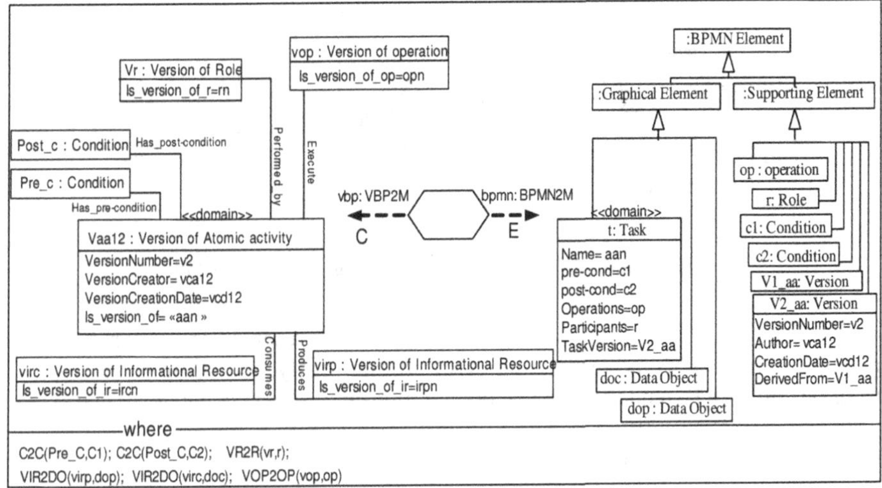

Fig. 5. Graphical Description of the VAA2T Relation

5 Implementation

This section gives a brief overview of the implementation we propose for the automatic mapping of VBP instances onto extended BPMN instances. It first describes the principles of generation of extended BPMN instances from corresponding VBP ones, and then illustrates this principle through an example.

5.1 Extending the BPMN Modeller Plug-In

As indicated in the introduction, VerFlexFlow includes $\text{VerFlexFlow}_{\text{design}}$ for supporting a process designer in specifying versions of business processes using the VBP meta-model. Schemas of the modelled BP versions are stored in a specific database that serves as a starting point for generating and visualising versions of BPs according to the extended BPMN meta-model. More precisely, $\text{VerFlexFlow}_{\text{design}}$ includes a specific eclipse plug-in to visualize BP versions. This plug-in is an extension of the already existing Eclipse BPMN Modeller plug-in: it completes this later by integrating new attributes, elements (both supporting and graphical elements –see section3-) and specific icons for representing versions.

Figure 6 below presents the method we use for producing new Business Process Diagrams (BPD) using the Extended BPMN meta-model. In fact, each BPD is described using the two following XML files: <Process_name>*.BPMN* and <Process_name>*.BPMN_DIAGRAM*. The first file defines the elements of the modelled BP version (for instance Pool, Lane, Data Object) while the second one describes the graphical features of these elements, such as their width, height or colour. So, in order to visualize versions of BPs using our Eclipse Extended BPMN Modeller plug-in, we need to automatically generate their associated files (i.e. .BPMN and .BPMN_DIAGRAM files) performing the following steps. The first one consists in querying a database storing schemas of BP versions in order to select a specific BP

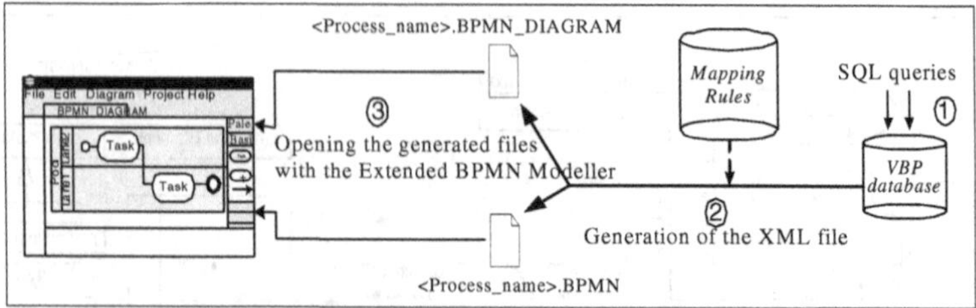

Fig. 6. Method for producing BPD using Extended BPMN

version. The second step refers to the mapping rules presented in section 4 to automatically generate its corresponding XML files. Finally, we open these two files using our Eclipse Extended BPMN Modeller plug-in to visualize the generated BPD.

5.2 Illustrative Example

To illustrate the automatic generation of a BPD representing a BP version, we use an example introduced in [9], and extended in [6]. This example describes a production business process and involves a factory, which owns one production pipeline following the BP shown in figure 7(a). It includes several activities: production scheduling, production using a work centre, quality checking and packaging. In order to increase its productivity, the factory decides to add a new work centre. The BP is then updated as shown in figure 7(b). If one of the two work centres, for instance work centre#1 (Pc#1), has a technical problem and consequently is out of order, two alternative solutions are proposed to attempt keeping the production output: fixing unqualified products or using employees for manual production. The business process is then updated as shown in figure 7(c) and 7(d).

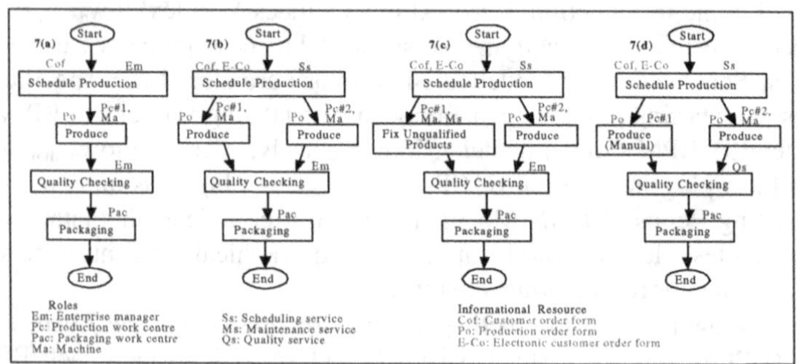

Fig. 7. Evolution in the Production Business Process

The four versions of the same Production BP are defined as instances of the VBP meta-model. Because of space limitation, we do not illustrate this instantiation and interested readers can consult [6] for information about it. For instance, to automatically generate the BPD of the first version 7(a) of the Production business process, we first perform a set of SQL queries to identify the different versions of atomic activities, operations, roles and informational resources which are involved in the definition of the Production BP version 7(a) along with their corresponding non versionable information (i.e. preconditions, post conditions, control patterns). Then, we automatically generate the two XML files according to the transformation rules introduced before. These two files are then used to produce the corresponding BPD. Figure 8 below visualises the derived BPD using the Eclipse Extended BPMN Modeller plug-in.

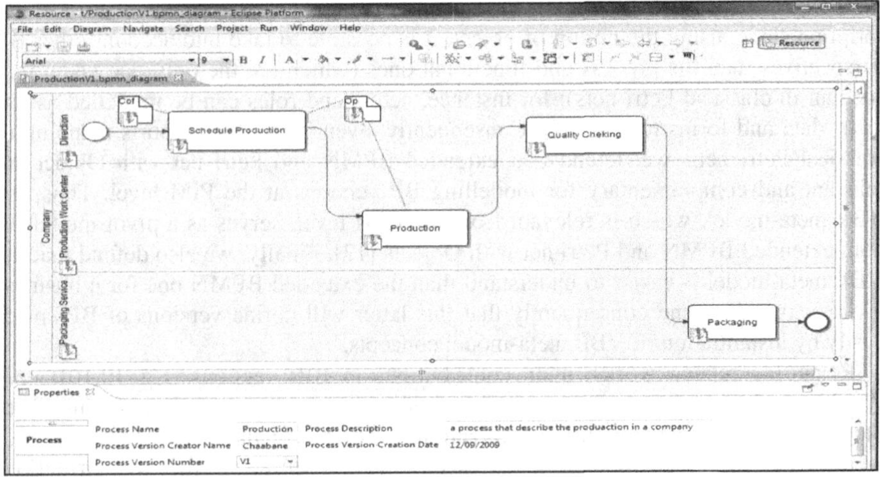

Fig. 8. BPD of the first version of the Production Business Process

6 Conclusion

This paper has presented a solution to model versions of BPs using an extension of BPMN. This solution is integrated into a more general framework supporting a process designer for modelling and specifying flexible business processes using the version concept. This framework advocates a MDE approach considering (i) at the CIM level, a specific meta-model, the Version Business Process (VBP) meta-model for modelling versions of BPs (ii) at the PIM level, an extension of the BPMN meta-model for visualizing and user validating the modelled BP versions, and finally, (iii) at the PSM level, several meta-models for implementing versions of BPs (e.g. XPDL and BPEL meta-models). This paper mainly focuses on the automatic mapping from the CIM level onto the PIM level (i.e. the extension of the BPMN meta-model) using a model driven engineering approach. Its contributions are the following:

- The specification of an extension of BPMN in order to model versions of BPs.
- An automatic mapping of versions of BPs modelled using the VBP meta-model onto BP versions modelled with extended BPMN meta-model.
- An implementation of this mapping extending the Eclipse BPMN Modeller plug-in in order to take into account version specificities.

A question deserves perhaps to be discussed: *why proposing two meta-models for modelling versions of business process and why not only extending BPMN to support versions modelling*? In fact, we use two different formalisms at the PIM level for both visualizing and validating versions of BPs. On the one hand, BPMN is used for graphic representation of modelled BP versions. Indeed, BPMN is a notation readily understandable by business users and it is recognized as a standard. Moreover, it will serve as a pivot model for the automatic derivation of specifications of BP versions (using XPDL or BPEL). On the other hand, the Petri net with Object formalism is used for formal specifications of BP versions, and the Renew platform supports their simulation and validation. Such a formalism is recognized as convenient for BP description since, using the notion of object, it is possible to take into account other BP perspectives than the process and functional ones (which are the only one taken into account in classical Petri nets): for instance, actors and roles can be modelled as objects, data and forms too [12,17]. Consequently, even if BPMN supports mapping to classical Petri nets, we defend that extended BPMN and Petri net with Object are relevant and complementary for modelling BP versions at the PIM level. Thus, the VBP meta-model, which is relevant from the CIM level, serves as a pivot model for both extended BPMN and Petri net with Objects [12]. Finally, we also defend that the VBP meta-model is easier to understand than the extended BPMN one for a business process modeller, and consequently that this latter will define versions of BPs more easily by instantiation of VBP meta-model concepts.

Regarding related works, main contributions in BPs versions (e.g. [9,10]) only consider two perspectives (process and functional), and do not take into account three other perspectives (operational, organizational and informational) which are considered as relevant for BP modelling and execution [11]. Moreover, theses contributions do not address the automatic mapping of modelled BP versions from a CIM level to a PIM level. On the other hand, contributions that address the automatic mapping of BPMN specifications into executable ones do not consider versions of business processes (e.g. [18]). Finally, to the best of our knowledge, it does not exist any contribution in the literature addressing the integration of the version notion in BPMN.

Our future works will take two directions. On the one hand, we will go on our efforts on VerFlexFlow. First, regarding $\text{VerFlexFlow}_{\text{design}}$,we will map BP version modelled using the extended BPMN meta-model onto versions of BPs described using language relevant from the PSM level of our MDA-based framework: XPDL and BPEL, which are the de-facto standard for implementing BPs. Second, we will address execution of specified BP versions through $\text{VerFlexFlow}_{\text{run}}$. On the other hand, we also planed to investigate another perspective of business processes: the intentional perspective. Our objective is to integrate this perspective into the VBP meta-model in order to enable a process designer to indicate why he defines a BP version. This objective is somewhat related to the notion of context introduced in [19] and [20].

References

1. Reijers, H.: Workflow Flexibility: the Forlon Promise. In: Int. Workshop on Enabling Technologies: Infrastructure for Collaborative Enterprises, Manchester, United Kingdom, June 2006, pp. 271–272 (2006)
2. Nurcan, S., Schmidt, R., Soffer, P.: Int. Workshop on Business Process Management, Design and Support, at Int. Conference on Advanced Information Systems, Montpellier, France (June 2008)

3. Sadiq, S., Weber, B., Reichert, M.: Beyond Rigidity: Lifecycle Management for Dynamic Processes. In: Tutorial at Int. Conference on Business Process Management, Brisbane, Australia (September 2007)
4. Nurcan, S.: A Survey on the Flexibility Requirements related to Business Process and Modeling Artifacts. In: Hawaii Int. Conference on System Sciences, Waikoloa, Big Island, Hawaii, USA, January 2008, p. 378 (2008)
5. Schoneneberg, H., Mans, R., Russell, N., Mulyar, N., van der Aalst, W.: Process Flexibility: A Survey of Contemporary Approaches. In: Int. Workshop on CIAO/EOMAS, at Int. Conf. on Advanced Information Systems, Montpellier, France, June 2008, pp. 16–30 (2008)
6. Chaabane, M.A., Andonoff, E., Bouzguenda, L., Bouaziz, R.: Versions to address business process flexibility issue. In: Grundspenkis, J., Morzy, T., Vossen, G. (eds.) ADBIS 2009. LNCS, vol. 5739, pp. 2–14. Springer, Heidelberg (2009)
7. Faure, C., Andonoff, E., Hanachi, C., Sibertin-Blanc, C., Salatge, N.: Flexibilité de processus de gestion de crise par intégration de protocoles d'interaction. In: National Conference on Informatique des Organisations et des Systèmes de Décision, Toulouse, France, May 2009, pp. 77–92 (2009)
8. Sciore, E.: Versioning and Configuration Management in Object-Oriented Databases. Int. Journal on Very Large Databases 3(1), 77–106 (1994)
9. Zhao, X., Liu, C.: Version Management in the Business Change Context. In: Int. Conference on Business Process Management, Brisbane, Australia, September 2007, pp. 198–213 (2007)
10. Kammer, P., Bolcer, G., Taylor, R., Bergman, M.: Techniques for supporting Dynamic and Adaptive Workflow. Int. Journal on Computer Supported Cooperative Work 9(3-4), 269–292 (1999)
11. van der Aalst, W.: Business Process Management Demystified: A Tutorial on Models, Systems and Standards for Workflow Management. In: Desel, J., Reisig, W., Rozenberg, G. (eds.) Lectures on Concurrency and Petri Nets. LNCS, vol. 3098, pp. 1–65. Springer, Heidelberg (2004)
12. Chaabane, M.A., Bouzguenda, L., Bouaziz, R., Andonoff, E.: Dealing with Business Process Evolution using Versions. In: Int. Conference on E-Business, Porto, Portugal, July 2008, pp. 267–278 (2008)
13. Renew: the Reference Net Workshop, `http://www.renew.de`
14. Business Process Management Initiative, Object Management Group, Business Process Modelling Notation, `http://www.bpmn.org`
15. Business Process Modelling Notation, Version 1.2., `http://www.omg.org/spec/BPMN/1.2`
16. Meta Object Facility MOF 2.0 Query/View/Transformation Specification, `http://www.omg.org/spec/QVT/1.0/PDF/`
17. Andonoff, E., Bouzguenda, L., Hanachi, C.: Specifying Workflow Web Services for Finding Partners in the context of Loose Inter-Organizational Workflow. In: Int. Conference on Business Process Management, Nancy, France, September 2005, pp. 120–136 (2005)
18. White, S.: Using BPMN to model a BPEL process, `http://www.bpmn.org/Documents/Mapping_BPMN_to_BPEL_Example.pdf`
19. Bessai, K., Claudepierre, B., Saidani, O., Nurcan, S.: Context Aware Business Process Evaluation and Redesign. In: Int. Workshop on Business Process Management, Design and Support, at Int. Conf. on Advanced Information Systems, Montpellier, France, June 2008, pp. 86–95 (2008)
20. Adams, M., ter Hofstede, A., Edmond, D., van der Aalst, W.: Worklets: A Service-Oriented Implementation of Dynamic Flexibility in Workflows. In: Int. Conference on Cooperative Information Systems, Montpellier, France, November 2006, pp. 291–306 (2006)

Value Propositions in Service Oriented Business Models for ERP: Case Studies

Håkan Enquist[1] and Gustaf Juell-Skielse[2]

[1] School of Business, Economics and Law, University of Gothenburg
hakan.enquist@handels.gu.se
[2] Stockholm University
gjs@dsv.su.se

Abstract. Service systems challenge traditional on-premise installations and create opportunities for new business models in the ERP market. In this paper, six case studies are analyzed to identify attributes and patterns of service oriented business models for Enterprise Resource Planning. The business models are analyzed with a focus on value proposition. Two patterns of service oriented business models for ERP are identified: *holistic* and *niche*. In addition to analyze business model patterns, we identified and applied categorizations of elementary offering types, ERPII layers and generic value proposition types. Hereby, the applied business model framework is enriched to broaden understanding of service oriented business models for ERP.

Keywords: Enterprise resource planning, business model, service systems, software as a service, business model ontology.

1 Introduction

Enterprise resource planning systems (ERP-systems) are the infrastructural information backbone of most western companies of any size and industry [1]. ERP represent an important market for vendors and consultants. The traditional monolithic design as well as the on-premise installations of ERP-systems is now challenged by Software as a service (SaaS). SaaS is a new view on ERP-systems as being an orchestrated collection of software services [2, 3] and is increasing its share of the ERP market [4]. Therefore there is a need for studies on emerging business models for service oriented ERP.

In this paper we report findings from six comparative case studies. The purpose is to identify patterns of service oriented business models for enterprise resource planning. Therefore we explore:

– *What value propositions can be found in the cases of service oriented business models for ERP?*

Three areas are described and analyzed to find answers to the main question:

1. Content of value propositions found in the case studies.
2. Assumed customer value.
3. Patterns of business model components.

W. Abramowicz and R. Tolksdorf (Eds.): BIS 2010, LNBIP 47, pp. 268–279, 2010.

The patterns and cases of service oriented business models for ERP will serve as a basis for researchers and practitioners to better understand and develop applied business models of specific firms. The use of additional frameworks and theories is a basis for extending the Business Model Ontology [5] to service orientation and ERP.

The paper is organized as follows. In the next chapter we discuss a theoretical framework for business models, service orientation and enterprise systems. In chapter three the method is outlined. In chapter four the cases and findings are presented followed by conclusions and future research in chapter five.

2 Theoretical Framework

In this chapter we present previous research in the areas of business models, service orientation and enterprise resource planning (ERP).

2.1 Service Orientation

According to Spohrer et al. [6, p.72] "Service systems comprise service providers and service clients working together to co-produce value in complex value chains or networks." Traditionally a service has been identified as something opposed to a product. It is intangible, heterogeneous and not possible to store. It is also difficult to separate service consumption from production [7, 8]. "A service 'is something that can be bought and sold but which you cannot drop on your foot'." [9, p. 22]. This way of portraying services has recently been challenged by another view where service is seen as a perspective on value creation rather than a category of market offerings [10]. In this perspective the focus is on customer value and service is the interactive, processual, experiential and relational nature of co-creation between consumer and producer. There are two aspects of this perspective to consider: the *customer logic* and the *provider logic* [11]. The using organization utilizes services according to *customer logic* to orchestrate business processes. Business processes serve as mediums for the using organization to coordinate activities between different professional realms for creating customer value [12]. The service providers follow *provider logic* and create interactive contacts with the using organization in order to co-create value with them and for them [11].

2.2 Enterprise Resource Planning

Enterprise Resource Planning (ERP) systems are standard software packages designed to meet demands from different users [13]. ERP systems include administrative functions for finance, human resources, production, logistics and sales and marketing. The various components or modules are integrated through a central database [14]. ERP provides support to coordinate the work along business processes and to monitor activities spanning large organizational and geographical distance [15]. ERP has evolved from a core of functions, to cover more or less all parts of a business [16]. In connection with this development the knowledge and experience from many companies have been built into the software packages and the large investments have been split between many companies. Extended ERP (ERPII) builds on the functional heart of ERP with advanced features for supply chain management and customer relationship management and use of the integration possibilities that the Internet offers [4]. Möller defines four layers of ERP: Foundation, Process, Analytical and Portal.

The life cycle of an ERP system can range from a few years up to 10-15 years and includes the selection, set-up, implementation, use and operation (including upgrades) and settlement [16]. Major implementations can last for several years and cost hundreds of millions of dollars. Implementation of ERP has proved to be complex and risky projects and are often more expensive and takes longer time than expected. ERP research has been focused on identifying critical success factors for reducing these risks (e.g. refer to [17] for a summary).

2.3 ERP and Service Orientation

The introduction of a service-oriented architecture opens up the possibility of replacing the traditional, monolithic architecture with distributed services [18]. The service-based business systems can more easily adapt to changing business demands and become less expensive for small-and medium-sized enterprises [19]. In a prototype solution, Brehm and Marx-Gomez demonstrate what such a federated ERP system (FERP) can look like. The core of the system follows the definitions of Möller [4] with a database and a workflow system for the management of business processes. Business logic is then added to the system in the form of web services that are bought real time and paid for per use. Process models that are used to orchestrate processes based on the web services are also treated as services.

2.4 Business Model and Value Proposition

According to Osterwalder [5 p.19] the main use and contribution of business models are for managers to "capture, understand, communicate, design, analyze, and change the business logic of their firms". Hence, the business model becomes a common language for expressing the characteristics of a firm's business logic, but also an instrument to change the business logic as a response to market opportunities. On a conceptual level a business model includes taxonomies for elements and relationships and several researchers have suggested generic business model concepts, for example [20, 21, 22].

In the Business Model Ontology (BMO), Osterwalder [5] decomposes a business model in four areas or "pillars": value proposition, customer interface, infrastructure management and financial aspects. For each pillar there are one or more building blocks, i.e. value proposition consists of one building block *value proposition* while financial aspects consists of two building blocks: *cost structure* and *revenue model.* The building block *value proposition* is characterized by its attributes *description, reasoning, value level* and *price level.* It is further decomposed into a set of *elementary offerings.* In turn an *elementary offering* is described by its attributes *description, reasoning, life cycle, value level* and *price level.* Customer value is produced when *assumed customer value* matches *perceived customer value* after the consumption of a *value proposition* or an *elementary offering.* The building block *revenue model* describes how a company makes money on a *value proposition.* A revenue model consists of a set of *revenue streams* and *pricing* for one or several *elementary offerings. Revenue streams and pricing* is described by its attributes *stream type* and *pricing method.*

In this paper, we primarily focus on value propositions of service oriented business models for enterprise resource planning. Value propositions represent what companies do for their customers better or differently than their competitors [23]. Previous research distinguishes between four generic value propositions. Porter [24] makes a distinction between *low-cost* value propositions and *differentiated* value propositions. According to Treacy and Wiersema [25] *differentiated* value propositions can be divided in *customer intimacy* and *product leadership. Customer intimacy* is sometimes referred to as *complete customer solution* [23]. Furthermore, Hax and Wilde [26] identify *lock-in* as a fourth generic value proposition. Treacy and Wiersema [25] claim that market leading companies must excel in one generic value proposition and be satisfactory in the other ones.

3 Case Analysis Approach

The approach in this paper is to analyze data on value propositions from multiple cases of service oriented business models for ERP. Six comparative case studies [27, 28, 29, 30] were performed in order to gather information about emerging business models. A form was designed to support the information gathering from the cases. The form contains four sections: author information, case background, case description and case evaluation. The form was tested on two pilot case studies and discussed with a reference group consisting of 15 organizations including ERP suppliers, consultants and organizations using ERP systems. The cases were selected in cooperation with the members of the reference group and documented during February to June 2009.

In the case analysis, a predefined structure based on Osterwalder's business model ontology [5] is used. The following sections describe the analysis approach and instruments used to address each area of investigation.

3.1 Content of the Value Propositions Found in the Case Studies

The content analysis was based on a comparison of case data searching for similarities and variations in the *value propositions* of the business models. Findings were made regarding:

- Content of *elementary offerings* as part of *value proposition.*
- Categories of *generic value propositions.*
- Layers of ERP content found in *elementary offerings.*

The value propositions were described using the attributes *description* and *offering* taken from the business model ontology [5]. They were categorized using four generic value propositions: *low total cost, product leadership, complete customer solution and lock-in* [23]. ERP functionality included in the offerings was categorized using four ERP layers: *foundation, process, analytical* and *portal* [4].

3.2 Assumed Customer Value

The analysis was based on data regarding *assumed customer value* and *customer relation* looking for: categories of customer needs; groups of cases with similar needs;

stakeholders in *customer relation* i.e. who made the decision on *consumption* or *purchase* of the *value proposition*. Furthermore, types of *revenue streams* and methods of *pricing* found in *revenue models* are described.

3.3 Patterns of Business Models

Business model *patterns* in terms of taxonomy types [20] were identified using a cross-case pattern search [28]. The taxonomy types are analyzed based on the concepts of:

- BMO [5]: value proposition, elementary offering, customer segment, relation, assumed customer value, revenue stream, pricing method.
- ERPII framework [4]: ERPII layer.
- generic value proposition [23]: primary generic value proposition.

Due to the delineation of scope to *value proposition* in this paper the taxonomy type elements are delimited to *value proposition* and elements directly linked to *value proposition*.

4 Findings

This chapter provides an overview of the cases and a presentation of analysis and findings according to three areas of investigation:

1. content of the value propositions found in the case studies.
2. assumed customer value.
3. patterns of business model components according to BMO.

4.1 Case Overview

This section presents an overview and introduction to the cases, see Table 1, including case name, provider and case selection rationale.

Table 1. Case studies of service oriented business models for ERP. Size of organization based on European Commission's definition [31].

Case	Customer	Size of Organization	Supplier	Case Provider
A	Västra Götalandsregionen	Large	Projectplace	KPMG
B	Global transportation company	Large	Salesforce	Accenture
C	Lidingö municipality	Large	Logica	Lidingö municipality
D	Real estate company	Small	Hogia	Hogia
E	Travel agencies	Small to medium	Scandisys	Microsoft
F	Manufacturing companies	Medium	Systeam	Systeam

Case A - Project Management in Regional Public Administration. The case was provided by the consulting and auditing firm KPMG. It includes the use of a project management service offered by Projectplace at Västra Götalandsregionen. Projectplace is a Swedish software service provider and Västra Götalandsregionen is a Swedish government region with 50.000 employees mainly in healthcare. The case study was prepared by the project coordinator from Västra Götalandsregionen and the key account manager for Västra Götalandsregionen at KPMG. Motivation: A well established SaaS-service that has been implemented in VGR for a number of years.

Case B - Customer Relationship Management Support in Global Transportation. The case was provided by the consulting firm Accenture. It includes the use of a customer relationship management support service offered by Salesforce at a transportation company. The transportation company performs business in more than 50 countries. The case study was prepared by the project manager and two project members from Accenture involved in the implementation project at the transportation company. Motivation: One of the largest SaaS projects in Europe.

Case C - E-Service Platform for Public Administration. The case was provided by the municipality of Lidingö. It includes the use of an e-service platform offered by Logica at the municipality of Lidingö. Lidingö has approximately 46.000 inhabitants and 2.600 employees. The case study was prepared by the chief information officer at the municipality of Lidingö. Motivation: E-service implementations in many Swedish municipalities use the described e-service platform.

Case D - Full IS/IT Service Supply in Real Estate Management. The case was provided by the ERP-vendor Hogia, a Swedish ERP-vendor with a focus on small and medium sized companies. The case study includes the use of a full IS/IT service offered by Hogia at a real estate management firm with 20 employees. The case study was prepared by a sales manager at Hogia. Motivation: A growing interest among customers for an ERP service with monthly and more transparent costs.

Case E - Enterprise Resource Planning for Travel Agencies. The case was provided by Microsoft. The case study includes the use of a service offered by Scandisys to separate travel agencies or travel departments in larger organizations. Scandisys is a small Swedish firm offering a full ERP-service for travel agencies built on Microsoft Dynamics AX and several travel industry services such as Amadeus. The case study was prepared by Microsoft's product manager for Dynamics AX in cooperation with the owner of Scandisys. Motivation: The solution is competitive due to its strong industry domain focus. It has been available for several years and is easy to evaluate.

Case F - Full IS/IT Service Supply in Manufacturing. The case was provided by Systeam, a Nordic consulting firm. The case study includes a full IS/IT service offered by Systeam to a medium sized international manufacturing company. The case was prepared by two key account managers at Systeam. Motivation: A growing interest among customers for ERP as a service with usage based payment models.

4.2 Content of Value Propositions Found in the Case Studies

This section provides a presentation of value proposition descriptions and elementary offerings included in the value propositions, see Table 2. In Table 3, generic value propositions and layers of ERP content are identified for each case. Furthermore, for each table, comparisons between the cases are made.

Table 2. Descriptive data on value propositions found in case studies

Case	Value Proposition Description	Elementary Offerings
A	Collaborative workspace supporting project management and project work according to customer specific project guidelines.	– Project management – Project work – Project model and templates – User Support
B	Common customer relationship management support based on aggregated transport management information.	– Customer relationship management – Integration development – Implementation – Development and test environments – Support is offered to both end-users and developers
C	Secure information management between government entities, citizens and organizations.	– Information management according to the SHS standard – Electronic signature and authentication – Implementation – Development and test environment for electronic forms
D	Full IS/IT Service Supply in Real Estate Management.	– Office applications – Business applications – Business-to-business integration – Implementation – User Support – Financing
E	Enterprise Resource Planning for travel agencies.	– ERP – Integration with various travel service providers (e.g. Amadeus for flights) – Integration with payment services (credit cards, banks)
F	Full IS/IT Service Supply in Manufacturing.	– Office applications – Business applications – Business-to-business integration – Development services – IT-management services – Implementation – User Support

Three cases (D, E and F) demonstrate similar value propositions including full support for ERP and two of these cases (D and F) also provide support for all business IT, see table 2. These three cases focus on specific industries: real estate management, travel agencies and manufacturing. The three remaining cases (A, B and C) offer specific ERP functions rather than full ERP. Two of these cases (B and C) assume integration with the customer's information systems while the third (A) is used stand-alone without integration with the customer's information systems.

All six cases offer ERP content as services. Two cases also offer other business IT content as services (D and F). Two cases offer development environments as services (B and C). Four of the cases include services traditionally labeled as "consulting services". These include integration development (B) and implementation (B, C, D and F). Some cases also report additional non-ERP services bundled in the value offering. These services include finance services (D) and business operations services (A and D). Business operations services include project management (A) and accounting (D).

Table 3. Analysis of ERP content and types of generic value propositions

Case	Size of Customer Organization	ERP II Layer	Primary Generic Value Proposition
A	Large	Process	Product Leadership
B	Large	Analytical, Portal	Low-cost
C	Large	Portal	Low-cost
D	Small	Foundation, Process, Portal	Complete customer solution
E	Small to Medium	Foundation, Process, Portal	Complete customer solution
F	Medium	Foundation, Process, Analytical, Portal	Complete customer solution

The function oriented value offerings reside within one layer of the ERPII framework (A, B and C) while the three cases offering full ERP support (D, E and F) include at least three layers of the ERPII framework. The three full ERP support cases all include foundation, process and portal which indicate a focus on core ERP complemented with external business relations. Only one of these three cases includes the analytical layer (F).

Regarding generic value proposition, three cases (D, E and F) provide a complete customer solution, while two provide a low-cost value proposition (B and C) and one (A) provide product leadership. The complete customer solutions (D, E and F) also tend to lock-in their customers due to the difficulties in switching from one full IS/IT provider to other solutions.

4.3 Assumed Customer Value

The assumed customer values are specific and directly related to the ERP function offered in the three cases A, B and C, see Table 4. The three cases D, E and F all comprise more complex sets of needs including broad ERP functionality, other business IT

Table 4. Descriptive data on assumed customer value, customer relation and revenue model

Case	Assumed Customer Value	Customer Relation	Revenue Model
A	Improve project and project portfolio management.	CIO driven, central buying decision	Sell. Fixed prizing: pay-per-use + subscription. Key service paid for per number of users and time period.
B	Provide a shared global view of customer relations to improve analysis of customers, markets and countries.	CIO driven, central buying decision	Sell. Fixed prizing: pay per use + subscription. Salesforce operation: user/month/one year in advance. Salesforce development: time and material. Accenture: Project budget based on time and material
C	Secure information exchange between public authorities and citizens.	CIO driven	Sell. Fixed prizing: Pay-per-use + subscription. Start-up fee + monthly fee + fee per transaction
D	Full IS/IT support while avoiding binding own human and financial resources in IS/IT investments.	CEO driven	Sell. Fixed prizing: Pay-per-use + subscription. User/month in 36 months.
E	Turn-key ERP including integrations with key travel service providers.	CEO driven	Sell. Fixed prizing: Pay-per-use + subscription User/month. Differential : content dependent
F	Variable IS/IT support while avoiding binding own human and financial resources in IS/IT investments.	CEO driven	Sell. Fixed prizing: Pay-per-use + subscription. Content/user/month

functionality, and IT management and financing services. Non-functional user needs such as flexibility and scalability are not mentioned explicitly.

In all cases, consumption decision appears to originate from top management, CIO or CEO. In cases with delimited function, (A, B and C) decision is taken by CIO/ IT organization while the cases with full ERP support are decided by CEO. The latter cases also may exclude or significantly alter the need for a specific CIO in the user organizations.

Regarding pricing, all cases are based on subscription: monthly fee. All cases, except B and C, charge per user /month (pay-per-use) while B and C charge for an aggregate of licenses/users (pay-per-use). Case C has a transaction fee (pay-per-use) while case E can vary the fee dependent on what content is used (differential prizing). Only case C applies a startup fee. In conclusion the fee variables appear to be; per content use, per user, per month and possibly in combination i.e. variations of mostly *fixed prizing* but also some cases of *differential prizing*.

4.4 Patterns of Business Model Components

Based on a cross-case analysis according to section 3.3, two taxonomy types of value propositions of service oriented business models for ERP are identified, see Table 5. The taxonomy types are called: *Holistic approach* and *Niche approach*. The taxonomy types consist of identified patterns of business model elements. The Holistic approach is used by suppliers to address the needs of customers who want a comprehensive solution including full support for ERP and even full IT-support with broad variety of elementary offering types. This value proposition is primarily directed toward small and medium sized organizations. The Niche approach is directed toward large organizations and offers one or a few specific functions of ERP which are delivered as services. The customer uses its own IT resources and information systems expertise to integrate the function(s) into its operations and IT architecture. In both types (all cases) the Revenue stream is "Sell" and the prizing model is "Fixed" indicating the service providers tend to remain in well known revenue models.

Table 5. Patterns of business models

Taxonomy type Elements	Niche approach Case A, B, C	Holistic approach Case D, E, F
Value proposition	Niche, single function within ERPII	Holistic, complete ERPII and complementary offering types
Elementary offerings ERPII content	Either of Process, Analytical and/or Portal	Foundation Process Analytical Portal
Elementary offering types/ blend	IS/IT services (ERPII etc); User support, Development, Implementation	IS/IT services (ERPII etc); User support, Development, Implementation; Integration with payment, booking and other services; IT-management; Financing
Primary generic value proposition	Product leadership (1) Low cost (2)	Complete customer solution Lock-in
Customer type	Large organizations	SME
Decision maker	CIO driven	CEO driven
Assumed customer values	Resolve customers needs in specific business process or function	Resolve the customer's needs for Business IT support
Revenue stream	Sell	Sell
Pricing model	Fixed prizing	Fixed prizing

5 Conclusions and Future Research

In this study we have found two business model taxonomy types, *Holistic approach* and *Niche approach*, based on cases of applied service oriented business models for ERP.

In addition, we have applied supporting categorizations in terms of elementary offering types, ERPII content [4] and generic value proposition [23] thereby enriching the Business Model Ontology [5] to better describe service oriented business models for ERP.

In the continued research of patterns of business models, further elements of BMO and additional cases will be analyzed with a focus on the three remaining pillars of BMO, adding content to the two identified business model taxonomy types and possibly identifying additional taxonomy types.

References

1. Bhattacharaya, S., Behara, R.S., Gundersen, D.E.: Business risk perspectives on information systems outsourcing. International journal of accounting information systems 4(1), 75–93 (2003)
2. Brehm, N., Gomez, J.M., Rautenstrauch, C.: An ERP solution based on web services and peer-to-peer networks for small and medium enterprises. International Journal of Information Systems and Change Management 1(1), 99–111 (2006)
3. Möller, C.: ERP II: a conceptual framework for next-generation enterprise systems? Journal of Enterprise Information Management 18(4), 483–497 (2005)
4. Dubey, A., Wagle, D.: Delivering Software as Services. The McKinsey Quarterly, Web exclusive (May 2007)
5. Osterwalder, A.: The business model ontology – a proposition in a design science approach. Dissertation, University of Lausanne, Switzerland (2004)
6. Spohrer, J., Maglio, P.P., Bailey, J., Gruhl, D.: Steps toward a science of service systems. IEEE Computer Society 40, 71–77 (2007)
7. Vargo, S.L., Morgan, F.W.: Services in Society and Academic Thought: An Historical Analysis. Journal of Macromarketing 25(1), 42–53 (2005)
8. Grönroos, C.: Service Management and Marketing: Managing the Moments of Truth in Service Competition. Lexington Books, Lexington, MA (1990)
9. Gummesson, E.: Lip Service – A Neglected Area in Services Marketing. The Journal of Services Marketing, Summer 1987, 19–23 (1987)
10. Edvardsson, B., Gustafsson, A., Roos, I.: Service Portraits in Service Research: A Critical Review. International Journal of Service Industry Management 16(1), 107–121 (2005)
11. Grönroos, C.: Service logic revisited: who creates value? And who co-creates? European Business Review 20(4), 298–314 (2008)
12. Beretta, S.: Unleashing the integration potential of ERP systems: the role of process-based performance measurement systems. Business Process Management Journal 8(3), 254–277 (2002)
13. Nilsson, A.G.: Using Standard Application Packages in Organisations - Critical Success Factors. In: Nilsson, A.G., Pettersson, J.S. (eds.) On Methods for Systems Development in Professional Organisations, Studentlitteratur, Lund, pp. 208–230 (2001)
14. Davenport, T.H.: Putting the enterprise into the enterprise system. Harvard Business Review, 121–131 (July-August 1998)
15. Al-Mashari, M.: Enterprise Resource Planning Systems: A Research Agenda. Industrial Management and Data Systems 102(3), 165–170 (2002)
16. Sumner, M.: Enterprise Resource Planning. Prentice Hall, Upper Saddle River (2004)
17. Grabski, S., Leech, S.: Complementary controls and ERP implementation success. International Journal of Accounting Information Systems 8(1), 17–39 (2007)

18. Abels, S., Brehm, N., Hahn, A., Gomez, J.M.: Change management issues in Federated ERP systems: an approach for identifying requirements and possible solutions. International Journal of Information Systems and Change Management 1(3), 318–335 (2006)
19. Brehm, N., Marx Gómez, J.: Web Service-Based Specification and Implementation of Functional Components in Federated ERP-Systems. In: Abramowicz, W. (ed.) BIS 2007. LNCS, vol. 4439, pp. 133–146. Springer, Heidelberg (2007)
20. Osterwalder, A., Pigneur, Y., Tucci, C.: Clarifying Business Models: Origins, present and Future of the Concept. In: Communications of the Association for Information Science (CAIS), vol. 15, pp. 751–775 (2005)
21. Hedman, J., Kalling, T.: The business model concept: theoretical underpinnings and empirical illustrations. European Journal of Information Systems 12(1), 49–59 (2003)
22. Mahadevan, B.: Business models for internet-based e.commerce: an anatomy. California management review 42, 55–69 (2000)
23. Kaplan, R., Norton, D.: Strategy Maps: converting intangible assets into tangible outcomes. Harvard Business School Publishing, Boston(2004)
24. Porter, M.: Competitive advantage. Free Press, New York (1985)
25. Treacy, M., Wiersema, F.: The Discipline of Market Leaders. McGraw-Hill, New York (1995)
26. Hax, A., Wilde, D.: The Delta Project: Discovering New Sources of Profitability in a Networked Economy. Palgrave, New York (2001)
27. Lillis, A.M., Mundy, J.: Cross-sectional field studies in management accounting research—closing the gaps between surveys and case studies. Journal of Management Accounting Research 17, 119–141 (2005)
28. Eisenhardt, K.M.: Building theories from case study research. Academy of Management Review 14(4), 532–550 (1989)
29. Yin, R.: Case study research. Sage Publications, Beverly Hills (1984)
30. Hevner, A.R., March, S.T., Park, J., Ram, S.: Design science in information systems research. MIS Quarterly 28(1), 75–106 (2004)
31. European Commission: Commission Recommendation of concerning the definition of micro, small and medium-sized enterprises. Official Journal of the European Union, L 124, 36–41 (2003)

Event-Driven Business Intelligence Architecture for Real-Time Process Execution in Supply Chains

Markus Linden, Sebastian Neuhaus, Daniel Kilimann, Tanja Bley, and Peter Chamoni

University of Duisburg-Essen, Mercator School of Management
Department of Technology and Operations Management
Chair of Information Systems and Operations Research
Lotharstraße 63, 47057 Duisburg, Germany
Markus.Linden@uni-due.de,
Sebastian.Neuhaus@uni-due.de,
Daniel.Kilimann@uni-due.de,
Tanja.Bley@uni-due.de,
Peter.Chamoni@uni-due.de

Abstract. This paper gives an insight perspective for developing a business intelligence architecture to satisfy permanently growing controlling requirements in complex distribution networks. Supply Chain Management (SCM), as a part of management science concerning intelligent synchronization of supply and demand, is the basis for the development of flexible, proactive and adaptive real-time information systems, called Operational Business Intelligence (OpBI) systems, which offer a significant support for decision making on operational level. Application scenarios including concrete decision-problems are analyzed regarding system implementation and in consideration of supply chain performance. The conclusion reflects the development process in order to allow a foresight.

Keywords: Operational Business Intelligence, Supply Chain Management, Event-Driven Architecture, Radio Frequency Identification.

1 Introduction

Since the last decades the term *logistic efficiency* is a keyword in organizations aspiring cost-leadership. But in the sense of global and dynamic markets as well as a result of growing customer demands and shortened product life cycles, concentration on the efficiency perspective only has to be marked as inadequate. The constantly growing complexity asks for a trade off between the cost-leadership paradigm and required effectiveness. Claims for flexibility, reactivity and reliability encourage the change to process-oriented system thinking and flat organization hierarchies. As a result, not only companies but value networks compete against each other [4].

The main objective of this paper is to point out an intersectoral business intelligence architecture to satisfy permanently growing controlling requirements in complex distribution networks. Supply Chain Management (SCM), as a part of management

W. Abramowicz and R. Tolksdorf (Eds.): BIS 2010, LNBIP 47, pp. 280–290, 2010.

science concerning intelligent synchronization of supply and demand, is the basis of the development of flexible, proactive and adaptive real-time information systems called Operational Business Intelligence (OpBI) systems, which offer a significant support for decision making on operational level. Current processes are controlled on the basis of analytical information and strategic objectives either semi-or fully automated.

The conceptual design of the information system results from a functional perspective. In the following chapter the theoretical basis, concerning SCM in general and its related performance measures, will be exposed. After a theoretical foundation of the term OpBI, the system components are specified consecutively. The following explanations will be related to the entire architecture. Application scenarios including concrete decision-problems are analyzed regarding system implementation and in consideration of supply chain performance. Thus, the research contribution of this paper is a conceptual business intelligence architecture for process execution, which integrates different components identified in a literature review and satisfies the requirements of the SCM use case scenario.

2 Use Case for Supply Chain Logistics

At the beginning of the development process possible application scenarios within the multifunctional SCM paradigm have to be extracted. It should be a general intersectoral application scenario and should fit into general logistic trends. Subsequently, the classification criteria of the supply chain perspective, infrastructure as well as the structure of commodities and distribution strategies will be differentiated. Considering trends concerning vendor independent planning and control of distributive supply chain systems the focus has to be on the outbound logistic service provider's perspective, who takes over the distribution- and redistribution functions between manufacturers and retailers. The logistic service provider is a system server (Third Party Logistics, 3PL). This means that the service provider is responsible for outbound logistics' planning and control without retaining further subcontractors. From now on it is called a network integrator. Practical examples are provided by courier-, express- and package service providers, which have expanded in the past into the sector of industrial contract logistics and value added logistics.

Due to simplification only double-staged local or regional supply chains are considered, which means that three distributive network stages appear: manufacturer, network integrator and retailer [11]. The network integrator has to control the convergent transport flows originating from the manufacturers, as well as the divergent transport flows to the retailers. Therefore, the system is comparable to a hub-and-spoke network without direct transport. Stock levels are only taken into consideration by the network integrator and retailers depending on the structure of commodities and implicit distribution strategies. Concerning capital expenditure the network integrator possesses resources concerning vehicle fleet, storage equipment and information technology. Because the following architecture focuses on a neutral network integrator it allows a comprehensive integration of different structures of commodities and distribution strategies. From a strategic perspective efficiency is achieved by means of forecasting and optimal lot sizing. Moreover, reactivity and flexibility are provided within make-to-order (m-t-o) paradigms.

Subsequently, with regard to the derived objectives of the OpBI system the focus is put on the control processes of the network integrator. A distribution center has to consider internal procurement processes and supply processes as well as retour processes within make-to-order and make-to-stock (m-t-s) paradigms. Stock keeping, as being a characteristic function, is taken into consideration within procurement processes referring to the reference processes of the Supply Chain Operation Reference Model (SCOR). Intra- and inter-organizational planning processes, which may determine order policies between network actors temporally, will only be considered as a framework of operational control processes. This means that results from tactical demand and inventory planning only serve as restrictions, thresholds or control variables of the operational information system.

3 Operational Business Intelligence

The explanation below provides a theoretical classification of the OpBI approach. Concerning enhancements of classical Business Intelligence (BI) approaches precise system requirements can be derived. Referring to the consensus parts of former definitions, OpBI can be summarized as an approach for fast, flexible and adaptive process control and decision support on the basis of analytical BI methods [5,15]. Therefore, OpBI follows recent trends in operational and organizational structures of companies. In doing so, decision making is simplified or automated at the operational level addressing a broad range of users. OpBI is directly connected to many existing approaches. Regarding operational process control it can be linked to Business Activity Monitoring (BAM) as well as Business Performance Management (BPM), which can be seen as requirements in order to monitor and to control processes continuously. Supply Chain Event Management (SCEM) is an approach to integrate planning and executive operations by identification of events causing disturbance [1,11]. In this context, OpBI can be seen as a technical enabler or implementation of a proactive real-time BPM- or SCEM-Paradigm [7].

Recommendations of integrated operational and analytical functions, which have been published, use concepts like real-time data warehousing [2] or active data warehousing [10,13]. Both approaches focus on a reduced decision-action time in order to enhance the decision's business value. Latencies cover a period between event appearance and reaction. This contains data latency, analytical latency and decision latency [10]. While real-time data warehousing concepts try to improve analytical systems' actuality by accelerating information system's loading time, the active data warehousing concepts focus on an improvement of the ability to give feedback to actions directly. This implies closed loop data processing between operational and analytical systems.

Moreover, OpBI can be seen as a concept that combines important topics covered by the mentioned approaches. This means Operational BI implicates process transparency, synchronization of strategic and operational control quantities, shortening of latency time as well as real-time data processing and not least the feedback of operational systems and decision makers. OpBI denotes an explicit change of traditional BI located at tactical level. Within this focus, at least daily data uploads from operational to analytical systems took place [8]. As a result decision making support or process control could only occur reactively on the basis of analytical aggregated information.

To achieve a proactive connection between analytical methods and operational process control regarding predestinated aims, OpBI has to close the time lags between event identification and reaction. Moreover, OpBI has to bridge the information gap between operational, tactical and strategic level. In the following these challenges, which determine the structure and effectiveness of an OpBI system, are described. Performance in the context of logistics is difficult to grasp as a theoretical construct including its cause-and-effect connections. As a result, objectives on the strategic, tactical and operational levels diverge in practice. Control approaches, which allow a holistic view of business environments, e.g. Balanced Scorecards, are only sufficient for a performance definition [14]. A proactive, semi- or fully automated process control needs predefined logical causalities concerning performance attributes and performance indicators, in order to control real-time events and problems precisely. Therefore, decision artifacts at the lowest level of granularity are focused in contrast to classical BI. OpBI has to guarantee a continuous congruency regarding physical decision artifacts and virtual process information.

A coupling of analytical and operational real-time systems implicates a bridging of existing time gaps related to latency [12]. Concerning existing decentralized operational system environments, especially in the context of SCM, the biggest challenge for an OpBI system is to minimize the time lag. The classical approach to update data daily only allows ex-post analysis. While operational dashboards and composite applications already constitute first steps concerning real-time decision support, analytical event-controlled platforms are regarded as promising proactive control instruments.

4 Concept of Operational Business Intelligence for Increasing Supply Chain Performance

The synchronization of operational and strategic control quantities within a performance measurement system represents a specific perspective for the implementation of an OpBI system regarding SCM. From a network integrator's perspective standardization of performance measurement has to be preferred, because it can be adopted beyond business boundaries. The SCOR model being a normative control model offers a complete transparency of value adding processes and a standardized framework for the definition of causalities concerning strategic objectives. In doing so, performance indicators from operational systems as well as from applications regarding event registration will be extracted, transformed and enhanced. Afterwards they will be loaded into a data mart consisting of the SCOR performance indicators on the basis of the core data warehouse.

4.1 Operational Business Intelligence Architecture for Supply Chain Management

The subsystems of an OpBI architecture will be combined with the classical BI architecture. Thereby, connections and interdependencies of subsystems are described using a five layer architecture, consisting of the following layers data sources, data acquisition, data storage, data provision and data analysis, as well as data presentation. The data source layer offers event-based data of control processes from operational transaction systems, e.g. directly from the central application regarding Electronic Product

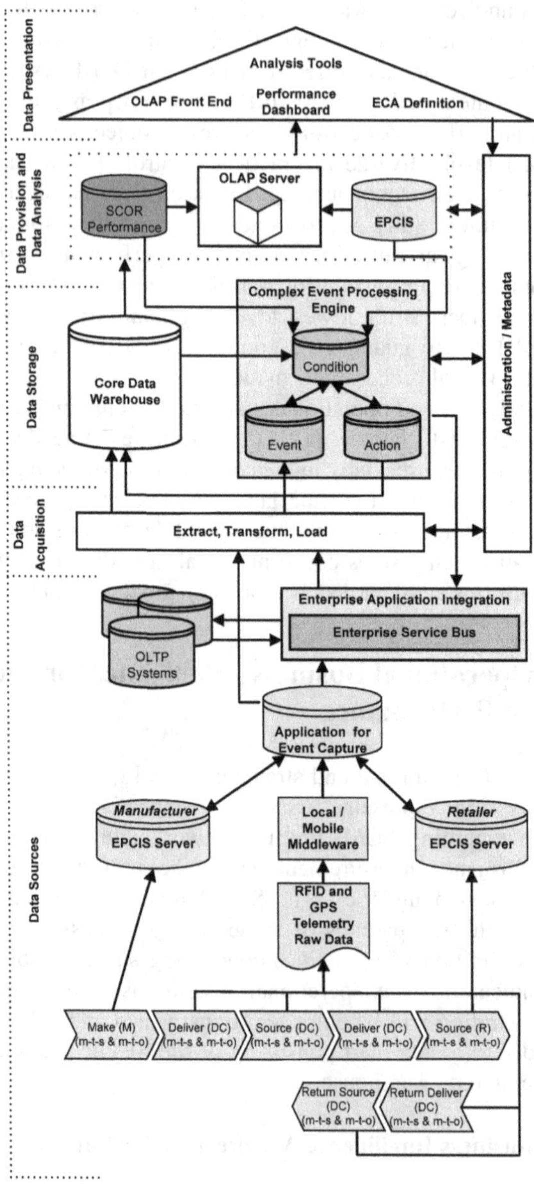

Fig. 1. Operational BI Architecture for Supply Chain Management

Code Information Services (EPCIS) event survey and query. The central EPCIS application filters and aggregates data incoming from internal Radio Frequency Identification (RFID) systems as well as from external EPCIS applications and is part of the preprocessing. Conditioned Electronic Product Code (EPC) event objects are transferred to On-Line Transaction Processing (OLTP) systems via Enterprise Application Integration (EAI) platforms. An EAI platform orchestrates incoming basic events by means of an Enterprise Service Bus (ESB). Moreover, it can ensure a high performance data integration from different operational applications.

Extract, Transform, Load (ETL) tools process data directly into the analytical data level. Predefined EPCIS event objects represent time-critical data of operational processes, which will be extracted and loaded continuously. On the one hand the data storage layer contains the Event, Condition, Action (ECA) component, which activates certain actions regarding incoming events dependent on conditions. On the other hand it contains the Core Data Warehouse, which stores subject-oriented, integrated data. Rule-based follow-up actions can be e.g. feedback to operational systems via ESB (closed-loop).

The data provision and data analysis layer sustains data from EPCIS and SCOR data marts, which are relevant for OpBI decisions. Via the On-Line Analytical Processing (OLAP) server data is transformed into problem specific OLAP cubes in order to query performance indicators and EPCIS histories.

The presentation layer provides an analysis and reporting system regarding all management levels by means of a web-based portal. Tactical and strategic management still have access to relevant data marts interactively. Other users, mainly on the operational management level, can use an early warning system via performance dashboards and can access administrative ECA configurations.

4.2 Event-Driven Process Components

The following scenarios refer to reference networks concerning a network integrator inside a multilateral product system. There will be no specific SCM planning concepts modeled, but transparency of outbound stocks inside the network integrator's responsibility is assumed.

The following explanations do not consider potentials regarding operational process optimization (e.g. use of mass data extraction, automated inventory, inventory management options, etc.) and they do not consider potentials concerning the deployment of planning algorithms (e.g. use of adaptive, dynamic real-time algorithms). Further explanations focus on an evaluation of operational real-time events regarding analytical aggregated data warehouse data within OLAP queries. The real-time events will be restricted to EPCIS events, which have been generated by an information system. Events from other operational transaction systems are not considered. Analytical data warehouse systems contain SCOR ratios and EPCIS histories in a data mart, as well as control parameters of tactical planning algorithms (e.g. thresholds from the Core Data Warehouse). Every control process which is in responsibility of the network integrator is considered:

S1:	Source m-t-s-products
S2:	Source m-t-o-products
D1:	Deliver m-t-s-products
D2:	Deliver m-t-o-products
SR1:	Source Return defective products
DR1:	Deliver Return defective products

Decisions based on plan variance (remarkable events) demonstrate a concrete application scenario within a control process. Decision making based on plan variance pursues an increase or a preservation of performance. The assurance of or increase in performance can be regarded as an instrument to ensure quality and can be viewed as an adaptive control instrument within OpBI. In this case, it is important to identify unanticipated events at an early stage. This means, perception latency has to be reduced, so that the manufacturer can already anticipate that his products might arrive at a later point in time. As a result a compensative action can be determined.

Such unexpected events within a reference network may occur during the whole process. This can happen at the manufacturer or at the retailer. Time critical processes proceed in m-t-o scenarios, but also in the distribution of m-t-s products at the network integrator or in out of stock situations. In this scenario every local middleware, which can measure process status and forwards it to the operational EPCIS application, can be an event producer. At this point, preprocessing is already done by relating generated EPCIS object events to business logic. Therefore, events going into the analytical level can be limited to time critical processes. At the analytical level the process status is compared with a target performance value. As a prerequisite the strength of the relations between all relevant information points at the physical process level have to be quantified in a matrix. Those evaluations can be queried as a general pass-through time stored in the SCOR performance database. Therefore, a time critical process object event can be connected to a specific planning milestone. This aggregated view on different time critical EPCIS object events can be used to put focus on delayed processes. Such an event serves as the basis for an application referring to OpBI, because at that time the person in charge has to make a decision in order to avoid errors regarding order execution and performance loss.

Possible results:

- Event A: Delay product exit process of manufacturer XY attached.
- Event B: Delay transportation process from manufacturer XY to DC aggregation number 02 attached.
- Event C: Delay transportation process from DC to retailer ZY aggregation number 02 attached.

An event processing engine could provide a specific rule configuration for every potential relation in case of an occurring delay. This happens via EPCIS histories and SCOR performance at the level of aggregation numbers. A delay could be judged by the relevance of the receiver. If aggregated historic values regarding reliability, reactivity and flexibility fall below the defined planning values including tolerance limits, an adequate action has to be triggered, e.g. the information is send to the responsible manager immediately. Against this background the semi-automatic way of feedback in terms of an open loop to the manager should be preferred [3].

An event-based automation provides a decline of perception latency as well as analysis latency. Lower perception latency can be achieved by automatic identification of process delays. Lower analysis latency may be achieved via automated integration of receiver- and product-context information.

The reaction to plan variations at an early stage can help to achieve scheduled order deliveries, stock deliveries and impeccable orders. Delivery time can be improved by means of aggregated order lead time and further actions. The increase of the performance attributes reliability and reactivity will cause an increase in total costs.

On the basis of potential influences from OpBI supported process control, performance attributes can be controlled referring to cause and effect relations in order to provide a meta-regulation. Expected results have to be checked within defined time intervals using a target/performance comparison according to planned service standards and actual evolution. In case of negative plan variances or high costs, the decision maker is able to check or change analysis rules.

5 Appraisal of the Approach

This concept of a system architecture concerning OpBI in the context of distribution networks uses RFID and Event-Driven Architecture (EDA) as core technologies, whereas EPCIS events serve as a basis for process monitoring and SCOR performance indicators may function as rule based control parameters. The system architecture has been described considering the perspective of EDA. Under the terms of Service-oriented Architecture (SOA) as being a loosely coupled architecture all services of OLTP systems, collaborative services (EPCIS queries) as well as analytical services (OLAP queries) can be integrated within overall decision making services. The *high End* of a SOA could be an entire operational decision making service. A synchronic communication of all system components has to be required to achieve this vision [9].

The SCOR concept as a control instrument has been chosen because of its standardized requirements. But it has to be noted that SCOR performance indicators show defects. That means, the value-based shareholder perspective, the social employee perspective, as well as production and marketing point of views are not taken into consideration. Regarding a network integrator long-term competitiveness is important. Referring to this, value-based models already exist, but have not been combined with the SCOR standard [6]. Another objective of SCOR is the integrative evaluation of the entire supply chain. That means, if performance evaluation cross company's limits, the willingness to participate in information sharing has to be questioned. Concerning the application scenarios, the range of integration has been limited to outbound logistics. Within these scenarios, the network integrator is able to use generated performance data as a control and marketing instrument in order to control performance within the competition of networks and to use performance attributes as a benchmarking instrument of logistic services.

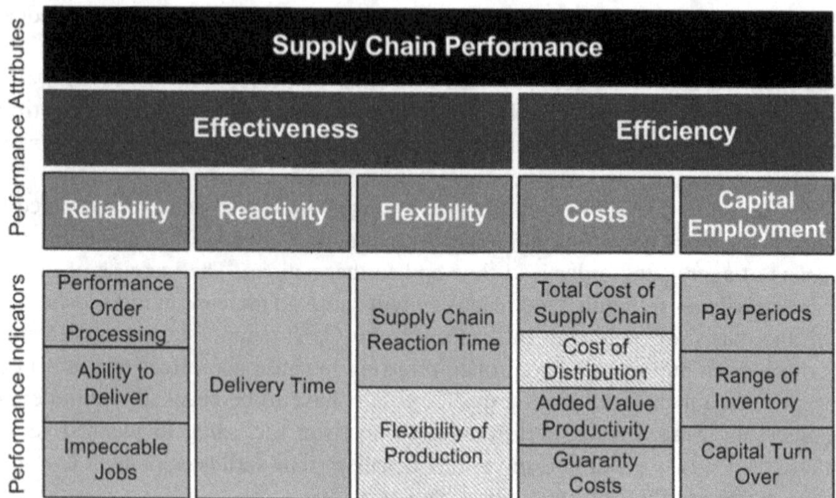

Fig. 2. Performance Attributes and Performance Indicators

The paper describes an intersectoral, fast, flexible and adaptive decision support system, which provides the ability of appropriate automated real-time decision making, in order to release the operational management. In doing so, transactional systems have to be enhanced with analytical BI functionalities. Therefore, the basic assumptions and decisions concerning the development of this system are discussed critically.

Integration of EAI and ETL regarding real-time requirements
An integration of EAI and ETL promises a technical and functional concentration on minimal real-time information within data and function integration. The data volume that has to be transferred is a determined success factor concerning potential performance restrictions. Looking into the future, further implementations regarding real-time data warehouse research are necessary, in order to generate references to technical system applications depending on real-time data.

RFID as an auto identification system based on article level and sensor functionality at charging level
RFID is a requirement for continuous congruency of physical material movement and virtual status information. As basic technology, it determines the potential efficiency of OpBI systems. The system technologies' market penetration is the prerequisite for the usage of OpBI systems, especially regarding article specific labeling.

EPCglobal as interorganizational communication network
The integration of the EPCglobal network promises the biggest standardization of RFID-based communication and is the most future orientated communication network regarding a multilateral network integrator. In order to implement more mature applications, further standardization concerning global services and interface definitions is required.

EDA, ECA mechanisms and optional service orchestration
Event-Driven Architectures support the flexibility, sensitivity and vitality of systems within an OpBI architecture. Platform independent integration and configuration tools are supposed to be important factors of success regarding future applications. These tools support a simple implementation and prepare an increase in the ability to integrate common OLTP solutions.

SCOR ratio system as controlling model
SCOR performance ratios and indicators within a standardized, functional and overall cause and effect model in the supply chain context serve as an implementation of an integrated execution and controlling framework. Looking at the future, adding new perspectives to the model could be an eligible improvement. Through the integration of value-based perspectives, decision problems could not only be evaluated by means of service levels or costs, but also by means of cost-/benefit analysis of decision making artifacts.

6 Conclusion

It can be stated, that an OpBI system can offer an effective instrument to support the operational management in a supply chain regarding requirements caused by the increasing complexity in value networks. The scenarios clarified application's flexibility, referring to multidimensional analytical execution and controlling parameters. The causal effects of control potentials have also been shown. Especially independent logistic service providers will use such a control model not only in order to optimize processes but also as a representative benchmarking and marketing instrument in consequence of standardized and transparent performance measurements. Looking at actual technological standardization and market penetration of the required basic technologies, especially RFID, an ad hoc realization of such a concept is not realistic. In fact, this approach reflects a long-term effort in order to optimize processes concerning RFID penetration.

References

1. Alvarenga, C.: A New Take on Supply Chain Event Management. Supply Chain Management Review 7(2), 28–35 (2003)
2. Azvine, B., Cui, Z., Nauck, D.: Towards Real-Time Business Intelligence. BT Technology Journal 23(3), 214–225 (2005)
3. Baars, H., Kemper, H., Siegel, M.: Combining RFID Technology and Business Intelligence for Supply Chain Optimization - Scenarios for Retail Logistics. In: Proceedings of the 41st Hawaii International Conference on System Science, pp. 1–10. IEEE Computer Society Press, Los Alamitos
4. Baumgarten, H.: Trends in der Logistik. In: Baumgarten, H., Darkow, I., Zadek, H. (eds.) Supply Chain Steuerung und Services, pp. 1–12. Springer, Heidelberg (2004)
5. Blasum, R.: Operational BI (2006), http://www.business-code.de/cms/uploads/media/BCD_Operational_BI_01.pdf (2010-02-07)

6. Bolstorff, P., Rosenbaum, R.: Supply Chain Excellence: A Handbook for Dramatic Improvement using the SCOR model. AMACOM, New York (2007)
7. Bucher, T., Dinter, B.: Business Performance Management. In: Chamoni, P., Gluchowski, P. (eds.) Analytische Informationssysteme: Business Intelligence-Technologien und -Anwendungen, pp. 23–50. Springer, Heidelberg (2006)
8. Eckerson, W.: Best Practices in Operational BI: Converging Analytical and Operational Processes (2007), http://www.tdwi.org (2010-02-07)
9. Gluchowski, P., Gabriel, R., Dittmar, C.: Management Support Systeme und Business Intelligence: Computergestützte Informationssysteme für Fach- und Führungskräfte. Springer, Heidelberg (2008)
10. Hackathorn, R.: Current Practices in Active Data Warehousing. Bolder Technology Inc. (2002), http://www.bolder.com/pubs/NCR200211-ADW.pdf (2010-02-07)
11. Jonsson, P.: Logistics and Supply Chain Management. McGraw-Hill, London (2008)
12. Schelp, J.: "Real"-Time Warehousing und EAI. In: Chamoni, P., Gluchowski, P. (eds.) Analytische Informationssysteme: Business Intelligence-Technologien und -Anwendungen, pp. 425–438. Springer, Heidelberg (2006)
13. Thalhammer, T., Schrefl, M., Mohania, M.: Active Data Warehouses: Complementing OLAP with Analysis Rules. Data & Knowledge Engineering 39(3), 241–269 (2001)
14. Weber, J.: Logistik und Supply Chain Controlling, Schäffer-Poeschel, Stuttgart (2002)
15. White, C.: The next Generation of Business Intelligence: Operational BI (2005), http://www.dmreview.com/issues/20050501/1026064-1.html (2010-02-07)

Production Inventory and Enterprise System Implementation: An Ex-ante No-Cost Based Evaluation

Salvatore Cannella[1], Elena Ciancimino[1], José David Canca Ortiz[2], and Rossitza Setchi[3]

[1] Faculty of Engineering, University of Palermo
viale delle Scienze, Parco d'Orleans,
90128 Palermo, Italy
{cannella,eciancimino}@unipa.it
[2] School of Engineering, University of Seville
Camino de los Descubrimientos s/n.
41092 Seville, Spain
dco@us.es
[3] Cardiff School of Engineering, Cardiff University
The Parade, Roath, Cardiff, South Glamorgan,
CF24, Cardiff, Wales, United Kingdom
setchi@cardiff.ac.uk

Abstract. The objective of this paper is to present an Enterprise System (ES) ex-ante no-cost based three step evaluation technique, which enables a pre-emptive analysis of the effects of an ES implementation using a system of referenced non financial performance metrics. The innovativeness is in the use of a simulation model fully integrated with the evaluation procedure. Researchers can extend the presented technique to further modelling approaches and test it on different market sectors. The analysis provides practitioners with a measurement system that enables an analysis of the effects of a given ES implementation and can be further employed in financial evaluations.

Keywords: IT investment; non financial measurement; supply chain; bullwhip; inventory management; continuous time differential equation model.

1 Context and Problem Statement

"If you're not careful, the dream of information integration can turn into a nightmare"[1]. With this cautionary statement, in 1998 Thomas H. Davenport commences the highly-cited paper "Putting the Enterprise into the Enterprise System (ES)". In his editorial, the world-famous business and technology analyst annotates exemplary "horror stories" about failed or out-of-control projects of implementation of ES, and advocates for managerial reflection: a speedy adoption of an ES may be a wise business move, but a rash implementation is not. The unsuccessful ES stories reported are mainly concerned with the enthusiasm of the company for adopting an attractive IT solution not accompanied by structured and careful estimation of hazards and

W. Abramowicz and R. Tolksdorf (Eds.): BIS 2010, LNBIP 47, pp. 291–303, 2010.

benefits. Davenport does not stigmatise ES adoption; on the contrary, he confirms the potential business gain, provided proper implementation.

In the last decade, several frameworks have been developed to support the management decision making on ES adoption and to identify key issues involved in its implementation [2]-[8]. One of the most referenced studies in this field is Markus and Tanis' research on ES life-cycle [9]. The authors state the key problem about ES from the perspective of an adopting organisation's executive leadership: will investment pay off? On the basis of this research question, Shang and Seddon [4] focus on the organisation gains resulting from the implementation of an ES and propose a benefit appraisal framework. They identify "five dimensions" of effectiveness measurement to evaluate the pay-off of an IT investment through the quantification of the enterprise systems benefits: (a) operational, (b) managerial, (c) strategic, (d) IT infrastructure, and (e) organisational. The measures employed in each of these dimensions are:

a) cost reduction, cycle time reduction, productivity improvement, quality improvement, and customer service improvement;
b) better resource management, improved decision making and planning, and performance improvement;
c) supporting business growth, supporting business alliance, building business innovation, building cost leadership, generating product differentiation, enabling worldwide expansion, providing benefits in B2B and B2C, generating and sustaining competitiveness;
d) building business flexibility, reducing IT costs, and increasing IT infrastructure capability;
e) supporting organisational change and coordination, facilitating business learning, empowering, building common visions and concentrating on core business.

In order to assess the described dimensions, financial and non-financial criteria as well as qualitative and quantitative metrics are needed. Traditionally, the evaluation of ES investments was mainly based on financial measures including Net Present Value, Internal Rate of Return, Return on Investment, and payback in time [7]. Nevertheless, there is a high percentage of Shang and Seddon's dimensions that are difficult to estimate with financial metrics, e.g. customer service improvement, better resource management, strategic decisions for market responsiveness [10].

Simulation based analysis is a suitable technique in support of the ex ante assessment of the ES implementation process [7].The virtual environment can enable inference on a subset of Shang and Seddon's dimensions that cannot be easily estimated through a cost-based evaluation.

In this paper we present a three step technique aimed at quantifying the benefit of adopting an ES according to Shang and Seddon's framework. To illustrate the three-step evaluation procedure, the technique is exemplified in a production/distribution network model.

This paper is organised as follows. Section 2 presents the production/distribution network model. In Section 3 the first step of the presented technique is described: the selection of expected benefits from Shang and Seddon's framework and their alignment to a set of non-cost based metrics are performed. In Section 4 the model is generated (second step). In Section 5 the output analysis and evaluation of ES investment are performed in step three. Section 6 provides conclusions and limitations of the study.

2 ES Three-Step Ex-ante Evaluation Procedure: Application to a Production Inventory Context

The ES three-step ex ante evaluation procedure is applied to a multi-tier production/distribution network. The choice of this particular business area is not accidental: the strategic, tactical and operational logistic coordination is an essential business process [11]. Enterprise Resource Planning effectiveness is affected by the distortion of information flows between trading partners: the *conditio sine qua non* for the single firm performance is the management and control of the network's information asynchronies [12]. Supply Chain Management systems provide functional cooperation as well as extended enterprise integration: the 21st century global operations strategy for achieving organisational competitiveness [13], [14].

A production/inventory control system transforms incomplete information about the market into coordinated plans for production and replenishment of raw materials [15]. An ES enables data sharing between trading partners and coordination of the network decision policies.

The example presented in this work is a make-to-stock four-tier serially-linked supply chain. In a generic traditional supply chain configuration, each firm receives only information on local stock, local work in progress levels, and local sales. The retailer forecasts customer demand on the basis of market time series and the remaining echelons take into account for their replenishment only downstream incoming orders. This decentralised supply chain configuration is extremely prone to the deleterious effect of network's information asynchronies and data distortion [16]. The most evident and costly consequence is a sudden and sharp increase in the variability of order sizes. This phenomenon is also known as false demand [17], demand amplification [18] or bullwhip effect [19]. The problem is well known in the real business world and its financial and economic consequences affect many global companies [19], [20], [21].

The ES adoption for the production/distribution systems provides a solution to information distortion: centralised operational data management allows each firm to implement order rules and inventory policies based on real-time network optimisation. In an ES Integrated logistic network, decision making is based on a real time database that integrates information on item position and sales data. Each echelon bases its replenishment on local information (local stock and work in progress level, local sales) and on network information (downstream incoming orders, actual market demand, inventory information and work in progress data incoming from downstream nodes).

The following three sections present the ES three-step ex-ante evaluation procedure for an ES Integrated logistic network application in a four-tier serially-linked supply chain.

3 Metrics and Benefits: The Selection and Alignment Process

The aim of this phase is to select a set of metrics that can provide a multi-faceted analysis of the effect of a given ES implementation. We quantify the benefit of adopting an ES according to Shang and Seddon's framework. As reported by the two researchers, the framework was created on the basis of an analysis of the features of enterprise systems, on the literature on information technology (IT) value, on data from 233 enterprise systems vendor-reported stories published on the Web and on interviews with managers of 34 organizations using ES. Their framework provides a detailed list of benefits that have reportedly been acquired through ES implementation. This list of benefits is consolidated into five benefits dimensions: operational, managerial, strategic, IT infrastructure and organizational.

In this phase, the Shang and Seddon's benefit framework is explored and a list of likely benefits is selected in relation to the ES expected performance. According to Shang and Seddon, the most appropriate management level for the evaluation of the ES is the middle level of Anthony's planning and control system pyramid [22]. Business managers have a comprehensive understanding of both the capabilities of ES and the business plans for system use.

Once a suitable subset of benefits is identified, corresponding quantitative metrics are selected. The selection activity is a critical point of the technique. As previously stated, a high percentage of Shang and Seddon's dimensions is difficult to estimate with traditional financial metrics. The research of proper measures is fundamental for the correct application of any evaluation procedure. The output of this phase is the "Alignment Table": the selected metric system is associated to the previously identified subset of Shang and Seddon's benefit dimensions.

One of the aims of ES Integrated logistic network is to avoid the effect of information distortion and provide coordination planning for supply chain stability. A cost function would not provide complete information on the effect of the ES implementation. Recently, the Operation Management community presented several no-cost based metrics suitable for the inference on a set of Shang and Seddon's dimensions concerning data coordination and stability in the network. One of the most important features of a performance measurement system for an Integrated logistic network is the ability to trace the links between the different performance measurement elements across the company [23].

The non-financial metrics chosen are the Order Rate Variance Ratio [24], the Inventory Variance Ratio [25], the Bullwhip Slope [26], the Inventory Instability Slope [27] and the Average Fill Rate. More specifically, the metrics assess three Shang and Seddon's dimensions, which coincide with the three decision levels of Anthony's Framework [22]: Operational, Managerial and Strategic.

$$ORVrR = \sigma_O^2 / \sigma_d^2 . \quad (1)$$

The Order Rate Variance Ratio (ORVrR) metric (1) is a quantification of the instability of orders in the network. The theoretical value of (1) is equal to 1 in case of absolute absence of demand amplification. σ_O^2 and σ_d^2 are the variance of the order quantity and the variance of the market demand, respectively. The higher the value of ORVrR, the greater the magnitude of demand amplification phenomenon along the production/distribution network is. In particular, a geometric or exponential increase of ORVrR in upstream direction is representative of the transmission of bullwhip effect [28].

$$IVrR = \sigma_I^2 / \sigma_d^2 . \tag{2}$$

The Inventory Variance Ratio (IVrR) metric (2) is a measure of warehouse instability [25], obtained by comparing the inventory variance magnitude σ_I^2 to the variance of the market demand. IVrR quantifies the fluctuations in actual inventory and permits investigating the benefit of centralised operational data management. The higher the value of Inventory Variance Ratio, the greater the inventory instability is. A geometric or exponential increase indicates a diffusion of buffer instability along the chain. In general inventory metrics are used in production/distribution system analysis in order to provide concise information on inventory investment. See for example, holding cost modelled as dependant from stock levels in [29]-[34].

One value of Order Rate Variance Ratio and Inventory Variance Ratio is computed for each echelon in the network. In order to quantify with a single value and compare alternative configurations, the Bullwhip Slope (ORVrR Slope) and the Inventory Instability Slope (IVrR Slope) are adopted. Slopes are calculated as the linear regression of the interpolated curves of ORVrR and IVrR measured over the echelons [27]. The slopes are indicative of the extent of inventory and order rates instability propagation [12]. A high positive value corresponds to a broad propagation of information distortion.

$$AverageFillRate = \frac{1}{T}\sum_{t=o}^{T} S_{\kappa}(t) / d(t) . \tag{3}$$

The Average fill rate is defined as the mean value in T, the observation time span, of the percentage of orders delivered ‘on time’, that is, no later than the delivery day requested by the customer [35]. The Average fill rate is a measure of customer service level history.

Furthermore, the presence of local stock and work in progress level, local sales, downstream incoming orders, actual market demand, inventory information and work in progress data sharing is evaluated with the Boolean variable Data Availability (DA).

The output of Step I of the ex ante evaluation of ES Integrated logistic network is the “Alignment Table”, in which the described metric set is associated to a subset of Operational, Managerial and Strategic benefit dimensions concerning data coordination and stability in the network. The subset is from Shang and Seddon’s framework (2002). The Alignment Table (table 1) is generated by the association of qualitative benefit and quantitative performance measures. The quantitative performance measures for the production-distribution networks above described are associated to the qualitative benefits derived from Shang and Seddon's dimension. According to their theory [4], the table is generated according to the industrial experience of the "middle manager". He can adopt different decision support systems to create the Alignment Table, such as multi-criterion techniques.

Table 1. Alignment Table

	ORVrR	*ORVrR Slope*	*IVrR*	*IVrR Slope*	*Averag Fill rate*	*DA*
OPERATIONAL						
▪ Supplier support activities in order processing, information exchanging and payment.	√	√		√		√
▪ Customer service					√	
▪ Data access and inquiries						√
MANAGERIAL						
▪ Asset management for physical inventory			√	√		
▪ Inventory management in shifting products where they were needed and responding quickly to surges or dips in demand.			√			√
▪ Managers able see the inventory of all locations in their region or across boundaries, making possible a leaner inventory				√		
▪ Production management for co-ordinating supply and demand and meeting production schedules at the lowest cost.	√	√				√
▪ Decision making and planning	√	√	√	√		
▪ Strategic decisions for market responsiveness		√		√	√	
▪ Management decisions for flexible resource management, efficient processes and quick response to operation changes.		√		√		
▪ Customer decisions with rapid response to customer demands and prompt service adjustments					√	
▪ Manufacturing performance monitoring, prediction and quick adjustments.	√		√			
▪ Overall operational efficiency and effectiveness management	√	√	√	√		
STRATEGIC						
▪ Building virtual corporations with virtual supply and demand consortia.		√		√		√
▪ Providing real-time and reliable data enquiries.						√

4 Methodology Selection and Business Modelling

The aim of this phase is to generate a business system model. Different methods are suited to different problems: no single technique is likely to prove a panacea [36] and the modelling approach is driven by the nature of the inputs and the objective of the study [37]. Gunasekaran and Kobu [13] highlight that the criteria to select a business system modelling methodology depend upon the nature of the decision areas and the data to be analysed. This phase consists of generating the model with an appropriate methodology, setting the operational parameters, running the model, and collecting data.

Several frameworks and guidelines exist in the literature for selecting a suitable modelling methodology [13], [36]-[39]. In the field of supply chain modelling and analysis, Riddalls et al. [36] identify four main categories of methodologies, namely: continuous time differential equation models, discrete time difference equation models, discrete event simulation systems and classical operational research (OR) methods. They state that OR techniques have their place at a local tactical level in the design of supply chains, while the implication of strategic design on supply chain performance is analysed by using the first three methodologies.

To assess the set of Shang and Seddon's dimensions concerning data coordination and stability in the network, methods based on the dynamics of the system fit well the aim of the analysis. Continuous time differential equation modelling is herein adopted to perform the ex ante evaluation of ES Integrated logistic network. In Operational Management this method is widely used to draw inferences on information distortion and efficacy of the solution techniques [18], [40]-[47].

Once the modelling methodological approach is identified, the second phase of this step is the generation of the models. A system of nonlinear repeated coupling of first-order differential equation represents herein the material and information flow of the production/distribution network under the ES implementation.

The mathematical formalism of the model is reported in the following. The generic echelon's position is represented by index i. Echelon i=1 stands for the manufacturer and i=K+1 for the final customer.

The system is modelled under the following assumptions:

a) K-stage production-distribution serial system. Each echelon in the system has a single successor and a single predecessor.
b) Unconstrained production-distribution capacity. No quantity limitations in production, buffering and transport are considered.
c) Single product. Aggregate production plans are assumed.
d) Non negative condition of order quantity. Products delivered can not be returned to the supplier.
e) Backlog allowed. Orders not fulfilled in time are backlogged so that inventory remains a positive or null value.
f) Uncapacitated raw material supply condition. Orders from echelon i=1 (producer) are always entirely fulfilled in time.
g) Market demand is visible to all echelons. All echelons adopt the exponential smoothing rule to forecast demand.
h) A generic echelon i receives information about order quantity from the downstream adjacent echelon i+1, on the up-to-date market demand d and on safety stock factors ε_j, lead times λ_j, inventory levels I_j, and work in progress levels W_j from all downstream echelons j=i+1…K..
i) Lead times and safety stock factors are equal for all echelons: h_j=h; c_j =c $\forall i$.

The mathematical formalism of the business network is as follows.

Work in progress	$W_i(t) = W_i(t-1) + S_{i-1}(t) - S_{i-1}(t-h)$.	(5)
Inventory	$I_i(t) = I_i(t-1) + S_{i-1}(t-h) - S_i(t)$.	(6)
Backlog	$B_i(t) = B_i(t-1) + O_{i+1}(t) - S_i(t)$.	(7)
Orders finally delivered	$S_i(t) = \min\{O_{i+1}(t) + B_{i+1}(t-1); I_{i+1}(t-1)S_{i-1}(t-h)\}$.	(8)
Demand forecast	$\hat{d}_i(t) = \alpha O_{i+1}(t-1) + (1-\alpha)\hat{d}_i(t-1)$.	(9)
	$O_{K+1}(t) = d_{market}(t)$.	(10)
Order quantity	$O_i(t) = \max\{\hat{d}(t) + \varphi(\hat{d}_K(t)\sum_{j=i}^{K} h_j - \sum_{j=i}^{K} W_j(t)) + \varphi(\hat{d}(t)\sum_{j=i}^{K} c_j - \sum_{j=i}^{K} I_j(t)); 0\}$.	(11)

The model nomenclature is shown in table 2.

Table 2. Nomenclature

W_i	*work in progress*	d	*customer demand*
I_i	*inventory of finished materials*	α	*forecast smoothing factor*
S_i	*delivered item*	h	*physical production/distribution lead time*
$\hat{d}$	*customer demand forecast*	c	*cover time for the inventory control*
O_i	*order quantity*	φ	*order rule proportional controller*
B_i	*backlog of orders*	K	*total number of echelons*
i	*echelon's position*		

The parameter setting concludes Step II of the ex-ante evaluation of an ES Integrated logistic network. Nine experiments are performed. Three values for each of the parameters α, h and φ are set. The parameter levels and state variable initial values are shown in table 3.

Table 3. Order Rate Variance Ratio and Inventory Variance Ratio

Set	α	h	c	φ	$W_i(0)$	$I_i(0)$	$B_i(0)$
1	1/6	1	3	2^{-1}	100	300	0
2	1/3	1	3	3^{-1}	100	300	0
3	2/3	1	3	4^{-1}	100	300	0
4	1/6	2	3	3^{-1}	200	300	0
5	1/3	2	3	4^{-1}	200	300	0
6	2/3	2	3	2^{-1}	200	300	0
7	1/6	3	3	4^{-1}	300	300	0
8	1/3	3	3	2^{-1}	300	300	0
G9	2/3	3	3	3^{-1}	300	300	0

The market demand is initialised at 100 units per time unit, until there is a pulse at t=10, increasing the demand value up to δ =200 units per time unit. The Euler-Cauchy method with order of accuracy Δt = 0.25 is adopted to approximate the solution for the initial-value problem. The serial system is composed by K=4 echelons. The simulation time is equal to 100 time units, with order of accuracy equal to Δt=0.25. Several mathematical toolboxes designed to solve a broad range of problems or ad-hoc applications, such as Vensim, Ithink, DYNAMO and Powersim [40-44], [46], [48], [49] exist to approximate the solution of the differential equations system. The simulation output is then collected to shift to the final phase of the evaluation procedure.

5 Performance Metric Analysis and Evaluation of ES Investment

This phase is devoted to the analysis of simulation output against the metrics identified in Step I and the estimation of the associated subset of Shang and Seddon's benefit dimensions. The output of Step III is one of the decision support systems for the ES investment evaluation.

Simulation output are collected and recorded in table 4 and table 5.

Table 4. Order Rate Variance Ratio and Inventory Variance Ratio

	Echelon 4		Echelon 3		Echelon 2		Echelon 1	
Set	*ORVrR*	*IVrR*	*ORVrR*	*IVrR*	*ORVrR*	*IVrR*	*ORVrR*	*IVrR*
1	2.98	20.96	6.54	17.90	7.59	14.67	5.34	14.23
2	1.49	19.98	2.54	18.33	3.32	16.55	3.55	15.78
3	1.50	19.62	2.51	17.74	3.38	15.73	3.76	14.92
4	1.69	29.23	3.11	27.58	3.68	25.66	3.17	23.57
5	1.91	30.11	3.54	25.85	4.29	23.16	3.79	21.87
6	7.17	38.87	15.84	26.50	16.58	21.82	7.09	20.92
7	2.01	37.54	4.01	38.93	4.68	33.49	3.39	28.03
8	10.39	49.86	22.49	38.56	22.07	33.03	6.51	27.39
9	6.34	46.56	13.01	33.50	15.73	30.89	7.47	26.89

Table 5 Order Rate Variance Ratio and Inventory Variance

Set	*ORVrR Slope*	*IVrR Slope*	*Average Fill Rate*
1	2.31	-3.14	0.99917
2	0.91	-1.71	0.99740
3	0.94	-1.94	0.99828
4	0.99	-1.78	0.98307
5	1.19	-3.47	0.98442
6	4.70	-8.53	0.98779
7	1.33	-2.03	0.96856
8	5.84	-8.42	0.97302
9	4.70	-7.83	0.97392

Results show that:

The ES implementation in the production-distribution network assures high customer care regardless the parameter setting. In the Alignment table, the Shang and Seddon's sub-dimension associated to the average fill rate is the customer service (operational dimension). Furthermore, results show that two managerial benefits, Customer decisions with rapid response to customer demands and Strategic decisions for market responsiveness, take advantage from the ES implementation.

ORVrR and IVvR reveal that the benefits are higher for short lead times. The reduction of lead time provided by the ES induces demand amplification avoidance, inventory stability and enhanced fulfilment of the actual market demand. This effect causes an improvement of several Shang and Seddon's managerial dimensions. Asset management for physical inventory, Inventory management in responding quickly to surges in demand and Decision making and planning benefit from ES implementation.

The numerical experiment reveals that, with respect to the improvement in the operational dimension and in particular in terms of customer service which is noticeably robust to lead time increments, the managerial benefits from ES implementation can be reduced by long lead times.

The technique shows that in ES implementation financial measurement cannot assess several aspects related to the dynamics of business. In our example of production-distribution network, lead time is a key element for system performance. Simulation output shows how an ES implementation on a network characterised by short physical distances and lean production system can benefit from collaboration systems based on hi-tech solutions. A real business case is represented by the Finnish Cloetta Fazer that successfully implemented an ES system with the distributors in its local markets [50]. On the contrary, the benefits for geographically dispersed networks are of minor significance.

Our example shows how the no-cost based benefits of Shang and Seddon's, quantified by the presented technique, should be assessed with relation to the specific market sector. The technique helps to understand the existent gap between the assessment provided by financial measurements and the no cost based consequences of ES implementation. The example shows as the ex-ante procedure is potentially applicable to any type of business in which the dynamics of information flows and material flows could strongly impact on performance.

6 Conclusion

The objective of this paper was to present an ES ex ante evaluation technique, developed in three steps.

STEP I. Metrics and Benefits: The Selection and Alignment Process. The aim of this phase was to select a set of metrics that can provide a multi-faceted analysis of the effect of a given ES implementation. The output of this phase is the "Alignment Table", in which the selected metric system is associated to the previously identified subset of Shang and Seddon's benefit dimensions.

STEP II. Methodology Selection and Modelling. The aim of this phase was to select the modelling methodology and generate a business system model. The output of this phase consisted in generating the model, setting the operational parameters, running the model, and collecting data.

STEP III. Performance Metric Analysis and Evaluation of ES Investment. The aim of this phase was the analysis of simulation output on basis of the metrics identified in Step I and the estimation of the associated subset of Shang and Seddon's benefit dimensions. The output of the phase was a set of performance metrics to be used as one of the decision support systems available for the ES investment evaluation.

In this work an example of three-step evaluation procedure was applied on a production/distribution network ES implementation. Numerical experiments show that benefits associated to customer service level are always assured and that several managerial sub-dimensions can suffer from long lead time.

Both researchers and practitioners are expected to benefit from the presented technique. Researchers can extend the technique to further modelling approaches and test it on different ESs. The no-cost based analysis and the Alignment Table provide practitioners with a measurement system that enables an exhaustive analysis of the effects of a given ES implementation.

The ex-ante procedure is potentially applicable to any type of business in which the dynamics of information flows and material flows could strongly impact on performance. The procedure is still under development and we hope to stimulate a fruitful scientific discussion on its applicability on real business world.

References

1. Davenport, T.H.: Putting the enterprise into the enterprise system. Harvard Business Review 76, 121–131 (1998)
2. Chang, S., Gable, G.: Major issues with SAP financials in Queensland government. In: Chung (ed.) The 2000 Americas Conference on Information Systems, Long Beach, CA, pp. 972–975 (2000)
3. Somers, T.M., Nelson, K., Ragowsky, A.: Enterprise Resource Planning (ERP) for the next millennium: development of an integrative framework and implications for research. In: Chung (ed.) The 2000 Americas Conference on Information Systems, Long Beach, CA, pp. 998–1004 (2000)
4. Shang, S., Seddon, P.B.: Assessing and managing the benefits of enterprise systems: the business manager's perspective. Information Systems Journal 12, 271–299 (2000)
5. Teltumbde, A.: A framework for evaluating ERP projects. International Journal of Production Research 38, 4507–4520 (2000)
6. Luo, W., Strong, D.M.: A framework for evaluating ERP implementation choices. IEEE Transactions on Engineering Management 51, 322–333 (2004)
7. Stefanou, C.J.: A framework for the ex-ante evaluation of ERP software. European Journal of Information Systems 10, 204–215 (2001)
8. Umble, E.J., Haft, R.R., Umble, M.M.: Enterprise resource planning: Implementation procedures and critical success factors. European Journal of Operational Research 146, 241–257 (2003)
9. Markus, L.M., Tanis, C.: The enterprise systems experience - from adoption to success. In: Zmud, R.W. (ed.) Framing the Domains of IT Research: Glimpsing the Future Through the Past, Pinnaflex Educational Resources, Cincinnati (2000)
10. Murphy, K.E., Simon, S.J.: Intangible benefits valuation in ERP projects. Information Systems Journal 12, 301–320 (2002)
11. Disney, S.M., Lambrecht, M.R.: On Replenishment Rules, Forecasting, and the Bullwhip Effect in Supply Chains. Foundations and Trends in Technology, Information and Operations Management 2, 1–80 (2008)

12. Ciancimino, E., Cannella, S.: Modelling the bullwhip effect dampening practices in a limited capacity production network. Lecture Notes in Business Information Processing, vol. 20, pp. 475–486 (2009)
13. Gunasekaran, A., Kobu, B.: Modelling and analysis of business process reengineering. European Journal of Production Research 40, 2521–2546 (2002)
14. Gunasekaran, A., Ngai, E.W.T.: Information systems in supply chain integration and management. European Journal of Operational Research 159, 269–295 (2004)
15. Axsäter, S.: Control theory concepts in production and inventory control. International Journal of Systems Science 16, 161–169 (1985)
16. Disney, S.M., Naim, M.M., Potter, A.T.: Assessing the impact of e-business on supply chain dynamics. The International Journal of Production Economics 89, 109–118 (2004)
17. Mitchell, T.: Competitive illusion as a cause of business cycles. Quarterly Journal of Economics 38, 631–652 (1923)
18. Forrester, J.: Industrial dynamics: a major breakthough for decision-makers. Harvard Business Review 36, 37–66 (1958)
19. Lee, H.L., Padmanabhan, V., Whang, S.: Information distortion in a supply chain: the bullwhip effect. Management Science 43, 546–558 (1997)
20. Cachon, G., Fisher, M.: Campbell Soup's continuous replenishment program: Evaluation and enhanced inventory decision rules. Production and Operations Management 6, 266–276 (1997)
21. Hammond, J.H.: Barilla SpA (A). Harvard Business School Case (1994)
22. Anthony, R.N.: Planning and control systems: a framework for analysis. Boston Division of Research Graduate School of Business Administration, Harvard University (1965)
23. Alfaro, J., Ortiz, A., Poler, R.: Performance measurement system for business processes. Production Planning and Control 18, 641–654 (2007)
24. Chen, F., Drezner, Z., Ryan, J.K., Simchi-Levi, D.: Quantifying the bullwhip effect in a simple Supply Chain: the impact of forecasting, lead-times and information. Management Science 46, 436–443 (2000)
25. Disney, S.M., Towill, D.R.: On the bullwhip and inventory variance produced by an ordering policy. Omega, the International Journal of Management Science 31, 157–167 (2003)
26. Cannella, S., Ciancimino, E., Márquez, A.C.: Capacity constrained supply chains: A simulation study. International Journal of Simulation and Process Modelling 4, 139–147 (2008)
27. Cannella, S., Ciancimino, E.: On the Bullwhip Avoidance Phase: Supply Chain Collaboration and Order Smoothing. International Journal of Production Research, first published on December 14, 2009 (iFirst) (2009), DOI: 10.1080/00207540903252308
28. Dejonckheere, J., Disney, S.M., Lambrecht, M.R., Towill, D.R.: The impact of information enrichment on the bullwhip effect in Supply Chains: A control engineering perspective. European Journal of Operational Research 153, 727–750 (2004)
29. Cachon, G.P., Fisher, M.: Supply chain inventory management and the value of shared information. Management Science 46(8), 1032–1048 (2000)
30. Disney, S.M., Grubbström, R.W.: Economic consequences of a production and inventory control policy. International Journal of Production Research 42, 3419–3431 (2004)
31. Shang, J.S., Li, S., Tadikamalla, P.: Operational design of a supply chain system using the Taguchi method, response surface methodology, simulation, and optimization. International Journal of Production Research 42, 3823–3849 (2004)
32. Chen, Y.F., Disney, S.M.: The myopic order-up-to policy with a proportional feedback controller. International Journal of Production Research 45, 351–368 (2007)

33. Poler, R., Hernandez, J.E., Mula, J., Lario, F.C.: Collaborative forecasting in networked manufacturing enterprises. Journal of Manufacturing Technology Management 19, 514–528 (2007)
34. Wright, D., Yuan, X.: Mitigating the bullwhip effect by ordering policies and forecasting methods. International Journal of Production Economics 113, 587–597 (2008)
35. Zipkin, P.H.: Foundations of Inventory Management. McGraw-Hill, New York (2000)
36. Riddalls, C.E., Bennett, S., Tipi, N.S.: Modelling the dynamics of supply chains. International Journal of System Science 31, 969–976 (2000)
37. Beamon, B.M.: Supply chain design and analysis: Models and methods. International Journal of Production Economics 55, 281–294 (1998)
38. Terzi, S., Cavalieri, S.: Simulation in the supply chain context: a survey. Computers in Industry 53, 3–16 (2004)
39. Kleijnen, J.P.C., Smits, M.T.: Performance metrics in supply chain management. The Journal of Operational Research Society 54, 507–514 (2003)
40. Sterman, J.D.: Modelling managerial behaviour: misperceptions of feedback in a dynamic decision-making experiment. Management Science 35, 321–339 (1989)
41. Wikner, J., Towill, D.R., Naim, M.M.: Smoothing supply chain dynamics. International Journal of Production Economics 22, 231–248 (1991)
42. Machuca, J.A.D., Del Pozo Barajas, R.: A computerized network version of the Beer Game via the Internet. System Dynamics Review 13, 323–340 (1997)
43. Ovalle, O.R., Marquez, A.C.: The effectiveness of using e-collaboration tools in the supply chain: An assessment study with system dynamics. Journal of Purchasing and Supply Management 9, 151–163 (2003)
44. Gonçalves, P., Hines, J., Sterman, J.: The impact of endogenous demand on push-pull production system. System Dynamics Review 21, 187–216 (2005)
45. Warburton, R.D.H.: An analytical investigation of the Bullwhip Effect. Production and Operations Management 13, 150–160 (2004)
46. Villegas, F.A., Smith, N.R.: Supply chain dynamics: Analysis of inventory vs. order oscillations trade-off. International Journal of Production Research 44, 1037–1054 (2006)
47. Kim, I., Springer, M.: Measuring endogenous supply chain volatility: Beyond the bullwhip effect. European Journal of Operational Research 189, 172–193 (2008)
48. Sterman, J.: Business Dynamics: Systems Thinking and Modelling for a Complex World. McGraw-Hill, New York (2000)
49. Ciancimino, E., Cannella, S., Canca Ortiz, J.D., Framinan, J.M.: Supply chain multi-level analysis: two bullwhip dampening approaches [Análisis multinivel de cadenas de suministros: Dos técnicas de resolución del efecto bullwhip]. Revista de Métodos Cuantitativos para la Economía y la Empresa 8, 7–28 (2009)
50. Holweg, M., Disney, S., Holmström, J., Småros, J.: Supply chain collaboration: Making sense of the strategy continuum. European Management Journal 23, 170–181 (2005)

Author Index